3-6-06   2|50

THE AMERICAN RAILWAY

ITS CONSTRUCTION, DEVELOPMENT, MANAGEMENT, AND APPLIANCES

BY

THOMAS CURTIS CLARKE

JOHN BOGART

M. N. FORNEY

E. P. ALEXANDER

H. G. PROUT

HORACE PORTER

THEODORE VOORHEES

BENJAMIN NORTON

ARTHUR T. HADLEY

THOMAS L. JAMES

CHARLES FRANCIS ADAMS

B. B. ADAMS, JR.

WITH AN INTRODUCTION BY

THOMAS M. COOLEY

CHAIRMAN OF INTERSTATE COMMERCE COMMISSION

Bramhall House • New York

THE LAST SPAN—READY TO JOIN.

CONTENTS.

PAGE

INTRODUCTION .... **xxi**

By THOMAS M. COOLEY,
Chairman Interstate Commerce Commission.

THE BUILDING OF A RAILWAY .... **I**

By THOMAS CURTIS CLARKE,
Civil Engineer.

Roman Tramways of Stone—First Use of Iron Rails—The Modern Railway
created by Stephenson's "Rocket" in 1830—Early American Locomo-
tives—Key to the Evolution of the American Railway—Invention of the
Swivelling Truck, Equalizing Beams, and the Switchback—Locating a Road
—Work of the Surveying Party—Making the Road-bed—How Tunnels are
Avoided—More than Three Thousand Bridges in the United States—Old
Wooden Structures—The Howe Truss—The Use of Iron—Viaducts of Steel
—The American System of Laying Bridge Foundations under Water—
Origin of the Cantilever—Laying the Track—How it is Kept in Repair—
Premiums for Section Bosses—Number of Railway Employees in the
United States—Rapid Railway Construction—Radical Changes which the
Railway will Effect.

FEATS OF RAILWAY ENGINEERING **47**

By JOHN BOGART,
State Engineer of New York.

Development of the Rail — Problems for the Engineer — How Heights are
Climbed—The Use of Trestles—Construction on a Mountain Side—Engi-
neering on Rope Ladders—Through the Portals of a Cañon—Feats on the
Oroya Railroad, Peru—Nochistongo Cut—Rack Rails for Heavy Grades—
Difficulties in Tunnel Construction—Bridge Foundations—Cribs and Pneu-
matic Caissons—How Men work under Water—The Construction of Stone

Arches—Wood and Iron in Bridge-building—Great Suspension Bridges—The Niagara Cantilever and the enormous Forth Bridge—Elevated and Underground Roads—Responsibilities of the Civil Engineer.

AMERICAN LOCOMOTIVES AND CARS 100

By M. N. FORNEY,

Author of " The Catechism of the Locomotive," Editor " Railroad and Engineering Journal," New York.

The Baltimore & Ohio Railroad in 1830—Evolution of the Car from the Conestoga Wagon—Horatio Allen's Trial Trip—The First Locomotive used in the United States—Peter Cooper's Race with a Gray Horse—The " De Witt Clinton," " Planet," and other Early Types of Locomotives—Equalizing Levers—How Steam is Made and Controlled—The Boiler, Cylinder, Injector, and Valve Gear—Regulation of the Capacity of a Locomotive to Draw—Increase in the Number of Driving Wheels—Modern Types of Locomotives—Variation in the Rate of Speed—The Appliances by which an Engine is Governed—Round-houses and Shops—Development of American Cars—An Illustration from Peter Parley—The Survival of Stage Coach Bodies—Adoption of the Rectangular Shape—The Origin of Eight-wheeled Cars—Improvement in Car Coupling—A Uniform Type Recommended—The Making of Wheels—Relative Merits of Cast and Wrought Iron, and Steel—The Allen Paper Wheel—Types of Cars, with Size, Weight, and Price—The Car-Builder's Dictionary—Statistical.

RAILWAY MANAGEMENT 149

By Gen. E. P. ALEXANDER,

President of the Central Railroad and Banking Company of Georgia.

Relations of Railway Management to all Other Pursuits—Developed by the Necessities of a Complex Industrial Life—How a Continuous Life is Given to a Corporation—Its Artificial Memory—Main Divisions of Railway Management—The Executive and Legislative Powers—The Purchasing and Supply Departments—Importance of the Legal Department—How the Roadway is Kept in Repair—The Maintenance of Rolling Stock—Schedule-making—The Handling of Extra Trains—Duties of the Train-despatcher—Accidents in Spite of Precautions—Daily Distribution of Cars—How Business is Secured and Rates are Fixed—The Interstate Commerce Law—The Questions of " Long and Short Hauls " and " Differentials "—Classification of Freight—Regulation of Passenger-rates—Work of Soliciting Agents—The Collection of Revenue and Statistics—What is a Way-bill—How Disbursements are Made—The Social and Industrial Problem which Confronts Railway Corporations.

CONTENTS.

SAFETY IN RAILROAD TRAVEL 187

By H. G. PROUT,

Editor " Railroad Gazette," New York.

The Possibilities of Destruction in the Great Speed of a Locomotive—The Energy of Four Hundred Tons Moving at Seventy-five Miles an Hour—A Look ahead from a Locomotive at Night—Passengers Killed and Injured in One Year—Good Discipline the Great Source of Safety—The Part Played by Mechanical Appliances—Hand-brakes on Old Cars—How the Air brake Works—The Electric Brake—Improvements yet to be Made—Engine Driver Brakes—Two Classes of Signals : those which Protect Points of Danger, and those which Keep an Interval between Trains on the Same Track—The Semaphore—Interlocking Signals and Switches—Electric Annunciators to Indicate the Movements—The Block Signal System—Protection for Crossings—Gates and Gongs—How Derailment is Guarded Against —Safety Bolts —Automatic Couplers—The Vestibule as a Safety Appliance —Car Heating and Lighting.

RAILWAY PASSENGER TRAVEL 228

By Gen. HORACE PORTER,

Vice-President Pullman Palace-Car Company.

The Earliest Railway Passenger Advertisement—The First Time-table Published in America—The Mohawk & Hudson Train—Survival of Stage-coach Terms in English Railway Nomenclature—Simon Cameron's Rash Prediction—Discomforts of Early Cars—Introduction of Air-brakes, Patent Buffers and Couplers, the Bell-cord, and Interlocking Switches—The First Sleeping-cars—Mr. Pullman's Experiments—The " Pioneer "—Introduction of Parlor and Drawing-room Cars—The Demand for Dining-cars—Ingenious Devices for Heating Cars—Origin of Vestibule-cars—An Important Safety Appliance—The Luxuries of a Limited Express—Fast Time in America and England—Sleeping-cars for Immigrants—The Village of Pullman—The Largest Car-works in the World—Baggage-checks and Coupon Tickets—Conveniences in a Modern Depot—Statistics in Regard to Accidents—Proportion of Passengers in Various Classes—Comparison of Rates in the Leading Countries of the World.

THE FREIGHT-CAR SERVICE 267

By THEODORE VOORHEES,

Assistant-General Superintendent, New York Central Railroad.

Sixteen Months' Journey of a Car—Detentions by the Way—Difficulties of the Car Accountant's Office—Necessities of Through Freight—How a Company's Cars are Scattered—The Question of Mileage—Reduction of the

PAGE

Balance in Favor of Other Roads—Relation of the Car Accountant's Work
to the Transportation Department—Computation of Mileage—The Record
Branch—How Reports are Gathered and Compiled—Exchange of " Junction Cards "—The Use of " Tracers "—Distribution of Empty Cars—Control of the Movement of Freight—How Trains are Made Up—Duties of
the Yardmaster—The Handling of Through Trains—Organization of Fast
Lines—Transfer Freight Houses—Special Cars for Specific Service—Disasters to Freight Trains—How the Companies Suffer—Inequalities in Payment for Car Service—The Per Diem Plan—A Uniform Charge for Car
Rental—What Reforms might be Accomplished.

HOW TO FEED A RAILWAY...................... 298

By BENJAMIN NORTON,

Second Vice-President, Long Island Railroad Company.

The Many Necessities of a Modern Railway—The Purchasing and Supply Departments—Comparison with the Commissary Department of an Army—
Financial Importance—Immense Expenditures—The General Storehouse—
Duties of the Purchasing Agent —The Best Material the Cheapest—Profits
from the Scrap-heap—Old Rails Worked over into New Implements—Yearly
Contracts for Staple Articles—Economy in Fuel—Tests by the Best Engineers and Firemen—The Stationery Supply—Aggregate Annual Cost of
Envelopes, Tickets, and Time-tables—The Average Life of Rails—Durability of Cross-ties—What it Costs per Mile to Run an Engine—The Paymaster's Duties—Scenes during the Trip of a Pay-car.

THE RAILWAY MAIL SERVICE 312

By THOMAS L. JAMES,

Ex-Postmaster General.

An Object Lesson in Postal Progress—Nearness of the Department to the Peo-
ple—The First Travelling Post-Office in the United States—Organization
of the Department in 1789—Early Mail Contracts—All Railroads made
Post-routes—Compartments for Mail Clerks in Baggage-cars—Origin of the
Present System in 1862—Important Work of Colonel George S. Bangs—
The " Fast Mail" between New York and Chicago—Why it was Suspended
—Resumption in 1877—Present Condition of the Service—Statistics—A
Ride on the " Fast Mail "—Busy Scenes at the Grand Central Depot—
Special Uses of the Five Cars—Duties of the Clerks—How the Work is
Performed—Annual Appropriation for Special Mail Facilities—Dangers
Threatening the Railway Mail Clerk's Life—An Insurance Fund Proposed
—Needs of the Service—A Plea for Radical Civil Service Reform.

PAGE

THE RAILWAY IN ITS BUSINESS RELATIONS....... 344
By ARTHUR T. HADLEY,
Professor of Political Science in Yale College, Author of " Railroad Transportation."

Amount of Capital Invested in Railways—Important Place in the Modern Industrial System—The Duke of Bridgewater's Foresight—The Growth of Half a Century—Early Methods of Business Management—The Tendency toward Consolidation—How the War Developed a National Idea—Its Effect on Railroad Building—Thomson and Scott as Organizers—Vanderbilt's Capacity for Financial Management—Garrett's Development of the Baltimore & Ohio—The Concentration of Immense Power in a Few Men—Making Money out of the Investors—Difficult Positions of Stockholders and Bondholders—How the Finances are Manipulated by the Board of Directors—Temptations to the Misuse of Power—Relations of Railroads to the Public who Use Them—Inequalities in Freight Rates—Undue Advantages for Large Trade Centres—Proposed Remedies—Objections to Government Control—Failure of Grangerism—The Origin of Pools—Their Advantages—Albert Fink's Great Work—Charles Francis Adams and the Massachusetts Commission—Adoption of the Interstate Commerce Law—Important Influence of the Commission—Its Future Functions—Ill-judged State Legislation.

THE PREVENTION OF RAILWAY STRIKES 370
By CHARLES FRANCIS ADAMS,
President of the Union Pacific Railroad.

Railways the Largest Single Interest in the United States—Some Impressive Statistics—Growth of a Complex Organization—Five Divisions of Necessary Work—Other Special Departments—Importance of the Operating Department—The Evil of Strikes—To be Remedied by Thorough Organization—Not the Ordinary Relation between Employer and Employee—Of what the Model Railway Service Should Consist—Temporary and Permanent Employees—Promotion from one Grade to the Other—Rights and Privileges of the Permanent Service—Employment during Good Behavior—Proposed Tribunal for Adjusting Differences and Enforcing Discipline—A Regular Advance in Pay for Faithful Service—A Fund for Hospital Service, Pensions, and Insurance—Railroad Educational Institutions—The Employer to Have a Voice in Management through a Council—A System of Representation.

THE EVERY-DAY LIFE OF RAILROAD MEN 383
By B. B. ADAMS, Jr.,
Associate Editor, "Railroad Gazette," New York.

The Typical Railroad Man—On the Road and at Home—Raising the Moral Standard—Characteristics of the Freight Brakeman—His Wit the Result of

CONTENTS.

Meditation—How Slang is Originated—Agreeable Features of his Life in Fine Weather—Hardships in Winter—The Perils of Hand-brakes—Broken Trains—Going back to Flag—Coupling Accidents—At the Spring—Advantages of a Passenger Brakeman—Trials of the Freight Conductor—The Investigation of Accidents—Irregular Hours of Work—The Locomotive Engineer the Hero of the Rail—His Rare Qualities—The Value of Quick Judgment—Calm Fidelity a Necessary Trait—Saving Fuel on a Freight Engine—Making Time on a Passenger Engine—Remarkable Runs—The Spirit of Fraternity among Engineers—Difficult Duties of a Passenger-train Conductor—Tact in Dealing with Many People—Questions to be Answered —How Rough Characters are Dealt with—Heavy Responsibilities—The Work of a Station Agent—Flirtation by Telegraph—The Baggage-master's Hard Task—Eternal Vigilance Necessary in a Switch-tender—Sectionmen, Train Despatchers, Firemen, and Clerks—Efforts to Make the Railroad Man's Life Easier.

STATISTICAL RAILWAY STUDIES.................... 425

ILLUSTRATED WITH THIRTEEN MAPS AND NINETEEN CHARTS.

By FLETCHER W. HEWES.

Author of " Scribner's Statistical Atlas."

Railway Mileage of the World—Railway Mileage of the United States—Annual Mileage and Increase—Mileage compared with Area—Geographical Location of Railways—Centres of Mileage and of Population—Railway Systems —Trunk Lines Compared : By Mileage ; Largest Receipts ; Largest Net Results—Freight Traffic—Reduction of Freight Rates—Wheat Rates—The Freight Haul—Empty Freight Trains—Freight Profits—Passenger Traffic— Passenger Rates—Passenger Travel—Passenger Profits—General Considerations—Dividends—Net Earnings per Mile and Railway Building— Ratios of Increase—Construction and Maintenance—Employees and their Wages — Rolling Stock—Capital Invested.

INDEX.. ··· 449

LIST OF ILLUSTRATIONS.

FULL-PAGE ILLUSTRATIONS.

Title.	Designer.	Page
THE LAST SPAN (Frontispiece)	A. B. Frost	11
ALPINE PASS. AVOIDANCE OF A TUNNEL	*From a photograph*	5
BIG LOOP, GEORGETOWN BRANCH OF THE UNION PACIFIC, COLORADO	*From a photograph*	11
SNOW-SHEDS, SELKIRK MOUNTAINS, CANADIAN PACIFIC	J. D. Woodward	19
RAIL MAKING	Walter Shirlaw	39
LOOP AND GREAT TRESTLE NEAR HAGERMAN'S, ON THE COLORADO MIDLAND RAILWAY	J. D. Woodward	51
PORTAL OF A TUNNEL IN PROCESS OF CONSTRUCTION	Otto Stark	65
AT WORK IN A PNEUMATIC CAISSON—FIFTY FEET BELOW THE SURFACE OF THE WATER	Walter Shirlaw	73
BELOW THE BROOKLYN BRIDGE	J. H. Twachtman	83
THE ST. LOUIS BRIDGE DURING CONSTRUCTION	M. E. Sands & R. Blum	95
A TYPICAL AMERICAN PASSENGER LOCOMOTIVE	*From a photograph*	111
INTERIOR OF A ROUND-HOUSE	M. J. Burns	130
VIEW IN LOCOMOTIVE ERECTING SHOP	J. D. Woodward & R. Blum	135

Title.	Designer.	Page
DIAGRAM USED IN MAKING RAILWAY TIME-TABLES		161
THE GENERAL DESPATCHER	M. J. Burns	165
MANTUA JUNCTION, WEST PHILADELPHIA, SHOWING A COMPLEX SYSTEM OF INTERLACING TRACKS	W. C. Fitler	169
DANGER AHEAD!	A. B. Frost	189
INTERLOCKING APPARATUS FOR OPERATING SWITCHES AND SIGNALS BY COMPRESSED AIR, PITTSBURG YARDS, PENNSYLVANIA RAILROAD	*From a photograph*	211
PULLMAN VESTIBULED CARS	*From a photograph*	247
IN A BAGGAGE-ROOM	W. C. Broughton	255
"SHOW YOUR TICKETS!"	Walter Shirlaw	261
FREIGHT YARDS OF THE NEW YORK CENTRAL & HUDSON RIVER RAILROAD, WEST SIXTY-FIFTH STREET, NEW YORK	W. C. Fitler	285
FREIGHT FROM ALL QUARTERS — SOME TYPICAL TRAINS	W. C. Fitler	291
AT A WAY-STATION—THE POSTMASTER'S ASSISTANT	Herbert Denman	321
TRANSFER OF MAIL AT THE GRAND CENTRAL STATION, NEW YORK	Herbert Denman	327
SORTING LETTERS IN CAR NO. 1—THE FAST MAIL	Herbert Denman	333
A BREAKDOWN ON THE ROAD	A. B. Frost	405
IN THE WAITING ROOM OF A COUNTRY STATION	A. B. Frost	413
THE TRIALS OF A BAGGAGE-MASTER	A. B. Frost	417

ILLUSTRATIONS IN THE TEXT.

PAGE

First Locomotive.. 2
Locomotive of To-day... 3
A Sharp Curve—Manhattan Elevated Railway, 110th Street, New York........... 7
A Steep Grade on a Mountain Railroad.................................. 8
A Switchback... 9
Plan of Big Loop... 10
Profile of the Same.. 10
Engineers in Camp... 14
Royal Gorge Hanging Bridge, Denver and Rio Grande, Colorado............... 16
Veta Pass, Colorado.. 17
Sections of Snow-sheds (3 cuts)..................................... 18
Making an Embankment.. 21
Steam Excavator... 21
Building a Culvert.. 22
Building a Bridge Abutment.. 22
Rock Drill... 23
A Construction and Boarding Train.................................... 24
Bergen Tunnels, Hoboken, N. J....................................... 25
Beginning a Tunnel... 26
Old Burr Wooden Bridge... 2~
Kinzua Viaduct ; Erie Railway....................................... 30
Kinzua Viaduct... 32
View of Thomas Pope's Proposed Cantilever (1810)...................... 34
Pope's Cantilever in Process of Erection.............................. 35
General View of the Poughkeepsie Bridge.............................. 36
Erection of a Cantilever.. 37
Spiking the Track.. 38
Track Laying 41
Temporary Railway Crossing the St. Lawrence on the Ice................. 44
View Down the Blue from Rocky Point, Denver, South Park and Pacific Railroad ; showing successive tiers of railway................................. 49
Denver and Rio Grande Railway Entering the Portals of the Grand River Cañon, Colorado.. 54
The Kentucky River Cantilever, on the Cincinnati Southern Railway.......... 55
Truss over Ravine, and Tunnel, Oroya Railroad, Peru.................... 56
The Nochistongo Cut, Mexican Central Railway......................... 57
The Mount Washington Rack Railroad................................. 58
Trestle on Portland and Ogdensburg Railway, Crawford Notch, White Mountains.. 58
A Series of Tunnels.. 59

PAGE

Tunnel at the Foot of Mount St. Stephen, on the Canadian Pacific............... 60

Peña de Mora on the La Guayra and Carácas Railway, Venezuela................ 61

Perspective View of St. Gothard Spiral Tunnels, in the Alps..................... 62

Plan of St. Gothard Spiral Tunnels.. 63

Profile of the Same.. 63

Portal of a Finished Tunnel ; showing Cameron's Cone, Colorado................ 64

Railway Pass at Rocky Point in the Rocky Mountains........................... 67

Bridge Pier Founded on Piles... 68

Pneumatic Caisson... 70

Transverse Section of Pneumatic Caisson...................................... 71

Pier of Hawkesbury Bridge, Australia... 75

Foundation Crib of the Poughkeepsie Bridge................................... 76

Transverse Section of the Same....... 76

Granite Arched Approach to Harlem River Bridge in Process of Construction...... 77

The Old Portage Viaduct, Erie Railway, N. Y.................................. 78

The New Portage Viaduct.. 79

The Britannia Tubular Bridge over the Menai Straits, North Wales.............. 80

Old Stone Towers of the Niagara Suspension Bridge............................ 82

The New Iron Towers of the Same... 82

Truss Bridge of the Northern Pacific Railway over the Missouri River at Bismarck,
 Dak.—Testing the Central Span.. 87

Curved Viaduct, Georgetown, Col. ; the Union Pacific Crossing its own Line...... 88

The Niagara Cantilever Bridge in Progress.................................... 90

The Niagara Cantilever Bridge Completed.... 91

The Lachine Bridge, on the Canadian Pacific Railway, near Montreal, Canada..... 92

The 510-feet Span Steel Arches of the New Harlem River Bridge, New York, during
 Construction... 97

London Underground Railway Station... 98

Conestoga Wagon and Team... 101

Baltimore & Ohio Railroad, 1830–35.. 101

Boston & Worcester Railroad, 1835... 102

Horatio Allen... 103

Peter Cooper's Locomotive, 1830... 104

" South Carolina," 1831, and Plan of its Running Gear........................ 105

The " De Witt Clinton," 1831.. 105

" Grasshopper " Locomotive.. 106

The " Planet "... 107

John B. Jervis's Locomotive, 1831, and Plan of its Running Gear 108

Campbell's Locomotive... 109

Locomotive for Suburban Traffic... 110

Locomotive for Street Railway... 110

Four-wheeled Switching Locomotive... 113

PAGE

Driving Wheels, Frames, Spurs, etc., of American Locomotive.................. 114
Longitudinal Section of a Locomotive Boiler...................................... 115
Transverse Section... 115
Rudimentary Injector... 116
Injector Used on Locomotives... 117
Sections of a Locomotive Cylinder.. 118
Eccentric.. 118
Eccentric and Strap.. 118
Valve Gear... 119
Turning Locomotive Tires... 121
Six-wheeled Switching Locomotive... 122
Mogul Locomotive... 123
Ten-wheeled Passenger Locomotive... 123
Consolidation Locomotive (unfinished) 124
Consolidation Locomotive... 124
Decapod Locomotive 125
" Forney " Tank Locomotive... 126
"Hudson " Tank Locomotive 127
Camden & Amboy Locomotive, 1848.. 129
Cab End of a Locomotive and its Attachments...................................... 133
Interior of Erecting Shop, showing Locomotive Lifted by Travelling Crane 137
Forging a Locomotive Frame... 138
Mohawk & Hudson Car, 1831 139
Early Car.. 139
Early Car on the Baltimore & Ohio Railroad....................................... 140
Early American Car, 1834... 140
Old Car for Carrying Flour on the Baltimore & Ohio Railroad...................... 141
Old Car for Carrying Firewood on the Baltimore & Ohio Railroad................... 141
Old Car on the Quincy Granite Railroad... 141
Janney Car Coupler, showing the Process of Coupling 142
Mould and Flask in which Wheels are Cast... 143
Cast-iron Car Wheels... 144
Section of the Tread and Flange of a Car Wheel................................... 145
Allen Paper Car Wheel.. 145
Modern Passenger-car and Frame 147
Snow-plough at Work.. 154
A Type of Snow-plough.. 155
A Rotary Steam Snow-shovel in Operation.. 156
Railway-crossing Gate.. 157
Signal to Stop... 162
Signal to Move Ahead... 162
Signal to Move Back.. 163

PAGE

Signal that the Train has Parted... 163

Entrance Gates at a Large Station.. 167

Central Switch and Signal Tower.. 168

Interior of a Switch-tower, showing the Operation of Interlocking Switches........ 171

Stephenson's Steam Driver-brake, patented 1833................................. 192

Driver-brake on Modern Locomotive... 192

English Screw-brake, on the Birmingham and Gloucester Road, about 1840........ 193

English Foot-brake on the Truck of a Great Western Coach, about 1840.......... 193

Plan and Elevation of Air-brake Apparatus...................................... 196

Dwarf Semaphores and Split Switch... 202

Semaphore Signal with Indicators.. 203

Section of Saxby & Farmer Interlocking Machine.............................. 204

Diagram of a Double-track Junction with Interlocked Switches and Signals........ 205

Split Switches with Facing-point Locks and Detector-bars...................... 206

Derailing Switch... 207

Torpedo Placer... 213

Old Signal Tower on the Philadelphia & Reading, at Phœnixville................. 214

Crossing Gates worked by Mechanical Connection from the Cabin............... 217

Some Results of a Butting Collision—Baggage and Passenger Cars Telescoped..... 218

Wreck at a Bridge 219

New South Norwalk Drawbridge.   Rails held by Safety Bolts.................... 220

Engines Wrecked during the Great Wabash Strike.............................. 222

Link-and-pin Coupler 224

Janney Automatic Coupler applied to a Freight Car............................. 224

Signals at Night... 225

Stockton & Darlington Engine and Car... 229

Mohawk & Hudson Train 231

English Railway Carriage, Midland Road.   First and Third Class and Luggage
    Compartments 232

One of the Earliest Passenger Cars Built in this Country ; used on the Western Rail-
    road of Massachusetts (now the Boston & Albany).......................... 233

Bogie Truck... 233

Rail and Coach Travel in the White Mountains................................. 234

Old Time Table, 1843... 235

Old Boston & Worcester Railway Ticket (about 1837)........................... 236

Obverse and Reverse of a Ticket used in 1838, on the New York & Harlem Railroad 236

The " Pioneer."   First Complete Pullman Sleeping-car......................... 240

A Pullman Porter... 241

Pullman Parlor Car 243

Wagner Parlor Car... 244

Dining-car (Chicago, Burlington & Quincy Railroad)............................. 245

End View of a Vestibuled Car.. 249

PAGE

Pullman Sleeper on a Vestibuled Train... 250

Immigrant Sleeping-car (Canadian Pacific Railway) 251

View of Pullman, Ill.. 252

Railway Station at York, England, built on a Curve............................. 257

Outside the Grand Central Station, New York.................................... 258

Boston Passenger Station, Providence Division, Old Colony Railroad............. 259

A Page from the Car Accountant's Book 277

Freight Pier, North River, New York.. 280

Hay Storage Warehouses, New York Central & Hudson River Railroad, West
    Thirty-third Street, New York.. 282

" Dummy " Train and Boy on Hudson Street, New York......................... 287

Red Line Freight-car Mark.. 288

Star Union Freight-car Mark.. 288

Coal Car, Central Railroad of New Jersey....................................... 289

Refrigerator-car Mark... 289

Unloading a Train of Truck-wagons, Long Island Railroad...................... 290

Floating Cars, New York Harbor.. 295

Postal Progress, 1776–1876.. 313

The Pony Express—The Relay... 314

The Overland Mail Coach—A Star Route.. 315

Mail Carrying in the Country... 316

Loading for the Fast Mail, at the General Post-Office, New York............... 324

At the Last Moment... 326

Pouching the Mail in the Postal Car.. 329

A Very Difficult Address—known as a " Sticker.".............................. 331

Distributing the Mail by States and Routes..................................... 332

Pouching Newspapers for California—in Car No. 5............................. 335

Catching the Pouch from the Crane... 339

George Stephenson.. 345

J. Edgar Thomson.. 349

Thomas A. Scott... 350

Cornelius Vanderbilt... 352

John W. Garrett.. 355

Albert Fink.. 366

Charles Francis Adams.. 367

Thomas M. Cooley. 369

" Dancing on the Carpet ".. 386

Trainman and Tramps... 387

Braking in Hard Weather... 389

Flagging in Winter... 391

Coupling... 392

The Pleasant Part of a Brakeman's Life... 395

PAGE

At the Spring.. 397
Just Time to Jump... 403
Timely Warning... 407
The Passenger Conductor... 409
Station Gardening... 416
In the Yard at Night.. 419
A Track-walker on a Stormy Night.. 421
A Crossing Flagman.. 423
A Little Relaxation... 424

MAPS.

Mileage compared with Area.. 429
Railways, 1830, 1840, 1850, and 1860.. 430
Railways, 1870.. 431
Railways, 1880.. 432
Railways, 1889.. 433
Five Railway Systems... 434, 435

CHARTS.

Principal Railway Countries... 425
Mileage to Area in New Jersey... 426
Total Mileage and Increase, 1830–1888... 429
Mileage by States, 1870... 431
Mileage by States, 1880... 432
Mileage by States, 1888... 433
Largest Receipts, 1888.. 435
Largest Net Results, 1888... 435
Freight Rates of Thirteen Trunk Lines, 1870–1888................................ 436
Wheat Rates, by Water and by Rail, 1870–1888.................................... 438
The Freight Haul, 1882–1888... 439
East-bound and West-bound Freight, 1877–1888.................................... 439
Freight Profits, 1870–1888.. 440
Passenger Rates, 1870–1888.. 441
Passenger Travel, 1882–1888... 442
Passenger Profits, 1870–1888.. 442
Average Dividends, 1876–1888.. 443
Net Earnings and Mileage Built, 1876–1888....................................... 444
Increase of Population, Mileage, and Freight Traffic, 1870–1888................. 446

INTRODUCTION.

By THOMAS M. COOLEY.

THE railroads of the United States, now aggregating a hundred and fifty thousand miles and having several hundred different managements, are frequently spoken of comprehensively as the railroad system of the country, as though they constituted a unity in fact, and might be regarded and dealt with as an entirety, by their patrons and by the public authorities, whenever the conveniences they are expected to supply, or the conduct of managers and agents, come in question. So far, however, is this from being the case, that it would be impossible to name any other industrial interest where the diversities are so obvious and the want of unity so conspicuous and so important. The diversities date from the very origin of the roads ; they have not come into existence under the same laws nor subject to the same control. It was accepted as an undoubted truth in constitutional law from the first that the authority for the construction of railroads within a State must come from the State itself, which alone could empower the promoters to appropriate lands by adversary proceedings for the purpose. The grant of corporate power must also come from the State, or, at least, have State recognition and sanction ; and where the proposed road was to cross a State boundary, the necessary corporate authority must be given by every State through or into which the road was to run. It was conceded that the delegated powers of the General Government did not comprehend the granting of charters for the construction of these roads within the States, and even in the Territories charters were granted by the local legislatures. The case of the transcontinental roads was clearly exceptional ; they were to be constructed in large part over the public domain, and subsidies were to be granted by Congress for the purpose. They were also, in part at least, to be constructed for governmental reasons as national agencies ; and invoking State authority for the purpose seemed to be as inconsistent as it would be inadequate. But, though these were exceptional cases, the magnitude and importance of the Pacific roads are so immense that the agency of the General Government in making provision for this method of transportation must always have prominence in railroad history and railroad statistics.

Not only have the roads been diverse in origin, but the corporations which have constructed them have differed very greatly in respect to their powers and rights, and also to the obligations imposed by law upon them. The early grants of power were charter-contracts, freely given, with very liberal provisions ; the public being more anxious that they be accepted and acted upon than distrustful of their abuse afterward. Many of them were not subject to alteration or repeal, except with the consent of the corporators ; and some of them contained provisions intended to exclude or limit competition, so that, within a limited territory, something in the nature of a monopoly in transportation would be created. The later grants give evidence of popular apprehension of corporate abuses; the legislature reserves a control over them, and the right to multiply railroads indefinitely is made as free as possible, under the supposition that in this multiplication is to be found the best protection against any one of them abusing its powers. In very many cases the motive to the building of a new road has been antagonism to one already in existence, and municipalities have voted subsidies to the one in the hope that, when constructed, it would draw business away from the other. The anomaly has thus been witnessed of distrust of corporate power being the motive for increasing it; and the multiplication of roads has gone on, without any general supervision or any previous determination by competent public authority that they were needed, until the increase has quite outrun in some sections any proper demand for their facilities.

Roads thus brought into existence, without system and under diverse managements, it was soon seen were capable of being so operated that the antagonism of managers, instead of finding expression in legitimate competition, would be given to the sort of strife that can only be properly characterized by calling it, as it commonly is called, a war. From such a war the public inevitably suffers. The best service upon the roads is only performed when they are operated as if they constituted in fact parts of one harmonious system; the rates being made by agreement, and traffic exchanged with as little disturbance as possible, and without abrupt break at the terminals. But when every management might act independently, it sometimes happened that a company made its method of doing business an impediment instead of a help to the business done over other roads, recognizing no public duty which should preclude its doing so, provided a gain to itself, however indirect or illegitimate, was probable. Many consolidations of roads have had for their motive the getting rid of this power to do mischief on the part of roads absorbed.

In nothing is the want of unity so distinctly and mischievously obvious as in the power of each corporation to make rates independently. It may not only make its own local rates at discretion, but it may join or refuse to join with others in making through rates; so that an inconsiderable and otherwise insignificant road may be capable of being so used as to throw rates for a large section of the country into confusion, and to render the making of profit by other roads impossible. It is frequently said in railroad circles that roads are sometimes constructed for no other reason than because, through this power of mischief, it will be possible to levy contributions upon others, or to compel others, in self-protection, to buy them up at extravagant prices. Cases are named in which this sort of scheming is supposed to have succeeded, and others in which it is now being tried.

Evils springing from the diversities mentioned have been cured, or greatly mitigated, by such devices as the formation of fast-freight lines to operate over many roads; by allowing express companies to come upon the roads with semi-independence in the transportation of articles, where, for special reasons, the public is content to pay an extra price for extra care or speed ; and by arrangements with sleeping-car companies for special accommodations in luxurious cars to those desiring them. These collateral arrangements, however, have not been wholly beneficial ; and had all the roads been constructed as parts of one system and under one management, some of them would neither have been necessary nor defensible. They exist now, however, with more or less reason for their existence ; and they tend to increase the diversities in railroad work.

The want of unity which has been pointed out tended to breed abuses specially injurious to the public, and governmental regulation was entered upon for their correction. Naturally the first attempts in this direction were made by separate States, each undertaking to regulate for itself the transportation within its own limits. Such regulation would have been perfectly logical, and perhaps effectual, had the roads within each State formed a system by themselves ; but when State boundaries had very little importance, either to the roads themselves or to the traffic done over them, unless made important by restrictive and obstructive legislation, the regulation by any State must necessarily be fragmentary and imperfect, and diverse regulation in different States might be harmful rather than beneficial. It must be said for State regulation that it has in general been exercised in a prudent and conservative way, but it is liable to be influenced by a sensitive and excitable public opinion ; and as nothing is more common than to find gross abuses in the matter of railroad transportation selfishly defended in localities, and even in considerable sections, which are supposed to receive benefits from them, it would not be strange if the like selfishness should sometimes succeed in influencing the exercise of power by one State in a manner that a neighboring State would regard as unfriendly and injurious.

The Federal Government recently undertook the work of regulation, and in doing so accepted the view upon which the States had acted, and so worded its statute that the transportation which does not cross State lines is supposed to be excluded. The United States thus undertakes to regulate interstate commerce by rail, and the States regulate, or may regulate, that which is not interstate. It was perhaps overlooked at first that, inasmuch as Government control may embrace the making of classifications, prescribing safety and other appliances, and naming rates, any considerable regulation of State traffic and interstate traffic separately must necessarily to some extent cause interference. The two classes of traffic flow on together over the same lines in the same vehicles under the management of the same agencies, with little or no distinction based on State lines ; the rates and the management influenced by considerations which necessarily are of general force, so that separate regulation may without much extravagance be compared to an attempt in the case of one of our great rivers to regulate the flow of the waters in general, but without, in doing so, interfering with an independent regulation of such portion thereof as may have come from the springs and streams of some particular section. This is one of many reasons for looking upon all existing legislation as merely tentative.

No doubt the time will come when the railroads of the country will constitute, as they do not now, a system. There are those who think this may, sufficiently for practical purposes, be accomplished by the legalization of some scheme of pooling ; but this is a crude device, against which there is an existing prejudice not easily to be removed. Others look for unity through gradual consolidations, the tendency to which is manifest, or through something in the nature of a trust, or by means of more comprehensive and stringent national control. Beyond all these is not infrequently suggested a Government ownership.

Of the theories that might be advanced in this direction, or the arguments in their support, nothing further will be said here ; the immediate purpose being accomplished when it is shown how misleading may be the term *system*, when applied to the railroads of the country as an aggregate, as now owned, managed, and controlled.

Every man in the land is interested daily and constantly in railroads and the transportation of persons and property over them. The price of whatever he eats, or wears, or uses, the cost and comfort of travel, the speed and convenience with which he shall receive his mail and the current intelligence of the day, and even the intimacy and extent of his social relations, are all largely affected thereby. The business employs great numbers of persons, and the wages paid them affect largely the wages paid in other lines of occupation. The management of the business in some of its departments is attended by serious dangers, and thousands annually lose their lives in the service.

Other thousands annually are either killed or injured in being transported; the aggregate being somewhat startling, though unquestionably this method of travel is safer than any other. The ingenuity which has been expended in devices to make the transportation rapid, cheap, and safe may well be characterized as marvellous, and some feats in railroad engineering are the wonder of the world. With all these facts and many others to create a public interest in the general subject, the editor of *Scribner's Magazine*, some little time ago, applied to writers of well-known ability and competency to prepare papers for publication therein upon the various topics of principal interest in the life and use of railroads, beginning with the construction, and embracing the salient facts of management and service. He was successful in securing a series of papers of high value, the appearance of which has been welcomed from month to month, beginning with June, 1888, with constant and increasing interest. These papers have a permanent value; and, in obedience to a demand for their separate publication in convenient form for frequent reference, the publishers now reproduce them with expansions and additions. A reference to the several titles will convince anyone at all familiar with the general subject that the particular topic is treated in every instance by an expert, entitled as such to speak with authority.

THE BUILDING OF A RAILWAY.

By THOMAS CURTIS CLARKE.

Roman Tramways of Stone—First Use of Iron Rails—The Modern Railway created by Stephenson's "Rocket" in 1830—Early American Locomotives—Key to the Evolution of the American Railway—Invention of the Swivelling Truck, Equalizing Beams, and the Switchback—Locating a Road—Work of the Surveying Party—Making the Road-bed—How Tunnels are Avoided—More than Three Thousand Bridges in the United States—Old Wooden Structures—The Howe Truss—The Use of Iron—Viaducts of Steel—The American System of Laying Bridge Foundations under Water—Origin of the Cantilever—Laying the Track—How it is Kept in Repair—Premiums for Section Bosses—Number of Railway Employees in the United States—Rapid Railway Construction—Radical Changes which the Railway will Effect.

THE world of to-day differs from that of Napoleon Bonaparte more than his world differed from that of Julius Cæsar; and this change has chiefly been made by railways.

Railways have been known since the days of the Romans. Their tracks were made of two lines of cut stones. Iron rails took their place about one hundred and fifty years ago, when the use of that metal became extended. These roads were called tram-roads, and were used to carry coal from the mines to the places of shipment. They were few in number and attracted little attention.

The modern railway was created by the Stephensons in 1830, when they built the locomotive "Rocket." The development of the railway since is due to the development of the locomotive. Civil engineering has done much, but mechanical engineering has done more.

The invention of the steam-engine by James Watt, in 1773, attracted the attention of advanced thinkers to a possible steam locomotive.   Erasmus Darwin, in a poem published in 1781, made this remarkable prediction :

"Soon shall thy arm, unconquered steam! afar
Drag the slow barge, or drive the rapid car."

The first locomotive of which we have any certain record was invented, and put in operation on a model circular railway in London, in 1804, by Richard Tre-

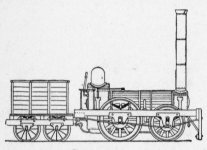

First Locomotive.

vithick, an erratic genius, who invented many things but perfected few.   His locomotive could not make steam, and therefore could neither go fast nor draw a heavy load.   This was the fault of all its successors, until the competitive trial of locomotives on the Liverpool and Manchester Railway, in 1829.   The Stephensons, father and son, had invented the steam blast, which, by constantly blowing the fire, enabled the "Rocket," with its tubular boiler, to make steam enough to draw ten passenger cars, at the rate of thirty-five miles an hour.

Then was born the modern giant, and so recent is the date of his birth that one of the unsuccessful competitors at that memorable trial, Captain John Ericsson, was until the present year (1889) living and actively working in New York.   Another engineer, Horatio Allen, who drove the first locomotive on the first trip ever made in the United States, in 1831, still lives, a hale and hearty old man, near New York.

The earlier locomotives of this country, modelled after the "Rocket," weighed five or six tons, and could draw, on a level, about 40 tons.   After the American improvements, which we shall describe, were made, our engines weighed 25 tons, and could draw, on a level, some sixty loaded freight cars, weighing 1,200 tons.   This was a wonderful advance, but now we have the "Consolidation" locomotive, weighing 50 tons, and able to draw, on a level, a little over 2,400 tons.

And this is not the end.   Still heavier and more powerful engines are being designed and built, but the limit of the strength of the track, according to its present forms, has nearly been reached. It is very certain we have not reached the limit of the size and power of engines, or the strength of the track that can be devised.

After the success of the " Rocket," and of the Liverpool and Manchester Railway, the authority of George Stephenson and his son Robert became absolute and unquestioned upon all subjects of railway engineering. Their locomotives had very little side play to their wheels, and could not go around sharp curves. They accordingly preferred to make their lines as straight as possible, and were willing to spend vast sums to get easy grades. Their lines were taken as models and imitated by other engineers. All lines in England were made with easy grades and gentle curves. Monumental bridges, lofty stone viaducts, and deep cuts or tunnels at every hill marked this stage of railway construction in England, which was imitated on the European lines.

As it was with the railway, so it was with the locomotive. The Stephenson type, once fixed, has remained unchanged (in Europe), except in detail, to the present day. European locomotives have increased in weight and power, and in perfection of

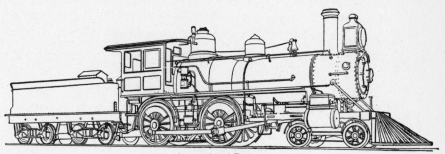

Locomotive of To-day.

material and workmanship, but the general features are those of the locomotives built by the great firm of George Stephenson & Son, before 1840.

When we come to the United States we find an entirely different state of things. The key to the evolution of the American railway is the contempt for authority displayed by our engineers, and the untrammelled way in which they invented and applied whatever they thought would answer the best purpose, regardless of precedent. When we began to build our railways, in 1831, we followed English patterns for a short time. Our engineers soon saw that unless vital changes were made our money would not hold out, and our railway system would be very short. Necessity truly became the mother of invention.

The first, and most far-reaching, invention was that of the swivelling truck, which, placed under the front end of an engine, enables it to run around curves of almost any radius. This enabled us to build much less expensive lines than those of England, for we could now curve around and avoid hills and other obstacles at will. The illustration opposite shows a railroad curving around a mountain and supported by a retaining wall, instead of piercing through the mountain with a tunnel, as would have been necessary but for the swivelling truck. The swivelling truck was first suggested by Horatio Allen, for the South Carolina Railway, in 1831; but the first practical use of it was made on the Mohawk and Hudson Railroad, in the same year. It is said to have been invented by John B. Jervis, Chief Engineer of that road.

The next improvement was the invention of the equalizing beams or levers, by which the weight of the engine is always borne by three out of four or more driving-wheels. They act like a three-legged stool, which can always be set level on any irregular spot. The original imported English locomotives could not be kept on the rails of rough tracks. The same experience obtained in Canada when the Grand Trunk Railway was opened, in 1854–55. The locomotives of English pattern constantly ran off the track; those of American pattern hardly ever did so. Finally, all their locomotives were changed by having swivelling trucks put under their forward ends, and no more trouble occurred. The equalizing levers were patented in 1838, by Joseph Harrison, Jr., of Philadelphia.

These two improvements, which are absolutely essential to the success of railways in new countries, and have been adopted in Canada, Australia, Mexico, and South America,* to the exclusion

---

* It is proper here to say that English engineers now appreciate the merits of the American swivelling truck or bogie. In the article on Railways in the last edition of the " Encyclopædia Britannica,"

Alpine Pass. Avoidance of a Tunnel.

of English patterns, are also of great value on the smoothest and best possible tracks. The flexibility of the American machine increases its adhesion and enables it to draw greater loads than its

A Sharp Curve—Manhattan Elevated Railway, 110th Street, New York

English rival. The same flexibility equalizes its pressure on the track, prevents shocks and blows, and enables it to keep out of the hospital and run more miles in a year than an English locomotive.*

Equally valuable improvements were made in cars, both for passengers and freight. Instead of the four-wheeled English car, which on a rough track dances along on three wheels, we owe to Ross Winans, of Baltimore, the application of a pair of four-wheeled swivelling trucks, one under each end of the car, thus enabling it to accommodate itself to the inequalities of a rough track and to follow its locomotive around the sharpest curves. There

speaking of locomotives, the author of the article, who is an English engineer of high authority, says: "American practice, many years since, arrived at two leading types of locomotive for passenger, and for goods traffic. The passenger locomotive has eight wheels, of which four in front are framed in a bogie, and the four wheels behind are coupled drivers. *This is the type to which English practice has been approximating.*" The italics are ours.

* The statistics of ten leading English and ten leading American lines, given by Dorsey, show the following results: 1. The cost per year of the rations, wages, fuel of an American locomotive is $3,590; of an English locomotive, $3,080. 2. Average yearly number of train-miles run by American locomotive, 23,928; English locomotive, 17,539. 3. Yearly earnings: American locomotive, $14,860; English locomotive, $10,940, although the English freight charges are much greater than those of the United States.

A Steep Grade on a Mountain Railroad.

are, on our main lines, curves of less than 300 feet radius, while, on the Manhattan Elevated, the largest passenger traffic in the world is conducted around curves of less than 100 feet radius. There are few curves of less than 1,000 feet radius on European railways.

The climbing capabilities of a locomotive upon smooth rails were not known until, in 1852, Mr. B. H. Latrobe, Chief Engineer of the Baltimore and Ohio Railroad, tried a temporary zigzag gradient of 10 per cent.—that is 10 feet rise in 100 feet length, or 528 feet per mile—over a hill about two miles long, through which the Kingwood Tunnel was being excavated. A locomotive weighing 28 tons on its drivers took one car weighing 15 tons over this line in safety. It was worked for passenger traffic for six months. This daring feat has never been equalled. Trains go over 4 per cent. gradients on the Colorado system, and there is one short line, used to bring ore to the Pueblo furnaces, which is worked by locomotives over a 7 per cent. grade. These are believed to be the steepest grades worked by ordinary locomotives on smooth rails.

Another American invention is the switchback. By this plan

the length of line required to ease the gradient is obtained by running backward and forward in a zigzag course, instead of going
straight up the mountain.   As a full stop has to be made at the
end of every piece of line, there is no danger of the train running
away from its brakes.   This device was first used among the hills
of Pennsylvania over forty years ago, to lower coal cars down into
the Nesquehoning Valley.   It was afterwards used on the Callao,
Lima, and Oroya Railroad in Peru, by American engineers, with
extraordinary daring and skill.   It was employed to carry the
temporary tracks of the Cascade Division of the Northern Pacific
Railroad over the "Stampede" Pass, with grades of 297 feet per
mile, while a tunnel 9,850 feet long was being driven through the
mountains.

With the improvement of brakes and more reliable means of

A Switchback.

stopping trains upon steep grades, came a farther development of
the above device, which was first applied on the Denver and Rio
Grande Railroad in Colorado, and has since been applied on a
grand scale on the Saint Gothard road, the Black Forest railways
of Germany, and the Semmering line in the Tyrol.   This device is
to connect the two lines of the zigzag by a curve at the point

where they come together, so that the train, instead of going alternately backward and forward, now runs continuously on.   It
becomes possible for the line to return above itself in spiral form,
sometimes crossing over the lower level by a tunnel, and sometimes by a bridge.   A notable instance of this kind of location is
seen on the Tehachapi Pass of the Southern Pacific, where the line

PLAN.

Plan of Big Loop.

NOTE: *The Figures denote Radii of Curves in Feet.*

ascends 2,674
feet in 25 miles,
with eleven tun-
nels, and a spi-
ral 3,800 feet
long.

The " Big Loop," as it is called, on the Georgetown branch of
the Union Pacific, in Colorado, between Georgetown and a mining
camp called Silver Plume, has been chosen to illustrate this point.
The direct distance up the valley is 1¼ miles and the elevation 600
feet, requiring a gradient of 480 feet per mile.   But by curving the
line around in a spiral, the length of the line is increased to 4 miles
and the gradient reduced to 150 feet per mile.   Zigzags were used
first for foot-paths, then for common roads, lastly for railways.
Their natural sequence, spirals, was a railway device entirely, and
confirms the saying of one of our engineers : " Where a mule can
go, I can make a locomotive go."   This may be called the poetry
of engineering,
as it requires
both imagina-
tion to conceive
and skill to ex-
ecute.

Profile of the Same.

There is one
thing more
which distin-
guishes the American railway from its English parent, and that is
the almost uniform practice of getting the road open for traffic in
the cheapest manner and in the least possible time, and then completing it and enlarging its capacity out of its surplus earnings, and
from the credit which these earnings give it.

Big Loop, Georgetown Branch of the Union Pacific, Colorado.

The Pennsylvania Railroad between Philadelphia and Harris-burg is a notable example of this. Within the past few years it has been rebuilt on a grand scale, and in many places relocated, and miles of sharp curves and heavy gradients, originally put in to save expense, have been taken out. This system has been followed everywhere, except on a few branch lines, and upon one monumen-tal example of failure—the West Shore Railroad, of New York. The projectors of that line attempted in three years to build a double-track railroad up to the standard of the Pennsylvania road, which had been forty years in reaching its present excellence. Their money gave out, and they came to grief.

II.

WE have thus briefly reviewed the development of our railways to show what they are, and how they came to be what they are, before describing the processes of building, in order that the reasons may be clearly understood why we do certain things, and why we fail to do other things which we ought to do.

In the building of a railway the first thing is to make the sur-veys and locate the position of the intended road upon the ground, and to make maps and sections of it, so that the land may be bought and the estimates of cost be ascertained. The engineer's first duty is to make a survey by eye without the aid of instruments. This is called the "reconnoissance." By this he lays down the general position of the line, and where he wants it to go if possi-ble. Great skill, the result of long experience, or equally great ignorance may be shown here. After the general position of the line, or some part of it, has been laid down upon the pocket map, the engineer sends his party into the field to make the preliminary survey with instruments.

In an old-settled country the party may live in farm-houses and taverns, and be carried to their daily work by teams. But a sur-veying party will make better progress, be healthier and happier, if they live in their own home, even if that home be a travelling camp of a few tents. With a competent commissary the camp can be well supplied with provisions, and be pitched near enough to the probable end of the day's work to save the tired men a long walk.

Engineers in Camp.

When they get to camp and, after a wash in the nearest creek, find a smoking-hot supper ready—even though it consist of fried pork and potatoes, corn-bread and black coffee—their troubles are all forgotten, and they feel a true satisfaction which the flesh-pots of Delmonico's cannot give. One greater pleasure remains—to fill the old pipe, and recline by the camp-fire for a jolly smoke.

A full surveying party consists of the front flag-man, with his corps of axe-men to cut away trees and bushes; the transit-man, who records the distances and angles of the line, assisted by his chain-men and flag-men; and lastly the leveller, who takes and records the levels, with his rod-men and axe-men. The chief of the party exercises a general supervision over all, and is sometimes assisted by a topographer, who sketches in his book the contours of the hills and direction and size of the watercourses.

One tent contains the cook, the commissary, and the provisions; another tent or two the working party, and another the superior engineers, with their drawing instruments and boards. In a properly regulated party the map and profile of the day's work should be plotted before going to bed, so as to see if all is right. If it turns out that the line can be improved and easier grades got, or other changes made, now is the time to do it.

After the preliminary lines have been run, the engineer-in-chief takes up the different maps and lays down a new line, sometimes coinciding with that surveyed, and sometimes quite different. The parties then go back into the field and stake out this new line, called the "approximate location," upon which the curves are all run in. In difficult country the line may be run over even a third or fourth time; or in an easy country, the "preliminary" surveys may be all that is wanted.

The life of an engineer, while making surveys, is not an easy one. His duties require the physical strength of a drayman and the mental accuracy of a professor, both exerted at the same time, and during heat and cold, rain and shine.

An engineer, once on a time, standing behind his instrument, was surrounded by a crowd of natives, anxious to know all about it. He explained his processes, using many learned words, and flattered himself that he had made a deep impression upon his hearers. At last, one old woman spoke up, with an expression of great contempt on her face, "Wall! If I knowed as much as you do, I'd quit ingineerin' and keep a grocery!"

A large part of the financial difficulties of our railways results from not taking time enough to properly locate the line. It must be remembered that a cheaply constructed line can be rebuilt, but with a badly located line nothing can be done except to abandon it entirely.

Royal Gorge Hanging Bridge, Denver and Rio Grande, Colorado.

It is well therefore to consider carefully what is the true problem of location.   It is so to place and build a line of railway that it
shall get the greatest amount of business out of the country through
which it passes, and at the same time be able to do that business
at the least cost, including both expenses of operating and the
fixed charges on the capital invested.   The mere statement of this
problem shows that it is not an easy one.   Its solution is different

in a new and unsettled country from that in an old-settled region. In the new country, the shortest, cheapest, and straightest line possible, consistent with the easiest gradients that the to-

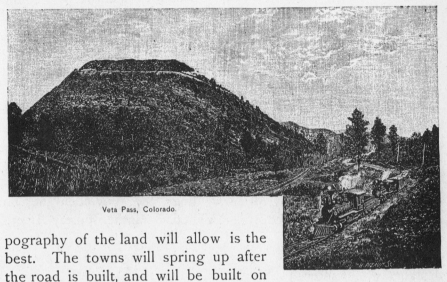

Veta Pass, Colorado.

pography of the land will allow is the best. The towns will spring up after the road is built, and will be built on its line, and generally at the places where stations have been fixed.

In a mountainous country, like Colorado, the problem is how to reach the important mining camps, regardless of the crookedness and increased length given to the line. The Denver and Rio Grande has been compared to an octopus. This is really a compliment to its engineers. It sucks nutriment from every place where nutriment is to be found. To do this it has been forced to climb mountains, where it was thought locomotives could never climb. In one place, called the Royal Gorge, the difficulties of blasting a road-bed into the side of the mountain were so great that it was thought expedient to carry the track upon a bridge, and this bridge was hung from two rafters, braced against the sides of the gorge. In surveying some parts of the lines the engineers were suspended by ropes from the top of the mountains and made their measurements swinging in mid-air.

The problem of location is different in an old-settled country, where the position of the towns as trade-centres has been fixed by natural laws that cannot be overruled. In this case the best thing the engineer can do is to get the easiest gradient possible consist-

ent with the topography of the country, and let the curves take
care of themselves; always to strike the important towns, even if
the line is made more crooked and longer thereby; to so place
the line in these towns as to accommodate the public, and
still be able to buy plenty of land; also to locate
for under or over, rather than grade crossings.

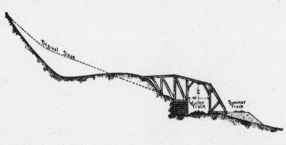

In all countries, old and new, mountainous and level, the rule should be to
keep the level of track well
above the surface of the
ground, in order to insure
good drainage and freedom
from snow-drifts.

Sections of Snow-sheds.

The question of avoidance of obstruction by snow is a very serious one upon the Rocky Mountain lines, and they could not be
worked without the device of snow-sheds—another purely American invention. There
are said to be six miles
of stanchly built snow-
sheds on the Cana-
dian Pacific and sixty
miles on the Central
Pacific Railway. The
quantity of snow fall-
ing is enormous, sometimes amounting to 250,000 cubic yards,
weighing over 100,000 tons, in one slide. It is stated by the engineers of the Canadian Pacific, that the force of the air set in
motion by these ava-
lanches has mown
down large trees, not
struck by the snow

itself. Their trunks, from one to two feet in diameter, remain,
split as if struck by lightning.

After the railway line has been finally located, the next duty of
the engineers is to prepare the work for letting. Land-plans are
made, from which the right of way is secured. From the sections,
the quantities are taken out. Plans of bridges and culverts are

Snow-sheds, Selkirk Mountains, Canadian Pacific. The winter track under cover; the outer track for summer use.

Making an Embankment.

made; and a careful specification of all the works on the line is drawn up.

The works are then let, either to one large contractor or to several smaller ones, and the labor of construction begins. The duties of the engineers are to stake out the work for the contractors, make monthly returns of its progress, and see that it is well done and according to the specifications and contract. The line is divided into sections, and an engineer, with his assistants, is placed in charge of each. Where the works are heavy, the contractors build shanties for their men

Steam Excavator.

and teams near the heavy cuttings or embankments. It is the custom to take out heavy cuttings by means of the machine called a steam shovel, which will dig as many yards in a day as 500 men.

On the prairies of the West the road-bed is thrown up from ditches on each side, either by men with wheelbarrows and carts, or by means of a ditching-machine, which can move 3,000 yards of earth daily. In this case the track follows immediately after the embankment, and the men live in cars fitted up as boarding-shanties, and moved forward as fast as required. If the country contains suitable stone, the culverts and bridge abutments are built by gangs

Building a Culvert.

of masons and stone-cutters, who move from point to point. But the general practice is to put in temporary trestle-work of timber resting upon piles, which trestle-work is renewed in the shape of stone culverts covered by embankments, or iron bridges resting on stone abutments and built after the road is running.

The pile-driver plays a very important part therefore in the construction of our railroads, and has been brought to great perfection. It is worked by a small boiler and engine, and gives its blows with great rapidity. It drags the piles up to leaders and lifts them into place by steam-power, so that it is worked by a small gang of men. Finally, it is as portable as a pedler's cart, and as soon as it has finished one job it is taken to pieces, packed upon w a g o n s, and moved on to the next job.

Tunnels are neither so long nor so frequent upon American railways as upon those of Europe. The longest are from two to two and a half miles long, except one, the Hoosac, about four miles. Sometimes they are unavoidable.

Rock Drill.

The ridge called Bergen Hill, west of Hoboken, N. J., is a case in p o i n t. T h i s is pierced by the tunnels of the West Shore, of the Delaware, Lackawanna, and Western, and of the Erie, the last two of which, as shown on page 25, are placed at different levels to enable one road to pass over the other.

It is by our system of using sharp curves that we avoid tunnels. It may be said, in general terms, that American engineers have shown more skill in avoiding the necessity of tunnels than could possibly be shown in constructing them. When we are obliged to use tunnels, or to make deep cuttings in rocks, our labors are greatly assisted by the use of power-drills worked by compressed air and by the use of high explosives, such as dyna-

A Construction and Boarding Train.

mite, giant powder, rend-rock, etc. Rocks can now be removed in less than half the time formerly required, when ordinary blasting-powder was used in hand-drilled holes.*

III.

From data furnished by Mr. D. J. Whittemore, chief engineer of the Chicago, Milwaukee, and St. Paul system (which had a total length of 5,688 miles on January 1, 1888), the length of open bridges on these lines was $115\frac{91}{100}$ miles, and of culverts covered over with embankment, $39\frac{2}{10}$ miles. "Everything," says Mr. Whittemore, "not covered with earth, except cattle guards, be the span 10 or 400 feet, is called a bridge. Everything covered with earth is called a culvert. Wherever we are far removed from suitable quarries, we build a wooden culvert in preference to a pile bridge, if we can get six inches of filling over it. These cul-

* The writer has obtained many of the statistics used in this article from A. M. Wellington's "Economic Theory of Railway Location," a perfect mine of valuable information upon all such matters.

Bergen Tunnels, Hoboken, N. J.

verts are built of roughly squared logs, and are large enough to draw an iron pipe through them of sufficient diameter to take care of the water. We do this because we believe that we lessen the liability to accident, and that the culvert can be maintained after decay has begun, much longer than a piled bridge with stringers to carry the track. Had we good quarries along our line, stone would be cheaper. Many thousands of dollars have been spent by this company in building masonry that after twenty to twenty-five years shows such signs of disintegration that

we confine masonry work now only to stone that we can procure
from certain quarries known to be good."

Mr Whittemore is an engineer of great experience, skill, and

Beginning a Tunnel.

judgment, and there is food for much reflection in these words of
his : First—that it is better to use temporary wooden structures,
to be afterward renewed in good stone, rather than to build of the
stone of the locality, unless first-class.   Second—that a structure
covered with earth is much safer than an open bridge ; which, if
short and apparently insignificant, may be, through neglect, a most
serious point of danger, as was shown in the dreadful accident of
1887 on the Toledo, Peoria, and Western road in Illinois, where
one hundred and fifty persons were killed and wounded, and by
the equally avoidable accident on the Florida and Savannah line,
in March, 1888.   Had these little trestles been changed to culverts
covered with earth, many valuable lives would not have been lost.

It was safely estimated that there were, in 1888, 208,749
bridges of all kinds, amounting in length to 3,213 miles, in the
United States.*

---

* The amount of permanent wood and iron truss bridges, and of temporary wooden trestles on the
Chicago, Milwaukee, and St. Paul is as follows :

Truss bridges,	700 spans,	average 93 feet,	12 $^4/_5$ miles.	
Trestle "	7,196 "	" 77 "	103$'/_{10}$ ".	
Total,	7,896		115$^9/_{10}$ "	

The approximate total number of bridges in the United States was in 1888 :

The wooden bridge and the wooden trestle are purely American products, although they were invented by Leonardo da Vinci in the sixteenth century. From the above statistics it will be seen how much our American railways owe to them, for without them over 150,000 miles could never have been built.

The art of building wooden truss-bridges was developed by Burr & Wernwag, two Pennsylvania carpenters, some of whose works are still in use after eighty years of faithful duty (p. 28). A bridge built by Wernwag across the Delaware in 1803 was used as a highway bridge for forty-five years, was then strengthened and used as a railway bridge for twenty-seven years more, and was finally superseded by the present iron bridge in 1875.

These old bridge-builders were very particular about the quality of their timber, and never put any into a bridge less than two years old. But when we began to build railways, everything was done in a hurry, and nobody could wait for seasoned timber. This led to the invention of the Howe truss, by the engineer of that name, which had the advantage of being adjustable with screws and nuts, so that the shrinkage could be taken up, and which had its parts connected in such a way that they were able to bear the heavy concentrated weight of locomotives without crushing. This bridge was used on all railways, new and old, from 1840 to about 1870. Had it been free from liability to decay and burn up, we should probably not be building iron and steel bridges now, except for long spans of over 200 feet; and as the table opposite shows, the largest number of our spans are less than 100 feet long.

The Howe truss forms an excellent bridge, and is still used in the West on new roads, with the intention of substituting iron trusses after the roads are opened.

After 1870, the weights both of locomotives and other rolling stock began to be increased very rapidly. This, together with

Iron and wood truss bridges,	61,562 spans,	1,086 miles.
Wooden trestles,	147,187	2,127 "
Total,	208,749	3,213 "

Probably three-fourths of the truss bridges are now of iron or steel, and may be considered perfectly safe so long as the trains remain upon the rails and do not strike the side trusses. The wooden trestles are a constant source of danger from decay or burning or from derailed trains, and should be replaced by permanent structures as fast as time and money will allow.

Freight Yards of the New York Central & Hudson River Railroad, West Sixty-fifth Street, New York.

general dimensions, and also the loads to be carried and the maximum strains to be allowed. The contracting engineer was left perfectly free to design his bridge, and he strained every nerve to find the form of truss and the arrangement of its parts that should give the required strength with the least number of pounds weight per foot, so that he could beat his competitors. When the different plans were handed in, an expert examined them and rejected those whose parts were too small to meet the strains. Of those found to be correctly proportioned, the lowest bid took the work.

By the rule of the survival of the fittest all badly designed forms of trusses disappeared and only two remained: one the original truss designed by Mr. Whipple, and the other, the well-known triangular, or "Warren" girder, so called after its English inventor.

It speaks well for the skill and honesty of American bridge engineers that many of their old bridges are still in use, designed for loads of 2,500 pounds per lineal foot, and now daily carrying loads of 4,000 pounds and over per foot. Sometimes the floor has been replaced by a stronger one, but the trusses still remain and do good service. The writer may be permitted to point to the bridge over the Mississippi River at Quincy, Ill., built in 1869, as an example. Most bridge-accidents can be traced to derailed trains striking the trusses and knocking them down. Engineers (both those specially connected with bridge works, and those in charge of railways) know much better now what is wanted, and the managers of railways are willing to pay for the best article. The introduction of mild steel is a great step in advance. This material has an ultimate strength, in the finished piece, of 63,000 to 65,000 pounds per square inch, or forty per cent. more than iron, and it is tough enough to be tied in a knot, or punched into the shape of a bowl, while cold. With this material it is as easy to construct spans of 500 feet as it was spans of 250 feet in iron.

Bridges are now designed to carry much heavier loads than formerly. The best practice adopts riveted connections except at the junction of the chord-bars and the main diagonals, where pins and eyes are still very properly used. Plate girders below the track are preferred up to 60 or 70 feet long, then riveted lattice up

Kinzua Viaduct; Erie Railway.

to 125 feet. The wind strains also are now provided for with a considerable excess of material, amounting in very long spans to nearly as much as the strains due to gravity. Observing the rule that no bridge can be stronger than its weakest part, a vast deal of care and skill has been applied in perfecting the connections of the parts of a truss, and many valuable experiments have been made which have greatly enlarged our knowledge of this difficult subject. The introduction of riveting by the power of steam or compressed air is another very great improvement.*

Valleys and ravines are now crossed by viaducts of iron and steel, of which the Kinzua viaduct, illustrated here, is an example. A branch line from the Erie, connecting that system with valuable coal-fields, strikes the valley of the Kinzua, a small creek, about 15 miles southwest of Bradford, Pa. At the point suitable for crossing, this ravine is about half a mile wide and over 300 feet deep. At first it was proposed to run down and cross the creek at a low level by some of the devices heretofore illustrated in this article. But finally the engineering firm of Clarke, Reeves & Co. agreed to build the viaduct, shown above, for a much less sum than

* See following article on "Feats of Railroad Engineering," page 86.

any other method of crossing would have cost. This viaduct was built in four months. It is 305 feet high and about 2,400 feet long. The skeleton piers were first erected by means of their own posts, and afterward the girders were placed by means of a travelling scaffold on the top, projecting over about 80 feet. No staging of any kind was used, nor even ladders, as the men climbed up the diagonal rods of the piers, as a cat will run up a tree.

The Manhattan Elevated Railway, about 34 miles long, is nothing but a long viaduct, and is as strong and durable as iron viaducts on railways usually are, while from the slower speed of its trains it is much safer.

It may not be out of place for the writer to state here what, in his belief, is the next series of steps to be taken to insure safety in travelling over our bridges : Replace, wherever possible, all temporary trestles by wood or stone culverts covered with earth. Where this cannot be done, build strong iron or steel bridges and viaducts with as short spans as possible and having no trusses above the track where it can possibly be helped. Cover these and all new bridges with a solid deck of rolled-steel corrugated plates, coated with asphalt to prevent rusting. Place on this broken

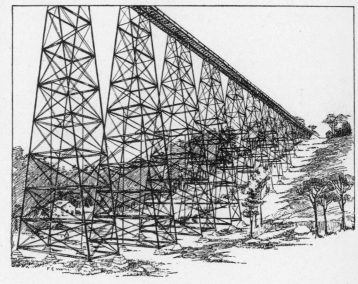

Kinzua Viaduct.

stone ballast, and bed the ties in it as in the ordinary form of road-bed.

By this means the usual shock felt in passing from the elastic embankment to the comparatively solid bridge will be done away.

Has a crack formed in a wheel or axle, this shock generally develops it into a break, the car or engine is derailed, and if it strikes the truss the bridge is wrecked. The cost of this proposed safety floor is insignificant, compared with the security resulting from it.

The improvements in the processes of putting in the foundations of bridges have been as great as those above water. All have shortened greatly the time necessary, and have made the results more certain. The American system may briefly be described as an abandonment of the old engineering device of coffer-dams, by which the bed of the river is enclosed by a water-tight fence and the water pumped out. For this we substitute driving piles and sawing them off under water; or sinking cribs down to a hard bottom through the water. In both cases we sink the masonry, built in a great water-tight box (called a caisson) with a thick bottom of solid timber, until it finally rests on the heads of the piles sawn to a level, or on the top of a crib which is filled with stone, dumped out of a barge. Sometimes it is filled with concrete lowered through the water by special apparatus.*

Another process, developed within the last twenty years, is to sink cribs through soft or unreliable material to a harder stratum by compressed air. This is an improvement on the old diving-bell. The air, forced into the bell-shaped cavity, expels the water and allows the men to work and remove the material, which is taken up by a device called an air-lock. The crib slowly sinks, carrying the masonry on its top.

By this means the foundations of the Brooklyn bridge and of the St. Louis bridge were sunk a little over 100 feet below water. A recent invention is that of a German engineer, Herr Poetsch, who freezes the sand by inserting tubes filled with a freezing mixture, and then excavates it as if it were solid rock.

The process of sinking open cribs through the water by weighting them and dredging out the material was followed at the new bridge recently built over the Hudson at Poughkeepsie, where the cribs were sunk 130 feet below water, and at the bridge building over the Hawkesbury River, in Australia. The Hawkesbury piers are sunk to a depth of 175 feet below water, and are the deepest

* For fuller description of work in a caisson see " Feats of Railway Engineering," page 69.

foundations yet put in. The writer (who derives his knowledge from being one of the designing and executive engineers of both these bridges) sees no difficulty in putting down foundations by this process of open dredging to even much greater depths. The compressed-air process is limited to about 110 feet in depth.

IV.

THE most notable invention of latter days in bridge construction is that of the cantilever bridge, which is a system devised to dispense with staging, or false works, where from the great depth, or the swift current, of the river, this would be difficult, or, as in the case of the Niagara River, impossible to make. The word cantilever is used in architecture to signify the lower end of a rafter, which projects beyond the wall of a building, and supports the roof above. It is from an Italian word, taken from the Latin *cantilabrum* (used by Vitruvius), meaning *the lip of the rafter*. If two beams were pushed out from the shores of a stream until they met in the centre, and these two beams were long enough to run back from the shores until their weight, aided by a few stones, held them down, we should have a primitive form of the cantilever, but one which in principle would not differ from the actual cantilever bridges. This is another American invention, although it has been developed by British engineers—Messrs. Fowler & Baker—in their huge bridge now building across the Forth, in Scotland, of a size which dwarfs everything hitherto done in this country, the Brooklyn bridge not excepted.

The first design of which we have any record was that of a bridge planned by Thomas Pope, a ship carpenter of New York, who, in 1810, published a book giving his designs for an arched bridge of timber across the North River at Castle Point, of 2,400 feet span. Mr. Pope called this an arch, but his description clearly shows it to have been what we now call a cantilever. As was the fashion of the day, he indulged in a poetical description:

> " Like half a Rainbow rising on yon shore,
> While its twin partner spans the semi o'er,
> And makes a perfect whole that need not part
> Till time has furnish'd us a nobler art."

View of Thomas Pope's Proposed Cantilever (1810).

The first railway cantilever bridge in the world was built by the late C. Shaler Smith, C.E., one of our most accomplished bridge engineers. This was a bridge over the deep gorge of the Kentucky River.* The next was a bridge on the Canadian Pacific, in British Columbia, designed by C. C. Schneider, C.E. A very similar bridge is that over the Niagara River, designed by the same engineer in conjunction with Messrs. Field & Hayes, Civil Engineers. This bridge was the first to receive the distinctive name of cantilever.

The new bridge at Poughkeepsie has three of these cantilevers, connected by two fixed spans, as shown in the illustration (pg. 36). The fixed spans have horizontal lower chords, and really extend beyond each pier and up the inclined portions, to where the bottom chord of the cantilever is horizontal. At these points the junctions between the spans are made, and arranged in such a way, by means of movable links, that expansion and contraction due to changes of temperature can take place. The fixed spans are 525 feet long. Their upper chord, where the tracks are placed, is 212 feet above water. These spans required stagings to build them upon. These stagings were 220 feet above water, and rested on piles, driven through 60 feet of water and 60 feet of mud, making the whole height of the temporary staging 332 feet, or within 30 feet of the height of Trinity Church steeple, in New York. The

* See "Feats of Railway Engineering," page 55.

time occupied in building one of these stagings and then erecting the steel-work upon it was about four months.

The cantilever spans were erected, as shown in the illustration on page 37, without any stagings at all below, and entirely from the two overhead travelling scaffolds, shown in the engraving. These scaffolds were moved out daily from the place of beginning over the piers, until they met in the centre. The workmen hoisted up the different pieces of steel from a barge in the river below and put them into place, using suspended planks to walk upon. The time saved by this method was so great that one of these spans of 548 feet long was erected in less than four weeks, or one-seventh of the time which would have been required if stagings had been used.

At the Forth Bridge, all the projecting cantilevers will be built from overhead scaffolds, 360 feet above the water. It contains two spans of 1,710 feet each. When spans of this length are used, the rivets become very long—seven inches—and it would be impossible to make a good job by hand riveting. Hence a power-riveter is used in riveting the work upon the staging. A steam-engine raises up a heavy mass of cast-iron, called "the accumulator;" the weight of this in descending is transmitted through tubes of water, and its power in-creased by

Pope's Cantilever in Process of Erection. (From his " Treatise on Bridge Architecture.")

contracting the area of pressure, until some twenty tons can be applied to the head of each rivet. One rivet per minute can be put in with this tool.

It will be seen that most of the great saving of time in modern construction of bridges and other parts of railways is due to im-proved machinery. The engineer of to-day is probably not more skilful than his ancestor, who, in periwig and cue, breeches and

General View of the Poughkeepsie Bridge.

silk stockings, is represented in old prints supervising a gang of
laborers, who slowly lift the ram of a pile-driver by hauling on one
end of a rope passed over a pulley-wheel. The modern engineer
has that useful servant, steam, and the history of modern engineering is chiefly the history of those inventions by which steam has
been able to supersede manual labor—such as pile-drivers, steam-
shovels, steam-dredges, and other similar tools.

After the road-bed of a railway is completed and covered with
a good coat of gravel or stone-ballast, and after all the temporary
structures have been replaced by permanent ones, that part of the
work may be said to be done, requiring only that the damages of
storms should be repaired. But the track of a railway is never
done. It is always wearing out and always being replaced.

Some of the early English engineers, not appreciating this, endeavored to lay down solid stone walls coped with stone cut to a
smooth surface, on which they laid their rails. They called this
"permanent way," as distinguished from the temporary track of
rails and cross-ties used by contractors in building the lines. But
experience soon showed that the temporary track, if supported by

a bed of broken stone, always kept itself drained and was always elastic, and remained in much better order than the more expensive so-called "permanent way." When the increase in the weight of our rolling stock began to take place, dating from about 1870, iron rails were found to be wearing out very fast. Some railway men declared that the railway system had reached its full development. But in this world the supply generally equals the demand. When a thing is very much wanted, it is sure to come, sooner or later. The process of making steel invented by, and named after, Henry Bessemer, of England, and perfected by A. L. Holley, of this country, gave us a steel rail which at the present time costs less than one of iron, and has a life five or six times as long, even

Erection of a Cantilever.

under the heavy loads of to-day. We are now approaching very near the limit of what the rail will carry, while the joints are becoming less able to do their duty. Bad joints mean rough track. Rough track means considerably greater expenditure both for its maintenance and that of all the rolling stock, as the blows and shocks do reciprocal damage, both to the rails and to that which runs on them.   Hence all railway managers are now devoting more care and attention to their tracks.

In laying track on a new railway, if it be in an old-settled country where other railroads are near and the highways good, the ties are delivered in piles along the line where wanted, and the haul of the rails is comparatively short. The ties are laid down, spaced and bedded, adzed off to a true

Spiking the Track.

bearing, and the rails laid upon them; the workmen being divided into gangs, each doing a different part of the work.   After the track is laid, the ballast-trains come along and cover the roadbed with gravel.   The track is raised, the gravel tamped well under the ties, and the track is ready for use.

The road is then divided into sections about five miles long. On each section there is a section-boss, with four to six laborers. Their duty is to pass over the track at least twice a day in their hand-car, to examine every joint, and where one is found low or out of line, to bring it back to its true position by tamping gravel under it and moving the track.   They have also to see that all

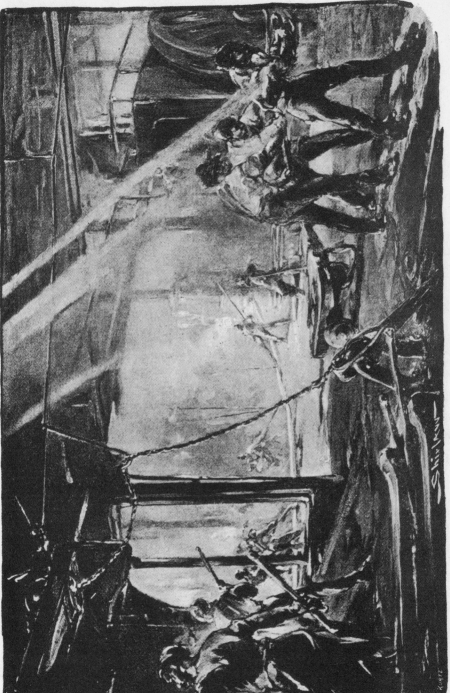

Rail Making.

ditches are kept clear of water, a most essential point, as without good drainage the ground under gravel ballast becomes soft, and

Track Laying.

the mud is churned up into the gravel, and the whole soon gets into bad order.

They have to see that the fences are all right, that trees and telegraph poles do not fall across the track, that wooden bridges do not burn down, that iron and stone bridges are not undermined by freshets, and always to set up danger signals to warn the trains.

It is admitted by competent judges, that the track of the Pennsylvania Railroad is the best in this country, and one of the best in the world. It is kept up to its high standard of excellence by a system of competitive examinations.

About the first of November, in each year, after the season's work has been done, a tour of inspection is made over all the lines, on a train of cars expressly prepared, consisting of two or more cars not unlike ordinary box cars with the front end taken out. Each car is pushed in front of an engine, and goes slowly over the line, by daylight only, so that the inspecting party may have a full view of the road.

The Pennsylvania road is divided into Grand Divisions, Superintendents' Divisions, of about 100 miles long, Supervisors' Divisions, of about 30 miles, and Subdivisions, of $2\frac{1}{2}$ miles.

The examining committee for each Supervisor's Division consists of the supervisors of other divisions. As they pass along, they mark on a card. One sub-committee marks the condition of the alignment and surfacing of the rails; another the condition of the joints and the spacing of the ties; another the ballast, switches, and sidings; another the ditches, road-crossings, station grounds. The marks range from 1 to 10, 0 being very bad, 5 medium, and 10 perfection. When the trip is done these reports are all collected and the average is taken for each division.

As an inducement to the supervisors and the foremen of the Subdivisions to excel on their division, premiums are given as follows :

$100 to the supervisor having the best yard on his Grand Division.

$100 each to the supervisors having the best Supervisor's Division on each Superin-tendent's Division of 100 miles.

$75 to the foreman having the best subdivision of 2¼ miles on each Grand Division.

$60 to each foreman having the best subdivision on his Superintendent's Division, including yards.

$50 to the foreman having the best subdivision on each Supervisor's Division.

In addition to the above there are two premiums of honor given by the general manager, which bring into competition with each other those parts of the main line lying on either side of Philadelphia, viz. :

$100 to the supervisor having the best line and surface between Pittsburg and Jersey City.

$50 to the second best ditto.

If a supervisor or foreman of subdivision receives one of the higher premiums, he is not allowed to be a competitor for any others premiums, except the premiums of honor.

The advantages of these inspections and premiums are these : Every man knows exactly what the standard of excellence is, and strives to have his section reach it. Under the old system, a man never got off of his own section, and had no means of comparison, and like all untravelled persons, became conceited.

The standard of excellence becomes higher and higher every year. Perfect fairness prevails, as the men themselves are the judges. The officers of the road make no marks, but usually look on and see that there is fair play.

This brings the officers and men nearer together, and shows the men how all are working for the common good. An agreeable break is made in the monotony of the men's lives. They have something to look forward to better than a spree.

It is by the adoption of such methods as these that strikes will be prevented in the future. It encourages an *esprit de corps* among the men, and educates them in every way.

This system was first devised and put in operation on the Pennsylvania Railroad in 1879, by Mr. Frank Thomson, General Manager, to whom the credit of it is justly due.

V.

I HAVE thus endeavored to trace the history of the building of a railway ; and it must have been seen, from what has been said, that the evolution of the railway and of its rolling stock follows the same laws which govern the rest of the world: adaptation to circumstances decides what is fittest, and that alone survives. The scrap-heap of a great railway tells its own story.

Our railways have now reached a development which is wonderful. The railways of the United States, if placed continuously, would reach more than half-way to the moon. Their bridges alone would reach from New York to Liverpool. Notwithstanding the number of accidents that we read of in the daily papers, statistics show that less persons are killed annually on railways than are killed annually by falling out of windows.

Railways have so cheapened the cost of transportation that, while a load of wheat loses all of its value by being hauled one hundred miles on a common road, meat and flour enough to supply one man a year can, according to Mr. Edward Atkinson, be hauled 1,500 miles from the West to the East for one day's wages of that man, if he be a skilled mechanic. If freight charges are diminished in the future as in the past, this can soon be done for one day's wages of a common laborer.

The number of persons employed in constructing, equipping, and operating our railways is about two millions.

The combined armies and navies of the world, while on peace footing, will draw from gainful occupations 3,455,000 men.

Those create wealth—these destroy it. Is it any wonder that America is the richest country in the world?

The rapidity with which it is possible to build railways over the prairies of the West is extraordinary. It is true that the

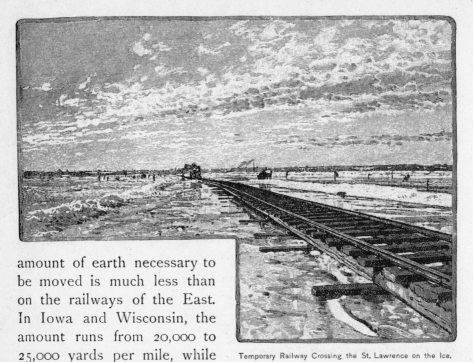

Temporary Railway Crossing the St. Lawrence on the Ice.

amount of earth necessary to be moved is much less than on the railways of the East. In Iowa and Wisconsin, the amount runs from 20,000 to 25,000 yards per mile, while in Dakota it is only 12,000 to 15,000 yards per mile. After making all due allowance for this, the result is still remarkable.

The Manitoba system was extended in 1887 through Dakota and Montana a distance of 545 miles. A small army of 10,000 men, with about 3,500 teams, commanded by General D. C. Shepard, of St. Paul, a veteran engineer and contractor, did it all between April 2 and October 19. All materials and subsistence had to be hauled to the front, from the base of supplies. The army slept in its own tents, shanties, and cars. The grading was cast up from the side ditches, sometimes by carts, and sometimes by the digging machine.

Everything was done with military organization, except that what was left behind was a railway and not earth-work lines of defence. Assuming that this railway, ready for its equipment, cost $15,100 per mile, or $8,175,000, and if it be true, as statisticians tell us, that every dollar expended in building railways in a new country adds ten to the value of land and other property, then this six months' campaign shows a solid increase of the wealth of our country of over eighty millions of dollars. Had it been necessary for our Government to keep an army of observation of the same size on the Canadian frontier, there would have been a dead loss of over eight millions of dollars, and the only result would have been a slight reduction of the Treasury surplus.

It must be remembered that this railway was built after the American system : when the rails were laid, so as to carry trains, it was not much more than half finished ; the track had to be ballasted, the temporary wooden structures replaced by stone and iron, and many buildings and miles of sidings were yet to be constructed. But it began to earn money from the very day the last rail was laid, and out of its earnings, and the credit thereby acquired, it will complete itself.

And this is only one instance out of many. The armies of peace are working all over our country, increasing our wealth, and binding all parts into a common whole. We have here the true answer to the Carlyles and the Ruskins who ask : "What is the use of all this ? Is a man any better who goes sixty miles an hour than one who went five miles an hour ? " " Were we not happier when our fields were covered with their golden harvests, than now, when our wheat is brought to us from Dakota ? "

The grand function of the railway is to change the whole basis of civilization from military to industrial. The talent, the energy, the money, which is expended in maintaining the whole of Europe as an armed camp is here expended in building and maintaining railways, with their army of two millions of men. Without the help of railways the rebellion of the Southern States could never have been put down, and two great standing armies would have been necessary. By the railways, aided by telegraphs, it is easy to extend our Federal system over an entire continent, and thus dispense forever with standing armies.

The moral effect of this upon Europe is great, but its physical effect is still greater. American railways have nearly abolished landlordism in Ireland, and they will one day abolish it in England, and over the continent of Europe. So long as Europe was dependent for food upon its own fields, the owner of those fields could fix his own rental. This he can no longer do, owing to the cheapness of transportation from Australia and from the prairies of

America, due to the inventions of Watt, the Stephensons, Besse-mer, and Holley.

With the wealth of the landlord his political power will pass away. The government of European countries will pass out of the hands of the great landowners, but not into those of the rabble, as is feared. It will pass into the same hands that govern America to-day—the territorial democracy, the owners of small farms, and the manufacturers and merchants. When this comes to pass, attempts will be made to settle international disputes by ar-bitration instead of war, following the example of the Geneva arbi-tration between the two greatest industrial nations of the world. Whether our Federal system will ever extend to the rest of the world, no one knows, but we do know that without railways it would be impossible.

When we consider the effects of all these wonderful changes upon the sum of human happiness, we must admit that the engineer should justly take rank with statesmen and soldiers, and that no greater benefactors to the human race can be named than the Stephensons and their American disciples—Allen, Rogers, Jervis, Winans, Latrobe, and Holley.

FEATS OF RAILWAY ENGINEERING.

By JOHN BOGART.

Development of the Rail—Problems for the Engineer—How Heights are Climbed—The Use of Trestles—Construction on a Mountain Side—Engineering on Rope Ladders—Through the Portals of a Cañon—Feats on the Oroya Railroad, Peru—Nochistongo Cut—Rack Rails for Heavy Grades—Difficulties in Tunnel Construction—Bridge Foundations—Cribs and Pneumatic Caissons—How Men work under Water—The Construction of Stone Arches—Wood and Iron in Bridge-building—Great Suspension Bridges—The Niagara Cantilever and the enormous Forth Bridge—Elevated and Underground Roads—Responsibilities of the Civil Engineer.

THERE are one hundred and fifty thousand miles of railway in the United States : three hundred thousand miles of rails—in length enough to make twelve steel girdles for the earth's circumference. This enormous length of rail is wonderful—we do not really grasp its significance. But the rail itself, the little section of steel, is an engineering feat. The change of its form from the curious and clumsy iron pear-head of thirty years ago to the present refined section of steel is a scientific development. It is now a beam whose every dimension and curve and angle are exactly suited to the tremendous work it has to do. The loads it carries are enormous, the blows it receives are heavy and constant, but it carries the loads and bears the blows and does its duty. The locomotive and the modern passenger and freight cars are great achievements ; and so is the little rail which carries them all.

The railway to-day is one of the matter-of-fact associations of our active life. We use it so constantly that it requires some little effort to think of it as a wonderful thing ; a creation of man's ingenuity, which did not exist when our grandfathers were young. Its long bridges, high viaducts, and dark tunnels may be remarked and remembered by the traveller, but the narrow way of steel, the road itself, seems but a simple work. And yet the problem of location, the determination, foot by foot and mile by mile, of where the line must go, calls in its successful solution for the highest skill of the engineer, whose profession before the railway was created hardly existed at all. Locomotives now climb heights which a few years ago no vehicle on wheels could ascend. The writer, with some engineer friends, was in the mountains of Colorado during the summer of 1887, and saw a train of very intelligent donkeys loaded with ore from the mines, to which no access could be had but by those sure-footed beasts. Within a year one of that party of engineers had located and was building a railway to those very mines. No heights seem too great to-day, no valleys too deep, no cañons too forbidding, no streams too wide; if commerce demands, the engineer will respond and the railways will be built.

The location of the line of a railway through difficult country requires the trained judgment of an engineer of special experience, and the most difficult country is not by any means that which might at first be supposed. A line through a narrow pass almost locates itself. But the approach to a summit through rolling country is often a serious problem. The rate of grade must be kept as light as possible, and must never exceed the prescribed maximum. The cuttings and the embankments must be as shallow as they can be made—the quantities of material taken from the excavations should be just about enough to make adjacent embankments. The curves must be few and of light radius—never exceeding an arranged limit. The line must always be kept as direct as these considerations will allow—so that the final location will give the shortest practicable economical distance from point to point. Many a mile of railway over which we travel now at the highest speed has been a weary problem to the engineer of location, and he has often accomplished a really greater success by securing a line which seems to closely fit the country over which it runs without marking itself sharply upon nature's moulding, than if he had with apparent boldness cut deep into the hills and raised embankments and viaducts high over lowlands and valleys.

View Down the Blue from Rocky Point, Denver, South Park and Pacific Railroad; showing successive tiers of railway.

But roads must run through many regions where very different measures must be taken to secure a location practicable for traffic. For instance, a line at a high elevation approaches a wide valley which it must cross. The rate of descent is fixed by the established maximum grade, and the sides of the valley are much steeper than that rate. Then the engineer must gain distance — that is to say, he must make the line long enough to overcome the vertical height. This can often be accomplished by carrying it up the valley on one side and down on the other.

Tributary valleys can be made use of if necessary, and the desired crossing thus accomplished. But at times even these expedients will not suffice. Then the line is made to bend upon itself and wind down the hillside upon benches cut into the earth, or rock, curving at points where nature affords any sort of opportunity, and reaching the valley at last in long convolutions like the path of a great serpent on the mountain side. These lines often show several tiers of railway, one directly above the other, as may be seen in the illustrations on pages 49 and 51.

The long trestle shown in the illustration opposite is an example of an expedient often of the greatest service in railway construction. These trestles are built of wood, simply but strongly framed together, and are entirely effective for the transport of traffic for a number of years. Then they must be renewed, or, what is better, be replaced by embankment, which can be gradually made by depositing the material from cars on the trestle itself. The trestle illustrated is interesting as conforming to the curve of the line, which in that country, the mountains of Colorado, was probably a necessity of location.

Where the direct turning of a line upon itself may not be necessary, there may and often must be bold work done in the construction of the road upon a mountain side. It must be supported where necessary by walls built up from suitable foundations, often only secured at a great depth below the grade of the road. Projecting points of rock must be cut through, and any practicable natural shelf or favorable formation must be made use of, as in the picture on page 61. In some of the mountain locations, galleries have been cut directly into the rock, the cliff overhanging the roadway, and the line being carried in a horizontal cut or niche in the solid wall.

The Oroya and the Chimbote railways in South America demanded constant locations of this character. At many points it was necessary to suspend the persons making the preliminary measurements from the cliff above. The engineer who made these locations told the writer that on the Oroya line the galleries were often from 100 to 400 feet above the base of the cliff, and were generally reached from above. Rope ladders were used to great advan-

Loop and Great Trestle near Hagerman's, on the Colorado Midland Railway.

tage. One 64 feet long and one 106 feet long covered the usual practice, and were sometimes spliced together. The side ropes were ¾ and 1¼ inches in diameter, and the rounds of wood 1¼ inches in diameter, and 16 inches and 24 inches long. These were notched at the ends and passed through the ropes, to which they were after-ward lashed. These ladders could be rolled up and carried about on donkeys or mules. When swung over the side of a cliff and secured at the top, and when practicable at the bottom, they formed a very useful instrument in location and construction. For simple examination of the cliff, and for rough or broken slopes not exceed-ing 70 to 80 degrees, an active fellow would, after some experience, walk up and down such a slope simply grasping the rope in his hands. If required to do any work he would secure the rope about his body, or wind it around his arm, leaving his hands com-paratively free for light work.

The boatswain's chair—consisting of a wooden seat 6 inches wide and two feet long, through the ends of which pass the side ropes, looped at the top, and having their ends knotted—is a par-ticularly convenient seat to use where cliffs overhang to a slight degree. The riggers were generally Portuguese sailors, who seemed to have more agility and less fear than any other men to be found. At Cuesta Blanca, on the Oroya, a prominent discolora tion on the cliff served as a triangulation point for locating the chief gallery. Men were swung over the side of the cliff in a cage about 2½ feet by 6 feet, open at the top and on the side next the rock. This was a peculiar cliff about 1,000 feet high, rising from the river at a general slope of about 70 degrees. The grade line of the road was 420 feet above the river. The Chileno miners climbed up a rope ladder to a large seam near the grade, where they lived ; pro-visions, water, etc., being hoisted up to them. The first men sent over the cliff to begin the preliminary work were lowered in a cage and took their dinners with them, for fear they would not return to the work, and that unless a genuine start was made others could not be induced to take their places. It is safe to say that 80 per cent. of the sixty odd tunnels on the Oroya and the seven tunnels on the Chimbote lines were located and constructed on lines determined by triangulation, and the results were so satisfactory that the method may be depended upon as the best system for

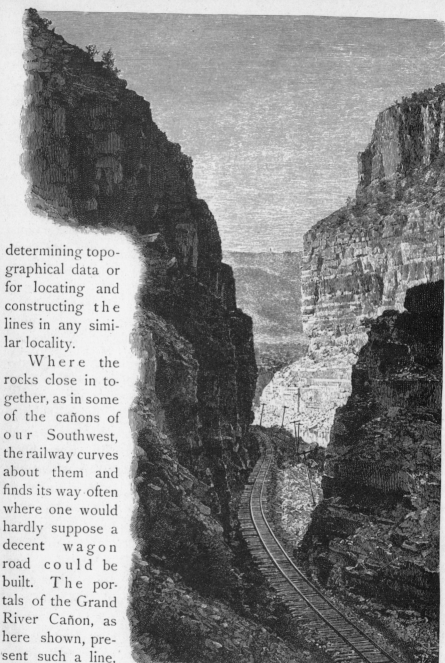

determining topo-
graphical data or
for locating and
constructing t h e
lines in any simi-
lar locality.

Where the
rocks close in to-
gether, as in some
of the cañons of
o u r Southwest,
the railway curves
about them and
finds its way often
where one would
hardly suppose a
decent wagon
road could be
built. T h e por-
tals of the Grand
River Cañon, as
here shown, pre-
sent such a line,
passing through

Denver and Rio Grande Railway Entering the Portals of the Grand River Cañon, Col.

narrow gateways of rock rising precipitously on either side to
enormous heights.

When such a cañon or a narrow valley directly crosses the line of the road, it must be spanned by a bridge or viaduct. The Kentucky River Bridge, shown below, is an instance. The Verrugas Bridge, on the Lima and Oroya Railroad in Peru, is another. This bridge is at an elevation of 5,836 feet above sea-level. It crosses a

The Kentucky River Cantilever, on the Cincinnati Southern Railway.

ravine at the bottom of which is a small stream. The bridge is 575 feet long, in four spans, and is supported by iron towers, the central one of which is 252 feet in height. The construction was accomplished entirely from above, the material all having been delivered at the top of the ravine, and the erection was made by lowering each piece to its position. This was done by the use of two wire-rope cables, suspended across the ravine from temporary towers at each end of the bridge.

On the line of the same Oroya Railroad is a striking example of the difficulties encountered in such mountain country and of the method by which they have been overcome. A tunnel reaches a narrow gorge, a truss is thrown across, and the tunnel continued.

Truss over Ravine, and Tunnel, Oroya Railroad, Peru.

Nature's wildest scenery the deep ravine, the mountain cliffs, and the graceful truss carrying the locomotive and train safely **over** what would seem an impossible pass, here combine to give a **vivid** illustration of an engineering feat.

The location of a part of the Mexican Central Railway through the cut of Nochistongo is peculiarly interesting. Far underneath the level of this line of railway there was skilfully constructed, **in** 1608, a tunnel which at that period was a very bold piece of engineering. It was designed to drain the Valley of Mexico, which has no natural outlet. This tunnel was more than six miles long and ten feet wide. It was driven through the formation called *tepetate*,

The Nochistongo Cut, Mexican Central Railway.

a peculiar earth with strata of sand and marl. It was finished in eleven months. At first excavated without a lining, it was afterward faced with masonry. It was not entirely protected when a great flood came, the dikes above gave way, and the tunnel became obstructed. The City of Mexico was flooded, and it was decided that, instead of repairing the tunnel an open cut should be made. The engineer who had constructed the tunnel, Enrico Martinez, was put in charge of this enormous undertaking, and others took his place after his death. The cut is believed to be the largest ever made in the world. For more than a century the work was continued. Its greatest depth is now 200 feet. It was cut deeper, but has partially filled with the washings from the slopes. The cost was enormous, more than 6,000,000 dollars in silver having been actually disbursed! Wages for workmen were then from 9 to 12 cents a day. All convicts sentenced to hard labor were put at work in the great cut. The loss of life was very great. Writers of the time state that more than 100,000 Indians perished while engaged in the work.

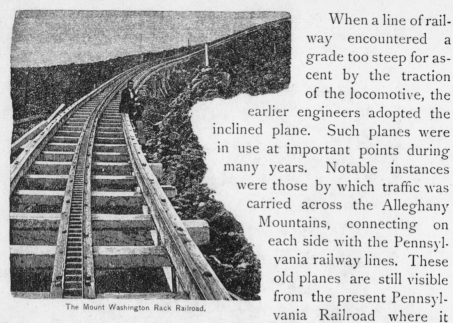

The Mount Washington Rack Railroad.

When a line of railway encountered a grade too steep for ascent by the traction of the locomotive, the earlier engineers adopted the inclined plane. Such planes were in use at important points during many years. Notable instances were those by which traffic was carried across the Alleghany Mountains, connecting on each side with the Pennsylvania railway lines. These old planes are still visible from the present Pennsylvania Railroad where it crosses the summit west of Altoona. The planes were operated by stationary engines acting upon cables attached to the cars. These cables passed around drums at the head of the planes, the weight of the cars on one track partially balancing those on the other. Similar planes were in use also at Albany, Schenectady, and other places.

Another effective expedient is the central rack rail. No better or more successful example of this method of construction can be given than the Mount Washington Railway, illustrated above. The road was completed in 1869. Its length is 3⅓ miles and

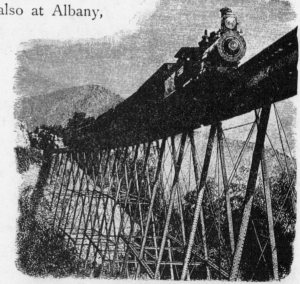

Trestle on Portland and Ogdensburg Railway, Crawford Notch, White Mountains.

its total rise 3,625 feet. Its steepest grade is about 1 foot rise in every 3 feet in length; the average grade is 1 in 4. It is built of heavy timber, well bolted to the rock. Low places are spanned by substantial trestle work. The gauge of the road is 4 feet 7½ inches, and it is provided with the two ordinary rails and also the central rack rail, which is really like an iron ladder, the sides being of angle iron and the cross-pieces of round iron 1½ inches in diameter and 4 inches apart. Into these plays the central cog-wheel on the locomotive, which thus climbs this iron ladder with entire safety. Very complete arrangements are made to control the descent of the train in case of accident to the machinery. The locomotive is always below the train, and pushes it up the mountain. Many thousands of passengers have been transported every year without accident.

The rack railroad ascending the Righi, in Switzerland, was copied after the Mount Washington line. Some improvements in the construction of the rack rail and attachments have been introduced upon mountain roads in Germany, and this system seems very advantageous for use in exceptionally steep locations.

A Series of Tunnels.

When a line of railway meets in its course a barrier of rock, it is often best to cut directly through. If the grade is not too far below the surface of the rock, the cut is made like a great trench with the sides as steep as the nature of the material will allow. Very deep cuts are, however, not desirable. The rains bring down upon their slopes the softer material from above, and the frost detaches pieces of rock which, falling, may result in serious accidents to trains. Snow lodges in these deep cuts, at times entirely stopping traffic, as in the blizzard near New York, in March, 1888. A tunnel, therefore, while perhaps greater in first cost than a moderately deep cut, is really often the more economical expedient.

Tunnel at the Foot of Mount St. Stephen, on the Canadian Pacific.
(The glacier 8,200 feet above the Railway.)

And here is as good a place, perhaps, as any other in this chapter, to say that true engineering is the economical adaptation of the means and opportunities existing, to the end desired. Civil engineering was defined, by one of the greatest of England's engineers, as "the art of directing the great sources of power in nature for the use and convenience of man," and that definition was adopted as a fundamental idea in the charter of the English Institution of Civil Engineers. But the development of engineering-works in America has been effected successfully by American engineers only because they have appreciated another side of the problem presented to them. A past president of the American Society of Civil Engineers, a man of rare judgment and remarkable executive ability, the late Ashbel Welch, said, in discussing a great undertaking proposed by an eminent Frenchman : " That is the best engineering, not which makes the most splendid, or even the most perfect, work, but that which makes a work that answers the purpose well, at the least cost." And it may be remarked. as to the project which he was then discussing, that after a very large expenditure and an experience of eight years since that discussion, the plans of the work were modified and the identical suggestions made by Mr. Welch of a radical economical change were adopted in 1888.* Another eminent American engineer, whose practical experience has been gained in the construction and engineering supervision of more than five thousand miles of railway, said, in his address as President of the American Society of Civil Engineers : "The high object of our profession is to consider and determine the most economic use of time, power, and matter."

Peña de Mora
on the La Guayra and Carácas Railway, Venezuela.

* Reference is made to the substitution of locks in the Panama Canal for the original project of a canal at the sea-level.

Perspective View of St. Gothard Spiral Tunnels, in the Alps.

That true economy, which finally secures in a completed work the best results from the investment of capital, in first cost and continued maintenance, is an essential element in the consideration of any really great engineering feat.

The difficulties involved in the construction of a tunnel, after the line and dimensions have been determined, depend generally upon the nature of the material found as the work advances. Solid rock presents really the fewest difficulties, but it is seldom that tunnels of considerable length occur without meeting material which requires special provision for successful treatment. In some cases great portions of the rock, where the roof of the tunnel is to be, press downward with enormous weight, being detached from the adjacent mass by the occurrence of natural seams.

At other places soft material may be encountered, and the passage then is attended with great difficulty. Temporary supports, generally of timber, and of great strength, have often to be used at every foot of progress to prevent the material from forcing its way into the excavation already made.

In long tunnels the ventilation is a difficult problem, although the use of compressed air drills has aided greatly in its solution.

Among the great tunnels which have been excavated, the St.

Gothard is the most remarkable. It is 9¼ miles long, with a section 26¼ feet wide by 19⅔ feet high. The work on this tunnel was continuous, and it required 9¼ years for its completion.

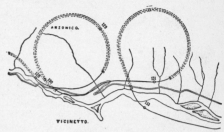

Plan of St. Gothard Spiral Tunnels.

The Mont Cenis tunnel, 8⅓ miles in length, was completed in 12 years.

The Hoosac Tunnel, 4¾ miles in length, 26 feet wide and 21½ feet high, was not prosecuted continuously; it was completed in 1876. These tunnels are notable chiefly on account of their great length; there are others of more moderate extent which have peculiar features; one, illustrated on the preceding page, is unique. This tunnel is a portion of the St. Gothard Railway, and not very far distant from the great tunnel referred to above. In the descent of the mountain it was absolutely necessary to secure a longer distance than a straight line or an ordinary curve would give; the line was therefore doubly curved upon itself. It enters the mountain at a high elevation, describes a circle through the rock and, constantly descending, reappears under itself at the side; still descending, it enters the mountain at another point and continues in another circular tunnel until it finally emerges again, under itself, but at a comparatively short horizontal distance from its first entry, having gained the required descent by a continued grade through the tunnels. The profile above shows the descent, upon a greatly reduced scale, the heavy lines marking where the line is in the tunnel.

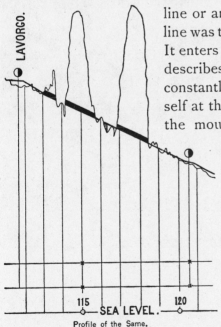

Profile of the Same.

The remarkable success achieved by engineers in securing suitable foundations at great depths is, of course, hardly known to

Portal of a Finished Tunnel; showing Cameron's Cone, Colorado.

the thousands who constantly see the structures supported on those foundations, but in any fair consideration of such engineering achievements this must not be omitted. The beautiful bridge built by Captain Eads over the Mississippi River at St. Louis, bold in its design and excellent in its execution, is an object of ad-

Portal of a Tunnel in Process of Construction.

miration to all who visit it, but the impression of its importance would be greatly magnified if the part below the surface of the water, which bears the massive towers, and which extends to a

Railway Pass at Rocky Point in the Rocky Mountains.

depth twice as great as the height of the pier above the water, could be visible.

The simplest and most effective foundation is, of course, on solid rock. In many localities reliable foundations are built upon earth, when it exists at a suitable depth and of such a character as properly to sustain the weight. Foundations under water, when rock or good material occurs at moderate depth, are constructed frequently by means of the coffer-dam, which is simply an enclosure made water-tight and properly connected with the bottom of the stream. The water is then pumped out and the foundation and masonry built within this temporary dam. When the material is not of a character to sustain the weight, the next expedient is the use of piles, which are driven into the ground, often to a very considerable depth, and sustain the load placed upon them by the friction upon the sides of the piles of the material in which they are driven. It is seldom that dependence is placed upon the load being transferred from the top to the point of the pile, even though the point may have penetrated to a comparatively solid material. Wood is generally used for piles, and where the ground is permanently saturated there seems to be hardly any known limit to

its durability.   The substructure of foundations, where it is certain that they will always be in contact with water, can be, and
generally is, of wood, and the permanency of such foundations
is well established.   An exception to this, however, occurs in
salt-water, particularly in warmer countries, where the ravages of
the minute *Teredo Navalis*, and of the still more minute *Limnoria
Terebrans*, destroy the wood in a very short period of time.
These insects, however, do not work below the ground-line or bed
of the water.   In many special cases hollow
iron piles are used successfully.

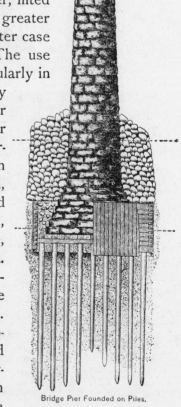

The ordinary method of forcing a pile into
the ground is by repeated blows of a hammer
of moderate weight ; better success being obtained by frequent blows of the hammer, lifted
to a slight elevation, than results from a greater
fall, there being danger also in the latter case
of injuring the material of the pile.   The use
of the water-jet for sinking piles, particularly in
sand, is interesting.   A tube, generally
of ordinary gas-pipe, open at the lower
end, is fastened to the pile ; the upper
end is connected by a hose to a powerful pump and, the pile being placed in
position on the surface of the sand,
water is forced through the tube and
excavates a passage for the pile, which,
by the application of very light pressure,
descends rapidly to the desired depth.
The stream of water must be continuous, as it rises along the side of the pile
and keeps the sand in a mobile state.
Immediately upon the cessation of pump-
ing, the sand settles about the pile, and
it is sometimes quite impossible to afterward move it.   The water-jet is used in
sinking iron piles by conducting the

Bridge Pier Founded on Piles.

water through the interior of the hollow pile and out of a hole at
its point.   The piles of the great iron pier at Coney Island were

sunk with great celerity in this way. The illustration opposite shows one of the piers of a bridge founded upon wooden piling.

In many cases it would be impossible to drive piling in such a way as to insure the durability of the structure above it. This is particularly true of the foundations of structures crossing many of our rivers, where the bottom is of material which, in time of flood, sometimes scours to very remarkable depths; the material often being replaced when the flood has subsided. The expedient adopted is the pneumatic tube, or the caisson. Both are merely applications of the well-known principle of the diving-bell. In the former case hollow iron tubes, open at the bottom, are sunk to considerable depths, the water being expelled by air pumped into the tubes at a pressure sufficient to resist the weight of the water. Entrance to the tubes is obtained by an air-lock at the top, the material is excavated from the inside, and sufficient weight placed upon the tube to force it gradually to the desired depth. When that depth is attained, the tubes are filled with concrete, and thus solid pillars of hydraulic concrete, surrounded by cast-iron tubing, are obtained.

The pneumatic caisson is an enlargement of this idea of the diving-bell. The caisson is simply a great chamber or box, open at the bottom; the outside bottom edges are shod and cased with iron so as to give a cutting surface; the roof and sides are made of timber, thoroughly bolted together, and of such strength as to resist the pressure of the structure to be finally founded upon it. The chamber in the open bottom is of sufficient height to enable the laborers to work comfortably in it. This caisson is generally constructed upon the shore in the vicinity of the structure and towed to the point where the foundation is to be sunk. Air is supplied by powerful pumps and is forced into the working chamber. The pressure of the air of course increases constantly as the caisson descends; it must always be sufficient to overbalance the weight of the water and thus prevent the water from entering the chamber.

Descent to the caisson is made through a tube, generally of wrought iron, and having, at a suitable point, an air-lock, which is substantially an enlargement of the tube, forming a chamber, and of sufficient size to accommodate a number of men. This air-lock is provided with doors or valves at the top and at the bottom, both opening downward, and also with small tubes connecting the air-lock with the chamber below and with the external air above.

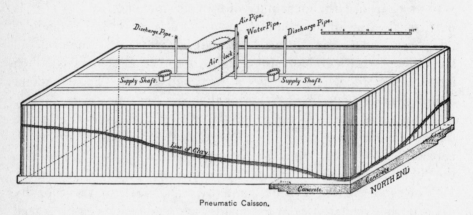

Pneumatic Caisson.

Entrance to the caisson is effected through this air-lock. The lower door, or valve, being at the bottom, closes and is kept closed by the pressure of the air in the caisson below. After the air-lock is entered the upper door or valve is shut, and held shut a few moments, and the tube connecting with the outer air is closed; a small valve in the tube connecting with the caisson is then opened gradually and the pressure in the air-lock becomes the same as that in the chamber below; as soon as this is effected the valve, or door, at the bottom of the air-lock falls open and the air-lock becomes really a part of the caisson.

A sufficient force of men is employed in the chamber to gradually excavate the material from its whole surface and from under the cutting edge, and the masonry structure is founded upon the top of the caisson and built gradually, so as to give constantly a sufficient weight to carry the whole construction down to its final location upon the stable foundation, which may be the bed-rock or may be some strata of permanent character.

The problem of lighting the chamber was until recently of considerable difficulty. The rapid combustion under great pressure made the use of lamps and candles very troublesome, particularly on account of the dense smoke and large production of lampblack.

The introduction of the electric light has greatly aided in the more comfortable prosecution of pneumatic foundation work.

The removal of rock, or any large mass, from the caisson is effected through the air-chamber ; but the removal of finer material, as sand or earth, is accomplished by the sand pump or by the pressure of the air.   A tube, extending from the top of the masonry and kept above the surface by additions, as may be required, enters the working chamber and is controlled by proper valves. Lines of tubing and hose extend to all portions of the chamber. A slight excavation is made and kept filled with water.   The bottom of the tube, or the hose connected with it, is placed in this excavation, and, the material being agitated so as to be in suspension in the water, the valve is opened, and the pressure of the air throws the water and the material held in suspension to the surface, through the tube, from the end of which it is projected with great velocity and may be deposited at any desired adjacent point. This method, however, exhausts the air from the caisson too rapidly for continuous service.   The Eads sand-pump is therefore generally used.   This is an ingenious apparatus, somewhat the

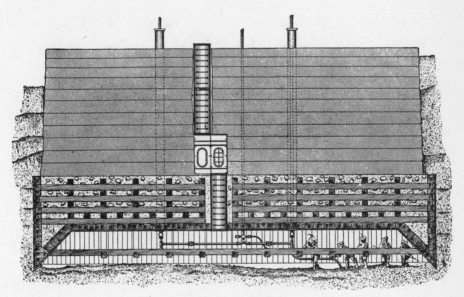

Transverse Section of Pneumatic Caisson.

same in principle as the injector which forces water into steam-boilers.   A stream of water is thrown by a powerful pump through a tube which, at a point near the inlet for the excavated material, is enlarged so as to surround another tube. The water is forced upward with great velocity into the second tube, through a conical annular opening, and, expelling the atmosphere, carries with it to the surface a continuous stream of sand and water from the bottom of the excavation.

This system has been used successfully in the foundations of piers and abutments of bridges in all parts of the world. The rapidity of the descent of the caisson varies with the material through which it has to pass. The speed with which such foundations are executed is remarkable, when one remembers with what delicacy and intelligent supervision they have to be balanced and controlled. In some instances it has been necessary to carry them to great depths, one at St. Louis being 107 feet below ordinary water level in the river.

The pressure of air in caissons at these depths is very great; at 110 feet below the surface of the water it would be 50 pounds to the square inch. Its effect upon the men entering and working in the caisson has been carefully noted in various works, and these effects are sometimes very serious; the frequency of respiration is increased, the action of the heart becomes excited, and many persons become affected by what is known as the "caisson disease," which is accompanied by extreme pain and in some cases results in more or less complete paralysis. The careful observations of eminent physicians who have given this disease special attention have resulted in the formulation of rules which have reduced the danger to a minimum.

The execution of work within a deep pneumatic caisson is worth a moment's consideration. Just above the surface of the water is a busy force engaged in laying the solid blocks of masonry which are to support the structure. Great derricks lift the stones and lay them in their proper position. Powerful pumps are forcing air, regularly and at uniform pressure, through tubes to the chamber below. Occasionally a stream of sand and water issues with such velocity from the discharge pipe that, in the night, the friction of the particles causes it to look like a stream of living fire. Far below is another busy force. Under the great pressure and abnormal supply of oxygen they work with an energy which makes it impossible to remain there more than a few hours. The water

At Work in a Pneumatic Caisson—fifty feet below the surface of the water.

from without is only kept from entering by the steady action of the pumps far above and beyond their control. An irregular settlement might overturn the structure. Should the descent of the caisson be arrested by any solid under its edge, immediate and judicious action must be taken. If the obstruction be a log, it must be cut off outside the edge and pulled into the chamber. Boulders must be undermined and often must be broken up by blasting. The excavation must be systematic and regular. A constant danger menaces the lives of these workers, and the wonderful success with which they have accomplished what they have undertaken is entitled to notice and admiration.

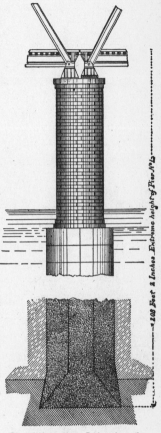

Another process, which has succeeded in carrying a foundation to greater depths than is possible with compressed air, is by building a crib or caisson, with chambers entirely open at the top, but having the alternate ones closed at the bottom and furnished with cutting edges. These closed chambers are weighted with stone or gravel until the structure rests upon the bottom of the river; the material is then excavated from the bottom through the open chambers, by means of dredges, thus permitting the structure to sink by its weight to the desired depth. When that depth is reached, the chambers which have been used for dredging are filled with concrete, and the masonry is constructed upon the top of this structure. The use of this system has enabled the engineer to place foundations deeper than has been accomplished by any other device, one recently built in Australia being 175 feet below the surface of the water. The illustrations above and on page 76 show this method of construction.

Pier of Hawkesbury Bridge, Australia.

Even more remarkable than the pneumatic caisson is this

method of sinking these great foundations. The removal of material must be made with such systematic regularity that the struct-

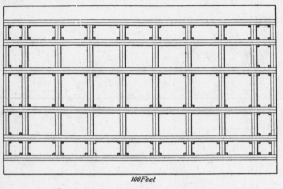

100 Feet

Foundation Crib of the Poughkeepsie Bridge.

ure shall descend even-
ly and always maintain
its upright position.
The dredge is handled
and operated entirely
from the surface. The
very idea is startling,
of managing an exca-
vation more than a
hundred feet below the
operator, entirely by
means of the ropes
which connect with the dredge, and doing it with such delicacy
that the movement of an enormous structure, weighing many tons,
is absolutely controlled. This is one of the latest and most interesting advances of engineering skill.

While it is true that the avoidance of large expenditure, when
possible, is a mark of the best engineering, yet great structures
often become absolutely necessary in the development of railway
communication. Wide rivers must be crossed, deep valleys must
be spanned, and much study has been given to the best methods
of accomplishing these
results. In the early
history of railways in
E u r o p e substantial
viaducts of brick and
stone masonry were
generally built; and in
this country there are
notable instances of
s u c h constructions.
The approach to the
depot of the Pennsyl-

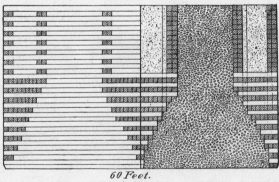

60 Feet.

Transverse Section of the same.

vania Railroad, in the city of Philadelphia, is an excellent example.
Each street crossed by the viaduct is spanned by a bold arch of

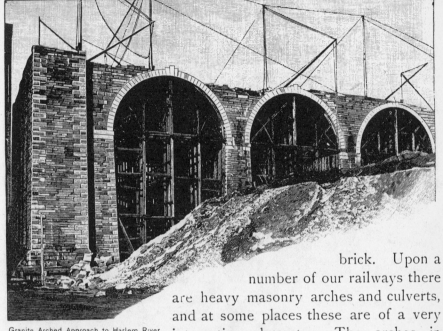

Granite Arched Approach to Harlem River Bridge in Process of Construction.

brick. Upon a number of our railways there are heavy masonry arches and culverts, and at some places these are of a very interesting character. The arches in the approach to the bridge over the Harlem Valley (recently completed) are shown above. They are of granite, having a span of 60 feet. The illustration shows also the method of supporting the stone work of such arches during construction. Braced timbers form what is called the centre, and support the curved frame of plank upon which the masonry is built, which, of course, cannot be self-supporting until the keystone is in place; then the centre is lowered by a loosening of the wedges which support it, and the stone work of the arch is permitted to assume its final bearing. It is generally considered that where it is practicable to construct masonry arches under railways there is a fair assurance of their permanency, but some engineers of great experience in railway construction advance the theory that the constant jar and tremor produced by passing railway trains is really more destructive to masonry work than has been supposed, and that it may be true that the elements of the best economy will be found in metal structures rather than in masonry. It is a fact that repairs and renewals of metal bridges are much more easily accomplished than of masonry constructions.

The Old Portage Viaduct, Erie Railway, N. Y.

In this country the wooden bridge has been an important, in fact an essential element in the successful building of our railways.

Timber is also used extensively in railroad construction in the form of trestles; one example of which has been alluded to on page 50. There were also constructed, years ago, some very bold viaducts in wood. One of the most interesting is shown above, being the viaduct at Portage, N. Y. This construction was over 800 feet long, and 234 feet high from the bed of the river to the rail. The masonry foundations were 30 feet high, the trestles 190 feet, and the truss 14 feet; it contained more than a million and a half feet, board measure, of timber. The timber piers, which were 50 feet apart, are formed by three trestles, grouped together. It was framed so that defective pieces could be taken out and replaced at any time. This bridge was finished in 1852 and was completely destroyed by fire in 1875. The new metal structure which took its place is shown on the opposite page, and is an interesting example of the American method of metal viaduct construction, an essential feature of that construction being the concentration of the material into the least possible number of parts. This bridge has ten spans of 50 feet, two of 100 feet, and one of 118 feet. The trusses are of what is called the Pratt pattern, and are supported

The New Portage Viaduct.

by wrought-iron columns, two pairs of columns forming a skeleton tower 20 feet wide and 50 feet long on the top. There are six of these towers, one of which has a total height from the masonry to the rail of 203 feet 8 inches. There are over 1,300,000 pounds of iron in this structure.

The fundamental idea of a bridge is a simple beam of wood. If metal is substituted it is still a beam with all superfluous parts cut away. This results in what is called an I beam. When greater loads have to be carried, the I beam is enlarged and built up of metal plates riveted together and thus becomes a plate girder. These are used for all short railway spans. For greater spans the truss must be employed.

Before referring, however, to examples of truss bridges, a description should be given of the Britannia Bridge, built by Robert

The Britannia Tubular Bridge over the Menai Straits, North Wales.

Stephenson in 1850, over the Menai Straits. This great construction carries two lines of rails and is built of two square tubes,
side by side, each being continuous, 1,511 feet long, supported at
each extremity and at three intermediate points, and having two
spans of 460 feet each and two spans of 230 feet each. The towers which support this structure are of very massive masonry, and
rise considerably above the top of the tubes. These tubes are
each 27 feet high and 14 feet 8 inches wide; they are built up of
plate iron, the top and bottom being cellular in construction, and
the sides of a single thickness of iron. The tubes for the long
spans were built on shore and floated to the side of the bridge and
then lifted by hydraulic presses to their final position. The rapid
current, and other considerations, made the erection of false works
for these spans impracticable. The beautiful suspension bridge,
built by Telford in 1820, over the Menai Straits, is only a mile
away from this Britannia Bridge, but, at the time of the construction of the latter, it was not deemed possible by English engineers
to erect a suspension bridge of sufficient strength and stability to
accommodate railway traffic.

The Victoria Bridge at Montreal is of the same general character of construction as the Britannia Bridge, but is built only for a single line of rails; this bridge also was built by Mr. Stephenson, in 1859. These two structures were enormous works; their strength is undoubted, but they lack that element of permanent economy which has been spoken of in this article; their cost was very great, and the expense of maintenance is also very great. A very large amount of rust is taken from these tubes every year; they require very frequent painting, and there are on the Victoria Bridge 30 acres of iron surface to be thus painted.

A remarkable and interesting contrast to these heavy tubes of iron is the Niagara Falls railway suspension bridge, completed in March, 1855. The span of this bridge is 821 feet, and the track is 245 feet above the water surface. It is supported by 4 cables which rested on the tops of two masonry towers at each end of the central span, the ends of the cables being carried to and anchored in the solid rock. The suspended superstructure has two floors, one above the other, connected together at each side by posts and truss rods, inclined in such a manner as to form an open trussed tube, not intended to support the load, but to prevent excessive undulations. The floors are suspended from the cables by wire ropes, the upper floor carrying the railroad track, and the lower forming a foot and carriage way. Each cable has 3,640 iron wires. This bridge carried successfully a heavy traffic for 26 years; it was then found that some repairs to the cable were required at the anchorage, the portions of the cables exposed to the air being in excellent condition. These repairs were made, and the anchorage was substantially reinforced. At the same time it was found that the wooden suspended superstructure was in bad condition, and this was entirely removed and replaced by a structure of iron, built and adjusted in such a manner as to secure the best possible results. For some time it had been noticed that the stone towers which supported the great cables of the bridge showed evidences of disintegration at the surface, and a careful engineering examination in 1885 showed that these towers were in a really dangerous condition. The reason for this was that the saddles over which the cables pass on the top of the towers had not the freedom of motion which was required for the action of the cables, caused by differences of temperature and by passing loads. These saddles had been placed upon rollers but, at some period, cement had been allowed to be put between these rollers, thus preventing their free motion. The result was a bending strain upon the towers which was too great for the strength and cohesion of the stone. A most interesting and successful feat was accomplished in the substitution of iron towers for these stone towers, without interrupting the traffic across the bridge. This was accomplished within a year or two by building a skeleton iron tower outside of the stone tower, and

Old Stone Towers of the Niagara Suspension Bridge.

transferring the cables from the stone to the iron tower by a most ingenious arrangement of hydraulic jacks. The stone towers were then removed. Thus, by the renewal of its suspended structure and the replacing of its towers, the bridge has been given a new lease of life and is in excellent condition to-day.

This Niagara railway suspension bridge has been so long in successful operation that it is difficult now to appreciate the general disbelief in the possibility of its success as a railway bridge, when it was undertaken. It was projected and executed by the late John A. Roebling. Before it was finished, Robert Stephenson said to him, "If your bridge succeeds,

The New Iron Towers of the Same.

mine is a magnificent blunder." The Niagara bridge did succeed.

We are so familiar with the great suspension bridge between New York and Brooklyn, that only a simple statement of some of

Below the Brooklyn Bridge.
From a painting by J. H. Twachtman.

its characteristic features will be given. Its clear span is 1,595½ feet. With its approaches its length is 3,455 feet. The clear waterway is 135 feet high. The towers rise 272 feet above high water and extend on the New York side down to rock 78 feet below. The four suspension cables are of steel wire and support six parallel steel trusses, thus providing two carriage ways, two lines of railway, and one elevated footway. The cables are carried to bearing anchorages in New York and in Brooklyn. The cars on the bridge are propelled by cables, and the amount of travel is now so great as to demand some radical changes in the methods for its accommodation, which a few years ago were supposed to be ample.

Except under special circumstances of location or length of span, the truss bridge is a more economical and suitable structure for railway traffic than a suspension bridge.

The advance from the wood truss to the modern steel structure has been through a number of stages. Excellent bridges were built in combinations of wood and iron, and are still advocated where wood is inexpensive. Then came the use of cast iron for those portions of the truss subject only to compressive strains, wrought iron being used for all members liable to tension. Many bridges of notable spans were built in this way and are still in use. The form of this combination truss varied with the designs of different engineers, and the spans extended to over three hundred feet. The forms bore the names of the designers, and the Fink, the Bollman, the Pratt, the Whipple, the Post, the Warren, and others had each their advocates. The substitution of wrought for cast iron followed, and until quite recently trusses built entirely of wrought iron have been used for all structures of great span. The latest step has been made in the use of steel, at first for special members of a truss and latterly for the whole structure. The art of railway bridge building has thus, in a comparatively few years, passed through its age of wood, and then of iron, and now rests in the application of steel in all its parts.

Two distinct ways of connecting the different parts of a structure are in common use, riveting and pin connections.

In riveted connections the various parts of the bridge are fastened at all junctions by overlapping the plates of iron or steel and inserting rivets into holes punched through all the plates to be connected. The rivets are so spaced as to insure the best result as to strength. The pieces of metal are brought together, either in the shop or at the structure during erection, and the rivets, which are round pieces of metal with a head formed on one end, are heated and inserted from one side, being made long enough to project sufficiently to give the proper amount of metal for forming the other head. This is done while the rivet is still hot, either by hammering or by the application of a riveting machine, operated by steam or hydraulic pressure. Ingenious portable machines are now manufactured which are hung from the structure during erection and connected by flexible hose with the steam power, by the use of which the rivet heads can be formed in place with great celerity. The connections of plates by rivets of proper dimensions and properly spaced give great strength and stiffness to such joints.

In pin connections the members of a structure are assembled at points of junction and a large iron or steel pin inserted in a pin-hole running through all the members. This pin is made of such diameter as to withstand and properly transmit all the strains brought upon it. Joints made with such pin connections have flexibility, and the strains and stresses can be calculated with great precision. Eye-bars are forged pieces of iron or steel, generally flat, and enlarged at the ends so as to give a proper amount of metal around the pin-hole or eye, formed in those ends.

Structures connected by pins at their principal junctions have, of course, many parts in which riveting must be used.

The elements which are distinctively American in our railway bridges are the concentration of material in few members and the use of eye-bars and pin connections in place of riveted connections. The riveted methods are, however, largely used in connection with the American forms of truss construction.

An excellent example of an American railway truss bridge is shown on the opposite page. This structure spans the Missouri River at its crossing by the Northern Pacific Railroad. It has three through spans of 400 feet each and two deck spans of 113 feet each. The bottom chords of the long spans are 50 feet above high water, which at this place is 1,636 feet above the level of the sea. The

Truss Bridge of the Northern Pacific Railway over the Missouri River at Bismarck, Dak.—Testing the central span.

foundations of the masonry piers were pneumatic caissons. The trusses of the through spans, 400 feet long, are 50 feet deep and 22 feet between centres. They are divided into 16 panels of 25 feet each. The truss is of the double system Whipple type, with inclined end posts. The bridge is proportioned to carry a train weighing 2,000 pounds per lineal foot, preceded by two locomotives weighing 150,000 pounds in a length of 50 feet. The pins connecting the members of the main truss are 5 inches in diameter.

This bridge is a characteristic illustration of the latest type of American methods. The extreme simplicity of its lines of construction, the direct transfer of the strains arising from loads, through the members, to and from the points where those strains are concentrated in the pin connections at the ends of each member, are apparent even to the untechnical eye. The apparent lightness of construction arising from the

Curved Viaduct, Georgetown, Col.; the Union Pacific crossing its own Line.

concentration of the material in so small a number of members, and the necessarily great height of the truss, give a grace and elegance to the structure, and suggest bold and fine development of the theories of mechanics.

An interesting viaduct is shown in the above illustration, where the railway crosses its own line on a curved truss.

The truss bridges which have been mentioned as types of the modern railway bridge are erected by the use of false works of timber, placed generally upon piling or other suitable foundation, between the piers or abutments, and made of sufficient strength to carry each span of the permanent structure until it is completed and all its parts connected, or, as is technically said, until the span is swung. Then the false works are removed and the span is left without intermediate support. But there are places where it would be impossible or exceedingly expensive to erect any false works. A structure over a valley of great depth, or over a river with very rapid current, are instances of such a situation.

A suspension bridge would solve the problem, but in many cases not satisfactorily. The method adopted by Colonel C. Shaler Smith at the Kentucky River Bridge [p. 55] shows ingenuity and boldness worthy of special remark. The Cincinnati Southern Railroad had here to cross a cañon 1,200 feet wide and 275 feet deep. The river is subject to freshets every two months, with a range of 55 feet and a known rise of 40 feet in a single night. Twenty years before, the towers for a suspension bridge had been erected at this point. The design adopted for the railroad bridge was based upon the cantilever principle. The structure has three spans of 375 feet each, carrying a railway track at a height of 276 feet above the bed of the river. At the time of its construction this was the highest railway bridge in the world, and it is still the highest structure of the kind with spans of over 60 feet in length. The bridge is supported by the bluffs at its ends and by two inter-mediate iron piers resting upon bases of stone masonry. Each iron pier is 177 feet high, and consists of four legs, having a base of $71\frac{1}{2} \times 28$ feet, and terminating at its top in a turned pin 12 inches in diameter under each of the two trusses. Each iron pier is a structure complete in itself, with provision for expansion and contraction in each direction through double roller beds interposed between it and the masonry, and is braced to withstand a gale of wind that would blow a loaded freight-train bodily from the bridge

The trusses were commenced by anchoring them back to the old towers, and were then built out as cantilevers from each bluff to a distance of one-half the length of the side spans, and at this point rested upon temporary wooden supports. Thence they were again extended as cantilevers until the side spans were com-pleted and rested upon the iron piers. This cantilever principle is simply the balancing of a portion of the structure on one side of a support by the portion on the opposite side of the same support. Similarly the halves of the middle span were built out from the piers, meeting with exactness in mid-air. The temporary support used first at the centre of one side span and then at the other, was the only scaffolding used in erecting the structure, none whatever being used for the middle span.

When the junction was made at the centre of the middle span, the trusses were continuous from bluff to bluff, and, had they been left in this condition, would have been subjected to constantly varying strains resulting from the rise and fall of the iron piers

The Niagara Cantilever Bridge in Progress.

due to thermal changes. This liability was obviated by cutting the bottom chords of the side spans and converting them into sliding joints at points 75 feet distant from the iron piers. This done, the bridge consists of a continuous girder 525 feet long, covering the middle span of 375 feet, and projecting as cantilevers for 75 feet beyond each pier, each cantilever supporting one end of a 300-foot span, which completes the distance to the bluff on each side.

A most interesting example of cantilever construction is the railway bridge built several years ago at Niagara, only a few rods from the suspension bridge and a short distance below the great falls. It is shown in the illustrations above and on page 91. The floor of the bridge is 239 feet above the surface of the water, which at that point has a velocity in the centre of 16½ miles per hour and forms constant whirlpools and eddies near the shores. The total length of the structure is 910 feet, and the clear span over the river between the towers is 470 feet. The shore arms of the cantilever, that is to say, those portions of the structure which extend from the top of the bank to the top of the tower built from the foot of the bank, are firmly anchored at their shore ends to a pier built upon the solid rock. These shore-arms were constructed on wooden false works, and serve as balancing weights to the other or river arms of the lever, which project out over the stream. These river-arms were built by the addition of metal, piece by piece, the weight being always more than balanced by the shore-arms. The separate members of the river-arms were run out on the top of the completed part and then lowered from the end by an overhanging travelling derrick, and fastened in place by men working upon a platform suspended below. This work was continued, piece by piece, until the river-arm of each cantilever was complete, and the structure was then finished by connecting these river-arms by a short truss suspended from them directly over the centre of the stream. This whole structure was built in eight months, and is an example both of a bold engineering work and of the facility with which a pin-connected structure can be erected. The materials are steel and iron. The prosecution of this work by men suspended on a platform, hung by ropes from a skeleton

The Niagara Cantilever Bridge Completed.

structure projecting, without apparent support, over the rushing Niagara torrent, was always an interesting and really thrilling spectacle.

The Lachine Bridge recently built over the St. Lawrence near Montreal, illustrated below, has certain peculiar features. It has a total length of 3,514 feet. The two channel spans are each 408 feet in length and are through spans. The others are deck spans.

Through spans are those where the train passes between the side trusses. Deck spans are those where the train passes over the top of the structure. These two channel

The Lachine Bridge. on the Canadian Pacific Railway, near Montreal, Canada.

spans and the two spans next them form cantilevers, and the channel spans were built out from the central pier and from the adjacent flanking spans without the use of false works in either channel. A novel method of passing from the deck to the through spans has been used, by curving the top and bottom chords of the channel spans to connect with the chords of the flanking spans. The material is steel.

This structure, light, airy, and graceful, forms a strong contrast to the dark, heavy tube of the Victoria Bridge just below.

The enormous cantilever Forth Bridge, with its two spans of 1,710 feet each, is in steady progress of construction and will when completed mark a long step in advance in the science of bridge construction.

Of entirely different design and principle from all these trusses are the beautiful steel arches of the St. Louis Bridge [p. 95], the great work of that remarkable genius, James B. Eads. This structure spans the Mississippi at St. Louis. Difficult problems were presented in the study of the design for a permanent bridge at that point. The river is subject to great changes. The variation between extreme low and high water has been over 41 feet. The current runs from $2\frac{3}{4}$ to $8\frac{1}{2}$ miles per hour. It holds always much matter in suspension, but the amount so held varies greatly with the velocity. The very bed of the river is really in constant motion. Examination by Captain Eads in a diving-bell showed that there was a moving current of sand at the bottom, of at least three feet in depth. At low water, the velocity of the stream is small and the bottom rises. When the velocity increases, a "scour" results and the river-bed is deepened, sometimes with amazing rapidity. In winter the river is closed by huge cakes of ice from the north, which freeze together and form great fields of ice.

It was decided to be necessary that the foundations should go to rock, and they were so built. The general plan of the super-structure, with all its details, was elaborated gradually and carefully, and the result is a real feat of engineering. There are three steel arches, the centre one having a span of 520 feet and each side arch a span of 502 feet. Each span has four parallel arches or ribs, and each arch is composed of two cylindrical steel tubes, 18 inches in exterior diameter, one acting as the upper and the other as the lower chord of the arch. The tubes are in sections, each about twelve feet long, and connected by screw joints. The thickness of the steel forming the tubes runs from $1\frac{3}{16}$ to $2\frac{1}{8}$ inches. These upper and lower tubes are parallel and are 12 feet apart, connected by a single system of diagonal bracing. The double tracks of the railroad run through the bridge adjacent to the side arches at the elevation of the highest point of the lower tube. The carriage road and footpaths extend the full width of the bridge and are carried, by braced vertical posts, at an elevation of twenty-three feet above the railroad. The clear headway is 55 feet above ordinary high water. The approaches on each side are masonry viaducts, and the railway connects with the City Station by a tunnel nearly a mile in length. The illustration shows vividly the method of erection of these great tubular ribs. They were built out from each side of a pier, the weight on one side acting as a counterpoise for the construction on the other side of the pier. They were thus gradually and systematically projected over the river, without support from below, till they met at the middle of the span, when the-last central connecting tube was put in place by an ingenious mechanical arrangement, and the arch became self-supporting.

The double arch steel viaduct recently built over the Harlem Valley in the city of New York [p. 97] has a marked difference from the St. Louis arches in the method of construction of the ribs. These are made up of immense voussoirs of plate steel, forming sections somewhat analogous to the ring stones of a masonry arch. These sections are built up in the form of great I beams, the top and bottom of the I being made by a number of parallel steel plates connected by angle pieces with the upright web, which is a single piece of steel. The vertical height of the I is 13 feet. The span of each of these arches is 510 feet. There are six such parallel ribs in each span, connected with each other by bracing. These great ribs rest upon steel pins of 18 inches diameter, placed at the springing of the arch. The arches rise from massive masonry piers, which extend up to the level of the floor of the bridge. This floor is supported by vertical posts from the arches and is a little above the highest point of the rib. It is 152 feet above the surface of the river—having an elevation fifty feet greater than the well-known High Bridge, which spans the same valley within a quarter of a mile. The approaches to these steel arches on each side are granite viaducts carried over a series of stone arches. The whole structure forms a notable example of engineering construction. It was finished within two years from the beginning of work upon its foundations, the energy of its builders being worthy of special commendation.

In providing for the rapid transit of passengers in great cities the two types of construction successfully adopted are represented

The St. Louis Bridge during Construction.

The 510-feet Span Steel Arches of the New Harlem River Bridge, New York, during construction.

by the New York Elevated and the London Underground railways. The New York Elevated is a continuous metal viaduct, supported on columns varying in height so as to secure easy grades. The details of construction differ greatly at various parts of the elevated lines, those more recently built being able to carry much heavier trains than the earlier portions. The roads have been very successful in providing the facilities for transit so absolutely necessary in New York. The citizens of that city are alive to the present necessity of adding very soon to those facilities, and it is now only a question of the best method to be adopted to secure the largest results in a permanent manner.

The London Underground road has also been very successful. Its construction was a formidable undertaking. Its tunnels are not only under streets but under heavy buildings. Its daily traffic is enormous. The difficult ques-

London Underground Railway Station.

tion in its management is, as in all long tunnels, that of ventilation, but modern science will surely solve that, as it does so many
other problems connected with the active life of man.

Many broad questions of general policy, and innumerable matters of detail are involved in the development of railway engineering. In the determination, for instance, of the location, the relations of cost and construction to future business, the possibilities
of extensions and connections, the best points for settlements and
industrial enterprises, the merits and defects of alternative routes
must be weighed and decided.

Where structures are to be built, the amount and delicacy of
detail requisite in their design and execution can hardly be described. Final pressures upon foundations must be ascertained
and provided for. Accurate calculations of strains and stresses,
involving the application of difficult processes and mechanical theo-

ries, must be made. The adjustment of every part must be secured with reference to its future duty. Strength and safety must
be assured and economy not forgotten. Every contingency must,
if possible, be anticipated, while the emergencies which arise during every great construction demand constant watchfulness and
prompt and accurate decision.

The financial success of the largest enterprises rests upon such
practical application of theory and experience. Even more weighty
still is the fact that the safety of thousands of human lives depends
daily upon the permanency and stability of railway structures.
Such are some of the deep responsibilities which are involved in
the active work of the Civil Engineer.

AMERICAN LOCOMOTIVES AND CARS.

By M. N. FORNEY.

The Baltimore and Ohio Railroad in 1830—Evolution of the Car from the Conestoga
Wagon—Horatio Allen's Trial Trip—The First Locomotive used in the United
States—Peter Cooper's Race with a Gray Horse—The " De Witt Clinton,"
" Planet," and other Early Types of Locomotives—Equalizing Levers—How Steam
is Made and Controlled—The Boiler, Cylinder, Injector, and Valve Gear—Regula-
tion of the Capacity of a Locomotive to Draw—Increase in the Number of Driving
Wheels—Modern Types of Locomotives—Variation in the Rate of Speed—The
Appliances by which an Engine is Governed—Round-houses and Shops—Develop-
ment of American Cars—An Illustration from Peter Parley—The Survival of Stage
Coach Bodies—Adoption of the Rectangular Shape—The Origin of Eight-wheeled
Cars—Improvement in Car Coupling—A Uniform Type Recommended—The
Making of Wheels—Relative Merits of Cast and Wrought Iron, and Steel—The
Allen Paper Wheel—Types of Cars, with Size, Weight, and Price—The Car-
Builder's Dictionary—Statistical.

AMONG the readers of this volume there
will be some who have reached the summit of the " divide " which separates the
spring and summer of life from its autumn
and winter, and whose first information about
railroads was received from Peter Parley's " First
Book of History," which was used as a school-
book forty or fifty years ago.   In his chapter on Maryland, he says :

But the most curious thing at Baltimore is the railroad.   I must tell you that there is
a great trade between Baltimore and the States west of the Alleghany Mountains.   The
western people buy a great many goods at Baltimore, and send in return a great deal of
western produce.   There is, therefore, a vast deal of travelling back and forth, and hundreds of teams are constantly occupied in transporting goods and produce to and from
market.*
Now, in order to carry on all this business more easily, the people are building what

* An engraving of a team and of a " Conestoga " wagon—which was used in this traffic—taken from
a photograph of one which has survived to the present day, is given opposite (Fig. 1).

is called a railroad. This consists of iron bars laid along the ground, and made fast, so that carriages with small wheels may run along upon them with facility. In this way, one horse will be able to draw as much as ten horses on a common road. A part of this

Fig. 1.—Conestoga Wagon and Team. (From a recent photograph.)

railroad is already done, and if you choose to take a ride upon it, you can do so. You will mount a car something like a stage, and then you will be drawn along by two horses, at the rate of twelve miles an hour.

The picture reproduced below (Fig. 2) of a car drawn by horses was given with the above description of the Baltimore & Ohio Railroad. The mutilated copy of the book from which the engraving and extract were copied does not give the date when it was written or published. It was probably some time between the years 1830 and 1835. That the car shown in the engraving was evolved from the Conestoga wagon is obvious from the illustrations.

This engraving and description, made for children, more than fifty years ago, will give some idea of the state of the art of railroading at that time; and it is a remarkable fact that the present wonderful development and the improvements in railroads and their equipments in this country have been made during the lives of persons still living.

In the latter part of 1827, the Delaware & Hudson Canal Company put the Carbondale Railroad under construction.

Fig. 2.—Baltimore & Ohio Railroad, 1830–35.

The road extends from the head of the Delaware & Hudson Canal at Honesdale, Pa., to the coal mines belonging to the Delaware & Hudson Canal Company at Carbondale, a distance of about sixteen

miles.   This line was opened, probably in 1829, and was operated
partly by stationary engines, and partly by horses.   The road is
noted chiefly for being the one on which a locomotive was first

Fig. 3.—Boston & Worcester Railroad, 1835.

used in this country.
This was the "Stour-
bridge Lion," which
was built in England
under the direction of
Mr. Horatio Allen,
who afterward was
president of the Nov-
elty Works in New York, and who is still (1889) living near
New York at the ripe age of eighty-seven.   Before the road
was opened, he had been a civil engineer on the Carbondale
line.   In 1828 Mr. Allen went to England, the only place where
a locomotive was then in daily operation, to study the subject
in all its practical details.   Before leaving this country he was
intrusted by the Delaware & Hudson Canal Company with the
commission to have rails made for that line, and to have three
locomotives built on plans to be decided by him when in England.   This, it must be remembered, was before the celebrated
trial of the "Rocket" on the Liverpool & Manchester Railway, which was not made until 1829.   Previous to that trial, it
had not been decided what type of boiler was the best for
locomotives.   The result of Mr. Allen's investigations was to
produce in his mind a decided confidence in the multitubular
boiler which is now universally used for locomotives.   Other
persons of experience recommended a boiler with small riveted
flues of as small diameter as could be riveted.   An order was
therefore given to Messrs. Foster, Rastrick & Co., at Stourbridge, for one engine whose boiler was to have riveted flues of
comparatively large size, and another order was given to Messrs.
Stephenson & Co., of Newcastle-on-Tyne, for two locomotives
with boilers having small tubes.   The engine built by Foster,
Rastrick & Co was named the "Stourbridge Lion."   It was sent
to this country and was tried at Honesdale, Pa., on August 9,
1829.   On its trial trip it was managed by Mr. Allen, to whom
belongs the distinction of having run the first locomotive that

was ever used in this country. In 1884 he wrote the following account of this trip:

When the time came, and the steam was of the right pressure, and all was ready, I took my position on the platform of the locomotive alone, and with my hand on the throttle-valve handle said : " If there is any danger in this ride it is not necessary that the life and limbs of more than one should be subjected to that danger."

The locomotive, having no train behind it, answered at once to the movement of the hand ; . . . soon the straight line was run over, the curve was reached and passed before there was time to think as to its not being passed safely, and soon I was out of sight in the three miles' ride alone in the woods of Pennsylvania. I had never run a locomotive nor any other engine before ; I have never run one since.

The two engines contracted for with Messrs. Stephenson & Co. were made by them, and Mr. Allen has informed the writer that they were built on substantially the same plans that were afterward embodied in the famous " Rocket." They were shipped to New York and for a time were stored in an iron warehouse on the east side of the city, where they were exhibited to the public. They were never sent to the Delaware & Hudson Canal Company's road, and it is not now known what ever became of them. If they had been put to work on their arrival here the use of engines of the " Rocket " type would have been anticipated on this side the Atlantic.

Horatio Allen.

The first railroad which was undertaken for the transportation of freight and passengers in this country, on a comprehensive scale, was the Baltimore & Ohio. Its construction was begun in 1828. The laying of rails was commenced in 1829, and in May, 1830, the first section of fifteen miles from Baltimore to Ellicott's Mills was opened. It was probably about this time that the animated sketch of the car given by Peter Parley was made. From 1830 to 1835 many lines were projected, and at the end of that year there were over a thousand miles of road in use.

Whether the motive power on these roads should be horses or

steam was for a long time an open question.   The celebrated trial
of locomotives on the Liverpool & Manchester Railway, in England,
was made in 1829.   Reports of these trials, and of the use of locomotive engines on the Stockton & Darlington line, were published
in this country, and, as Mr. Charles Francis Adams says, "The
country, therefore, was not only ripe to accept the results of the
Rainhill contest, but it was anticipating them with eager hope."

Fig. 4.—Peter Cooper's Locomotive
1830.

In 1829 Mr. Horatio Allen, who had been
in England the year before to learn all that
could then be learned about steam locomo-
tion, reported to the South Carolina Railway
Company in favor of steam instead of horse
power for that line.   The basis of that report, he says, "Was on the broad ground
that in the future there was no reason to
expect any material improvement in the
breed of horses, while, in my judgment, the
man was not living who knew what the breed of locomotives was
to place at command."

As early as 1829 and 1830, Peter Cooper experimented with a
little locomotive on the Baltimore & Ohio Railroad (Fig. 4).   At
a meeting of the Master Mechanics' Association in New York, in
1875—at the Institute which bears his name—he related with great
glee how on the trial trip he had beaten a gray horse, attached to
another car.   The coincidence that one of Peter Parley's horses is
a gray one might lead to the inference that it was the same horse
that Peter Cooper beat, a deduction which perhaps has as sound a
basis to rest on as many historical conclusions of more importance.

The undeveloped condition of the art of machine construction
at that time is indicated by the fact that the flues of the boiler of
this engine were made of gun-barrels, which were the only tubes
that could then be obtained for the purpose.   The boiler itself is
described as about the size of a flour-barrel.   The whole machine
was no larger than a hand-car of the present day.

In the same year that Peter Cooper built his engine, the South
Carolina Railway Company had a locomotive, called the "Best
Friend," built at the West Point Foundry for its line.   In 1831 this
company had another engine, the "South Carolina" (Fig. 5),

which was designed by Mr. Horatio Allen, built at the same shop. It was remarkable in having eight wheels, which were arranged in two trucks. One pair of driving-wheels, *D D* and *D' D'*, and a pair of leading-wheels, *L L* and *L' L'*, were attached to frames, *c d e f* and *g h i j*, which were connected to the boiler by kingbolts, *K K'*, about which the trucks could turn. Each pair of driving-wheels had one cylinder, *C C'*. These were in the middle of the engine and were connected to cranks on the axles *A* and *B*.

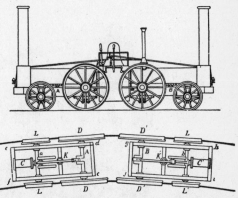

Fig. 5.—"South Carolina," 1831, and Plan of its Running Gear.

The "De Witt Clinton" (Fig. 6) was built for the Mohawk & Hudson Railroad, and was the third locomotive made by the West Point Foundry Association. The first excursion trip was made with passengers from Albany to Schenectady, August 9, 1831. This is the engine shown in the silhouette engraving of the "first* railroad train in America" which in recent years has been so widely distributed as an advertisement.

In 1831 the Baltimore & Ohio Railroad Company offered a premium of $4,000 "for the most approved engine which shall be delivered for trial upon the road on or before the 1st of June, 1831; and $3,500 for the engine which shall be adjudged the next best." The requirements were as follows:

Fig. 6.—The "De Witt Clinton," 1831.

The engine, when in operation, must not exceed three and one-half tons weight, and must, on a level road, be capable of drawing day by day fifteen tons, inclusive of the weight of wagons, fifteen miles per hour.

In pursuance of this call upon American genius, three locomotives were produced, but only one of these was made to answer

* It was not really the first train, as the Baltimore & Ohio and the South Carolina roads were in operation earlier.

any useful purpose.   This engine, the " York," was built at York, Pa., and was brought to Baltimore over the turnpike on wagons. It was built by Davis & Gartner, and was designed by Phineas

Fig. 7.—" Grasshopper " Locomotive.   (From an old photograph.)

Davis, of that firm, whose trade and business was that of a watch and clock maker.   After undergoing certain modifications, it was found capable of performing what was required by the company. After thoroughly testing this engine, Mr. Davis built others, which were the progenitors of the " grasshopper " engines (Fig. 7) which were used for so many years on the Baltimore & Ohio Railroad. It is a remarkable fact that three of these are still in use on that road, and have been in continuous service for over fifty years. Probably there is no locomotive in existence which has had so long an *active* life.

In August, 1831, the locomotive " John Bull," which was built by George & Robert Stephenson & Company, of Newcastle-upon-Tyne, was received in Philadelphia, for the Camden & Amboy Railroad & Transportation Company.   This is the old engine which was exhibited by the Pennsylvania Railroad Company at the Centennial Exhibition in 1876.   After the arrival of the " John Bull " a very considerable number of locomotives which were built by the Stephensons were imported from England. Most of them were probably of what was known as the "Planet" class (Fig. 8), which was a form of engine that succeeded the famous "Rocket."

The following quotation is from "The Early History of Locomotives in this Country," issued by the Rogers Locomotive & Machine Works:

These locomotives, which were imported from England, doubtless to a very considerable extent, furnished the types and patterns from which those which were afterward built here were fashioned. But American designs very soon began to depart from their British prototypes, and a process of adaptation to the existing conditions of the railroads in this country followed, which afterward "differentiated" the American locomotives more and more from those built in Great Britain. A marked feature of difference between American and English locomotives has been the use of a "truck" under the former.

In all of the locomotives which have been illustrated, excepting the "South Carolina," the axles were held by the frames so that the former were always parallel to each other. In going around curves, therefore, there was somewhat the same difficulty that there would be in turning a corner with an ordinary wagon if both its axles were held parallel, and the front one could not turn on the kingbolt. The plan of the wheels and running gear of the "South Carolina" shows the position that they assumed on a curved track (Fig. 5). It will be seen that, by reason of their connection to the boiler by kingbolts, *K K'*, the two pairs of wheels could adjust themselves to the curvature of

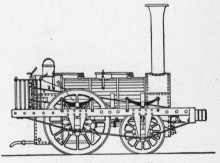

Fig. 8.—The "Planet."

the rails. This principle was afterward applied to cars, and nearly all the rolling-stock in this country is now constructed on this plan, which was proposed by Mr. Allen in a report dated May 16, 1831, made to the South Carolina Canal & Railroad Company; and an engine constructed on this principle was completed the same year.

In the latter part of the year 1831 the late John B. Jervis invented what he called "a new plan of frame, with a bearing-carriage for a locomotive engine," for the use of the Mohawk & Hudson Railroad. Jervis's engine is shown by Figure 9. In a letter

published in the *American Railroad Journal* of July 27, 1833, he
described the objects aimed at in the use of the truck as follows :

> The leading objects I had in view, in the general arrangement of the plan of the en-
> gine, did not contemplate any improvement in the power over those heretofore con-
> structed by Stephenson & Company,* but to make an engine that would be better
> adapted to railroads of less strength than
> are common in England ; that would travel
> with more ease to itself and to the rail on
> curved roads ; that would be less affected
> by inequalities of the rail, than is attained
> by the arrangement in the most approved
> engines.

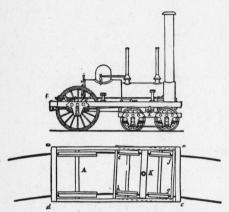

In Jervis's locomotive the
main driving-axle, *A*, shown in
the plan of the wheels and running gear, was rigidly attached
to the engine-frame, *a b c d*, and
only one truck, or "bearing-carriage," *e f g h*, consisting of the
two pairs of small wheels at-

Fig. 9.—John B. Jervis's Locomotive, 1831, and Plan of its
Running Gear.

tached to a frame, was used.   This was connected to the main
engine-frame by a kingbolt, *K*, as in Allen's engine.

The position of its wheels on a curve, and the capacity of the
truck, or "bearing-carriage," to adapt itself to the sinuosities of
the track are shown in the plan.   The effectiveness of the single
truck for locomotives, in accomplishing what Mr. Jervis intended it
for, was at once recognized, and its almost general adoption on
American locomotives followed.

In 1834, Ross Winans, of Baltimore, patented the application
of the principle which Mr. Allen had proposed and adopted for
locomotives "to passenger and other cars."   He afterward brought
a number of actions at law against railroads for infringement of his
patent, which was a subject of legal controversy for twenty years.
Winans claimed that his invention originated as far back as 1831,
and was completed and reduced to practice in 1834.   The dispute
was finally carried to the Supreme Court of the United States, and
was decided against the plaintiff, after an expenditure of as much
as $200,000 by both sides.   It involved the principle on which

* The truck was first applied by Mr. Jervis to an engine built by R. Stephenson & Co., of England.

nearly all cars in this country are now and were then built; and, as one of the counsel for the defendants has said, " It was at one time a question of millions, to be assured by a verdict of a jury."

In 1836, Henry R. Campbell, of Philadelphia, patented the use of two pairs of driving-wheels and a truck, as shown in Figure 10. The driving-wheels were coupled by rods, as may be seen below. This plan has since been so generally adopted in this country that it is now known as the " American type" of locomotive, and is the one almost universally used here for passenger, and to a considerable extent for freight, service. An example of a modern locomotive of this type is represented by Figure 11.

From these comparatively small beginnings, the magnificent equipment of our railroads has grown. From Peter Cooper's locomotive, which weighed less than a ton, with a boiler the size of a flour-barrel, and which had difficulty in beating a gray horse, we now have locomotives which will easily run sixty and can exceed seventy miles an hour, and others which weigh seventy-five tons and over. A comparison of the engraving of Peter Cooper's engine with that of the modern standard express passenger locomotive (Fig. 11) shows vividly the progress which has been made since that first experiment was tried—little more than half a century ago. In that period there have been many modifications in the design of locomotives to adapt them to the changed conditions of the various kinds of traffic of to-day. An express train travelling at a high rate of speed requires a locomotive very different from one which is designed for handling heavy freight trains up steep mountain-grades. A special class of engines is built for light trains making frequent stops, as on the elevated railroads in New York, and those provided for suburban

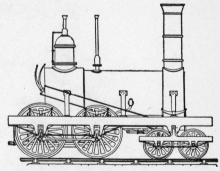

Fig. 10.—Campbell's Locomotive.

traffic (Fig. 12)—and still others for street railroads (Fig. 13), for switching cars at stations (Fig. 14), etc. [Pp. 110 and 113]. The process of differentiation has gone on until there are now as many different kinds of these machines as there are breeds of dogs or horses.

Fig. 12.—Locomotive for Suburban Traffic. By the Baldwin Locomotive Works, Philadelphia.

Nearly all the early locomotives had only four wheels.   In some cases one pair alone was used to drive the engine, and in others the two pairs were coupled together, so that the adhesion of all four could be utilized to draw loads.   The four-wheeled type is still used a great deal for moving cars at stations, and other purposes where the speed is comparatively slow.   But to run around

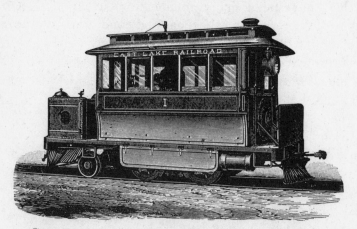

Fig. 13.—Locomotive for Street Railway. By the Baldwin Locomotive Works.

sharp curves the wheels of such engines must be placed near together, just as they are under an ordinary street-car.   This makes the wheel-base very short, and such engines are therefore very un-

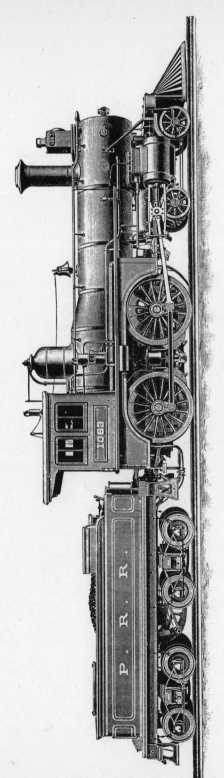

Fig. 11.—A Typical American Passenger Locomotive.

steady at high speeds, so that they are unsuited for any excepting slow service. They have the advantage, though, that the whole weight of the machine may be carried on the driving-wheels, and

Fig. 14.—Four-wheeled Switching Locomotive. By the Baldwin Locomotive Works, Philadelphia.

can thus be useful for increasing their friction, or adhesion to the rails. This gives such engines an advantage for starting and moving heavy trains, at stations or elsewhere, which is the kind of service in which they are usually employed.

If the front end of the engine is carried on a truck, as in Campbell's plan (Fig. 10)—which is the one that has been very generally adopted in this country—the wheel-base can be extended and at the same time the front wheels can adjust themselves to the curvature of the track. This gives the running-gear lateral flexibility. But as the tractive power of a locomotive is dependent upon the friction, or adhesion of the wheels to the rails, it is of the utmost importance that the pressure of the wheels on the rails should be uniform. For this reason the wheels must be able to adjust themselves to the vertical as well as the horizontal inequalities of the track.

Figure 15 shows the driving-wheels, axles, journal-boxes, and part of the frame and springs of an American type of engine—the circumference of the wheels only being shown.   The axles *A A* each have ournal-boxes or bearings, *B B*, in which they turn.

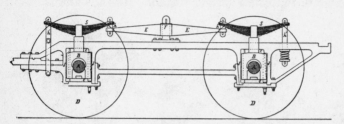

Fig. 15.—Driving Wheels, Frames, Spurs, etc., of American Locomotive.

These boxes are held between the jaws *J J J J* of the frames, and can slide vertically in the spaces *c c c c* between the jaws.   The frames are suspended on springs, *S S*, which bear on the boxes *B B*. The vertical motion of the boxes and the flexibility of the springs allow the wheels to adjust themselves to some extent to the unevenness of the track.   But, in order to distribute the weight equally on the two wheels, the springs *S S* on each side of the engine are connected together by an equalizing lever, *E E*.   These levers each have a fulcrum, *F*, in the middle, and are connected by iron straps or hangers, *h h*, to the springs.   It is evident that any strain or tension on one spring is transferred by the equalizing lever to the other spring, and thus the weight is equalized on both wheels.

But to give perfect vertical adjustment of such an engine to the track, still another provision must be made.   Everyone has observed that a three-legged stool will always stand firm on any surface, no matter how irregular, but one with four legs will not. Now if the back end of a locomotive should rest on the fulcrums of the equalizing levers, as shown in Figure 15, and the front end should rest on the two sides of the truck, it would be in the condition of the four-legged stool.   Therefore, instead of resting on the two sides of the truck, locomotives are made to bear on the centre of it, so that they are carried on it and on the two fulcrums of the equalizing levers, which gives the machine the adjustability due to the three-legged principle.   When more than four driving-wheels are used the springs are connected together by equalizing levers, as shown in Figure 29 (p. 124), which represents a consolidation engine as it appears before the wheels are put under it.

Having a vehicle which is adapted to running on a railroad track, it remains to supply the motive power.   This, in all but some very few exceptional cases, is the expansive power of steam. What the infant electricity has in store for us it would be rash to predict, but for locomotives its steps have been thus far weak and uncertain, and when we want a giant of steel or a race-horse of iron our only sure reliance is steam. This is the breath of life to the locomotive, which is inhaled and exhaled to and from the cylinders, which act as lungs, while the boiler fulfils functions analogous to the digestive organs of an animal. A locomotive is as dependent on the action of its boiler for its capacity for doing work as a human being on that of his stomach. The mechanical appliances of the one and the mental and physical equipment of the other are nugatory without a good digestive apparatus.

A locomotive boiler consists of a rectangular fireplace or fire-box, as shown at A, in Figure 16, which is a longitudinal section, and Figure 17 a transverse section through the fire-box. The fire-box is connected with the smoke-box B by a large number of small tubes, a a, through which the smoke and products of combustion pass from the fire-box to the smoke-box, and from the latter they escape up

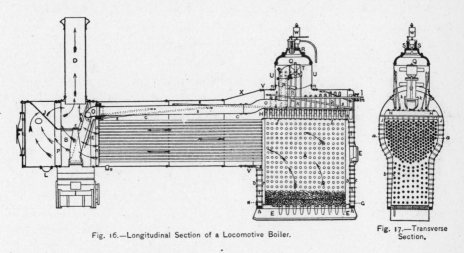

Fig. 16.—Longitudinal Section of a Locomotive Boiler.

Fig. 17.—Transverse Section.

the chimney D. The fire-box and tubes are all surrounded with water, so that as much surface as possible is exposed to the action of the fire. This is essential on account of the large amount of water which must be evaporated in such boilers. To create a strong draught, the steam which is exhausted from the cylinders is discharged up the chimney through pipes, and escapes at e.

This produces a partial vacuum in the smoke-box, which causes a current of air to flow through the fire on the grate, into the fire-box, through the tubes, and thence to the smoke-box and up the chimney.   Probably many readers have noticed, that of late years the smoke-boxes of locomotives have been extended forward in front of the chimneys.   This has been done to give room for deflectors and wire netting inside to arrest sparks and cinders, which are collected in the extended front and are removed by a door or spout, *L*, below.

To get the water into the boiler against the pressure of steam a very curious instrument, called an injector, has been devised. Formerly force-pumps were used, but these are now being abandoned.   The illustration (Fig. 18) shows what may be called a rudimentary injector.   *B* is a boiler and *E* a conical tube open at its lower end—and connected to a water-supply tank by a pipe, *C*.   A pipe, *A*, is connected with the steam-space of the boiler and terminates in a contracted mouth, *F*, inside of the cone *E*.   If steam is admitted to *A*, it flows through the pipe and escapes at *F*.   In doing so it produces a partial vacuum in E, and water is consequently drawn up the pipe *C* from the tank.   The current of steam now carries with it the water, and they escape at *G*.   After flowing for a few seconds the water has a high velocity and the steam, mingling with the water, is condensed. The momentum of the water soon becomes sufficient to force the valve *H* down against the pressure below it, and the jet of water then flows continuously into the boiler.   A very curious phenomenon of this somewhat mysterious instrument is that if steam of a low pressure is taken from one boiler it will force water into another against a higher pressure.   Figure 19 is a section of an actual injector used on locomotives.

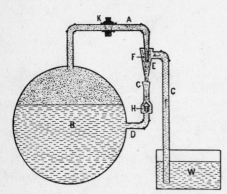

Fig. 18.—Rudimentary Injector.

Having explained how the steam is generated, it remains to show how it propels a locomotive.   It does this very much as a person on a bicycle propels it—that is, by means of two cranks the wheels are made to revolve, and the latter must then either slip or the vehicle will move. In a locomotive the driving-wheels are turned by means of two cylinders and pistons, which are connected by rods to the cranks attached to the driving-wheels or axles. These cranks are placed at right angles to each other, so that when one of them is at the "dead-point" the piston connected with the other can exert its maximum power to rotate the wheels. This enables the locomotive to start with the pistons in any position; whereas, if one cylinder only was used it would be impossible to turn the wheels if the crank should stop at one of its dead-points.

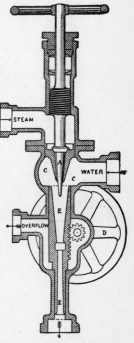

Fig. 19.—Injector used on Locomotives.

It will probably interest a good many readers to know how the steam gets into the cylinders and moves the pistons and then gets out again, and how a locomotive is made to run either backward or forward at pleasure.

Figure 20 (p. 118) shows a section of a cylinder, *A A'*, with the piston *B* and piston rod *R*. The cylinder has two passages, *c c* and *d d*, which connect its ends with a box, *U*, called a steam-chest, to which steam is admitted from the boiler by a pipe, *J*. The two passages *c* and *d* have another one, *g*, between them, which is connected with the chimney. These passages are covered by a slide-valve, *V*, which moves back and forth in the steam-chest, alternately uncovering the openings *c* and *d*. When the valve is in the position shown in Figure 20, obviously steam can flow into the front end *A* of the cylinder through the passage *c*, as indicated by the darts. The valve has a cavity, *H*, underneath it. When this cavity is over the passage *d* and *g*, it is plain that the steam in the back end *A'* of the cylinder can flow through *d* and *g* and then escape up the chimney. Under these circumstances the steam in the front end *A* of the cylinder will force the piston *B* to the back end. When it reaches the back end of the cylinder the valve is moved into the position shown in Figure 21, and steam can then enter *d* and will fill the back end *A'* while that in the front end escapes through *c* and *g*. The piston is then forced to the front end by the pressure of the steam behind it. It will thus be seen that the steam enters and escapes to and from the cylinder through the same openings.

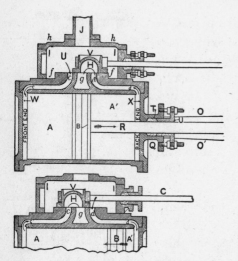

Figs. 20 (above) and 21.—Sections of a Locomotive Cylinder.

From what has been said it is obvious, too, that every time the piston moves from one end of the cylinder to the other the valve must also be moved back and forth in the steam-chest. This is done by what is called an eccentric.

An "eccentric" is a disk or wheel (Fig. 22) with a hole, *S*, the size of the axle of the locomotive to which it is attached. The centre *n* of the outside periphery of the eccentric is some distance from *S*, the centre of the shaft. A metal ring, *K K* (Fig. 23), made in two halves, embraces the eccentric, and the latter revolves inside of this ring. A rod, *L*, is attached to the strap, and is connected with the valve so that the motion of the eccentric is communicated to it. It is obvious that if the eccentric revolves it will impart a reciprocating motion to the rod *L*, which is communicated to the valve.

Fig. 22.—Eccentric.

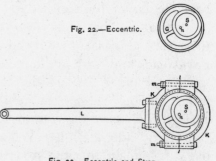

Fig. 23.—Eccentric and Strap.

If properly adjusted on the axle the eccentric will run the engine in one direction. To run the opposite way another eccentric must be provided. Therefore locomotives always have two eccentrics for each cylinder. These, *J* and *K*, are shown in Figure 24, which represents the "valve-gear" of a locomotive. *S* is a section of the main driving-axle, to which the eccentrics are attached by keys or screws. *C* is the eccentric rod of the forward-motion eccentric and D that of the one for running backward. As a locomotive must be run either backward or forward, and, as the one eccentric moves the valve to run forward and the other to run backward, we must be able to connect or disconnect the rods to and from the valve at will. The eccentric rods of the early locomotives had hooks on the ends by which they were attached to or detached from suitable pins connected with the valves. But these hooks were very uncertain in their action and therefore were abandoned, and now what is known as the

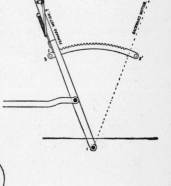

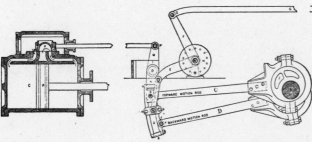

Fig. 24.—Valve Gear.

"link-motion" is almost universally used for the valve-gear of locomotives. It consists of a "link" ($a\ b$, Fig. 24) which has a curved opening or slot, k, in it in which a block, B, fits accurately, so that it can slide from end to end of the link. This block has a hole bored in the middle which receives a pin, c, which is attached to the end of the arm N of the "rocker" MON. The rocker has a shaft, O, which can turn in a suitable bearing, and two arms, M and $N;$ the latter, as explained, is connected to the link by the pin c and block B. The upper arm M has another pin, V, on its end, which is connected by a rod, $v\ V$, to the main slide-valve V. The rocker-arms, as will be seen, can vibrate about the shaft O.

The link is hung by a pendulous bar, $g\ h$, to the end g of the arm E, attached to the shaft A. This shaft has another upright arm, F, which is connected by a rod or bar, $G\ G'$, to a lever, $H\ I$, called a reverse lever, whose fulcrum is at I. To save room, in the engraving this lever and the cylinder G are drawn nearer to the main axle S than they would be on an engine. The lever is located inside the cab of the locomotive, and is indicated by the numbers 17 17' in Figure 36 on p. 133, which is a view looking from the tender at the back end of a locomotive. The lever has a trigger (*t*, Fig. 24) which is connected by a rod, *r*, to a latch, *l*, which engages in the notches of the sector *S S*. This latch holds the lever in any desired position and can be disengaged from the notches by grasping the upper end of the lever and the trigger.

It is plain that, by moving the upper end of the reverse lever, the link *a b* can be raised up or lowered at will. When the link is down, or in the position represented in the engraving, the forward eccentric rod imparts its motion to the block *B*, pin *c*, and thence to the rocker and valve, and the engine will run forward. If, however, the reverse lever is thrown back into the position indicated by the dotted line *f I*, the link would then be raised up so that the end *e* of the backward-motion rod would be opposite to the block *B* and pin *c* and would communicate its motion to the rocker and valve, and the wheels would then be turned backward instead of forward. It will thus be seen how the movement of the reverse lever effects the reversal of the engine.

A locomotive is started by admitting steam to the cylinders by means of what is called the "throttle-valve." This is usually placed in the upper part of the boiler at *T* (Fig. 16). The valve is worked by a lever at *l*, which is also shown at 14, 14' (Fig. 36). The steam is conveyed to the cylinders by a pipe (*s*, Fig. 16, p. 115).

If steam is admitted to the cylinders and the wheels are turned, one of two results must follow: either the locomotive will move backward or forward according to the direction of revolution, or the wheels will slip, as they often do, on the rails. That is, if the resistance of the cars or train is less than the friction or "adhesion" of the wheels on the rails, the engine and train will be moved; if the adhesion is less than the resistance the wheels will turn without moving the train.

The capacity of a locomotive to draw loads is therefore dependent on the adhesion, and this is in proportion to the weight or pressure of the driving-wheels on the rails. The adhesion also varies somewhat with the weather and the condition of the wheels and rails. In ordinary weather it is equal to about one-fifth of the

Fig. 25.—Turning Locomotive Tires.

weight which bears on the track; when perfectly dry, if the rails are clean, it is about one-fourth, and with the rails sanded about one-third. In damp or frosty weather the adhesion is often considerably less than a fifth.

It would, then, seem as though all that is needed to increase the capacity of a locomotive to draw loads would be to add to the weight on its driving-wheels, and provide engine-power sufficient to turn them—which is true. But it has been found that if the weight on the wheels is excessive both the wheels and rails will be injured. Even when they are all made of steel, they are crushed out of shape or are rapidly worn if the loads are too great. The weight which rails will carry without being injured depends somewhat on their size or weight, but ordinarily from 12,000 to 16,000 pounds per wheel is about the greatest load which they should carry.

For these reasons, when the capacity of a locomotive must be increased beyond a limit indicated by these data, one or more additional pairs of driving-wheels must be used. Thus, if a more powerful engine was required than that shown in Figure 14 (p. 113), another pair of wheels would be added, as shown in Figures 26, 27, and 28. Or, if you wanted a more powerful engine than these, still another pair of driving-wheels would be provided, as shown in Figure 30. In this way the Mogul, ten-wheeled and consolidation

Fig. 26.—Six-wheeled Switching Locomotive. By the Schenectady Locomotive Works.

engines have been developed from that shown in Figure 14. The Mogul locomotive (Fig. 27) has three pairs of driving-wheels, but only one pair of truck-wheels. The engravings shown in Figures 30 and 31 represent consolidation and decapod types of engines which have four and five pairs of driving-wheels.

From the illustrations, Figures 28, 30, and 31, it will be seen that when so many wheels are used, even if they are of small diameter, the wheel-base must necessarily be long, so that a limit is very soon reached beyond which the number of driving-wheels cannot be increased.

Improvements in the processes of manufacturing steel, which resulted in the general use of that material for rails and tires, have made it possible to nearly double the weight which was carried on each wheel when they were made of iron. The weight of rails has also been very much increased since they were first made of steel. Twenty or twenty-five years ago iron rails weighing 56 pounds per yard were about the heaviest that were laid in this

Fig. 27.—Mogul Locomotive. By the Schenectady Locomotive Works.

country. Low steel rails weighing 72 pounds are commonly used, and some weighing 85 pounds have been laid on American roads, and others weighing 10 pounds have been laid on the Continent of Europe.

Of late years urban and suburban traffic has created a demand for a class of locomotives especially adapted to that kind of service. One of the conditions of that traffic is that trains must stop and start often, and therefore, to "make fast time," it is essential to

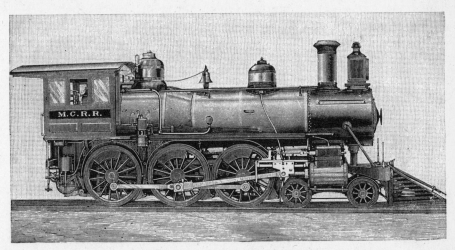

Fig. 28.—Ten-wheeled Passenger Locomotive. By the Schenectady Locomotive Works

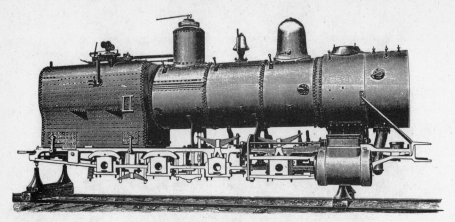

Fig. 29.—Consolidation Locomotive (unfinished).

start quickly.   Few persons realize the great amount of force which must be exerted to start any object suddenly.   A cannon-ball, for example, will fall through 16 feet in a second with no other resistance than the atmosphere.   The impelling force in that case is the weight of the ball.   If we want it to fall 32 feet during the first second, the force exerted on it must be equal to double its weight, and for higher speeds the increase of force must be in the same proportion.   This law applies to the movement of trains.   To start in half the time, double the force must be exerted.   For this reason, trains which start and stop often require engines with a great deal of weight on the driving-wheels.   In accordance with these conditions a class of engines has been designed which carry all, or nearly all, the weight of the boiler and machinery, and sometimes the

Fig. 30.—Consolidation Locomotive. By the Pennsylvania Railroad Company.

water and fuel, on the driving-wheels. For suburban traffic, the speed between stops must often be quite rapid, and consequently the engine must have a long wheel-base for steadiness, as well as considerable weight on the wheels for adhesion. Four-wheeled engines (Fig. 14) have all their weight on the driving-wheels, but the wheel-base is short.

Fig. 31.—Decapod Locomotive. By the Baldwin Locomotive Works, Philadelphia.

To combine the two features, engines have been built with the driving-wheels and axles arranged as in Figure 32. The frames are then extended backward, and the water-tank and fuel are placed on top of the frames, and their weight is carried by a truck underneath. This arrangement leaves the whole weight of the boiler and machinery on the driving-wheels, and at the same time gives a long wheel-base for steadiness. This plan of engine was patented by the author of this article in 1866, and has come into very general use—since the expiration of the patent. In some cases a two-wheeled truck is added at the opposite end, as shown in Figure 33. For street railroads, in which the speed is necessarily slow, engines such as Figure 13 (p. 110) are used. To hide the machine from view, and also to give sufficient room inside, they are enclosed in a cab large enough to cover the whole machine.

The size and weight of locomotives have steadily been increased ever since they were first used, and there is little reason for thinking that they have yet reached a limit, although it seems probable that some material change of design is impending which will permit of better proportions of the parts or organs of the larger sizes.

The decapod engines built at the Baldwin Locomotive Works, in Philadelphia, for the Northern Pacific Railroad, weigh in working order 148,000 pounds. This gives a weight of 13,300 pounds on each driving-wheel. Some ten-wheeled passenger engines, built at the Schenectady Locomotive Works for the Michigan Central Railroad, weigh 118,000 pounds, and have 15,666 pounds on each driving-wheel. Some recent eight-wheeled passenger locomotives for the New York, Lake Erie & Western Railroad weigh 115,000 pounds, and have 19,500 pounds on each driving-wheel. At the Baldwin Works, some "consolidation" engines have recently been built which are still heavier than the decapod engines.

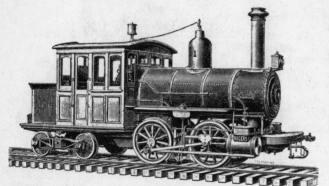

Fig. 32.—"Forney" Tank Locomotive. By the Rogers Locomotive and Machine Works, Paterson, N. J.

The following table gives dimensions, weight, price, and price per pound of locomotives at the present time. If we were to quote them at 8 to 8¼ cents per pound for heavy engines and 9 to 22¼ for smaller sizes, it would not be much out of the way.

Dimensions, Weights, and Approximate Prices of Locomotives.

Type.	Cylinders.		Diameter of driving-wheel.	Weight of engine in working order, exclusive of tender	Weight of engine and tender without water or fuel.	Approximate price.	Price per pound.
	Diam.	Stroke.	Inches.	Pounds.	Pounds.		Cents.
"American" Passenger....	18	24	62 to 68	92,000	110,000	$8,750	7.95
"Mogul" Freight..........	19	24	50 to 56	96,000	116,000	9,500	8.19
"Ten-wheel" Freight......	19	24	50 to 58	100,000	118,000	9,750	8.26
"Consolidation" Freight..	20	24	50	120,000	132,000	10,500	7.95
"Decapod" Freight........	22	26	46	150,000	165,000	13,250	8.03
Four-wheel Tank Switching	15	24	50	58,000	47,000	5,500	11.70
Six-wheel Switching, with tender................	18	24	50	84,000	98,000	8,500	8.89
"Forney" N. Y. Elevated..	11	16	42	42 000	34,000	4,500	13.23
Street-car Motor Locomotive	10	14	35	22,000	18,000	$3,500 to $4,000 according to design.	19.44 to 22 22

Fig. 33.—"Hudson" Tank Locomotive. By the Baldwin Locomotive Works.

The speed of locomotives, however, has not increased with their weight and size. There is a natural law which stands in the way of this. If we double the weight on the driving-wheels, the adhesion, and consequent capacity for drawing loads, is also doubled. Reasoning in an analogous way, it might be said that if we double the circumference of the wheels the distance that they will travel in one revolution, and consequently the speed of the engine, will be in like proportion. But, if this be done, it will require twice as much power to turn the large wheels as was needed for the small ones; and we then encounter the natural law that the resistance increases as the square of the speed, and probably at even a greater ratio at very high velocities. At 60 miles an hour the resistance of a train is four times as great as it is at 30 miles. That is, the pull on the draw-bar of the engine must be four times as great in the one case as it is in the other. But at 60 miles an hour this pull must be exerted for a given distance in half the time that it is at 30 miles, so that the amount of power exerted and steam generated in a given period of time must be eight times as great in the one case as in the other. This means that the capacity of the boiler, cylinders, and the other parts must be greater, with a corresponding addition to the weight of the machine.   Obviously, if the weight per wheel is limited, we soon reach a point at which the size of the driving-wheels and other parts cannot be enlarged; which means that there is a certain proportion of wheels, cylinders, and boiler which will give a maximum speed.

The relative speed of trains here and in Europe has been the subject of a good deal of discussion and controversy.   There appears to be very little difference in the speed of the fastest trains here and there; but there are more of them there than we have. From 48 to 53 miles an hour, including stops, is about the fastest time made by our regular trains on the summer time-tables.

When this rate of speed is compared with that of sixty or seventy miles an hour, which is not infrequent for short distances, there seems to be a great discrepancy.   It must be kept in mind, though, that these high rates of speed are attained under very favorable conditions.   That is, the track is straight and level, or perhaps descending, and unobstructed.   In ordinary traffic it is never certain that the line is clear.   A locomotive-runner must always be on the look-out for obstructions.   Trains, ordinary vehicles, a fallen tree or rock, cows, and people may be in the way at any moment.   Let anyone imagine himself in responsible charge of a locomotive and he will readily understand that, with the slightest suspicion that the line is not clear, he would slacken the speed as a precautionary measure.   For this reason fast time on a railroad depends as much on having a good signal system to assure the locomotive-runners that the line is clear, as it does on the locomotives.   If he is always liable to encounter, and must be on the look-out for, obstructions at frequent grade-crossings of common roads, or if he is not certain whether the train in front of him is out of his way or not, the locomotive-runner will be nervous and be almost sure to lose time.   If the speed is to be increased on American railroads, the first steps should be to carry all streets and common roads either over or under the lines, have the lines well fenced, provide abundant side-tracks for trains, and adopt efficient systems of signals so that locomotive-runners can know whether the line is clear or not.

In what may be called the period of adolescence of railroads there was a very decided predilection on the part of locomotive engineers for large driving-wheels.   Figure 34 represents one of the engines built as early as 1848 for the Camden & Amboy Railroad, with driving wheels 8 feet in diameter. Other engines with 6 and 7 feet wheels were not uncommon. In Europe many engines with very large wheels were made and are still in use. Here, as well as there, excessively large wheels have, however, been abandoned, and six feet in diameter is now about the limit of their size in this country.

So far as locomotives are concerned, fast time, especially with heavy trains, is generally dependent more upon the supply of steam than it is on the size of the wheels. Without steam to turn them, big wheels are useless; but with an abundant supply there is no difficulty in turning small wheels at a lively rate. Speed, therefore, is to a great extent a question of boiler capacity, and the general maxim has been formulated that " within the limits of weight and space to which a locomotive boiler must be confined, it cannot be made too big." But the maximum speed at which a locomotive can run when an adequate supply of steam is provided also depends on the perfection of the machinery. At 60 miles an hour a driving-wheel $5\frac{1}{2}$ feet in diameter revolves five times every second. The reciprocating parts of each cylinder of a Pennsylvania Railroad passenger engine, including one piston, piston-rod, cross-head, and

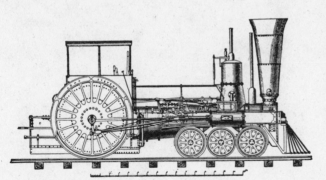

connecting rod, weigh about 650 pounds. These parts must move back and forth a distance equal to the stroke, usually two feet, every time the wheel revolves, or in a fifth of a second. It starts from a

Fig. 34.—Camden & Amboy Locomotive, 1848.

state of rest at each end of the stroke of the piston and must acquire a velocity of 32 feet per second, in one-twentieth of a second, and must be brought to a state of rest in the same period of time. A piston 18 inches in diameter has an area of $254\frac{1}{2}$ square inches. Steam of 150 pounds pressure per square inch would therefore

Fig. 35.— Interior of a Round-house.

exert a force on the piston equal to 38,175 pounds. This force is applied alternately on each side of the piston, ten times in a second. The control of such forces requires mechanism which works with the utmost precision and with absolute certainty, and it is for this reason that the speed and the economical working of a locomotive depend so much on the proportions of the valves and the "valve-gear" by which the "distribution" of steam in the cylinders is controlled.

The engraving (Fig. 36) on p. 133 represents the cab end of a locomotive of the New York Central & Hudson River Railroad, looking forward from the tender, and shows the attachments by which the engineer works the engine.* This gives an idea of the number of keys on which he has to play in running such a machine. There is room here for little more than an enumeration of the parts which are numbered:

1. Engine-bell rope.
2. Train-bell rope.
3. Train-bell or gong.
4. Lever for blowing whistle.
5. Steam-gauge to indicate pressure in boiler.
6. Steam-gauge lamp to illuminate face of gauge.
7. Pressure-gauge for air-brake ; to show pressure in air-reservoirs.
8. Valve to admit steam to air-brake pump.
9. Automatic lubricator for oiling main valves.
10. Cock for admitting steam to lubricator.
11. Handle for opening valves in sand-box to sand the rails.
12. Handle for opening the cocks which drain the water from the cylinders.
13. Valve for admitting steam to the jets which force air into the fire-box.
14, 14'. Throttle-valve lever. This is for opening the valve which admits steam to the cylinders.
15. Sector by which the throttle-lever is held in any desired position.
16. "Lazy-cock" handle. A "lazy-cock" is a valve which regulates the water-supply to the pumps and is worked by this handle.
17, 17'. Reverse lever.
18. Reverse-lever sector.
19, 19, 19. Gauge-cocks for showing the height of the water in the boiler ; 19' is a pipe for carrying away the water which escapes when the gauge-cocks are opened.
20, 20. Oil-cups for oiling the cylinders. †
21. Handle for working steam-valve of injector.
22. Handle for controlling water-jet of the injector.
23. Handle for working water-valve of injector.

* It should be mentioned that this is not one of the most recent types of engines. The arrangement of parts in the cab has been somewhat simplified in later locomotives.

† This engine had two different appliances for oiling the cylinders, a pair of oil-cups, 20, 20, and an automatic oiler, 9.

24. Oil-can shelf.
25. Handle for air-brake valve.
26. Valve for controlling air-brake.
27. Pipe for conducting air to brakes under the cars.
28. Pipe connected with air-reservoir.
29. Pipe-connection to air-pump.
30. Handle for working a valve which admits or shuts off the air for driving-wheel brakes.
31. Valve for driving-wheel brakes.
32, 32'. Lever for moving a diaphragm in smoke-box, by which the draught is regulated.
33. Handle for raising or lowering snow-scrapers in front of truck-wheels.
34. Handle for opening cock on pump to show whether it is forcing water into the boiler.
35. Lamp to light the water-gauge, 51, 51.
36. Air-hole for admitting air to fire-box.
37. Tallow-can for oiling cylinders.
38. Oil-can.
39. Shelf for warming oil-cans.
40. Furnace door.
41. Chain for opening and closing the furnace door.
42. Handles for opening dampers on the ash-pan.
43. Lubricator for air-pump.
44. Valve for admitting steam to the chimney to blow the fire when the engine is standing still.
45. Valve for admitting steam to the train-pipes for warming the cars.
46. Valve for reducing the pressure of the steam used for heating cars.
47. Cock which admits steam to the pressure-gauge, 48.
48. Pressure-gauge which indicates the steam-pressure in heater pipes.
49. Pipe for conducting steam to the train to heat the cars.
50. Cock for water-gauge, 51.
51, 51. Glass water-gauge to indicate the height of water in the boiler.
52. Cock for blowing off impurities from the surface of the water in the boiler.

Besides being impressive as a triumph of human ingenuity, there is much about the construction and working of locomotives which is picturesque. A shop where they are constructed or repaired is always of interest. An engine-house (Fig. 35) especially at night, is full of weird suggestions and food for the imagination. Figure 37 (p. 135) is an illustration from a photograph taken in the erecting shops of the Baldwin Locomotive Works in Philadelphia; and Figure 38 (p. 137) is a view of a similar shop of the Pennsylvania Railroad at Altoona, which suggests at a glance many of the processes of construction which go on in these great works. At Altoona are immense travelling cranes resting on brick arches and spanning the shop from side to side. These are power-

Fig. 36.—Cab End of a Locomotive and its Attachments.

ful enough to take hold of the largest locomotive and lift it bodily from the rails and transfer it laterally or longitudinally at will. A large consolidation engine is shown in Figure 38, swung clear of the rails, and in the act of being moved laterally. The hooks of the crane are attached to heavy iron beams, from which the locomotive is suspended by strong bars.   Figure 39 (p. 138) is a view in the blacksmiths' shop of the Baldwin Works, showing a steam hammer and the operation of forging a locomotive frame.

It is quite natural that the engineers, or "runners," as they generally call themselves, who have the care of locomotives should take a deep interest in and acquire a sort of attachment for them. In the earlier days of railroading this was much more the case than it is now.   Then each locomotive had an individuality of its own. It was rare that two engines were exactly alike.   Nearly always there was some difference in their proportions, or one engine had some device in it which the other had not.   Now, many locomotives are made exactly alike, or as nearly so as the most improved machinery will permit.   There is nothing to distinguish the one from the other.   Therefore Bony Smith can claim no superiority for his machine which Windy Brown has not the advantage of.   In the old days, too, each engine had its own runner and fireman, and it seldom fell into the hands of anyone else, and those in charge of it took as much pride in keeping it bright as the character in "Pinafore" did "in polishing up the handle of the big front door." On many roads—particularly the larger ones—engines are not assigned to special men.   The system of "first in first out" has been adopted ; that is, the engines are sent out in the order in which they come in, and the men take whichever machine happens to fall to their lot.   This naturally results in a loss of personal attachment to special engines.

Every change in the construction, alteration in the proportions, or addition to the attachments of locomotives is a subject of intense interest to the men and a topic of endless discussion at all times and places.   The theories which are propounded, and the yarns which are spun while sitting around hot stoves in round-houses, or waiting for passing trains on side-tracks, would fill many books. Jack never tires of telling what his engine did when "she was going up Rattlesnake Grade," and Smoky Bill grows excited when he describes how Ninety-six turned her wheels in making up forty-nine minutes time in the down run with the "electric express."

Locomotive engineers and firemen read with avidity everything which is explanatory of the construction or working of locomotives, but generally have a contempt for things which have no practical

Fig. 37.—View in Locomotive Erecting Shop.

Fig. 38.—Interior of Erecting Shop, Showing Locomotive Lifted by Travelling Crane.

bearing. They demand "lucidity" in what they read with as much vehemence as Matthew Arnold did, and some editors and college professors, whose writing and thinking are foggy, would be greatly benefited by the criticisms of the Locomotive Brotherhood.

Much might be written about the duties of locomotive-runners and firemen, and the qualifications required. It is the general opinion of locomotive superintendents that it is not essential that the men who run locomotives should be good mechanics. The best runners or engineers are those who have been trained while young as firemen on locomotives. Brunel, the distinguished civil engineer, said that he never would trust himself to run a locomotive because he was sure to think of some problem relating to his profession which would distract his attention from the engine. It is probably a similar reason which sometimes unfits good mechanics for being good locomotive-runners.

It will perhaps interest some readers to know how much fuel a locomotive burns. This, of course, depends upon the quality of fuel, work done, speed, and character of the road. With freight trains consisting of as many cars as a heavy locomotive can draw without difficulty, the consumption of coal will not exceed **from**

Fig. 39.—Forging a Locomotive Frame.

1 to 1½ pounds of coal per car per mile if the engine is carefully managed.   It takes from 15 to 20 pounds of coal per mile to move an engine and tender alone, the consumption being dependent upon the size of the engine, speed, grades, and number of stops.   If this amount of coal is allowed for the engine and tender, and the balance that is consumed is divided among the cars, it will reduce the quantity for hauling the cars alone to even less amounts than those given above.   In ordinary average practice the consumption is from 3 to 5 pounds per freight-car per mile, without making any allowance for the engine and tender.   With passenger trains, the cars of which are heavier and the speed higher, the coal consumption is from 10 to 15 pounds per car per mile.   A freight locomotive with a train of 40 cars will burn 40 to 200 pounds of coal per mile, the amount depending on the care with which it is managed, quality of the coal, grades, speed, weather, and other circumstances.

AMERICAN CARS.

Peter Parley's illustration (p. 101) of the Baltimore & Ohio Railroad represents one of the earliest passenger-cars used in this country. The accuracy of the illustration may, however, be questioned. Probably the artist depended upon his imagination and memory somewhat when he drew it. The engraving below (Fig. 40) is from a drawing made by the resident engineer of the Mohawk & Hudson Railroad, and from which six coaches were made by James Goold for the Mohawk & Hudson Railroad in 1831. It is an authentic representation of the cars as made at that time. Other old prints of railroad cars represent them as substantially stage-coach bodies mounted on four car-wheels, as shown by Figure 41. The next step in the development of cars was that of joining together several coach-bodies. This form was continued after the double-truck system was adopted, as shown by Figure 42, which represents an early Baltimore & Ohio Railroad car, having three sections, united. It was soon displaced by the rectangular body, as shown in Figure 43, which is a reproduction from an old print.

Figure 44 is an illustration of a car used for the transportation of flour on the Baltimore & Ohio Railroad, while horses were still used as the motive power. To show how nearly all progress is a process of evolution, it was asserted, in one of the trials of the validity of Winans' patent on eight-wheeled cars with two trucks, that

Fig. 40.—Mohawk & Hudson Car, 1831.
(From the original drawing by the resident engineer.)

Fig. 41.—Early Car.
(From an old print.)

before the date of his patent it was a practice to load firewood by connecting two such cars with long timbers, which rested on bolsters attached by kingbolts to the cars. The wood was loaded on top of these timbers, as shown in Figure 45. An old car (Fig. 46), which antedated Winans' patent and was used at the Quincy

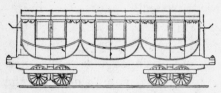

granite quarries for carrying large blocks of stone, was also introduced as evidence for the defendants in that suit. Although Winans was not able to establish the validity of his patent on eight-wheeled cars with two trucks, he was undoubtedly one of the first to put it into practical form, and did a great deal to introduce the system.

Fig. 42.—Early Car on the Baltimore & Ohio Railroad.

The progress in the construction of cars has been fully as great as in that of locomotives. If the old stage-coach bodies on wheels are compared with a vestibule train of to-day the difference will be very striking. Most of us who are no longer young can recall the days when sleeping-cars were unknown, when a journey from an Eastern city to Chicago meant forty-eight hours or more of sitting erect in a car with thirty or more passengers, and an atmosphere which was fetid. Happily those days are past, although the improvement in the ventilation of cars has been very slow, and is still very imperfect.

Improvement has also lagged in the matter of coupling cars. It has been shown by statistics and calculations that some hundreds

Fig. 43.—Early American Car, 1834.

of persons are killed and some thousands injured in this country annually in coupling cars. The use of automatic coupling, by which cars could be connected together without going between them, it has been supposed, would greatly lessen, if it would not entirely prevent, this fearful sacrifice of life and limb. To accomplish this end, though, it is essential that some one form of coupler shall be generally adopted by all railroads. One of the obstacles in the way of this has been the mechanical difficulty of finding a mechanism which

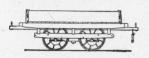

will satisfactorily accomplish the purpose for which it was intended. After thirty or forty years of invention and experiment, no automatic coupler has been produced, which has been approved by competent judges with a sufficient degree of unanimity to justify its

Fig. 44.—Old Car for Carrying Flour on the Baltimore & Ohio Railroad.

general adoption. The patents on that class of inventions are numbered by thousands, so that it is no light task to select the best one or even the best kind. Besides this difficulty, there is the other equally formidable one of inducing railroad men, of various degrees of knowledge, ignorance, and prejudice regarding this subject, and who are scattered all over the continent, to agree in adopting some one form or kind of automatic coupler. Various

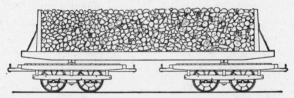

Fig. 45.—Old Car for Carrying Firewood on the Baltimore & Ohio Railroad.

cliques had also been organized on different roads in the interest of some patents, and in such cases argument and reason addressed to them were generally wasted. Public indignation was, however, aroused; and the stimulus of legislation in different States compelled railroad officers to give serious attention to the subject. After devoting some years to the investigation, the Master Car-Builders' Association—which is composed of officers of railroad companies, who are in charge of the construction and repair of cars on the different lines—has recommended the adoption of a coupler of the type represented by Figures 47 to 49, which has been already applied to many cars and the indications are that it will be very generally adopted for freight and probably for passenger cars.

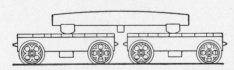

Fig. 46.—Old Car on the Quincy Granite Railroad.

If it should be, it will relieve railroad employees of the dangerous duty of going between cars to couple them. Figure 47 shows a plan looking down on the couplers with one of the latches, *A*, open; Figure 48 shows it with the two couplers partly engaged; and Figure 49 shows them when the coupling is completed.

One of the first problems which presented itself in the infancy of railroads was how to keep the cars on the rails.

Anyone who will stand close to a line of railroad when a train is rushing by at a speed of forty, fifty, or sixty miles an hour must wonder how the engine and cars are kept on the track; and even those familiar with the construction of railroad machinery often express astonishment that the flanges of the wheels, which are merely projecting ribs about $1\frac{1}{8}$ inches deep and $1\frac{1}{4}$ inches thick, are sufficient to resist the impetus and swaying of a locomotive or car at full speed. The problem of the manufacture of wheels which will resist this wear, and will not break, has occupied a great deal of the attention of railroad managers and manufacturers.

Locomotive driving-wheels in this country are always made of cast-iron, with steel tires which are heated and put on the wheels and then cooled. They are t h u s contracted and "shrunk" on the wheel. The tread, that is, the surface which bears on the rail, and the flange of the tire are then turned off in a lathe, shown in Figure 25, on p. 121, made especially for the purpose. For engine-truck, tender, and car-wheels, until within a few years, "chilled" cast-iron wheels have been used almost exclusively on American railroads.

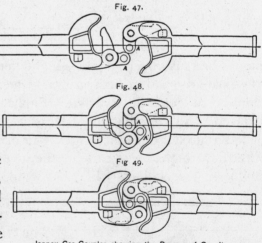

Janney Car Coupler, showing the Process of Coupling.

If the tread and flange of a wheel were made of ordinary cast-iron they would soon be worn out in service, as such iron has ordinarily little capacity for resisting the wear to which wheels are subjected. Some cast-iron, however, has the

singular property which causes it to assume a peculiar, hard crystalline form if, when it is melted, it is allowed to cool and solidify
in contact with a cold iron mould. The iron which is thus cooled
quickly, or "chilled," becomes very hard, and resists wear very
much better than iron which is not chilled. Car-wheels which are
made of this material are therefore cast in what is called a chill-
mould. Figure 50 represents a section of such a mould and flask in
which wheels are cast.

A A is the wheel, which is moulded in sand in the usual way.
The part *B B* of the mould, which forms the rim or tread of the
wheel, consists of a heavy cast-iron ring. The melted iron is poured
into this mould and
comes in contact
with *B B*. This
has the effect of
chilling the hot
iron, as has been
explained. In
cooling, the wheel
contracts; and for
that reason the part

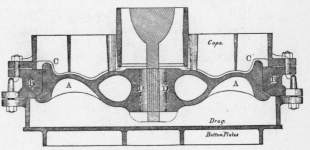

Fig. 50.—Mould and Flask in which Wheels are Cast.

between the rim *C* and the hub *D* is made of a curved form, as
shown in the section, so that if one part should cool more rapidly
than another these parts can yield sufficiently to permit contraction
without straining any portion of the wheels injuriously. For the
same reason the ribs on the back of the wheels, as shown in Figure 51, are also curved. As an additional safeguard to the unequal
contraction in cooling, the wheels are taken out of the mould while
they are red-hot, and placed in ovens where they are allowed to
remain several days so as to cool very slowly.

Figure 52, on p. 145, represents a section of the tread and
flange of a chilled wheel, showing the peculiar crystalline appearance of the chilled iron.

In making cast-iron wheels the quality of the iron used is of the
utmost importance. The difficulty in making good wheels lies in
the fact that most iron which is ductile and tough will not chill,
whereas hard white iron, which has the chilling property in a very
high degree, is brittle, and wheels which are made of it are liable

to break. There are some kinds of cast-iron produced in this country which have the two qualities combined, in a very remarkable degree; that is, they are ductile and tough, and will also chill.

Fig. 51—Cast-iron Car Wheels.

Wheel-founders also mix different qualities of irons to produce wheels with the required strength, and which will resist wear; that is, they use a certain amount of hard white iron which will chill, with that which is ductile and soft. By changing the proportions, any required amount of chill can be produced. The danger is that iron which has little strength or ductility will be fortified with hard chilling iron, and a very weak wheel will thus be the result. Thousands of such wheels have been bought and used because they are cheap, and many lamentable accidents are undoubtedly due to this cause. To guard against this, car-wheels should always be subjected to rigid tests and inspection.

In Europe wheels are made of wrought-iron, with tires which were also made of the same material before the discovery of the improved processes of manufacturing steel, but since then they have been made of the latter material. Owing to the breakage of a great many cast-iron wheels of poor quality, steel-tired wheels are now coming into very general use on American roads under passenger-cars and engines. A great variety of such wheels is now made. The "centres" or parts inside the tires of some of them are cast-iron, and others are wrought-iron constructed in various ways.

What is known as the Allen paper wheel is used a great deal in this country, especially under sleeping-cars. A section and front view of one of these wheels is shown by Figure 53. It consists of a cast-iron hub, A, which is bored out to fit the axle. An annular disk, *B B*, is made of layers of paper-board glued together and then subjected to an enormous pressure. The disk is then bored out to fit the hub, and its circumference is

Fig. 52.—Section of the Tread and Flange of a Car Wheel.

turned off, and the tire *C C* is fitted to it. Two wrought-iron plates, *P P*, are then placed on either side of it, and the disk, plates, tire, and hub are all bolted together. The paper, it will be seen, bears the weight which rests on the hub of the axle and the hub of the wheel.

Steel tires have the advantage that when they become worn their treads and flanges may be turned off anew, whereas chilled cast-iron wheels are so hard that it is almost impossible to cut them with any turning tool. For this reason machines have been constructed for grinding the tread with a rapidly revolving emery-wheel. In these the cast-iron wheel is made to turn slowly, whereas the emery-wheel revolves very rapidly. The emery-wheel is then brought

Fig. 53.—Allen Paper Car Wheel.

close to the cast-iron wheel, so that as they revolve the projections on the latter are cut away, and the tread is thus reduced to a true circular form.   These machines are much used for "truing-up" wheels which have been made flat by sliding, owing to the brakes being set too hard.

It would require a separate article to give even a brief description of the different kinds of cars which are now used.   The following list could be increased considerably if all the different varieties were included.

Baggage-car,	Drop-bottom car,	Inspection-car,	Postal-car,
Boarding-car,	Dump-car,	Lodging-car,	Refrigerator-car.
Box-car,	Express-car,	Mail-car,	Restaurant-car,
Buffet-car,	Flat or platform car,	Milk-car,	Sleeping-car,
Caboose or conduc-	Gondola-car,	Oil-car,	Sweeping-car,
tor's car,	Hand-car,	Ore-car,	Tank-car,
Cattle- or stock-car,	Hay-car,	Palace-car,	Tip-car,
Coal-car,	Hopper-bottom car,	Passenger-car,	Tool or wrecking car,
Derrick-car,	Horse-car,	Post-office car,	Three-wheeled hand-
Drawing-room car,	Hotel-car,	Push-car,	car.

The following table gives the size, weight, and price of cars at the present time.   The length given is the length over the bodies not including the platforms.

	Length, feet.	Weight, lbs.	Price.
Flat-car......................	34	16,000 to 19,000	$380
Box-car.....................	34	22,000 to 27,000	$550
Refrigerator-car..............	30 to 34	28,000 to 34,000	$800 to $1,100
Passenger-car	50 to 52	45,000 to 60,000	$4,400 to $5,000
Drawing-room car	50 to 65	70,000 to 80,000	$10,000 to $20,000
Sleeping-car..................	50 to 70	60,000 to 90,000	$12,000 to $20,000
Street-car...................	16	5,000 to 6,000	$800 to $1,200

Some years ago the master car-builders of the different railroads experienced great difficulty in the transaction of their business from the fact that there were no common names to designate the parts of cars in different places in the country.   What was known by one name in Chicago had quite a different name in Pittsburg or Boston.   A committee was therefore appointed by the Master Car-Builders' Association to make a dictionary of terms used in car-construction and repairs. Such a dictionary has been prepared, and is a book of 560 pages, and has over two thousand illustrations. It has some peculiar features, one of which is de-

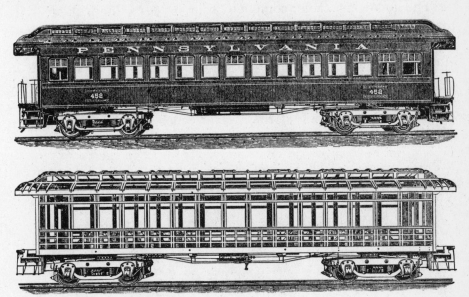

Fig. 54.—Modern Passenger-car and Frame.

scribed as follows in the preface: "To supply the want which demanded such a vocabulary, what might be called a double dictionary is needed. Thus, supposing that a car-builder in Chicago received an order for a 'journal-box'; by looking in an alphabetical list of words he could readily find that term and a description and definition of it. But suppose that he wanted to order such castings from the shop in Albany, and did not know their name; it would be impracticable for him to commence at A and look through to Z, or until he found the proper term to designate that part." To meet this difficulty the dictionary has very copious illustrations in which the different parts of cars are represented and numbered, and the names of the parts designated by the numbers are then given in a list accompanying the engraving. An alphabetical list of names and definitions is also given, as in an ordinary dictionary. The definition usually contains a reference to a number and a figure in which the object described is illustrated. In making the dictionary the compilers selected terms from those in use, where appropriate ones could be found. In other cases new names were devised. The book is a curious illustration of a more rapid growth of an art than of the language by which it is described.

The following table, compiled from "Poor's Manual of Railroads," gives the number of locomotives and of different kinds of cars in this country, beginning with 1876, and for each year thereafter. If the average length of locomotives and tenders is taken at 50 feet, those now owned by the railroads would make a continuous train 280 miles long; and the 1,033,368 cars, if they average 35 feet in length, would form a train which would be more than 6,800 miles long.

Statement of the Rolling Stock of Railroads in the United States; from "Poor's Manual" for 1889.

Year.	Miles of railroad.	Locomotives.	Passenger-train cars.		Freight cars.	Total.
			Passenger.	Baggage, mail, and Express.		
1876.........	76,305	14,562	....	....	358,101	358,101
1877.........	79,208	15,911	12,053	3,854	392,175	408,082
1878.........	80,832	16,445	11,683	4,413	423,013	439,109
1879.	84,393	17,084	12,009	4,519	480,190	496,718
1880.........	92,147	17,949	12,789	4,786	539,255	556,930
1881.........	103,530	20,116	14,548	4,976	648,295	667,819
1882.........	114,461	22,114	15,551	5,566	730,451	751,568
1883.	120,552	23,623	16,889	5,848	778,663	801,400
1884.........	125,152	24,587	17,303	5,911	798,399	821,613
1885.........	127,729	25,937	17,290	6,044	805,519	828,853
1886.........	133,606	26,415	19,252	6,325	845,914	871,491
1887.........	147,999	27,643	20,457	6,554	950,887	977,898
1888.........	154,276	29,398	21,425	6,827	1,005,116	1,033,368

The number of cars, it will be seen, has more than doubled in ten years, so that if the same rate of increase continues for the next decade there will be over two millions of them on the railroads of this country alone. Beyond a certain point, numbers convey little idea of magnitude. Our railroad system and its equipment seem to be rapidly outgrowing the capacity of the human imagination to realize their extent. What it will be with another half-century of development it is impossible even to imagine.

RAILWAY MANAGEMENT.

By E. P. ALEXANDER.

Relations of Railway Management to all Other Pursuits—Developed by the Necessities of a Complex Industrial Life—How a Continuous Life is Given to a Corporation—Its Artificial Memory—Main Divisions of Railway Management—The Executive and Legislative Powers—The Purchasing and Supply Departments—Importance of the Legal Department—How the Roadway is Kept in Repair—The Maintenance of Rolling Stock—Schedule-making—The Handling of Extra Trains—Duties of the Train-despatcher—Accidents in Spite of Precautions—Daily Distribution of Cars—How Business is Secured and Rates are Fixed—The Interstate Commerce Law—The Questions of "Long and Short Hauls" and "Differentials"—Classification of Freight—Regulation of Passenger-rates—Work of Soliciting Agents—The Collection of Revenue and Statistics—What is a Way-bill—How Disbursements are Made—The Social and Industrial Problem which Confronts Railway Corporations.

 HE world was born again with the building of the first locomotive and the laying of the first level iron roadway. The energies and activities, the powers and possibilities then developed have acted and reacted in every sphere of life—social, industrial, and political—until human progress, after smouldering like a spark for a thousand years, has burst into a conflagration which will soon leave small trace of the life and customs, or even the modes of thought, which our fathers knew. But, in it all, the railroad remains the most potent factor in every development. By bringing men more and more closely together, and supplying them more and more abundantly and cheaply with all the varied treasures of the earth, stored up for millions of years for the coming of this generation, it adds continually more fuel to the flame it originated. And as it is necessarily reacted upon equally by every new invention or

discovery, and by all progress in other departments of human activity, the demands upon it, and its points of contact with everyday life, are still increasing in geometrical progression.

Hence, in the practical management of railroad affairs, problems are of constant occurrence which touch almost every pursuit to which men give themselves, whether of finance, agriculture, commerce, manufactures, science, or politics; and the methods, forms, and principles under which current railroad management is being developed (for it is by no means at a stand-still) are the result of the necessities imposed by these multiplying problems acting within the constraints of corporate existences.

For while the life of a corporation is perpetual, its powers are constrained, and the individuals exercising them are constantly changing. It is but an artificial individual existing for certain purposes only, and, as it lacks some human qualities, all its methods of doing business are influenced thereby. The business affairs of an individual, for instance, are greatly simplified by his memory of his transactions from day to day and from year to year. But a corporation having no natural memory, all of its transactions and relations must be minutely and systematically noted in its archives. Every contract and obligation must be of record, all property bought or constructed must go upon the books, and, when expended or used up, must go off in due form; and especially must an accurate system of checks guard all earnings and expenditures, and a comprehensive system of book-keeping consolidate innumerable transactions into the great variety of boiled-down figures and statistics necessary for officers and stockholders to fully understand what the property is doing.

Under such circumstances, then, our railroads and their systems of organization and management, like the Darwinian Topsy, have not " been made " but have " growed."

Naturally, both the direction and extent of the development have varied in different localities and under different conditions. Within the limits of this article it would be impossible to give anything like an exhaustive or complete account of the organization, distribution of duties, systems of working, and of checks in the various departments of even a single road. Most roads publish more or less elaborate small volumes of regulations on such subjects for the use of their various employees. The task would also be endless to describe technically the variations of practice and of nomenclature in different sections and on different systems. The shades of difference, too, between managers, superintendents, or masters; comptrollers, auditors, book-keepers, and accountants; secretaries, cashiers, treasurers, and paymasters in different localities would be tedious to draw. A technical account of them would be almost a reproduction of the volumes above-mentioned. I can only attempt to outline and illustrate very briefly the general principles which underlie the present practice, and are more or less elaborated as circumstances may require.

The principal duties connected with the management of a railroad may be classified as follows:

1. The physical care of the property.
2. The handling of the trains.
3. The making rates and soliciting business.
4. The collection of revenue and keeping statistics.
5. The custody and disbursement of revenue.

The president is, of course, the executive head of the company, but in important matters he acts only with the consent and approval of the Board of Directors, or of an executive committee clothed with authority of the board, which may be called the legislative branch of the management. More or less of the executive power and supervision of the president may be delegated to one or more vice-presidents. Often all of it but that relating to financial matters is so delegated, but, as their functions are subdivisions of those of the president, they have no essential part in a general scheme of authority.

Of the five subdivisions of duties indicated above, the first four are usually confided to a general manager, who may also be a vice-president, and the fifth is in charge of a treasurer, reporting directly to the president.

The special departments under charge of the general manager are each officered by trained experts:

A superintendent of roadway or chief engineer has charge of the maintenance of the track, bridges, and buildings.

A superintendent of machinery has charge of the construction and maintenance of all rolling stock.

A superintendent of transportation makes all schedules, and has charge of all movements of trains.

A car accountant keeps record of the location, whereabout, and movements of all cars.

A traffic manager has charge of passenger and freight rates, and all advertising and soliciting for business.

A comptroller has charge of all the book-keeping by which the revenue of the company is collected and accounted for. All statistics are generally prepared in his office.

A paymaster receives money from the treasurer and disburses, under the direction of the comptroller, for all expenses of operation.

All dividend and interest payments are made by the treasurer, under direction of the president and board.

There are, besides the above, two general departments with which all the rest have to do, to a greater or less extent—the legal department and the purchasing department. The quantity and variety of articles used and consumed in the operation of a railroad are so great that it is a measure of much economy to concentrate all purchases into the hands of a single purchasing agent, rather than to allow each department to purchase for itself. This agent has nothing to do but to study prices and markets. His pride is enlisted in getting the lowest figures for his road, and the large amount of his purchases enables him to secure the best rates. And last, but not least, in matters where dishonesty would find so great opportunities, it is safer to concentrate responsibility than to diffuse it.

As I shall not again refer to this department, what remains of interest for me to say about it will be said here. As an adjunct to it, storehouses are established at central points in which stocks of articles in ordinary use are kept on hand. Whenever supplies are wanted in any other department—as, for instance, a bell-cord and lantern by a conductor—requisitions are presented, approved by a designated superior. These requisitions state whether the articles are to be charged to legitimate wear and tear, and if so, whether to the passenger or the freight service, and of which subdivision of the road; or whether they are to be charged to the conductor for other articles not properly accounted for. Without going into further detail, it can be readily seen how the comptroller's office can, at the end of each month, from these requisitions, have a complete check upon all persons responsible for the care of property. The purchasing agent, too, from his familiarity with prices, is usually charged with the sale of all condemned and worn-out material.*

Before returning to a more detailed review of the operating departments of a railroad, its legal department requires a few words. Not only is a railroad corporation, being itself a creation of the law, peculiarly bound to conform all its actions to legal forms and tenets, but it is also a favorite target for litigation. The popular prejudice against corporations, it may be said in passing, is utterly illogical. The corporation is the poor man's opportunity. Without it he could never share in the gains and advantages open to capital in large sums. With it a thousand men, contributing a thousand dollars each, compete on equal terms with the millionaire. Its doors are always open to any who may wish to share its privileges or its prosperity, and no man is denied equal participation according to his means and inclinations. It is the greatest "anti-poverty" invention which has ever been produced, and the most democratic. But, for all that, instead of possessing the unbounded power usually ascribed to it, no creature of God or man is so helpless as a corporation before the so-called great tribunal of justice, the American jury. It may not be literally true that a Texas jury gave damages to a tramp against a certain railroad because a section-master's wife gave him a meal which disagreed with him, but the story can be nearly paralleled from the experience of many railroads. Hence settlements outside of the law are always preferred where they are at all possible, and an essential part of an efficient legal organization is a suitable man always ready to repair promptly to the scene of any loss or accident, to examine the circumstances with the eye of a legal expert on liabilities.

But the management of claims, and of loss and damage suits, though a large part, is by no means all of the legal business connected with a railroad. Every contract or agreement should pass under scrutiny of counsel, and in the preparation of the various forms of bonds, mortgages, debentures, preferred stocks, etc.,

* See "How to Feed a Railway," page 302.

which the wants of the day have brought forth, the highest legal talent finds employment.   For, as development has multiplied the types of cars and engines to meet special wants, so have a great variety of securities been developed to meet the taste and prej-

udices of investors of all nations.   There is, in fact, a certain fashion in the forms of bonds, and the conditions incorporated in mortgages, which has to be observed to adapt any bond to its proposed market.

We shall now return to the operating departments under their respective heads, and glance briefly at the methods and detail pursued in each.

On roads of large mileage the general manager is assisted by general or division superintendents in charge of roadway, motive power, and trains of one or more separate divisions ; but for our purposes we may consider the different departments without reference to these superintendents.

The superintendent of roadway or chief engineer comes first, having charge of track, bridges, and buildings.   In his office are collected maps of all important stations and junction points, kept up to date with changes and additions ; scale drawings of all bridges and trestles, of all standard depots, tanks, switches, rails, fastenings, signals, and everything necessary to secure uniformity of patterns and practice over the entire road. Under him are supervisors of bridges and supervisors of road, each assigned to a certain territory. The supervisors of bridges make frequent and minute examinations of every piece or member of every bridge and trestle, report in advance all the repairs that become necessary, and make requisition for the material needed.

A Type of Snow-plough.

Under the bridge supervisor are organized "bridge gangs," each consisting of a competent foreman with carpenters and laborers skilled in bridge work and living in "house" or "boarding" cars, and provided with pile-drivers, derricks, and all appliances for handling heavy timbers and erecting, tearing down, and repairing bridges. These cars form a movable camp, going from place to place as needed, and being side-tracked as near as possible to the work of the gang. Long experience begets great skill in their special duties, and the feats which these gangs will perform are often more wonderful than many of the more showy performances of railroad engineering. It is an every-day thing with such gangs to take down an old wooden structure, and erect in its place an iron one, perhaps with the track raised several feet above the level of the original, while fifty trains pass every day, not one of which will be delayed for a moment.

Each of the supervisors of road has his assigned territory divided into "sections," from   five to eight miles in

A Rotary Steam Snow-shovel in Operation.
(From an instantaneous photograph.)

length. At a suitable place on each section are erected houses for a resident section-master and from six to twelve hands. These are provided with hand- and push-cars, and spend their whole time in keeping their sections in good condition. Upon many roads annual inspections are made and prizes offered for the best sections. At least twice a day track-walkers from the section-gangs pass over the entire line of road. To simplify reports and instructions, frequently every bridge or opening in the track is numbered, and the number displayed upon it; and every curve is also posted with its degree of curvature and the proper elevation to be given to the outer rail.

The work of the section-men is all done under regular system. In the spring construction-trains deliver and distribute ties and rails on each section, upon requisitions from supervisors. Then the section-force goes over its line from end to end, putting in first the new ties and then the new rails needed. Next the track is gone over with minute care and re-lined, re-surfaced, and re-ballasted, to repair the damages of frost and wet, the great enemies of a road-bed. Then ditches, grass, and the right-of-way have attention. These processes are continually repeated, and especially in the fall in preparation for winter. During the winter as little disturbance of track is made as possible, but ditches are kept clean, and low joints are raised by "shims" on top of joint ties. Essential parts of the equipment of any large road are snow-ploughs (pp. 154-5-6) and wrecking cars, with powerful derricks and other appliances for clearing obstructions. When wrecks or blockades occur these cars, with extra engines, section-hands, bridge gangs, and construction-trains, are rushed to the spot, and everything yields to the work of getting the road clear.

We come next to the superintendent of machinery, whose duty it is to provide and maintain locomotives and cars of all kinds to handle the company's traffic. His department is subdivided between a master mechanic, in charge of locomotives and machine-shops, and a master carbuilder, in charge of car-shops.

Railway-crossing Gate.

The master mechanic selects and immediately controls all engine-runners and firemen, and keeps performance sheets of all locomotives, showing miles run, cars hauled, wages paid, coal and oil consumed, and other details giving results accomplished by different runners and firemen, and by different types of engine, or on different divisions

Report of Performance of Engines, Repairs, and all other Costs

Number of Engine.	Miles Run. Passenger	Freight.	Gravel or Construction.	Switching.	Total.	Fuel. Eighth Cords of Wood.	Bushels Coal.	Cost of Fuel.	Oil, Waste and Other Stores. Gallons of Engine Oil.	Signal Oil	Head-Light Oil.	Lbs. of Cyl. Oil.	Car Grease.	Waste.	Packing.	Gallons Kerosene.	Cost of Stores.	Wages of Engineer and Fireman.
1	....	12,084	4,253	64	16,401	118	10,699	$ 1,090 25	124	10	29	59½	45	347	72		$ 87 64	$ 1,293 80
2	....	2,672	11,779	954	15,405	193	10,913	1,131 77	121½	13½	35½	69½	69	466	102	2	106 85	1,646 90
3	5,402	14,471	408	120	20,407	189	10,590	1,101 08	132½	10½	38	74½	69	350	61	.	93 85	1,489 65
4	28,643	4,168	....	....	32,811	297	11,875	1,212 20	258	14	49	125	106	659	76	..	171 85	1,719 55
5	28,275	4,490	.....	72	32,837	301	12,961	1,335 31	256	12	39	99½	75	622	82½	.	144 86	1,628 80
6	....	....	....	32,370	32,370	33	10,360	1,042 26	230½	12½	188½	111¼	....	298	160½	..	173 92	1,884 50
8	3,229	11,799	4,779	....	19,807	150	13,233	1,356 30	134	10½	41	65¼	60	327	98	..	97 34	1,593 05
9	1,050	23,203	.....	....	24,253	155	16,344	1,668 41	135	12½	45½	73	70	374	87	..	108 53	1,625 80
10	874	24,729	...	96	25,699	158	17,039	1,741 67	131½	13½	63	69	70	372	96	..	108 38	1,669 55
11	....	....	....	23,609	23,609	205	7,661	811 00	136	1¾	96	81	40	354	81	2	111 83	1,126 75
12	1,527	....	4,369	12,060	17,956	142	8,875	918 75	105	9¼	58	95½	20	360	75	..	106 31	1,405 10
30	41,345	....	....	....	41,345	237	17,702	1,821 37	223	23¾	44½	69	106	726	51	..	142 71	1,719 55
31	37,450	....	.....	....	37,450	215	16,695	1,716 56	243	15¼	46	92	110	660	66	1	152 16	1,554 55
32	4,233	13,516	.....	120	17,869	115	10,918	1,117 10	138	10½	41	71½	130	361	63	7	108 40	1,186 40
34	13,742	5,217	.....	1,224	20,183	149	6,691	704 07	186	10	32	71	75	409	43	2	109 17	1,059 50
	165,770	116,349	25,588	70,695	378,402	2657	182,556	$18,768 13	2,554	179½	846	1,226½	1045	6685	1214	14	1,823 80	22,603 45

or roads. Premiums are often paid the runners and firemen accomplishing the best results.

The master car-builder has charge of the shops where cars are built and repaired, and of the car-inspectors who are stationed at central and junction points to prevent defective cars being put into the trains.

Formerly each railroad used its own cars exclusively, and through freights were transferred at every junction point. This involved such delay and expense that railroads now generally permit all loaded cars to go through to destination without transfer, and allow each other a certain sum for the use of cars. Usually this is about three-quarters of a cent for each mile which the car travels on a foreign road. This involves a great scattering of cars, and an extensive organization to keep record of their whereabouts and of the accounts between the companies for mileage.* This organization will be referred to more fully in connection with the department of transportation. But the joint use of each other's cars

* See "The Freight-car Service," page 275.

makes it necessary that there should be at least enough similarity in their construction and their coupling appliances to permit their

Incident thereto, for the fiscal year ending June 30th, 1888.

Cost of Cleaning.	COST OF REPAIRS			Total Expenses and Repairs.	M'ls run to one			COST PER MILE RUN FOR.						Car Mileage.	Number of Engine.
	Labor	Material	Total Cost of Repairs.		Bushel Coal.	Gal. Engine Oil.	Pound of Tallow.	Repairs.	Fuel.	Stores.	Wages E. and F	Cleaning.	Total.		
$ 115 00	$ 223 40	$ 66 32	$ 289 72	$ 2,876 41	1.5	122 3	14.5	01.76	06 64	00 53	07.89	00 61	17.43	177,659	1
82 50	69 65	75 14	144 79	3,112 81	1.1	126 8	27.7	00 94	07 34	00 65	10 69	00.53	20.19	197,203	2
187 50	178 25	63 61	241 86	3,113 94	0.9	77 7	17 4	02.32	10 58	00.90	14.31	02 04	30 15	182,402	3
212 50	203 95	100 13	304 08	3,620 18	2 7	127.2	32 8	00.92	03 69	05 23	05 24	00 64	15 72	139,422	4
202 00	240 55	114 98	355 53	3,666 50	2 5	128 2	41 2	01 08	04.06	00 44	04 96	00.61	11 15	135,780	5
10 00	172 35	63 65	236 00	3,346 68	3 1	140 4	36.3	00.72	03.22	00 53	05 82	00 03	10.32	......	6
150 00	110 75	106 69	217 44	3,414 13	1 5	147.8	37.9	01.09	06 84	00 49	08.04	00.76	17.22	305,024	8
200 00	139 80	175 48	315 28	3,918 02	1 4	150.0	48 5	01 30	06 88	00 40	06 70	00 82	16 10	383,682	9
205 00	207 55	109 78	317 33	4,041 93	1 5	195.4	46 5	01 23	06 77	00 31	06 49	00.79	15 59	409,035	10
5 00	413 95	89 76	503 71	2,558 29	3 0	173 6	36.4	02 13	03.43	00.47	04.77	00 02	10 82	....	11
25 00	37 45	27 17	64 62	2,519 78	2.0	171.0	23.5	00 36	05 11	00 59	07.82	00.14	14 02	66,834	12
212 50	144 50	77 52	222 02	4,118 15	2.3	185 4	74 9	00 53	04 40	00.34	04.15	00.51	09 93	231,554	30
205 00	642 50	432 86	1,075 36	4,703 66	2.2	154.1	50 8	02.87	04 58	00 40	04 15	00.54	12 54	202,289	31
172 00	1,729 70	438 40	2,168 10	4,752 00	1.6	129 5	31 2	12.11	06.25	00.60	06 64	00.96	26.56	184,083	32
137 00	1,522 10	781 64	2,303 74	4,313 48	3 2	108.5	35.5	11.41	03.48	00 54	05 29	00.67	21 39	107,060	34
2,121 00	6,036 45	2.723 13	8,759 58	54,075 96	2 5	148 1	38.5	02 31	04.98	00 48	05 97	00 65	14 29	2,722,027	

indiscriminate use upon all roads. And conventions of master car-builders have recommended certain forms and dimensions as standards, which are now in general use.

There is much convenience in this, but one disadvantage. It requires almost unanimous action to introduce any change of form or of construction, however advantageous it may be. And to secure unanimous action in such matters is almost as hard as it would be to secure unanimity in a change in the spelling of English words. Still there is progress, though slow, toward several desirable reforms, the most important of which is the adoption of a standard automatic coupler (see p. 142).

Having shown how the property of all kinds is kept in efficient condition, we next come to its operation. This is called " conducting transportation," and the officer in charge is usually called the superintendent of transportation. All train-despatchers, conductors, train-men, and telegraph operators are under his immediate control. He makes all schedules and provides all extra and irregular service that the traffic department makes requisition for, himself calling upon the superintendent of machinery for the necessary locomotives, switching engines, and cars. It is his especial province to handle all trains as swiftly as possible, and to see that there are no collisions. It is impossible to detail fully the safeguards and precautions used to this end, but the general principles observed are as follows:

First, a general time-table or schedule is carefully made out for all regular trains upon each division, showing on one sheet the time of each train at each station.

This schedule is all that is needed so long as all trains are able to keep on time, and there are no extras. Trouble begins when regular trains cannot keep on schedule, or when extra trains have to be sent out, not provided for on the schedule. A diagram, or graphic representation of this schedule, upon a board or large sheet of paper, is an important feature of the office regulating train-movements. Twenty-four vertical lines divide the board into equal spaces representing the twenty-four hours of the day, numbered from midnight to midnight. Horizontal lines at proportionate distances from the top represent the stations in their order between the termini, represented by the top and bottom lines of the diagram. The course of every train can now be plotted on this diagram in an oblique line joining the points on each station line corresponding to the time the train arrives at and leaves that station. The cut on the opposite page will illustrate. It represents a road 130 miles long from A to N, with intermediate stations B, C, D, etc., at different distances from each other, and six trains are shown as follows:

A passenger train, No. 1, leaving A at 12 midnight and arriving at N at 4.05 A.M. A fast express, No. 2, leaving N at 12.45 and arriving at A at 3.30. A local passenger train, No. 4, which leaves N at 1.15, runs to E by 4 A.M., stops there until 4.10, and returns to N by 7 A.M.; being called No. 3 on the return, as the direction is always indicated by the train-number's being odd or even. No. 5 is a way freight, leaving A at 12.05 and making long stops at each station. No. 6 is an opposing train of the same character.

The diagram shows at a glance how, when, and where all these trains meet and pass each other, and where every train is at any

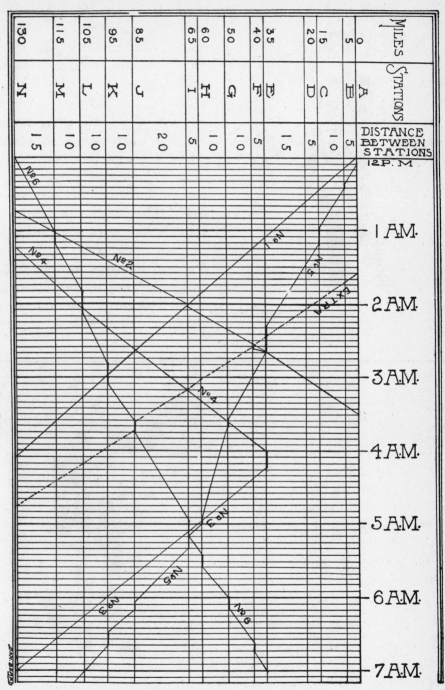

Diagram Used in Making Railway Time-Tables.

A lamp swung across the track is the signal to stop.

moment. Should it be desired to send an extra train at any time, a line drawn or a string stretched on the board will indicate what opposing trains must be guarded against. For instance, to send an extra through in three hours, leaving A between 1 and 2 A.M., a trial line will show that Nos. 5, 2, 4, and 6 must all be met or passed, and as (on a single-track road) this can only be done at stations, the extra must leave at 1.35 A.M., pass No. 5 at E, meet No. 2 at F, No. 4 at I, and No. 6 at J. A dotted line on the diagram indicates its run, and that No. 2 is held at F for 5 minutes

to let it pass. If the road is double-tracked, only trains going in the same direction need be regarded.*

But the more usual way of handling extra trains, when circumstances will permit, is to let them precede or follow a regular train upon the same schedule. The train is then said to be run in " sections," and a ten minutes' interval is allowed between them. That opposing trains may be informed, the leading section (and

* Of course, this "stringing" of an extra train is not always done in actual operation. Practice and experience will give as wonderful expertness to a train-despatcher in handling trains "in his head" as to a mathematician in solving problems, and often all trains on a road will be handled entirely "by order," or as extras. But the example given illustrates the principle upon which expert practice is based.

A lamp raised and lowered vertically is the signal to move ahead.

A lamp swung vertically in a circle across the track, when the train is standing, is the signal to move back.

when there are more than two all but the last) wears on its locomotive two green flags by day and two green lights by night, indicating that a train follows which is to be considered as a part of the train leading, and having the same rights.

So far the rules are very simple, and they would be all that is necessary if all trains could always be kept exactly on time. But as that cannot be, provision must be made for all the complications which will result. The first and most important rule is that no train must ever, under any circumstances, run *ahead* of

time. The next is that any train making a stop not on its schedule must immediately send out flagmen with red flags, lights, and torpedoes to protect it. This rule is a very difficult one to enforce without rigid discipline, and its neglect is the cause of a large percentage of the accidents " that will happen." The flagman who must go to the rear, often a half-mile, at night, across trestles and in storms, must frequently be left behind, to take his chances of getting home by being picked up by a following train. There is no one to watch him, and he will often take chances, and not

A lamp swung vertically in a circle at arm's length across the track, when the train is running, is the signal that the train has parted.

go as far back or as fast as he should; and if all goes well no one is ever the wiser.

Now, when a train is prevented from arriving on time at its meeting-point, we must have some rules by which the opposing train may proceed, or all business on the road would be suspended by the delay of a single train. Only the general principles of these rules can be stated within limits. They are as follows:

1. All freight trains must wait indefinitely for all passenger trains.

2. When one train only is behind time, the opposing train of the same class will wait for it a specified time, usually ten minutes, and five minutes more for possible variation of watches, then go ahead, keeping fifteen minutes behind its schedule.

3. But should such a train, running on delayed time, lose more time, or in any other way should both trains get behind time, then the one which is bound in a certain direction—for instance, north—has the right to the track, and the other must lie by indefinitely.

These principles, duly observed, will prevent collisions, but they will often cause trains to lose a great deal of time. The train-despatcher, therefore, has authority to handle extra and delayed trains by direct telegraphic order. Every possible precaution is taken to insure that such orders are received and correctly understood. As there are great advantages following uniformity of usages and rules among connecting roads, after years of conference, in conventions and by committees, approved forms of all running rules and signals have recently been adopted and are now in very general use over the United States. Yet, in spite of all possible precautions, accidents will sometimes happen. Richard Grant White gave a name to a mental habit which, in train despatchers, has caused many fatal accidents. It is "heterophemy," or thinking one thing while saying, hearing, or reading another. A case within my knowledge, which cost a dozen lives, was as follows: Two opposing trains were out of time, and the train-despatcher wished to have them meet and pass at a certain station we will call "I," as Nos. 1 and 2 are represented as doing on the diagram (see diagram of schedule board, p. 161). So he telegraphed the following message, to be delivered to No. 1 at "H"

The General Despatcher.

and to No. 2 at " J ": "Nos. 1 and 2 will meet at ' I.'" This message was correctly received at " J " and delivered to No. 2. But at
" H " the operator had just sold a passenger a ticket to " K," and,

Entrance Gates at a Large Station.

getting this name in his head, he wrote out the message: " Nos. 1
and 2 will meet at 'K.'" But the mistake was not yet past correction. The operator had to repeat the message back to the despatcher, that the latter might be sure it was correctly understood.
He repeated it as he had written it—" K." But the despatcher
was also "heterophemous." He *saw* "K," but he *thought* "I,"
and replied to the operator that the message was O. K.

So it was delivered to No. 1, and that train left " H " at full
speed, expecting to run thirty-five miles to " K " before meeting
No. 2. There was no telegraph office at " I," and there were no
passengers to get off or on, and it passed there without stopping,
and three miles below ran into No. 2 on a curve.

By one of those strange impulses which seem to come from
some unconscious cerebration, the train-despatcher meanwhile had
a feeling that something was wrong, and looked again at the message received from " H " and discovered his mistake. But the
trains were then out of reach. He still hoped that No. 2 might arrive at " I " first, or that they might meet upon a straight portion
of road, and as the time passed he waited at the instrument in a
state of suspense which may be imagined. When the news came
he left the office, and never returned.

Double tracks make accidents of this character impossible; but
introduce a new possibility, that a derailment from any cause upon

Central Switch and Signal Tower.

one track may obstruct the other track so closely ahead of an opposing train that no warning can be given.

Where trains become very numerous additional safeguards are added by multiplying telegraph stations at short intervals, and giving them conspicuous signals of semaphore arms and lanterns, until finally the road is divided into a number of so-called "blocks" of a few miles each; and no train is permitted to enter any block until the train preceding has passed out. And in the approaches to some of our great depots, where trains and tracks are multiplied and confused with cross-overs and switching service, all switches are set and all movements controlled by signals from a single central tower. Sometimes, by very expensive and complicated apparatus, it is made mechanically impossible to open a track for the movement of a train without previously locking all openings by which another train might interfere. The illustrations on pages 169, 171, and above will serve to give some general idea of these appliances.*

* See "Safety in Railroad Travel," page 204.

Mantua Junction, West Philadelphia, showing a Complex System of Interlacing Tracks.

There remains one other branch of the duties of the master of transportation—the proper daily distribution of cars to every station according to its needs, and the keeping record of their where-

Interior of a Switch-tower, showing the Operation of Interlocking Switches.

abouts. And now that the gauges of all roads are similar, and competition enforces through shipments, roads are practically making common property of each other's cars, and the detail and trouble of keeping record of them become enormous.

The records are made up from daily reports, by every conductor, of every car, home or foreign, handled in his train, and from every station-agent of all cars in his yard at certain hours. From these returns the car accountant reports to their respective owners all movements of foreign cars and gives the transportation department information where cars are lying. The honesty of each other's reports concerning car movements is generally relied upon by railroads, but "lost car agents" are kept travelling to hunt up estrays, and to watch how the cars of their roads are being handled.

It has been suggested that a great step in advance would be to have all the roads in the United States unite and put all cars into a common stock and let them be distributed, record kept of movements, and mileage paid through a general clearing house. This would practically form a single rolling-stock company owned by the roads contributing their cars to it. It could gradually introduce uniform patterns of construction, improved couplers, and air-brakes, and could concentrate cars in different sections of the country in large numbers as different crops required movement, thus avoiding the blockades which often occur in one section while cars are superabundant in another. Consolidations usually render more efficient and cheaper service than separate organizations can do, and this may come about in the course of time.*

We have now seen how the road is maintained and its trains safely handled. The next step in order is to see how business is secured and the rates to be charged are fixed. This department may be controlled by a traffic manager, with two assistants—the general freight agent and the general passenger agent—or the officers may report directly to the general manager without the intervention of a traffic manager. But it would be a more accurate expression to say, not that these officers "fix" the rates, for if they did few railroads would ever fail, but that they accept and announce the rates that are fixed by conditions of competition between different markets and products, and between different railroads and water lines. Among these complex forces a railroad freight agent is nearly as powerless to regulate rates as a professor of grammar is to regulate the irregularities of English verbs. He can accept them and use them, or he may let them alone, but the irregularities will remain, all the same. There is no eccentricity, for example, more idiotic or indefensible to the ordinary citizen than a habit railroads have of sometimes charging less money for a long haul than they charge for a shorter haul. Yet I believe there is not a railroad line in the United States which will not be found guilty of this apparent folly of charging "less for the long haul" if its rates to distant points are followed far enough. For if followed far enough we

* See " The Freight-car Service," page 288.

shall come to the ocean, and find the railroad accepting business between two seaports. For instance, all railroads running westward from New York through some of their connections finally reach San Francisco, and compete for freight between these ports. But the rates they are able to obtain are limited by steamers using the ocean for a highway, and sailing vessels using the wind for motive power, and able to carry heavy freights at one-tenth the average cost to railroads across mountains and deserts. This average cost must fix the average rates charged by the railroads to intermediate points, such as to Ogden, in Utah. So the railroad must either charge less for the long haul to San Francisco, or leave that business to be done solely by water. Yet it may be profitable to the railroad to accept the business at such rates as it can obtain; for, as in all business ventures, manufacturing or mercantile, *new* business can be profitably added at less than the average cost. And if profitable to the railroad its tendency is beneficial, even to the intermediate points which pay higher rates, as promoting better service, besides being advantageous to the whole Pacific Coast in tending to keep down the rates by water.

But it would lead too far from our subject to follow this and several other questions which are suggested by it. Only it may be said briefly that the original Interstate Commerce Bill, introduced by Mr. Reagan, absolutely prohibited "less for the long haul." The Senate amended by adding "under similar circumstances and conditions," and the Interstate Commerce Commission has held that "water competition" makes dissimilar circumstances and thus legalizes it.

And in this connection it may be added that the other Senate amendment to the Reagan bill, creating an Interstate Commerce Commission, was, next to the above amendment, the wisest measure of the bill. It forms a body of experts whose opinions and decisions must gradually educate the public, on the one hand, to a better understanding of transportation problems, and restrain the railroads, on the other, from many of the abuses incident to unchecked competition among them. For, however theorists may differ as to the advantages or disadvantages of competition in manufactures and commerce, either absolutely unchecked or checked only by high or low tariffs, I think all will agree that unchecked *railroad* competition is a great evil, because it results in fluctuating rates and private rebates to large shippers. The rebates, to be sure, are forbidden by law, but they can be disguised past recognition. I have known a case, for instance, where a receipt was given for 75 barrels of whiskey, when only 73 were shipped. The shipper was to make claim for two barrels lost and be paid an agreed value as a rebate on his freight bill. In another case, a road agreed with a certain shipper to pay his telegraph bills for a certain period in order to control his shipments. Understating the weight or class of the shipment is another common device for undercharging or rebating.

In nearly every foreign country there is either a railroad pool or a division of territory, to prevent this sort of competition, which is only pernicious. A merchant needs to feel assured that rates are stable and uniform to all, and not that he must go shopping for secret rates, in order to be on an equality with his competitor. In the United States the railroads had largely resorted to pools before the Interstate Commerce Law forbade them. The result of this prohibition has generally been very advantageous to the best lines, which, under the pool, really paid a sort of blackmail to the poorer lines to maintain rates. If the penalties of the law can restrain such lines from rebating and under-billing, to be rid of the pool will be a great blessing to the well-located roads. If not, then the roads will be driven into consolidation, for the end of fighting will be bankruptcy and sale. Fortunately consolidation has already gone so far in many sections of the country that the difficulties of abolishing rebates have been greatly reduced. And as far as it has gone it has proved of much advantage both to the public and to the stockholders.

Fortunately, too, the other results attendant upon consolidation have been sufficiently demonstrated to remove any intelligent fear of extortion in rates or deterioration of service. Who would to-day desire to undo the consolidations which have built up the Pennsylvania Railroad or the New York Central, and call back to life the numberless small companies which preceded them? The country has outgrown such service as they could render, and the local growth and development along the lines of these consolidated companies certainly indicates improved conditions. In this connection, too, the improvement in cost and character of service is instructive. In 1865 the average rate per ton per mile on the principal Eastern lines was about 2.900 cents; in 1887 it was 0.718 for a service twice as speedy and efficient.

There are many other live issues of great interest and importance in transportation suggested by this subject, such as "re-billing" or "milling in transit," and "differentials," but space forbids more than an explanation of the meaning of these two especially prominent ones.

A   B   C

Let A B and B C be two railroads connecting at B. Let the local rates A to B be 10 cents per 100 lbs. on grain, and B to C also 10 cents. Let the through rate A to C be 18, since longest hauls are usually cheapest per mile. Let A be a large grain market, such as Chicago. Now a merchant at C can save 2 cents per 100 lbs. by buying direct from A instead of buying from a merchant at B. For the grain will pay less for the single long haul than for the two short hauls. But perhaps the town of B has for many years enjoyed the trade of C, and there are large mills and warehouses erected there. B will then say it is "discriminated against," and will demand the privilege of "re-billing" or "milling in transit." That is to say, when a merchant or miller at B ships to C grain, or flour made of grain, which he received from A, the two roads consent to make a new way-bill and treat the shipment as a through shipment from A to C. The road B C charges but 8 cents, and the road A B gives B C one cent from the 10 it originally collected. This involves much trouble and a loss of revenue to the roads, and is, apparently, a discrimination against the home products of B, but roads frequently do it where there is competition at C by rival lines, and also at local points along their lines to build up mills, distilleries, and factories of all kinds in competition with those located elsewhere. As yet the Interstate Commerce Commission has not pronounced upon this practice.

The question of differentials is as follows: Suppose there are three lines, B, D, and E, between the cities A and C (Diagram, page 176). B, being the shortest, will get most of the business when

rates are the same (10 cents, for instance) by each line. But D
and E insist upon participating, so they demand that B shall allow

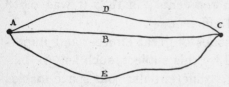

them to operate lower or "differential" rates—that is, B must
maintain his rate at 10 while allowing D to charge only 8 and
E 6 cents, on account of their
disadvantages. So that a differential is practically a premium
offered for business by an inferior line.

The foregoing will illustrate how the rivalry of railroads with
each other complicates the making of rates. But even more difficult to manage is the rivalry of markets, and of products, and of
new methods which threaten property invested in old methods; as,
for instance, the dressed-beef traffic from the West threatens the
investments in slaughter-houses and stock-yards in the East.

As the roads have found it necessary to act together in establishing running rules and regulations, so, in spite of all rivalries,
there must also be joint agreements reached in some way concerning rates. Usually the roads serving a certain territory form an
"association," and their freight agents form "rate committees,"
which fix and publish joint rates. A tariff published by one of the
trunk lines from the Eastern cities forms a good example. As the
result of many long and bitter wars and many compromises, it has
been agreed among these roads that the rates from New York to
Chicago shall form a basis for all other rates, and a scale has been
fixed showing the percentage of the Chicago rate to be used as
the rate to each important point in the West. Thus Pittsburgh,
Pa., is 60 per cent. of Chicago rate; Indianapolis is 93; Vandalia,
116. The tariff above referred to gives an alphabetical list of some
5,000 towns reached over these roads, and opposite each town the
figure showing its percentage of the Chicago rate. The list begins with Abanaka, O., 90, and ends with Zoar, O., 74.

The tariff next gives what is called the "Trunk Line Classification," which is a list comprising every article known to commerce,
in all the different conditions, shapes, and packages in which it is
offered for transportation, and opposite each article is given its assigned "class." This particular classification assigns every article
to one of six regular, or two special, classes, and the present rates

to Chicago in cents per 100 lbs. are given as 75, 65, 50, 35, 30, 25, 26, 21. The list of articles begins with Acetate of Lime, in carloads, 5th class; in less quantities, 4th; and ends with Zinc, in various forms from 1st to 6th—comprising in all nearly 6,000 articles. From these tables any desired rate readily appears. Thus, 500 pounds of acetate of lime would cost, from New York to Zoar, O., 74 per cent. of Chicago's 4th class rate, or 74 per cent. of 35—say, 26 cents per 100 lbs., or $1.30.

There is also given in the tariff pamphlet a list of some 300 manufacturing towns in New England, from each of which the same rates apply as from New York. So, on the whole, the pamphlet gives rates on about 6,000 articles from 300 points of origin to 5,000 destinations.

In different sections of the country different classifications are in use, some of them embracing twenty or more classes, and allowing finer shades of difference between articles according to their value, bulk, or many other varying conditions which determine the class into which each article is put.

Great efforts have been made to bring about a uniformity of classification over the whole United States, and the number of classifications in extensive use has been reduced from a very large number to perhaps a dozen.

But absolute uniformity cannot be obtained under the widely different conditions which prevail in different sections, without great loss and sacrifices somewhere. A road, for instance, competing with a river or canal must adjust the classification of the particular kinds of freight best adapted to river or canal transportation so as to secure the traffic in competition with boats. It must almost entirely disregard bulk, value, and all other conditions upon which a road not affected by this particular kind of competition arranges its classification. Uniformity would either force one of them to lose a legitimate business, or the other to reduce reasonable rates.

These rates and classifications are the battle-ground for all the innumerable rivalries of trade and commerce. Every city is here at war with every other city, every railroad with every other road, every industry with those which rival it, and every individual shipper is a skirmisher for a little special rate, or advantage, all to himself. State legislatures and commissions, Congress, and the Inter-

state Commerce Commission are the heavy artillery which different combatants manage to bring into the contest.   On these rates
probably a million dollars are collected every day, yet it is very
rarely that the *positive* rates are fought over or complained of.
Their average is considerably below that of the average rates of
any other country in the world, even though other nations have
cheaper labor and denser populations.   Fifty cents for carrying a
barrel of flour a thousand miles cannot be called exorbitant, and, indeed, the retail prices paid for bread and clothing would probably
not be reduced in the slightest were the transportation of all such
articles absolutely free.   But the battle is over the *comparative*
rates to different points, over different routes, and for different commodities.*

Passenger rates are established in much the same manner as
freight rates.   There are passenger-agents' associations and conventions, and they fight as do the freight men over comparative
rates and differentials, and commissions to agents.   The last within a few years has been a fearful abuse, and is not yet entirely
abolished.   This will illustrate :

The road A B has two connections, C and D, to reach E.   It
sells tickets over each at the same rate, and stands neutral between
them.   But C agrees with A's ticket-seller that he will give him a
dollar for every ticket he can sell over C's line.   D finds that he is

---

* An idea may be gained of the extent and minuteness of the classification, and of the constant
changes and adjustments, both of rates and classifications, perpetually going on from the following partial
list of subjects submitted to a recent meeting of the Rate Committee of the Southern Railway and
Steamship Association.

RATES.—Watermelon rates ; canned goods, Richmond to Atlanta ; rates on cement from Eastern
cities to Association territory ; rates on sulphuric acid from Atlanta ; rates from Atlanta, etc., to California and Transcontinental terminals ; special iron rates from Cincinnati, etc., to Carolina points ;
rates on earthenware, East Liverpool to S. E. territory ; rates on cotton bags to Memphis from Atlanta ; rates on fertilizers to Mobile, Ala. ; beer rates ; rates on special iron articles from Chattanooga ;
rates from the West to Camden, S C. ; rates from Evansville and Cairo, on business from points between Cairo, Evansville, and Chicago.

CLASSIFICATION.—Classification of paper twine ; beer packages, empty returned ; old machinery returned for repairs ; steel car springs ; cotton softener ; iron safes or vaults weighing over 12,000
lbs. ; toys, etc. ; portable powder magazines ; coffee extract ; empty lard tierces returned ; bolts and
nuts in barrels ; box and barrel material ; glass oil bottles in tin jackets ; cast-iron radiators ; malle-
able iron castings ; dried beef; sausage ; straw paper ; burlaps ; tobacco stems ; hinges ; straw braids ;
lawn hose reels ; excelsior ; car-load rates.

SUBJECTS NOT ON THE REGULAR LIST.—Demurrage rules ; adjustment of rates as per instructions from the Executive Board ; rates from Cincinnati to Columbus, Eufaula, Opelika, etc. ; classification of iron tanks ; classification of whiting ; rates to Eufaula, Ala., from East ; rates to Milledgeville,
Ga. ; classification of cast-iron cane mills ; classification of locomotives and tenders.

losing travel, and offers, privately, a larger commission. Neither knows what the other is doing. The ticket-seller gets his regular salary from A, and from C and D often enormous sums as commissions, and is interested, not in sending ignorant travellers over the line which might suit them best, but over the one paying him the largest secret commission. This should be held as against public policy, because it tends to prevent reductions in rates to the public by robbing the roads of much of their revenue, and it also demoralizes the officers who handle a business which is practically but the giving away of large sums of money as bribes.

There is another practice in the passenger business which is unfair at the best and is the source of many abuses. It is charging the same to the man with no baggage as to the man with a Saratoga trunk. If the baggage service were specially organized as a trunk express, it could be more efficiently handled and without any "baggage smashing," while the total cost of travelling to persons with baggage would be no more than at present, and to those without, much less.

As an illustration of the sort of abuses to which it is now liable, I may cite a single case. I have known a merchant buy a lot of twenty trunks for his trade, pack them all full of dry-goods, check them to a city 1,000 miles away by giving a few dollars to baggage-men, and himself buy a single ticket and go by a different route. The roads which handled that baggage imagined that it belonged to their passengers, and were never the wiser. While the baggage service is free, no efficient checks can be provided against such frauds.

Essential parts of both freight and passenger departments are the soliciting agents. They are like the cavalry pickets and scouts of an army, scattered far and wide over the country and looking after the interests of their lines, making personal acquaintances of all shippers and travellers, advertising in every possible manner, and reporting constantly all that the enemy—the rival lines—are doing, and often a great deal that they are not. For the great railroad wars usually begin in local skirmishes brought on by the zeal of these pickets when the officers in command would greatly prefer to live in peace.

Besides their receipts from freight and passenger traffic, rail-roads derive revenue also from the transportation of mails and ex-press freight on passenger trains, from the sleeping-car companies, and from news companies for the privilege of selling upon trains. Of the total revenue about 70 per cent. is usually derived from freight, 25 per cent. from passengers, and 5 per cent. from mail, ex-press, sleeping-cars, and privileges. When it is considered that high speed involves great risks and necessitates a far more perfect roadway, more costly machinery and appliances, and a higher grade and a greater number of employees, the fast passenger, mail, and express traffic hardly seems at present to yield its due proportion of income.

We have now followed the line of organization and manage-ment through the physical maintenance of the road and rolling stock, the safe handling of the trains, the establishment of rates, and solicitation of business. It only remains to show how the rev-enue is collected, how the expenses of operation are paid, and all statistics of the business prepared. These duties are usually united under charge of an officer called the comptroller, general auditor, or some equivalent title. His principal subordinates, whose duties are indicated by their titles, are the auditor of receipts, auditor of disbursements, local treasurer, paymaster, and clerk of statistics.

The record of a single shipment of freight will illustrate meth-ods, so far as limits will permit. A shipper sending freight for ship-ment sends with each dray-load a " dray ticket " in duplicate, show-ing the articles, weight, marks, and destination. If he has prepaid the freight, or advanced any charges which are to be paid at desti-nation, it is also noted on the dray ticket. When the drayman reaches the outbound freight depot with his load, he is directed to a certain spot where all freight for the same destination is being collected for loading. A receiving clerk checks off his load against the duplicate dray tickets, keeps one and files it, and gives the drayman the other, receipted. In case of any loss arising after-ward, the original dray ticket, made by the shipper himself, with his marks and instructions, becomes a valuable record. When the entire shipment has been delivered at the loading point, the ship-per takes the dray tickets representing it to the proper desk, and receives "a bill of lading." This bill of lading is made in triplicate. The original and a duplicate are given to the shipper. He keeps the last and sends the former to the consignee. It represents the obligation of the railroad to transport and deliver the articles named on it to the person named, or his assignee. It is negotiable, and banks advance money upon it. But the shipper may still, by a legal process, have the goods stopped *en route* should occasion arise, as, for instance, by the bankruptcy of the consignee. The goods are also liable for garnishments in certain cases, and there is much railroad and commercial law which it behooves the officials interested to be well posted in. When the goods arrive at destination the possession of the bill of lading is the evidence of the consignee's right to receive them.

Now we will return to the shipment itself and see how it is taken care of. The whole structure of the system of collecting freight revenue, holding accountable all agents who assess it and collect it, dividing it in the agreed proportions between all the railroads, boats, bridges, wharves, and transfer companies who may handle it in its journeys, even across the continent, and the tabulating of the immense mass of statistics which are kept to show, separately, the quantities of freight of every possible class and variety, by every possible route, and to and from every possible point of destination and departure—all this system, neither the magnitude nor the minute elaboration of which can be adequately described within limits, is founded upon a paper called the way-bill.

The theory of the way-bill is that no car must move without one accompanying it, describing it by its number and the initials of the road owning it, and showing its points of departure and destination, its entire contents, with marks and weights of each package, consignors and consignees, freight and charges prepaid or to be collected at destination, and the proportion of the same due to each carrier or transfer in the line. And not only must a way-bill accompany the car, but a duplicate of it must be sent immediately and directly, by the office making the original, to the office of the auditor of freight receipts. If the railroad is a member of any association, as the Trunk Line Association in New York, another duplicate is sent to its office, that it may supervise all rates, and see what each road is doing. The sum of all the way-bills is the total of a road's freight business. To facilitate taking copies they are printed with an ink which will give several impressions on strong, thin tissue-paper, forming " soft copies," while the " hard copy," or original, goes with the freight to be checked against it when the car is unloaded.

And while the original way-bill fulfils its important function of conducting the freight to destination and delivery, the duplicate which was forwarded directly to the auditor of freight receipts has no less important purposes. It is the initial record that freight has been earned, and it shows which agent of the company has been charged with its collection. Before making any entries from it its absolute correctness must be assured. For this purpose all its figures are first checked by a rate-clerk, who is kept constantly supplied by the traffic department with all current rates, classifications, and percentage tables by which through freights are divided. These way-bills, coming in daily by hundreds and thousands, are then the grist upon which the office of the auditor of receipts grinds, and from which come forth the accounts with every agent, showing his debits for freight received, and the consolidations showing the freight earnings of the road. Agents remit the moneys they collect direct to the treasurer, who makes daily reports of the credits due to each one. A travelling auditor visits every station at irregular intervals and checks the agent's accounts, requiring him to justify any difference between his debits and credits by an exhibit of undelivered freight.

The passenger earnings are obtained from daily reports by all conductors of their collections, and by all ticket-sellers of tickets sold. These reports are also checked by a passenger rate-clerk, and the travelling auditor frequently examines and verifies the tickets reported by agents as on hand unsold.

After the auditor of receipts has finished with the way-bills and ticket reports, they go to the statistical department, where are prepared the great mass and variety of statistics required by different officers to keep themselves thoroughly posted on the growth or decrease of business of every variety, and from and to every market reached by the road. Finally, the way-bills are filed away for reference in case of claims for overcharges, or lost or damaged goods.

The auditor of disbursements has supervision of all expenditures of money, which is only paid out by the paymaster or treasurer upon vouchers and pay-rolls approved by proper authority. The vouchers and pay-rolls then form the grist upon which his office works, and from which are produced the credits to be given all officers and agents who disburse money, and the classified records of expenses, and comparison of the same with previous months and years, and between different divisions.

I have thus outlined the skeleton of a railroad organization, and suggested briefly the relations between its most important parts, and some of the principles upon which its work is conducted. The scheme of authority is outlined in the diagram on page 185. But space is utterly lacking to clothe the skeleton with flesh and go into the innumerable details and adjustments involved in the economical and efficient discharge of all of its functions.

It seems a very simple matter for a railroad to place a barrel of flour in a car, to carry it to its destination, and to collect fifty cents for the service. It is done apparently so spontaneously that even the fifty cents may seem exorbitant, and I have actually heard appeals for free transportation on the ground that the cars were going anyhow. So it also seems a very simple matter for a man to pick up a stone and place it on a wall. But this simple act involves in the first place the existence of a bony frame, with joints, sinews, and muscles, sustained by a heart, lungs, and digestive system, with eyes to see, a brain to direct, nerves to give effect to the will-power, and a thousand delicate adjustments of organs and functions without which all physical exertion would soon cease. Similarly, a railroad organized to respond efficiently to all the varied demands upon it as a common carrier, by the public, and as an investment by its owners, becomes almost a living organism. That the barrel of flour may be safely delivered and the fifty cents reach the company's treasury, and a part of it the stockholder's pocket, the whole organization outlined in the diagram must thrill with life, and every officer and employee, from president to car-greaser, must discharge his special functions. All must be co-ordinated, and the organization must have and use its eyes and its ears, its muscle, its nerves, and its brain. It must immediately feel and respond to every demand of our rapidly advancing civilization.

Each road usually has its own individuality and methods, and its employees are animated with an *esprit de corps*, as are the soldiers in an army. There is much about the service that is attractive, and, on the whole, the wages paid railroad employees are probably in excess of the rates for similar talent in any other industry, although labor in every other industry in the United States is protected by high tariffs, while in this it is under the incubus of legislation as oppressive as constitutional limits will permit.

In Europe, where the pooling system practically prevails, the service is much more stable than in the United States, and in many instances there are pensions and insurances and disability funds, and regular rules for promotion and retirement, and provision for the children of employees being brought into service in preference to outsiders. Such relations between a company and its employees as must result from arrangements of this character are surely of great benefit to both. They are the natural outgrowth of *stability of business*. Their most advanced form is found in France, where each road is practically protected from dangerous competition by means of a division of territory. In the United States we are still in the midst of a fierce competition for territory and business, and, as pooling is forbidden, the railroad companies will be in unstable equilibrium until consolidation takes place. As that goes on, and large and rich corporations are formed, with prospects of stability in management and in business, we may hope to see similar relations established between our companies and their employees. Already there is a beginning upon some of the largest roads, such as the Baltimore & Ohio and the Pennsylvania Central. But the ground still needs preparation also on the employees' side, for our American spirit is aggressive and is sometimes rather disposed to resent, as interfering with its independence, any paternal relations with a corporation. And as we have before found railroad management in intimate contact with every problem of finance and commerce, it is here confronted with the social and industrial questions involved in labor unions and

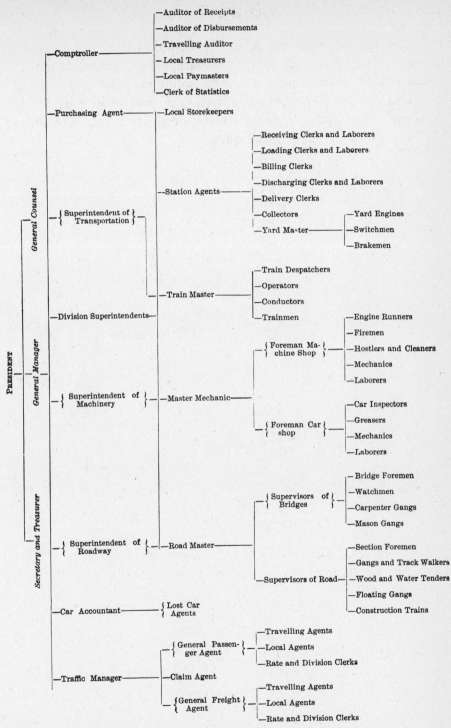

Diagram showing the Skeleton of a Railroad Organization, and Lines of Responsibility.

problems of co-operation. As to the results, we can only say that, as war is destructive, no state of warfare, even between capital and labor, can be permanent. Peaceful solutions must prevail in the end, and progress toward stability, peace, and prosperity in railroad operation and ownership will be progress toward the happy solution of many vexed social questions.

SAFETY IN RAILROAD TRAVEL.

By H. G. PROUT.

The Possibilities of Destruction in the Great Speed of a Locomotive—The Energy of Four Hundred Tons Moving at Seventy-five Miles an Hour—A Look ahead from a Locomotive at Night—Passengers Killed and Injured in One Year—Good Discipline the Great Source of Safety—The Part Played by Mechanical Appliances—Hand-brakes on Old Cars—How the Air brake Works—The Electric Brake—Improvements yet to be Made—Engine Driver Brakes—Two Classes of Signals : those which Protect Points of Danger, and those which Keep an Interval between Trains on the Same Track—The Semaphore—Interlocking Signals and Switches—Electric Annunciators to Indicate the Movements—The Block Signal System—Protection for Crossings—Gates and Gongs—How Derailment is Guarded Against—Safety Bolts –Automatic Couplers—The Vestibule as a Safety Appliance—Car Heating and Lighting.

IN 1829, when Ericsson's little locomotive " Novelty," weighing two and a half tons, ran a short distance at the rate of thirty miles an hour, a writer of the time said that " it was the most wonderful exhibition of human daring and human skill that the world had ever seen." To-day trains weighing four hundred tons thunder by at seventy-five miles an hour, and we hardly note their passage. We take their safety as a matter of course, and seldom think of the tremendous possibilities of destruction stored up in them. But seventy-five miles an hour is one hundred and ten feet a second, and the energy of four hundred tons moving at that rate is nearly twice as great as that of a 2,000-pound shot fired from a 100-ton Armstrong gun. This is the extreme of weight and speed now reached in passenger service, and, indeed, is very rarely attained, and then but for short distances ; but sixty miles is a common speed, and a rate of forty or fifty miles is attained daily on

almost every railroad in the country. We cannot tell from the
time-tables how fast we travel. The schedule times do not indicate the delays that must be made up by spurts between stations.
The traveller who is curious to know just how fast he is going,
and likes the stimulus of thinking that he is in a little danger, may
find amusement in taking the time between mile-posts ; and when
these are not to be seen, he can often get the speed very accurately by counting the rails passed in a given time. This may be
done by listening attentively at an open window or door. The
regular clicks of the wheels over the rail-joints can usually soon be
singled out from the other noises, and counted. The number of
rail-lengths passed in twenty seconds is almost exactly the number of miles run in an hour.

But if one wants to get a lively sense of what it means to rush
through space at fifty or sixty miles an hour, he must get on a
locomotive. Then only does he begin to realize what trifles stand
between him and destruction. A few months ago a lady sat an
hour in the cab of a locomotive hauling a fast express train over a
mountain road. She saw the narrow bright line of the rails and
the slender points of the switches. She heard the thunder of the
bridges, and saw the track shut in by rocky bluffs, and new perils
suddenly revealed as the engine swept around sharp curves. The
experience was to her magnificent, but the sense of danger was
almost appalling. To have made her experience complete, she
should have taken one engine ride in a dark and rainy night. In
a daylight ride on a locomotive, we come to realize how slender is
the rail and how fragile its fastenings, compared with the ponderous machine which they carry. We see what a trifling movement
of a switch makes the difference between life and death. We learn
how short the look ahead must often be, and how close danger
sits on either hand. But it is only in a night ride that we learn
how dependent the engineer must be, after all, upon the faithful
vigilance of others. We lean out of the cab and strain our eyes
in vain to see ahead. The head-light reveals a few yards of glis-
tening rail, and the ghostly telegraph poles and switch targets.
Were a switch open, a rail taken up, or a pile of ties on the track,
we could not possibly see the danger in time to stop. The
friendly twinkle of a signal lamp, shining faintly, red or white, tells

Danger Ahead !

the engineer that the way is blocked or is clear, and he can only rush along trusting that no one of a dozen men on whom his life depends has made a mistake.

When one reflects upon the destructive energy which is contained in a swiftly moving train, and sees its effects in a wreck; when he understands how many minute mechanical details, and how many minds and hands must work together in harmony to insure its safe arrival at its destination, he must marvel at the safety of railroad travel. In the year 1887, the passengers killed in train accidents in the United States were 207 ; those injured were 916. The employees killed were 406, and injured 890.* These were in train accidents only, it must be remembered, and do not include persons killed at crossings, or while trespassing on the track, or employees killed and injured making up trains. As will be seen later, the casualties in these two classes are much greater than those from train accidents. The total passenger movement in 1887 was equal to one passenger travelling 10,570,306,710 miles. That is to say, a passenger might have travelled 51,000,000 miles before being killed, or 12,000,000 miles before being injured. Or he might travel day and night steadily at the rate of 30 miles an hour for 194 years before being killed. Mark Twain would doubtless conclude from this that travelling by rail is much the safest profession that a man could adopt. It is unquestionably true that it is safer than travelling by coach or on horseback, and probably it is safer than any other method of getting over the earth's surface that man has yet contrived, unless it may be by ocean steamer. If one wants anything safer he must walk.

In considering the means that have been adopted to make railroad travel safe, it must be remembered that there are very few devices in use that are purely safety appliances. Nearly everything used on a railroad has an economic or mechanical value, and if it promotes safety that is but part of its duty. The great source of safety in railroad working is good discipline. Of all the train accidents which have happened in the United States in the last

---

* The statistics of train accidents used in this article are those collected and published monthly for many years by the *Railroad Gazette*. In the nature of things such statistics cannot be absolutely accurate, but no others are in existence for the whole country. These are sufficiently accurate for all practical purposes.

sixteen years, nearly ten per cent. were due to negligence in operation, and seventeen per cent. were unexplained.   Of these no
doubt many were due to negligence, and many that were attributed
to defects of track and equipment
would have been prevented, had
men done their duty.   The value
of mechanical appliances for safety is perhaps as often overrated
as underrated.   Undoubtedly the
best, and in the long run the
cheapest, practice will be that
which combines in the highest
degree both elements — disci-

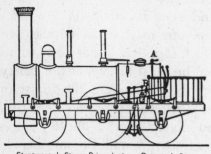

Stephenson's Steam Driver-brake.   Patented 833.

plined intelligence and perfection of mechanical details.

   First in importance among the mechanisms which demand attention here is the brake.   From the beginning of railroads the
necessity for brakes was apparent, and in 1833 Robert Stephenson
patented a steam driver-brake (the brake on the driving-wheels).
This was but four years after the Rainhill trials, which settled the
question of the use of locomotives on the Liverpool & Manchester
Railroad.   This
early brake con-
tained the princi-
ple of the driver-
brake, operated
by steam or air,
which has in late
years come into
wide use.   The
apparatus is so
simple that the
cut representing
it hardly needs
explanation. Ad-
mission of steam
into the cylinder

Driver-brake on Modern Locomotive.

raised the piston, which through a lever and rod raised the toggle-
joint between the brake-blocks and forced them against the treads

of the wheels. Essentially the same method of applying the retarding force can now be seen on most passenger engines, and
often, but not so commonly, on engines for freight service. **For**
various reasons Stephenson's
driver-brake did not come into
use.

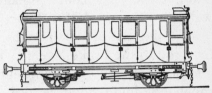

Innumerable devices for car-
brakes have been invented, but
they divide themselves into two
groups: those in which the re-

English Screw-brake, on the Birmingham and Gloucester
Road, about 1840.

tarding force is applied to the circumference of the wheel, and
those in which it is applied to the rail. The class of brakes in
which the retarding force is applied to the rail has been little used,
although various contrivances have been devised to transfer a portion of the weight of the car from the wheels to runners sliding on
the rails. There are many objections to the principle, and it will
probably never again be seriously considered by railroad men.
The apparatus is necessarily heavy, the power required to apply
it is great, and its action is slow. When brought into action it is
not as efficient as the brake applied to the tread of the wheels, and
the transfer of the load increases the chance of derailment.

Many different devices have been used to apply the brake-
shoes to the wheels, and various sources of power. Hand-power
brakes have been used, worked by
levers, or by screws, or by winding
a chain on a staff; or, in still other
forms, springs wound up by hand
are released and apply the brakes
by their pressure. The momen-

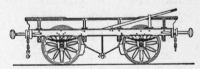

English Foot-brake on the Truck of a Great Western Coach, about 1840.

tum of the train has been employed to wind up chains by the rotation of the axles. This is the principle of the chain-brake, very
much used in England. This same source of power has been utilized by causing the drawheads, when thrust in as the cars run together, to wind up the brake-chains. Hydraulic pressure has been
used in cylinders under the cars; and finally air, either under pressure or acting against a vacuum, has been found to be the most
useful of all means of operating train-brakes. Early forms of hand-
brakes are seen in the illustrations of some old English cars. The

coach shows a hand-brake operated by a screw and system of levers. By turning a crank the guard puts in operation the system of levers which apply the brake with great force; but the operation is slow. The common hand-brake of the United States is too well known to need illustration. With this brake a chain is wound around the foot of a staff, and the pull of this chain is transmitted by a rod to the brake-levers. This apparatus is simple, and when a train is manned by a sufficient number of smart brakemen it is capable of doing good service. This simple form of hand-brake will probably be used in freight-car service until it is replaced by air-brakes, and the various forms of chain and momentum brakes do not appear likely to be much more used in the future than they have been in the past. Therefore, no further space will be given to them.

The expression, electric brake, is now often heard, and requires a word of explanation. There are various forms of so-called electric brakes which are practicable, and even efficient, working devices. In none of them, however, does electricity furnish the power by which the brakes are applied; it merely puts in operation some other power. In one type of electric brake the active braking force is taken from an axle of each car. A small friction-drum is made fast to the axle. Another friction-drum hung from the body of the car swings near the axle. If, when the car is in motion, these drums are brought in contact, that one which hangs from the car takes motion from the other, and may be made to wind a chain on its shaft. Winding in this chain pulls on the brake-levers precisely as if it had been wound on the shaft of the hand-brake. The sole function of electricity in this form of brake is to bring the friction-drums together. In a French brake which has been used experimentally for some years with much success, an electric current, controlled by the engine-driver, energizes an electro-magnet which forms part of the swinging-frame in which the loose friction-pulley is carried. This electro-magnet being vitalized, is attracted toward the axle, thus bringing the friction-drums in contact. In an American brake lately exhibited on a long freight train, a smaller electro-magnet is used, but the same end is accomplished by multiplying the power by the intervention of a lever and wheel. The other type of so-called electric brake is that in which the motive power is compressed air, and the function of the electric device is simply to manipulate the valves under each car, by which the air is let into the brake-cylinder or allowed to escape, thus putting on or releasing the brakes. All of these devices have this advantage, that, whatever the length of the train, the application of the brakes is simultaneous on all the wheels, and stops can be made from high speed with little shock. Up to two years ago it seemed as if this advantage might be a controlling one, and compel the introduction of electric brakes for freight service. Since then the new " quick-acting " form of the air-brake has been developed, by which the brakes are applied on the rear of a fifty-car train in two seconds, and there is no longer any necessity to turn to other devices. It is doubtful, therefore, if the additional complication of electricity is widely introduced into brake mechanism for many years, if ever.

It is now universally held that the brake, both for freight and for passenger service, must be continuous ; that is, it must be applied to every wheel of every car of the train from some one point, and ordinarily that point must be the engineer's cab. With the valve of an efficient continuous brake constantly under his left hand, the engine-driver can play with the heaviest and fastest train. Without that instrument his work is far more anxious, and much less certain.

The continuous brake which to day prevails all over the world, is the automatic air-brake. In the United States much the largest part of the rolling stock used in passenger service is equipped with the Westinghouse automatic brake. A few roads peculiarly situated use the Eames vacuum-brake. That brake is used on the elevated roads of New York, and on the Brooklyn bridge roads. The Westinghouse brake is also largely used in England, on the Continent of Europe, in India, Australia, and South America. In the United States it is being rapidly applied to freight cars also. This brake, therefore, being the highest development of the automatic air-brake, and the one most widely used, will be briefly described, as best representing the most approved type of the most important of all safety appliances.

The general diagram which is given on pages 196–97 shows all of the principal parts as applied to a locomotive, a tender, and a

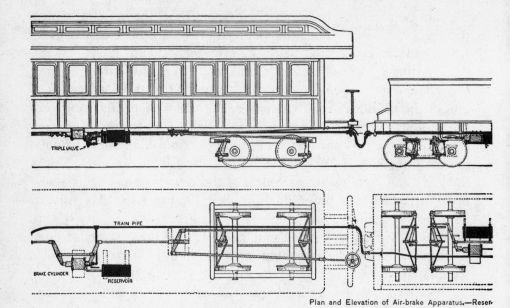

Plan and Elevation of Air-brake Apparatus.—Reser-

passenger car. The diagram is reduced from one prepared by Mr. M. N. Forney for a new edition of his " Catechism of the Locomotive." In the plan view are shown very clearly the hand-wheels, the chains, the rods, and the levers by which the brake is applied by hand. In passenger service the hand-wheels are rarely used, but they are retained for convenience in switching cars in the yard, and for those rare emergencies in which the air-brakes fail. Under the middle of the car the ordinary pull-rod of the old hand-brake is cut and two levers are inserted. One lever is connected with the brake-cylinder, and the other with the piston which slides in that cylinder. When air is admitted to the cylinder the piston is driven out, and the brakes are applied exactly as they would be were the chains wound up by turning the hand-wheels. Compressed air is supplied to the cylinder from the reservoir near it, in which pressure is maintained at from 70 to 80 pounds per square inch by a pump placed on one side of the locomotive. The pump fills the main reservoir on the engine, and also the car-reservoirs, by means of the train-pipe which extends under all the cars. When the brakes are off there is a full pressure of air in all of the car-reservoirs and train-pipes. It is a *reduction* of the pressure in the train-pipes which causes the brakes to be applied.

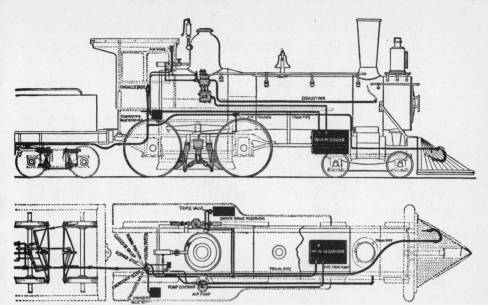

voirs and piping in solid black; brake gear shaded.

This fact must be borne in mind, for it is on this principle that the automatic action of the brakes depends. If a train parts, or if the air leaks out of the train-pipe, the brakes go on. This automatic principle is a vital one in most safety appliances, and it is secured in the case of the air-brake by one of the most ingenious little devices that man ever contrived, that is, the triple valve, which is placed in the piping system between the brake-cylinder and the car-reservoir. This triple valve has passages to the brake-cylinder, to the car-reservoir, to the train-pipe, and to the atmosphere. Which of these passages are open and which are closed depends upon the position of a piston inside of the triple valve, and the position of that piston is determined by the difference in air-pressure on either side of it. Thus, when the pressure in the train-pipe is greater than that in the car-reservoir, the triple valve piston is forced over, say to the left, a communication is opened from the train-pipe to the car-reservoir, and the air pressure in the latter is restored from the main reservoir on the locomotive. At the same time a passage is opened from the brake-cylinder to the atmosphere, the compressed air escapes, the brake-piston is driven back by a spring, and the brakes are released. If the pressure in the train-pipe is reduced, the triple-valve piston is driven to the right (we will assume) by the pressure from the car-reservoir, the passage to the atmosphere is closed, air flows freely from the car-reservoir to the brake-cylinder, and the brakes are applied.

The function of the engineer's valve is to control these operations. Naturally the runner's left hand rests on this instrument, which is fixed to the back head of the boiler. To apply the brakes he turns the handle to such a position as to allow air to escape from the train-pipe ; to release, he turns it to allow air to pass from the main or locomotive reservoir into the train-pipe, and thence into the car-reservoir. It is hardly necessary to say that the operation of the brake, which has been described for one car, is practically simultaneous throughout the train. The brakes on the driving-wheels of the engine are also automatically applied at the same time as those of the cars and the tender.

In the plan on page 197 the several different positions of the handle of the engineer's valve are indicated, and among them the service-stop and the emergency-stop positions. The quickness of the stop can be to some degree controlled by the rapidity with which the air-pressure in the train-pipe is reduced. To make a stop in the shortest possible time, the runner moves the throttle lever with his right hand and shuts off steam, and with his left hand moves the handle of the engineer's valve to the emergency position, then pulls the sand-rod handle to let sand down to the rails, and finally, if the engine is not fitted with driver-brakes, he must reverse the engine and again open the throttle. These movements must be made in order and with precision ; and to make them instantly and without mistake in the face of sudden danger requires coolness and presence of mind. It sometimes happens that an engine-runner reverses his engine before shutting off steam, in which case the cylinder-heads will very likely be blown out and the engine be instantly disabled. Then, if there are no driver-brakes, the locomotive is worse than useless, for instead of aiding in making the stop, its momentum adds to the work to be done by the train-brakes. Again, if the air-pressure in the brake-cylinders is so high, and the adjustment of the levers such that an instant application of the full pressure will stop the rotation of the wheels, and cause them to slide on the rails, the stop will take longer than if the wheels continued to revolve. The maximum braking effect is obtained when the pressure on the wheels is as great as it can be without causing them to slide, and it may happen that a quicker stop can be made by putting the engineer's valve to the service-stop position than by trying to make an emergency-stop. The runner must, therefore, be familiar with the special conditions of his brakes, and must have that kind of mind which can be depended upon to work clearly and quickly in a moment of tremendous responsibility. Fortunately, such minds are not very rare. The world is full of heroes who want only discipline, habit, and opportunity.

The pressure of air in the main reservoir and the train-pipe is maintained by the air-pump on the locomotive, the speed of which is automatically regulated by an ingenious governor. It is the throbbing of this vigilant machine which one hears during short stops at stations. The air-pressure has been reduced in applying the brakes, and the governor has set the pump at work.

All of those parts of the air-brake apparatus which are shown in the diagram (pp. 196–97) can be easily seen on a train standing at a station ; but the curious traveller must be careful not to mistake the gas-tank carried under some cars for the car-reservoir. The gas-tank is about eight feet long ; the car-reservoir is about thirty-three inches.

Although the air-brake can almost talk, it is still not perfect. There are several fortunes to be made yet in improving it. For instance, it is desirable, in descending long and steep grades, that the brake-pressure should be just sufficient to control the speed of the train, and should be steadily applied; otherwise the descent will be by a succession of jerks which may become dangerous. With the automatic the brakes must be occasionally released to re-charge the reservoirs, or when the speed of the train is too much reduced ; and it is difficult to keep a uniform speed. So far, the means devised to overcome this difficulty and keep a constant and light pressure on the wheels have been thought too costly or complicated for general use. With hand-brakes long trains are controlled by the brakes of but a few of the cars in any one train. It follows that in the descent of grades the braked wheels must often run for miles with the pressure as great as it can be without sliding the wheels. The rim of the wheel is rapidly heated by the friction of the brake-shoe, and the unequal expansion of the heated and the unheated parts of the wheel causes a fracture. This is why so many broken car-wheels are found at the foot of grades—of all places the worst for such an accident to happen. With " straight air," that is, with the pressure from the main reservoir, or the air-pump, going directly to the brake-cylinder, the engineer can apply the brakes to all the wheels of his train simultaneously, and with great delicacy of graduation; and by turning a three-way cock which is placed in the piping of each car, the air can be used "straight." This is regularly done on some mountain-roads. At summits the trains are stopped and the brakes are changed from "automatic" to "straight." This practice is dangerous, however, and is not approved by the best brake-experts, for if a hose bursts, or through some other accident the air in the train-pipe escapes, the brakes are useless. The automatic arrangement by which a reduction of air-pressure in the train-pipe applies the brakes, as previously explained, is much preferred, although no entirely satisfactory means has yet been devised for automatically regulating the air-pressure in the brake-cylinder.

There is not space here to enter into the history of the air-brake. It was first practically applied to passenger trains in 1868. The first great epoch in its subsequent development was the invention, by Mr. George Westinghouse, Jr., of the triple valve. The introduction of the triple valve at once reduced the time of full application of the brake for a ten-car train from twenty-five seconds to about eight seconds. This means, at forty miles an hour, a reduction by more than one thousand feet in the distance in which a train can be stopped. The next great epoch in the history of the air-brake was made by the celebrated Burlington brake-trials of 1886 and 1887. These trials were undertaken by a committee of the Master Car-builders' Association, to determine whether or not there was any power-brake fit for freight service. For general freight service the brake must be capable of arresting a very long train, with cars loosely coupled, running at a fair average passenger speed, without producing objectionable shocks in the rear of the train. The two series of trials were carried out in July, 1886, and May, 1887. The competing brake-companies brought to the trials trains of fifty cars each, equipped with their devices. Skilled mechanical engineers from various railroad and private companies assisted both years. These trials were most exhaustive, and have contributed more to the art of braking than any that preceded or have followed them. The first year's trials developed the fact that the air-brakes could not be applied on the rear of a fifty-car train in less than eighteen seconds, whereas the head of a train moving twenty miles an hour could be completely stopped in fifteen seconds. The result was that disastrous collisions between the cars of any one train were produced in the act of stopping. Men in the rear cars were thrown down and injured, and much damage was done to the cars. At the end of nineteen days the brake-companies went home to work another year over the new problem. In 1887 they reappeared on the same ground, and in eighteen days proved that no simple air-brakes, as then operated, could prevent disastrous shocks in a long train; but it was shown that by bringing in electricity to actuate the air-valves, the application of the brakes could be made practically simultaneous throughout the train. Mr. Westinghouse, however, during the summer following, made such modifications in the triple valve and in the train-pipe that he succeeded in applying the brakes throughout a fifty-car train in two seconds. That settled the matter. He at once equipped a train of fifty cars, and in October and November, 1887, that train made a journey of about three thousand miles, making exhibition stops at various cities. The journey was a splendid and conclusive demonstration that the air-brake is now a thoroughly efficient and reliable contrivance for freight as well as for passenger service. The result has been a very rapid application of the new quick-acting brake to freight cars. The performance of this train was to railroad men most impressive. A freight train of fifty cars is about one-third of a mile long. To see such a train, running forty miles an hour, smoothly stopped in one-third of its own length, without shock or fuss, was an object-lesson that no one could fail to understand or to remember. Some of the stops made by this train will give a fair notion of the relative power of hand- and air-brakes for quick stops. The following figures are averages of stops made in six different cities. They give the distances run in feet from the instant of applying the brakes till the train was brought to a stand-still:

                                                                    Feet.
Hand-brakes, 50 cars, 20 miles an hour...........................794
Air-brakes, 50 cars, 20 miles an hour............................166
Air-brakes, 50 cars, 40 miles an hour............................581
Air-brakes, 20 cars, 20 miles an hour............................ 99

With twenty cars at twenty miles an hour even shorter stops were made than those recorded above. In the Burlington trials the hand-brake stops, with fifty-car trains at forty miles an hour, were made in from two thousand five hundred to three thousand feet.

The air-brake is somewhat complicated, but the complicated mechanism is strong, has little movement, and is securely protected from dirt and the elements. It is therefore little liable to derangement. It is, however, becoming better understood that brake-gear must be good, and employees carefully instructed in the care and use of the air-brake to get its best results; and in recent years two or three elaborate instruction-cars have been fitted up for the education of the enginemen and trainmen.

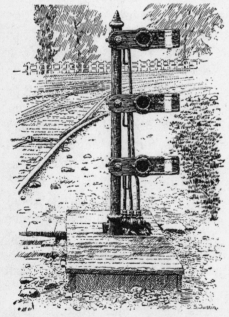

Dwarf Semaphores and Split Switch.

Space does not permit more than an allusion to driver-brakes, which are operated by steam and by air. The forms in constant use are made by the Eames, the American, the Westinghouse, and the Beals companies. Nor can much be said here of the water-brake, used to some extent on locomotives working heavy grades. It consists of a simple arrangement of admitting a little hot water, instead of steam, to the cylinders. The engine is reversed and the cylinder-cocks are opened to the air. The cylinders then act as air-pumps, and the retarding effect is due to the back pressure. The use of the water is to prevent overheating of the parts.

If it is important to have efficient means of stopping trains, it is scarcely less important to have timely information of the need of stopping them. To give such information is the function of signals, which, among safety appliances, must stand next after brakes. Signals fall naturally into two great classes: Those which protect points of danger and govern the movements of engines in yards, and those which keep an interval of space between two trains running on one track. For the protection of switches, crossings, junctions, and the like, signals in immense variety have been used, and, unfortunately, are still used ; but in the last ten or fifteen years the semaphore signal has become the general standard in the United States, as it long has been in England. This consists of a board, called the blade or arm, pivoted on the post, and back of the pivot is a heavy casting which carries a colored glass lens, either green or red. On the post is hung

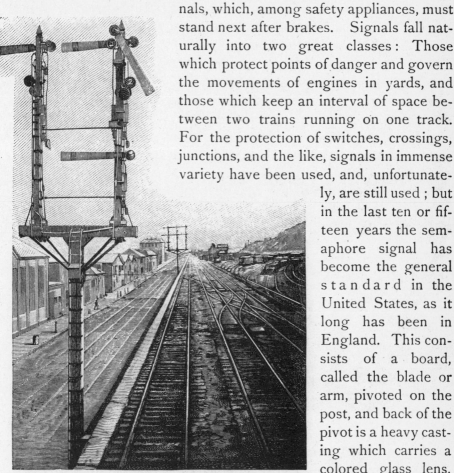

Semaphore Signal with Indicators.
(One arm governs several tracks. The number of the track which is clear is shown on the indicator disk.)

a lantern. The danger position is with the blade horizontal. In this position the lens is in front of the lamp, and the light shows red or green, as the case may be. The safety position is with the blade hanging about sixty degrees from the horizontal. In this position the light of the lantern shows white. Red is the universal danger color, and green the color of caution. Therefore, a semaphore signal at a point of danger shows by day a blade painted red, with the end of the blade cut square. At night it shows a red light. At a position some distance from the point of actual danger, but where it is desirable to warn an engine-runner that he is likely to find the danger signal against him, a caution signal is placed. This is a semaphore blade painted green, with the end notched in a V-shape, or, as it is called, a fish-tail. At night this signal shows a green light. There is nothing very remarkable about a piece of board arranged to wag up and down on a pin stuck through a post, but it is wonderful how much of good brains and good breath have been expended in getting these boards to wag harmoniously, and in getting railroad officers to understand that a plain board, having two possible positions, is a better signal than any more complicated form.

The arrangement of a group of signals and switches in such a way that their movements are made mutually dependent one upon the other, and so that it is impossible to make these movements in any but prearranged sequences, is called, in railroad vernacular, "interlocking," and in this sense the word will be used here. Interlocking has become a special art. The objects which it is sought to accomplish by interlocking, and the admirable way in which those objects are attained, may best be understood from an actual example. For that purpose we shall take a double-track junction completely equipped with signals, facing-point locks, and derailing switches (p. 205).

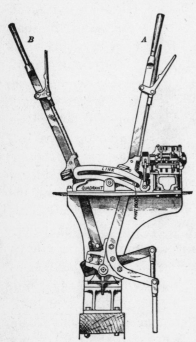

Section of Saxby & Farmer Interlocking Machine.
(Showing two levers and locking mechanism. A is normal, B is reversed.)

A general view of an interlocking frame was given on page 171 of this volume. Two levers from such a frame are here shown. The normal position of the levers is forward, as lever A. When pulled back, as lever B, the lever is said to be reversed.

Let it be supposed that a main-line train is to be passed east-

ward in the direction of the arrow *B*. The first movement of the
signalman in the signal-tower would naturally be to lower signals

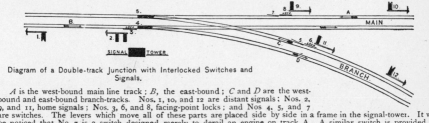

Diagram of a Double-track Junction with Interlocked Switches and
Signals.

A is the west-bound main line track ; *B*, the east-bound ; *C* and *D* are the west-
bound and east-bound branch-tracks. Nos. 1, 10, and 12 are distant signals ; Nos. 2,
9, and 11, home signals ; Nos. 3, 6, and 8, facing-point locks ; and Nos 4, 5, and 7
are switches. The levers which move all of these parts are placed side by side in a frame in the signal-tower. It will
be noticed that No. 7 is a switch designed merely to derail an engine on track A. A similar switch is provided on
track C, and is worked by the same lever which works junction switch No. 5. In the sketch all levers are supposed to
stand in their "normal" position, all signals are at danger, and the switches are set for the main line. The switches
themselves are not locked in this position of the facing-point lock levers.

1 and 2. He attempts to pull over lever 1, but cannot move it,
and, in spite of any effort or ingenuity on his part, that signal remains at danger. The reason is that lever 2 when normal locks
lever 1 normal. The logic of this will be at once apparent.
Clearing signal 1 is an indication to the engineer that the way is
clear, and that he may pass the junction at speed. So long as this
signal (which, it must be remembered, is a *caution* signal) stands
at danger he knows that he may pass it, but must be ready to stop
before he reaches No. 2, the home-signal. Therefore No. 1 must
never be lowered till all is arranged for passing the junction at
speed. As the signalman cannot lower signal 1, he attempts to
lower signal 2. Again he finds that he cannot budge the lever.
It is locked by lever No. 3. This lever works a facing-point lock,
which must be described just at this point (p. 206).

The front rod of the switch, that is, the rod which connects the
points of the two moving rails of the switch, is pierced with two
holes placed a distance apart just equal to the throw of the switch.
In front of these holes is a bolt which is worked by a lever in the
signal-tower. After the switch is set the lock-lever is reversed
and the bolt enters one of the holes, thus securely locking the
switch in position. There is one other interesting feature of this
facing-point lock. It has happened very often that a switch has
been thrown under a moving train, splitting the train and derailing
more or less of it. This class of accidents is especially likely to
happen when train movements are very frequent, and may be prevented by the use of the "detector-bar." This is a bar about forty

Split Switches with Facing-point Locks and Detector-bars.

(The rod on the right of the track is the mechanical connection to the lever in the signal-tower by which the locks and detector-bars are moved.)

feet long, placed alongside the rail, and carried on swinging links, like those of a parallel ruler, in such a way that any effort to move the bar lengthwise of the rail must raise it above the top of the rail. This bar is moved by the same lever which moves the locking-bolt. So long as there is a wheel on the rail above the detector-bar it cannot be moved, therefore the locking-bolt cannot be withdrawn, and the switch cannot be moved until the train has passed completely off it.

We left the signalman trying to lower signal No. 2 ; vainly, be-cause No. 3 lever was still normal and the switch unlocked (Dia-gram, p. 205).   Probably he would not have begun his operations

in the bungling way that has
been supposed, but would have
first reversed lever 3.   That
locks the switch by the fac-ing-point lock, and locks also
switch-lever 4 in the frame in
the signal-tower and releases
lever 2.   Then he reverses
lever 2.   That locks lever 3
and releases lever 1.   Then he
reverses lever 1, which locks
lever 2.   Now the way is made
for a train to pass east on the
main line, and the signals are
clear.   The last signal could
not have been lowered until

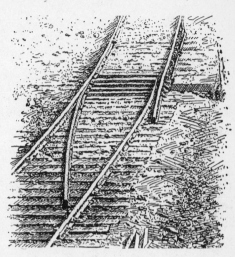

Derailing Switch.

the chain of operations was complete; none of the levers can now
be moved until lever 1 is again put normal and signal 1 made
to show danger.   There is one point of great danger in this partic-ular train-movement which has not been mentioned ; that is, the
crossing of main-line east-bound track *B* by the branch-line west-bound track *C*.   It will be noticed that with the levers normal, de-railing switch 5 is open, and it is impossible for a locomotive to
pass beyond it.   Lever 5 is interlocked in the tower with lever 4
in such a way that, before 5 can be reversed to let a train pass
west from *C*, lever 4 must be reversed to trap any train on *B* and
turn it down the branch *D*.   It must not be understood that the
use of "derailers" is universal.   In fact, they are not recommended
by the best signal engineers, except in special conditions.   In the
absence of derailer No. 5, signals 11 and 12 would be interlocked
with switch 4, so that, so long as that switch stands open for the
main line a clear signal cannot be given to a train coming west on
C.   It will be noticed that signal 2 carries two semaphores on one
post.   The upper one is for the main line and the lower one for
the branch.   Both are operated by one lever, 2, and whether re-

versing lever 2 lowers the main-line signal or the branch signal depends on the position of the switch. The switch is made to pick out its signal by an ingenious but very simple little arrangement, called a selector, which is placed somewhere in the line of ground connections.

It would be an interesting study, were there space, to follow the possible and proper combinations of movements to pass trains over the various tracks. It will be seen that, by concentrating the levers which move switches and signals in one place and interlocking them, it is made mechanically impossible for a signalman to give a signal which would lead to a collision or a derailment within the region under his control. The only danger at such points is that an engineer may overrun the signals. This description of the objects and the capacity of the system of interlocking is no fancy sketch. The system has been in use for many years, doing just what has been here described, and more. A recent close estimate gave the number of interlocked levers now in use in the United States as about eight thousand, and the number is rapidly increasing. Recent official reports showed that in Great Britain and Ireland there were thirty-eight thousand cases in which a passenger line was connected with or crossed by another line, siding, or cross-over. In eighty-nine per cent. of these cases the levers operating the switches and protecting signals were interlocked.

The example of interlocking which has been given is one of the simplest; the principle is capable of almost indefinite expansion, and any one lever may be made to lock any one or more levers among hundreds in the same frame. The greatest number of levers assembled in any one signal-tower in this country is one hundred and sixteen, at the Grand Central Station in New York. In the London Bridge tower there are two hundred and eighty levers. This is probably the greatest number in any one tower in the world. All of these levers may be more or less interlocked. The same principle is applied to the locking of two levers at a single switch, and to the protection of drawbridges and highway crossings.

The mechanism by which the interlocking is done is strong and comparatively simple, but a detailed description of it seems out of place here. Two levers from a Saxby & Farmer machine are shown on page 204, with lever *A* normal and *B* reversed. The locking mechanism is in front of the levers, and is actuated not by the levers themselves, but by their catch-rods. It follows that it is not the actual movement of a signal which prevents the movement of other signals, or of switches, but it is the intention to move that signal. This principle of "preliminary locking" is one of great importance.

Switches and signals are often worked at such distances from the tower that it is impossible for the operator to know whether or not the movement contemplated has taken place. The British Board of Trade does not permit switches to be worked more than 750 feet away. In this country there is no limit, but probably 800 feet is very rarely exceeded. Signals are worked in England up to 3,000 or 3,500 feet very commonly, and they are even worked a mile away, but not satisfactorily. This is with direct mechanical connection, by rod or wire, from the levers. It is obvious that a break in the connections between the lever and the switch or signal might take place, and the lever be pulled over, without having produced the corresponding movement at the far end. The locking mechanism in the tower would not be affected by such an accident, and consequently conflicting signals might be given. Even this contingency is provided against with almost perfect safety. If a signal connection breaks, the signal is counterweighted to go to danger. The worst that can happen is to delay traffic. If a switch connection breaks, the locking-bolt, in the latest form of facing-point lock, will not enter the hole in the switch-rod, and consequently warning is given in the tower that the switch has not moved. Electric annunciators are often placed in the signal-tower, to show on a board before the operator whether or not the movements of switches and signals have taken place.

Considerable work must be done in the movement of each lever. The ground connections must be put down with great care, as nearly straight and level as may be, well drained, and protected from ice and snow. All of these difficulties have been overcome in a beautiful pneumatic interlocking apparatus which has been introduced within the last two or three years. In this system the motive power is compressed air. Near each switch is a small cylinder, containing a piston which is attached directly to the switch movement. Compressed air admitted to or : side or the other of this piston moves the switch one way or the other. But, as it would take some time for the necessary quantity of air to flow from the signal-tower to a distant switch, a small reservoir is placed near the switch, and the air from this reservoir is admitted to one end or the other of the switch cylinder according to the position of a valve. For transmitting the motion from the tower to the valve compressed air might be used, but, as air is elastic, a quicker movement is got by using in the pipes some liquid which does not readily freeze, and which, being practically non-compressible, transmits an impulse given at one end almost instantly to the other. The signals are worked in essentially the same manner as the switches, except that the pneumatic valves are moved by electricity. The tower apparatus of a pneumatic system in the yard of the Pennsylvania Railroad at Pittsburg is shown in the engraving opposite. In the front of the apparatus is seen a rank of small handles, which can be turned from side to side with as much ease as the keys of a piano can be depressed. Turning one of these handles admits compressed air to the end of a pipe containing liquid. Instantly the pressure is transmitted 500 or 1,000 feet to the valve at the switch to be moved. The small levers are interlocked perfectly, and in that particular perform the duties of the ordinary machine. A model of the tracks controlled is placed before the operator, showing the switches and signals, and when a movement is made on the ground it is at once repeated back by electricity and duplicated on the model. This beautiful system is due to the same genius that gave us the perfected air-brake and the triple valve, and is the greatest improvement that has been made in interlocking in the last dozen years.

If the reader has grasped the full significance of interlocking, he understands that it makes it impossible to give a signal that would lead to a collision or to a derailment at a misplaced switch. The worst that a stupid, or drunken, or malicious signalman could do would be to delay traffic, if the signals were obeyed. Here comes in the failing case. The brake-power may be insufficient to stop a train after a danger signal is given. That is a rare oc-

Interlocking Apparatus for Operating Switches and Signals by Compressed Air, Pittsburg Yards, Pennsylvania Railroad.
(A model of the track is shown above the levers, on which the movements of the switches and signals are electrically indicated after they are completed.)

currence, but may happen. The engineer may not see the danger signal because of fog, or he may carelessly run past it. Provision against a failure to see and to obey a signal may be made by placing on the track a torpedo, which will explode with a loud report when struck by a wheel. The use of hand-torpedoes in fogs, and for emergencies in places unprovided with fixed signals, is very common. These are little disks filled with a detonating powder, and provided with tin straps that are bent down to clasp over the top of the rail. A simple and very efficient torpedo machine, which has been used for some years on the Manhattan Elevated and elsewhere, is here shown. This machine has a magazine holding five torpedoes.

Torpedo Placer.

(The torpedo is carried forward by the plunger and exploded by the depression of the hammer shown near the rail.)

It is connected to a signal-lever in such a way that, when the signal is put to danger, one torpedo is placed in a position to be exploded by the first passing wheel. When the signal returns to the clear position the torpedo, if unexploded, is withdrawn to the magazine. If the torpedo is exploded another one takes its place at the next movement of the signal-lever. One of these machines on the Elevated Road moves about five thousand times every day. In such a case a torpedo would soon be worn out if it was not exploded or frequently changed. When this apparatus is in operation, an unmistakable alarm is at once given to the engineer and to others if a danger signal is passed. On the Manhattan Elevated lines an engineman who overruns a danger signal and can show no good reason for it is suspended for the first offence, and discharged for the second. The torpedo makes it impossible for him to escape detection.

The second great class of signals comprises those which are intended to keep fixed intervals of space between trains running on the same track. These are block signals. The block system is used on a few of the railroads of the United States which have the heaviest a n d fastest traffic.   Much the most common practice in this country, however, is to run trains by time intervals, and under the constant control of the train despatcher.   In England the block system is almost universal. About ninety per cent. of all the passenger lines of that country are worked under the absolute block system.

When the block system is not used, it is quite common to protect particularly dangerous points, such as curves and deep cuts, by stationing watchmen there with flags or with some form of fixed sig-

Old Signal Tower on the Philadelphia & Reading, at Phœnixville.

nal.   The watchman can notify an approaching engine-runner that a preceding train has or has not passed beyond his own range of vision ; or can notify him that it has been gone a certain time. Travellers by the Philadelphia & Reading must have noticed the queer structures, with revolving vanes on top, looking like a feeble sort of windmill, which appear in positions to command a view of cuts, curves, etc.   These are examples of the devices for local protection.   The non-automatic block signal develops naturally from the protection of scattered points.   Instead of placing watchmen at points of especial danger, they are placed at regular intervals of one mile, two miles, or five miles.   Instead of the

watchman looking to see that a train has disappeared from his
field of vision before he lets another train pass, he uses the eyes
of the next watchman ahead, who telegraphs back that the train
has passed his station.   Suppose A, B, and C to be three block-

A   B   C
_____

signal stations placed at intervals of two miles.   When a train
passes A, the operator at that point at once puts a signal to danger
behind it.   This signal stands at danger until the train passes B,
and the operator puts his signal to danger, and telegraphs back to
A to announce that train No. 1 has passed out of the block A B,
and is protected by the signal at B.   Then, and not until then, the
operator clears the signal at A and allows train No. 2 to enter the
block.   Meanwhile train No. 1 is proceeding through the block
B C, its rear protected at B; and the same sequence of events
happens when it arrives at C as happened at B.   This is the simplest form of block signalling.   In the more elaborate form there
are at each block-station three signals—the distant, the home, and
the starting.   The signals are often electrically interlocked, from
one station to another, in such a way that it is mechanically impossible for the operator at A to give a signal for a train to pass that
station until the signal at B has been put to danger behind the
preceding train.

It is seen that no two trains can be in the same block and on
the same track at the same time.   If all run at a uniform speed,
they will be kept just the length of a block apart.   If No. 2 is
faster than No. 1, it will arrive at B before No. 1 gets to C, but
will have to wait there.   The block system, therefore, while it
gives security, does not always facilitate traffic.   The longer the
blocks the greater will be the delay to trains; but the shorter the
blocks, the greater the cost of establishment, maintenance, and
operation.

Various systems have been contrived to have block signals displayed automatically by the passage of trains.   This, if it can be
done reliably, will do away with the wages of part of the operators,
and will also eliminate the dangers arising from human carelessness.   But there are very great objections to relying solely upon

the automatic action of signals, and automatic block signals are little used except as auxiliary to a system employing operators also. So used, they are of decided advantage, as they make sure that a danger signal is set behind every train in spite of the operator and that it cannot be again set to the all-clear position till the train has passed out of the block. All this is accomplished by electricity.

Brakes, interlocking, and the apparatus of signalling have been considered at length because they are very much the most important of all the appliances which go to increase the safety of operating railroads. They act chiefly to prevent collisions, but often prevent or mitigate accidents from derailments and other causes. Of all train-accidents happening in the last sixteen years, over one-third have been from collisions, and more than one-half from derailments.

After brakes and signals, the devices next in importance as means of saving life are those for the protection of highway crossings at the grade of railroads. In years to come, as wealth increases and as traffic becomes more crowded, we may suppose there will be few such crossings; but their abolition must be slow, and meantime the loss of life at them is great. The most accurate and complete statistics bearing on this matter are those collected by the Railroad Commissioners of Massachusetts. In 1888, of all those killed in the operation of the railroads of the State, seven per cent. were passengers, thirty-three per cent. were employees, and sixty per cent. were others. The others include trespassers, forty-seven per cent.; and killed at grade crossings, eleven per cent. More trespassers were killed than any other class; but the deaths at highway crossings considerably exceeded those among passengers. The difficulty of preventing this class of accidents is strikingly shown by the fact that, of all crossing accidents, forty-two per cent. were due to the victims' disregard of warnings given by closed gates or flags. It is evident that the efforts of the railroad companies to save people's lives at crossings are largely nullified by the carelessness of the public, and the lack of proper laws to punish those who venture upon railroad tracks when they should keep off them. Still, it remains the duty and the policy of the railroads to protect street crossings by all practicable means. The best protection is afforded by gates with watchmen, and of all forms of gate the most common, because it is the simplest and most convenient to operate, is the familiar arm-gate. This is usually worked

Crossing Gates worked by Mechanical Connection from the Cabin.

by a man turning a crank, but it is also worked by compressed air. On this page is shown a group of gates worked from an elevated cabin by a mechanical connection. A bell fixed at a crossing, to be rung by an approaching train, is a very useful auxiliary to gates and to watchmen with flags, and is considerably used where the traffic does not warrant the expense of maintaining a watchman. There are several good devices of this sort, either electric or magneto-electric. One of the latter class has a lever alongside the rail, which is depressed by each wheel that passes over it. This lever is geared to a fly-wheel, which is set rapidly revolving and causes an armature to revolve in the field of a magnet, and thus generates a current and rings a gong, precisely as is done with the familiar magnetic bell used with the telephone.

About thirteen per cent. of the train-accidents in the United States, in the last sixteen years, were derailments due to defects of road. These include not only defective rails, switches, and frogs, but bridge wrecks. There are, however, few devices used in the track, other than those already mentioned, that can be called safety appliances. This class of accidents is to be provided against only by good material, good workmanship, and unceasing care. Many so-called safety switches and safety frogs are offered to railroad officers, but those actually in wide use are confined to a very few standard forms. The split-switch, which is shown in the engravings on pages 206 and 207, has gradually replaced the old

Some Results of a Butting Collision—Baggage and Passenger Cars Telescoped.

stub-switch, as well as most of the " safety " switches that have been from time to time introduced ; although the stub-switch is still in considerable use in yards where movements are slow, and in the main tracks of the less progressive roads. It consists of a pair of moving rails the ends of which are brought opposite to the

Wreck at a Bridge.

ends of the main-line rails, or to those of the turnout, as the case may be. It follows that but one of these tracks is continuous at any one time, and a train reaching the switch by the other track must be derailed. The distressing accident which happened at Rio, Wis., in 1886, where seventeen people lost their lives, was a derailment of this sort. Since that time the railroad on which the accident happened has taken out all stub-switches on thousands of miles of main-line track. The split-switch provides against such derailments, for if the switch is set for the turnout, and a train approaches it from the main line in the "trailing" direction, the flanges of the wheels move the switch-rails to make the track continuous. The terms "facing" and "trailing," as applied to switches, are almost self-explanatory. If a train approaches toward the points of the moving rails, the switch is said to be facing. If it runs through the switch from the rear of the moving rails, the switch is said to be trailing. This will be made clear by reference to the illustration on page 206. If a train were coming from the bridge, the first switch reached by it would be a trailing and the second a facing switch. In the newspaper reports an accident will very often be assigned to one of two causes, failure

New South Norwalk Drawbridge.   Rails held by safety bolts.

of the air-brakes or spreading of the rails.   The chances are that
it will be found on investigation to be due to neither of these
causes.   Those interested to maintain the credit of the air-brake
or of the track department are not often on the ground when the
reporter gets his information, and the temptation is always great
to shift the responsibility to the shoulders of the absent.   Probably
the displacement of the rail will have taken place after the derailment; but rails do sometimes spread.   Loose spikes and rotten
ties allow the outer edge of the rail-flange to sink into the wood,
and the rail to roll outward enough to let the wheels drop.   Sound
ties are the first safeguard against such accidents.   Metal plates
under the rails are useful also; but one of the most efficient means
of preventing displacement of the rails is the interlocking bolt
shown above.   These bolts cross in the timber, and slots cut in

the two bolts engage with each other in such a way that when the nuts are screwed down on the rail-flange it is impossible to pull the bolts out. They can only be moved by tearing through the wood contained in the angle between them. This bolt is much used on bridges and trestles, where it is of vital importance that the rails should be held in place and no part of the floor broken.

In 1853 an express train went through an open draw at South Norwalk, Conn., and forty-six lives were lost. This, one of the most serious railroad accidents that ever happened, is still remembered as an historical calamity. The bridge which stands on the same site is shown opposite. In May, 1888, a west-bound express train, consisting of an engine and seven cars, was derailed just as it was entering the draw-span. The train ran three hundred feet on the sleepers before it was stopped. Then it was found that all of the driving-wheels of the engine had regained the rails, but all the other wheels were off, except those of two sleeping-cars in the rear. This was a remarkable escape from a bad accident, and much of the credit of it has been given to the interlocking bolts with which the rails were fastened. They are supposed to have prevented the rails being crowded aside, and thus to have made possible the rerailing of the engine. Besides, they helped the oak guard-timbers to hold the ties in place. The destruction of a bridge in an accident frequently begins by the ties bunching in front of the wheels and allowing the wheels to drop through and strike the floor-beams below. For this reason guard-timbers, notched down over the ties, should always be used.

The traveller will have noticed, on all bridges of various roads, two rails placed inside the track-rails, and curved to meet in a point at either end of the bridge. These are known as inside guard-rails, and their function is to keep derailed trucks in line till the train can be stopped. Besides the bunching of the ties, there is danger in a bridge derailment that a truck may swing around and strike one of the trusses. Then the bridge is very likely to be wrecked. A further provision for the protection of bridges is the rerailing frog invented by the late Charles Latimer, whose name is dear to railroad men all over America. This consists of a pair of castings combined with inside guard-rails, designed to raise the derailed wheels and guide them on to the rails. There is no

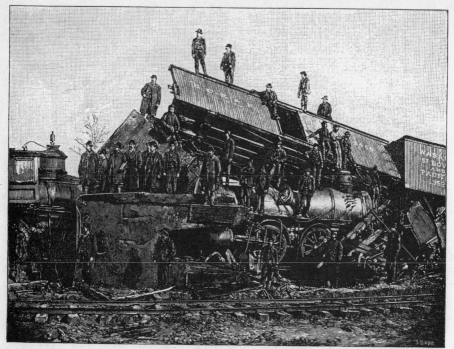

Engines Wrecked during the Great Wabash Strike.

doubt that it has prevented several wrecks, although it has never
been widely used.   The subject of bridges should not be left without a word of explanation of the stout timber-posts often seen at
either end placed in line with the trusses.   These are designed to
stop any derailed vehicle which might otherwise strike against and
destroy a truss.

There is one track-fixture that has no duty or value except as
it promotes safety.   It helps only one humble class of railroad employees.   That device is the foot-guard.   At all places where two
rails cross or approach each other, as at frogs and guard-rails,
dangerous boot-jacks are formed by the rail-heads.   The overhang
of the heads of the rail makes it easy for one to so fasten his foot
in one of those boot-jacks that it is hard to get it out.   If a man
finds himself in this position in front of an approaching train, he
sometimes has the alternative of standing up to be struck by the
engine or lying down and having his foot cut off.   Fortunately
this class of accidents is comparatively rare ; probably not more

than two or three per cent. of all deaths and injuries to passengers and employees is caused in this way. Nevertheless, the means of guarding against accidents of this class is so cheap that it should be more generally adopted than it is. It consists simply in partly filling the space between the rail-heads by putting in wooden blocks or strips of metal, or even packing with cinders, gravel, or any sort of ballast. Various wooden and metal foot-guards have been patented. They are all too simple to require description.

Of all accidents to employees the most numerous are those which arise in coupling and uncoupling cars. In Massachusetts, in 1888, the employees killed and injured were 391 ; of these casualties 154 occurred in coupling accidents. The commissioners of other States, especially of Iowa, have for years published statistics showing nearly the same ratio. Fortunately accidents of this class, although numerous, are not proportionately fatal. Far the greater part of them result in the loss of part of a hand ; but they are so frequent as to have caused much discussion, legislation, and invention. Several States have, one time and another, passed laws requiring the use of automatic couplers ; and two or three years ago there were on record in the United States over four thousand coupler patents. The laws have been futile because impracticable ; and most of the patents have been worthless for the same reason. It was obvious that the business of supplying couplers for the one million freight cars of the country could not be put into the hands of some one patentee unless his device was manifestly and preeminently superior to all others. It became important, therefore, to select as a standard some type of coupler general enough to include the patents of various men, and at the same time so definite that all couplers made to conform to the standard could work together interchangeably. Those who read Mr. Voorhees' story *
of the wanderings of a freight car will understand that any one freight car in the United States or Canada should be prepared to run in the same train with any other car. A few years ago a committee of the Master Car-builders' Association was appointed to choose and recommend a type of coupler to be adopted as the standard of the association. After prolonged and careful study of

* See " The Freight-car Service," page 267.

the subject, the committee recommended the type of which the
Janney is the best known example, and that has now become the

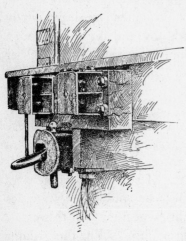
Link-and-pin Coupler.

standard of the association. This
action does not give a monopoly to
the Janney company, as there are already half a dozen couplers which
conform to the type. This coupler
is shown by diagrams in the article
by M. N. Forney, page 142. A perspective view is herewith given. This
device couples automatically, and thus
does away with the necessity for the
brakeman going between the cars.
It can also be unlocked by the rod
shown extending to the side of the
car, and the locking device can be set
not to couple, to facilitate switching
and yard work. The mechanical principles of this coupler are a
great and important improvement upon any form of link-and-pin
coupler ; and the coupler question has now come to this point:
A type of coupler has been selected by a technical body representing most of the railroads of the United States. It is general

enough to avoid the
evils of a patent mo-
nopoly. It promises
to be economical in
operation, and will
certainly do away
with the terrible loss
of life and limb which
results from the use
of the non-automatic
coupler. The rail-
roads are adopting it
with reasonable
speed, perhaps, but

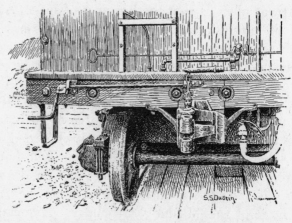
Janney Automatic Coupler applied to a Freight Car.

not as rapidly as simple considerations of humanity would dictate.

Closely related to the coupler is the vestibule, which within the last two years has become so fashionable. The vestibule is not merely a luxury, but has a certain value as a safety device.* The

Signals at Night.

full measure of this value has not yet been proved. Occasionally lives are lost by passengers falling from or being blown from the platforms of moving trains. Such accidents the vestibule will prevent, and, further, it decreases the oscillation of the cars, and thus to some degree helps to prevent derailment. It is also some protection against telescoping. A few months ago a coal train on a double-track road was derailed, and four cars were thrown across in front of a solid vestibule train of seven Pullman cars approaching on the other track. The engine of the vestibuled train was completely wrecked. Even the sheet-iron jacket was stripped off it. The engineer and fireman were instantly killed, but not another person on the train was injured. They escaped partly because the cars were strong, and partly, doubtless, because the vestibules helped to keep the platforms on the same level and in line, and thus to prevent crushing of the ends of the cars.

The number of passengers burned in wrecks is greatly exaggerated in the public mind; but that fate is so horrible that it is

* See " Railway Passenger Travel," page 249.

not wonderful that "the deadly car-stove" should be the object of persistent and energetic attacks by the press and in State legislatures. The result has been the development, in the last three years, of the entirely new business of inventing and trying to sell systems of heating by steam or hot water from the locomotive, and even by electricity. In fact, the manufacture of such apparatus has already become an industry of some importance, several thousand cars being equipped with it. This whole matter of steam-heating is still in a somewhat crude state, and it does not seem desirable to force it by legislation. It has been demonstrated that it is the cheapest way of heating trains, and the most easily regulated; and it has become a good advertisement to attract passengers. Consequently the whole subject may be safely left in the hands of the railroad companies, and allowed to develop itself naturally in a business way. There is not yet any system of continuous heating so perfected that a railroad company could without hardship be compelled to adopt it for all its passenger equipment.

Fires in wrecked trains have originated probably quite as often from kerosene lamps as from the stoves. The danger of fire from this source, and the desire to give passengers the luxury of sufficient light, have led to methods of lighting by gas and, more recently by electricity. Lighting by compressed gas ceased years ago to be an experiment. In Germany it is almost universal, but in this country it has been brought into use very slowly. The system is almost absolutely safe, not unreasonably expensive, and may be made to give satisfactory and even brilliant illumination ; but the ideal light for railroad trains will probably be found in electricity. It is even safer than gas, and is the most adaptable of any known method of lighting. Some sleeping-cars that have been recently put in service on the Chicago, Milwaukee & St. Paul Railway are provided with small electric lamps in the sides of the car, between each two adjoining seats, so that the occupants can read comfortably either when sitting in their seats or lying in their berths.

It is not to be supposed that so large a subject as that of safety appliances can be exhaustively treated within the limits of one article. It has been thought best, therefore, to give most of the space available to the two or three devices of greatest and most useful application. There remain various others that are in daily use, and that have important offices, which have not even been mentioned. If the reader has gleaned from these very incomplete notes some clearer notions than he had before of the means by which the power of the locomotive is guided into safe and useful paths, the writer's object has been accomplished.

RAILWAY PASSENGER TRAVEL.

By HORACE PORTER.

The Earliest Railway Passenger Advertisement—The First Time-table Published in America—The Mohawk and Hudson Train—Survival of Stage-coach Terms in English Railway Nomenclature—Simon Cameron's Rash Prediction—Discomforts of Early Cars—Introduction of Air-brakes, Patent Buffers and Couplers, the Bell-cord, and Interlocking Switches—The First Sleeping-cars—Mr. Pullman's Experiments—The "Pioneer"—Introduction of Parlor and Drawing-room Cars—The Demand for Dining-cars—Ingenious Devices for Heating Cars—Origin of Vestibule-cars—An Important Safety Appliance—The Luxuries of a Limited Express—Fast Time in America and England—Sleeping-cars for Immigrants—The Village of Pullman—The Largest Car-works in the World—Baggage-checks and Coupon Tickets—Conveniences in a Modern Depot—Statistics in Regard to Accidents—Proportion of Passengers in Various Classes—Comparison of Rates in the Leading Countries of the World.

FROM the time when Puck was supposed to utter his boast to put a girdle round, about the earth in forty minutes to the time when Jules Verne's itinerant hero accomplished the task in twice that number of days, the restless ingenuity and energy of man have been unceasingly taxed to increase the speed, comfort, and safety of passenger travel. The first railway on which passengers were carried was the "Stockton & Darlington," of England, the distance being 12 miles. It was opened September 27, 1825, with a freight train, or, as it is called in England, a "goods" train, but which also carried a number of excursionists. An engine which was the result of many years of labor and experiment on the part of George Stephenson was used on this train. Stephenson mounted it and acted as driver; his bump of caution was evidently largely developed, for, to guard against accidents from the recklessness of the speed, he arranged to have a signalman on horseback ride in advance of the engine to warn the luckless trespasser

Stockton & Darlington Engine and Car.

of the fate which awaited him if he should get in the way of a
train moving with such a startling velocity. The next month,
October, it was decided that it would be worth while to attempt
the carrying of passengers, and a daily "coach," modelled after
the stage-coach and called the "Experiment," was put on, Monday, October 10, 1825, which carried six passengers inside and
from fifteen to twenty outside. The engine with its light load
made the trip in about two hours. The fare from Stockton to
Darlington was one shilling, and each passenger was allowed fourteen pounds of baggage. The limited amount of baggage will appear to the ladies of the present day as niggardly in the extreme,
but they must recollect that the
bandbox was then the popular
form of portmanteau for women,
the Saratoga trunk had not been
invented, and the muscular bag-
gage-smasher of modern times
had not yet set out upon his
career of destruction. The advertisement which was published

Stockton & Darlington
Railway.
The Company's
◆ COACH ◆
CALLED THE
EXPERIMENT.

in the newspapers of the day is here given, and is of peculiar interest
as announcing the first successful attempt to carry passengers by rail.

The Liverpool & Manchester road was opened in 1829. The first train was hauled by an improved engine called the "Rocket," which attained a speed of 25 miles an hour, and some records put it as high as 35 miles. This speed naturally attracted marked attention in the mechanical world, and first demonstrated the superior advantages of railways for passenger travel. Only four years before, so eminent a writer upon railways as Wood had said : " Nothing can do more harm to the adoption of railways than the promulgation of such nonsense as that we shall see locomotives travelling at the rate of 12 miles an hour."

America was quick to adopt the railway system which had had its origin in England. In 1827 a crude railway was opened between Quincy and Boston, but it was only for the purpose of transporting granite for the Bunker Hill Monument. It was not until August, 1829, that a locomotive engine was used upon an American railroad suitable for carrying passengers. This road was constructed by the Delaware & Hudson Canal Company, and the experiment was made near Honesdale, Pa. The engine was imported from England and was called the " Stourbridge Lion."

In May, 1830, the first division of the Baltimore & Ohio road was opened. It extended from Baltimore to Ellicott's Mills, a distance of 15 miles. There being a scarcity of cars, the regular passenger business did not begin till the 5th of July following, and then only horse-power was employed, which continued to be used till the road was finished to Frederick, in 1832. The term Relay House, the name of a well-known station, originated in the fact that the horses were changed at that place.

The following notice, which appeared in the Baltimore newspapers, was the first time-table for passenger railway trains published in this country :

RAILROAD NOTICE.

A sufficient number of cars being now provided for the accommodation of passengers, notice is hereby given that the following arrangements for the arrival and departure of carriages have been adopted, and will take effect on and after Monday morning next the 5th instant, viz. :

A brigade of cars will leave the depot on Pratt St. at 6 and 10 o'clock A. M., and at 3 to 4 o'clock P. M., and will leave the depot at Ellicott's Mills at 6 and 8½ o'clock A. M., and at 12½ and 6 P. M.

Way passengers will provide themselves with tickets at the office of the Company in

Baltimore, or at the depots at Pratt St. and Ellicott's Mills, or at the Relay House, near Elk Ridge Landing.

The evening way car for Ellicott's Mills will continue to leave the depot, Pratt St., at 6 o'clock P. M. as usual.

N. B.   Positive orders have been issued to the drivers to receive no passengers into any of the cars without tickets.

P. S   Parties desiring to engage a car for the day can be accommodated after July 5th.

It will be seen that the word train was not used, but instead the schedule spoke of a "brigade of cars."

The South Carolina Railroad was begun about the same time as the Baltimore & Ohio, and ran from Charleston to Hamburg, opposite Augusta. When the first division had been constructed, it was opened November 2, 1830.

Peter Cooper, of New York, had before this constructed a locomotive and made a trial trip with it on the Baltimore & Ohio Railroad, on the 28th of August, 1830, but, not meeting the requirements of the company, it was not put into service.

A passenger train of the Mohawk & Hudson Railroad which was put on in October, 1831, between Albany and Schenectady, attracted much attention. It was hauled by an English engine named the "John Bull," and driven by

Mohawk & Hudson Train.

an English engineer named John Hampson. This is generally regarded as the first fully equipped passenger train hauled by a steam-power engine which ran in regular service in America. During 1832 it carried an average of 387 passengers daily. The accompanying engraving is from a sketch made at the time.

It was said by an advocate of mechanical evolution that the modern steam fire-engine was evolved from the ancient leathern fire-bucket; it might be said with greater truth that the modern railway car has been evolved from the old-fashioned English stagecoach.

England still retains the railway carriage divided into compartments, that bear a close resemblance inside and outside to stagecoach bodies with the middle seat omitted. In fact, the nomenclature of the stage-coach is in large measure still preserved in England.   The engineer is called the driver, the conductor the guard, the ticket-office is the booking-office, the cars are the car-

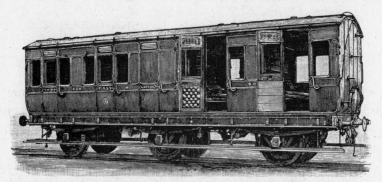

English Railway Carriage, Midland Road.   First and Third Class and Luggage Compartments.

riages, and a rustic traveller may still be heard occasionally to object to sitting with his back to the horses.   The earlier locomotives, like horses, were given proper names, such as Lion, North Star, Fiery, and Rocket; the compartments in the round-houses for sheltering locomotives are termed the stalls, and the keeper of the round-house is called the hostler.   The last two are the only items of equine classification which the American railway system has permanently adopted.

America, at an early day, departed not only from the nomenclature of the turnpike, but from the stage-coach architecture, and adopted a long car in one compartment and containing a middle aisle which admitted of communication throughout the train. The car was carried on two trucks, or bogies, and was well adapted to the sharp curvature which prevailed upon our railways.

The first five years of experience showed marked progress in the practical operation of railway trains, but even after locomotives had demonstrated their capabilities and each improved engine had shown an encouraging increase in velocity, the wildest flights of fancy never pictured the speed attained in later years.

When the roads forming the line between Philadelphia and Harrisburg, Pa., were chartered in 1835, and town meetings were held to discuss their practicability, the Honorable Simon Cameron, while making a speech in advocacy of the measure, was so far carried away by his enthusiasm as to make the rash prediction that there were persons within the sound of his voice who would live to see a passenger take his breakfast in Harrisburg and his supper in

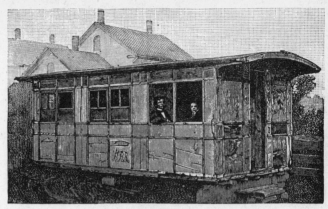

One of the Earliest Passenger Cars Built in this Country; used on the Western Railroad of Massachusetts (now the Boston & Albany).

Philadelphia on the same day. A friend of his on the platform said to him after he had finished: "That's all very well, Simon, to tell to the boys, but you and I are no such infernal fools as to believe it." They both lived to travel the distance in a little over two hours.

The people were far from being unanimous in their advocacy of the railway system, and charters were not obtained without severe struggles. The topic was the universal subject of discussion in all popular assemblages. Colonel Blank, a well-known politician in Pennsylvania, had been loud in his opposition to the new means of transportation. When one of the first trains was running over the Harrisburg & Lancaster road, a famous Durham bull belonging to a Mr. Schultz became seized with the enterprising

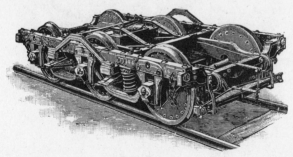

Bogie Truck.

spirit of Don Quixote, put his head down and tail up, and made a desperate charge at the on-coming locomotive, but his steam-breathing opponent proved the better butter of the two and the bull was ignominious-

ly defeated. At a public banquet held soon after in that part of the State, the toast-master proposed a toast to " Colonel Blank

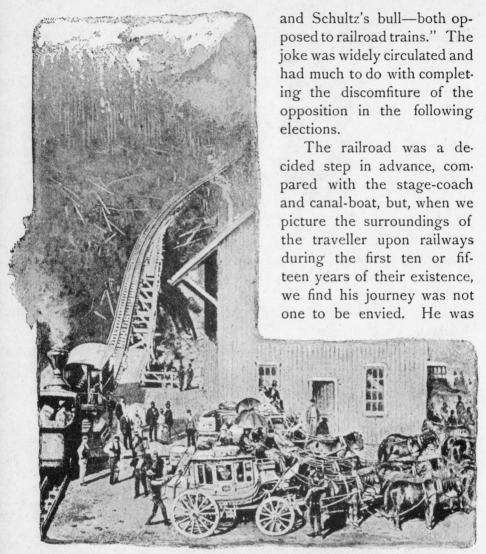

and Schultz's bull—both opposed to railroad trains." The joke was widely circulated and had much to do with completing the discomfiture of the opposition in the following elections.

The railroad was a decided step in advance, compared with the stage-coach and canal-boat, but, when we picture the surroundings of the traveller upon railways during the first ten or fifteen years of their existence, we find his journey was not one to be envied. He was

Rail and Coach Travel in the White Mountains.

jammed into a narrow seat with a stiff back, the deck of the car was low and flat, and ventilation in winter impossible. A stove at each end did little more than generate carbonic oxide. The passenger roasted if he sat at the end of the car, and froze if he sat in the middle. Tallow candles furnished a "dim religious light," but the accompanying odor did not savor of cathedral incense. The dust was suffocating in dry weather; there were no adequate spark-arresters on the engine, or screens at the windows, and the begrimed passenger at the end of his journey looked as if he had spent the day in a blacksmith-shop. Recent experiments in obtaining a spectrum-analysis of the component parts of a quantity of dust collected in a railway car show that minute particles of iron form a large proportion, and under the microscope present the appearance of a collection of tenpenny nails. As iron administered to the human system through the respiratory organs in the form of tenpenny nails mixed with other undesirable matter is not especially recommended by medical practitioners, the sanitary surround-

ings of the primitive railway car cannot be commended. There were no double tracks, and no telegraph to facilitate the safe despatching of trains. The springs of the car were hard, the jolting intolerable, the windows rattled like those of the modern omnibus, and conversation was a luxury that could be indulged in only by those of recognized superiority in lung power. The brakes were clumsy and of little service. The ends of the flat-bar rails were cut diagonally, so that when laid down they would lap and form a smoother joint. Oc-

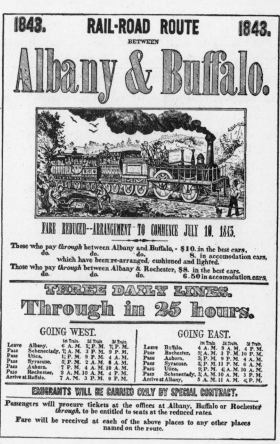

From an Old Time-table (furnished by the "A B C Pathfinder Railway Guide").

casionally they became sprung; the spikes would not hold, and the end of the rail with its sharp point rose high enough for the wheel to run under it, rip it loose, and send the pointed end through the floor of the car. This was called a "snake's head,"

Old Boston & Worcester Railway Ticket (about 1837).

and the unlucky being sitting over it was likely to be impaled against the roof. So that the traveller of that day, in addition to his other miseries, was in momentary apprehension of being spitted like a Christmas turkey.

Baggage-checks and coupon tickets were unknown. Long trips had to be made over lines composed of a number of short independent railways ; and at the terminus of each the bedevilled passenger had to transfer, purchase another ticket, personally pick out his baggage, perhaps on an uncovered platform in a rain-storm, and take his chances of securing a seat in the train in which he was to continue his weary journey.

After the principal companies had sent agents to Europe to gather all the information possible regarding the progress made there, they soon began to aim at perfecting what may justly be called the American system of railways.   The roadbed, or what in England is called the "permanent way," was constructed in such a manner as to conform to the requirements of the new country, and the equipment was adapted to the wants of the people.   In no branch of industry has the inventive genius of the race been more skilfully or more successfully employed than in the effort to bring railway travel to its present state of per-

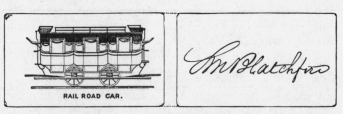

RAIL ROAD CAR.

Obverse and Reverse of a Ticket Used in 1838, on the New York & Harlem Railroad.

fection.   Every year has shown progress in perfecting the comforts and safety of the railway car.   In 1849 the Hodge hand-brake was introduced, and in 1851 the Stevens brake.   These enabled the cars to be controlled in a manner which added much to the economy and safety of handling the trains. In 1869 George Westinghouse patented his air-brake, by which power from the engine was transmitted by compressed air carried through hose and acting upon the brakes of each car in the train.* It was under the control of the engineer, and its action was so prompt and its power so effectual that a train could be stopped in an incredibly short time, and the brakes released in an instant. In 1871 the vacuum-brake was devised, by means of which the power was applied to the brakes by exhausting the air.

A difficulty under which railways suffered for many years was the method of coupling cars. The ordinary means consisted of coupling-pins inserted into links attached to the cars. There was a great deal of "slack," the jerking of the train in consequence was very objectionable, and the distance between the platforms of the cars made the crossing of them dangerous. In collisions one platform was likely to rise above that of the adjoining car, and "telescoping" was not an uncommon occurrence.

The means of warning passengers against standing on the platform were characteristic of the dangers which threatened, and were often ingenious in the devices for attracting attention. On a New Jersey road there was painted on the car-door a picture of a new-made grave, with a formidable tombstone, on which was an inscription announcing to a terrified public that it was " Sacred to the memory of the man who had stood on a platform."

The Miller coupler and buffer was patented in 1863, and obviated many of the discomforts and dangers arising from the old methods of coupling. This was followed by the Janney coupler † and a number of other devices, the essential principle of all being an automatic arrangement by which the two knuckles of the coupler when thrust together become securely locked, and a system of springs which keep the buffers in close contact and prevent jerking and jarring when the train is in motion.

The introduction of the bell-cord running through the train and enabling conductors to communicate promptly by means of it with the engineer, and signal him in case of danger, constitutes another source of safety, but is still a wonder to Europeans, who cannot un-

---

* See " Safety in Railroad Travel," page 195.
† See " Safety in Railroad Travel," page 224; also, " American Locomotives and Cars," page 142.

derstand why passengers do not tamper with it, and how they can resist the temptation to give false signals by means of it.   The only answer is that our people are educated up to it, and being accustomed to govern themselves, they do not require any restraint to make them respect so useful a device.   Aside from the inconveniences which used to arise occasionally from a rustic mistaking the bell-cord for a clothes-rack, and hanging his overcoat over it, or from an old gentleman grabbing hold of it to help him climb into an upper berth in a sleeping-car, it has been singularly exempt from efforts to pervert it to unintended uses.

The application of the magnetic telegraph to railways wrought the first great revolution in despatching trains, and introduced an element of promptness and safety in their operation of which the most sanguine of railroad advocates had never dreamed.   The application of electricity was gradually availed of in many ingenious signal devices for both day and night service, to direct the locomotive engineer in running his train, and interpose precautions against accidents.   Fusees have also been called into requisition, which burn with a bright flame a given length of time; and when a train is behind time and followed by another, by igniting one of these lights, and leaving it on the track, the train following can tell by noting the time of burning about how near it is the preceding train. Torpedoes left upon the track, which explode when passed over by the wheels of a following train and warn it of its proximity to a train ahead, are also used.

In the early days more accidents arose from switches than from any other cause; but improvement in their construction has progressed until it would seem that the dangers have been effectually overcome.   The split-rail switch prevents a train from being thrown off the track in case the switch is left open, and the result is that in such an event the train is only turned on another track.   The Wharton switch, which leaves the main line unbroken, marks another step in the march of improvement.   Among other devices is a complete interlocking-switch system, by means of which one man standing in a switch-tower, overlooking a large yard with numerous tracks, over which trains arrive and depart every few minutes, can, by moving a system of levers, open any required track and by the same motion block all the others, and prevent the possibility of collisions or other accidents resulting from trains entering upon the wrong track.*

The steam-boats on our large rivers had been making great progress in the comforts afforded to passengers. They were providing berths to sleep in, serving meals in spacious cabins, and giving musical entertainments and dancing parties on board. The railroads soon began to learn a lesson from them in adding to the comforts of the travelling public.

The first attempt to furnish the railway passenger a place to sleep while on his journey was made upon the Cumberland Valley Railroad of Pennsylvania, between Harrisburg and Chambersburg. In the winter season the east-bound passengers arrived at Chambersburg late at night by stage-coach, and as they were exhausted by a fatiguing trip over the mountains and many wished to continue their journey to Harrisburg to catch the morning train for Philadelphia, it became very desirable to furnish sleeping accommodations aboard the cars. The officers of this road fitted up a passenger car with a number of berths, and put it into service as a sleeping-car in the winter of 1836–37. It was exceedingly crude and primitive in construction. It was divided by transverse partitions into four sections, and each contained three berths—a lower, middle, and upper berth. This car was used until 1848 and then abandoned.

About this time there were also experiments made in fitting up cars with berths something like those in a steam-boat cabin, but these crude attempts did not prove attractive to travellers. There were no bedclothes furnished, and only a coarse mattress and pillow were supplied, and with the poor ventilation and the rattling and jolting of the car there was not much comfort afforded, except a means of resting in a position which was somewhat more endurable than a sitting posture.

Previous to the year 1858 a few of the leading railways had put on sleeping-cars which made some pretensions to meet a growing want of the travelling public, but they were still crude, uncomfortable, and unsatisfactory in their arrangements and appointments.

In the year 1858 George M. Pullman entered a train of the

* See "Safety in Railroad Travel," page 204.

Lake Shore Railroad at Buffalo, to make a trip to Chicago. It happened that a new sleeping-car which had been built for the

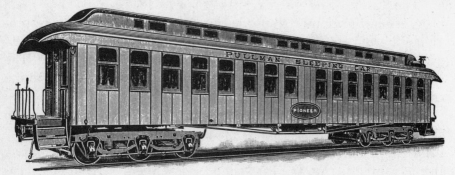

The "Pioneer." First complete Pullman Sleeping-car.

railroad company was attached to this train and was making its first trip. Mr. Pullman stepped in to take a look at it, and finally decided to test this new form of luxury by passing the night in one of its berths. He was tossed about in a manner not very conducive to the "folding of the hands to sleep," and he turned out before daylight and took refuge upon a seat in the end of the car. He now began to ponder upon the subject, and before the journey ended he had conceived the notion that, in a country of magnificent distances like this, a great boon could be offered to travellers by the construction of cars easily convertible into comfortable and convenient day or night coaches, and supplied with such appointments as would give the occupants practically the same comforts as were afforded by the steam-boats. He began experiments in this direction soon after his arrival in Chicago, and in 1859 altered some day-cars on the Chicago & Alton Railroad, and converted them into sleeping-cars which were a marked step in advance of similar cars previously constructed. They were successful in meeting the wants of passengers at that time, but Mr. Pullman did not consider them in any other light than experiments. One night, after they had made a few trips on the line between Chicago and St. Louis, a tall, angular-looking man entered one of the cars while Mr. Pullman was aboard, and after asking a great many intelligent questions about the inventions, finally said he thought he would try what the thing was like, and stowed himself away in an upper berth. This proved to be Abraham Lincoln.

In 1864 Mr. Pullman perfected his plans for a car which was to be a marked and radical departure from any one ever before attempted, and that year invested his capital in the construction of what may be called the father of the Pullman cars. He built it in a shed in the yard of the Chicago & Alton Railroad at a cost of $18,000, named it the "Pioneer," and designated it by the letter "A." It did not then occur to anyone that there would ever be enough sleeping-cars introduced to exhaust the whole twenty-six letters of the alphabet. The sum expended upon it was naturally looked upon as fabulous at a time when such sleeping-cars as were used could be built for about $4,500. The constructor of the "Pioneer" aimed to produce a car which would prove acceptable in every respect to the travelling public. It had improved trucks and a raised deck, and was built a foot wider and two and a half feet higher than any car then in service. He deemed this necessary for the purpose of introducing a hinged upper berth, which, when fastened up, formed a recess behind it for stowing the necessary bedding in the daytime. Before that the mattresses had been piled in one end of the car, and had to be dragged through the aisle when wanted. It was known to him that the dimen-

sions of the bridges and station-platforms would not admit of its passing over the line, but he was singularly confident in the belief that an attractive car, constructed upon correct principles, would find its way into service against all obstacles. It so happened that soon after the car was finished, in the spring of 1865, the body of President Lincoln arrived at Chicago, and the "Pioneer" was wanted for the funeral train which was to take it to Springfield. To enable the car to pass over the road, the station-platforms and other obstructions were reduced in size, and thereafter the line was in a condition to put the car into service. A few months afterward General Grant was making a trip West to visit his home in Galena, Ill., and as the railway companies were anxious to take him from Detroit to his destination in the car which had now become quite celebrated, the station-platforms along the line were widened for the purpose, and thus another route was opened to its passage.

The car was now put into regular service on the Alton road. Its popularity fully realized the anticipations of its owner, and its size became the standard for the future Pullman cars as to height and width, though they have since been increased in length.

The railroad company entered into an agreement to have this car, and a number of others which were immediately built, operated upon its lines. They were marvels of beauty, and their construction embraced patents of such ingenuity and originality that they attracted marked attention in the railroad world and created a new departure in the method of travel.

In 1867 Mr. Pullman formed the Pullman Car Company and devoted it to carrying out an idea which he had conceived, of organizing a system by which passengers could be carried in luxurious cars of uniform pattern, adequate to the wants of both night and day travel, which would run through without change between far-distant points and over a number of distinct lines of railway, in charge of responsible through agents, to whom ladies, children, and invalids could be safely intrusted. This system was especially adapted to a country of such geographical extent as America. It supplied an important want, and the travelling public and the railways were prompt to avail themselves of its advantages.

Parlor or drawing-room cars were next introduced for day runs, which added greatly to the luxury of travel, enabling passengers to secure seats in advance, and enjoy many comforts which were not found in ordinary cars. Sleeping and parlor cars were soon recognized as an essential part of a railway's equipment and became known as " palace cars."

The Wagner Car Company was organized in the State of New York, and was early in the field in furnishing this class of vehicles. It has supplied all the cars of this kind used upon the Vanderbilt system of railways and a number of its connecting roads.   Several smaller palace-car companies have also engaged in the business at

Pullman Parlor Car.

different times.   A few roads have operated their own cars of this class, but the business is generally regarded as a specialty, and the railway companies recognize the advantages and conveniences resulting from the ability of a large car-company to meet the irregularities of travel, which require a large equipment at one season and a small one at another, to furnish an additional supply of cars for a sudden demand, and to perform satisfactorily the business of operating through cars in lines composed of many different railways.

Next came a demand for cars in which meals could be served. Why, it was said, should a train stop at a station for meals any more than a steamboat tie up to a wharf for the same pur-

Wagner Parlor Car.

pose? The Pullman Company now introduced the hotel-car, which was practically a sleeping-car with a kitchen and pantries in one end and portable tables which could be placed between the seats of each section and upon which meals could be conveniently served. The first hotel-car was named the " President," and was put into service on the Great Western Railway of Canada, in 1867, and soon after several popular lines were equipped with this new addition to the luxuries of travel.

After this came the dining-car, which was still another step beyond the hotel-car. It was a complete restaurant, having a large kitchen and pantries in one end, with the main body of the car fitted up as a commodious dining-room, in which all the passengers in the train could enter and take their meals comfortably. The first dining-car was named the " Delmonico," and began running on the Chicago & Alton Railroad in the year 1868.

The comforts and conveniences of travel by rail on the main lines now seemed to have reached their culmination in America.

The heavy **T**-rails had replaced the various forms previously used; the improved fastenings, the reductions in curvature, and the greater care exercised in construction had made the trip delightfully smooth, while the improvements in rolling-stock had obviated the jerking, jolting, and oscillation of the cars. The roadbeds had been properly ditched, drained, and ballasted with broken stone or gravel, the dust overcome, the sparks arrested, and cleanliness, that attribute which stands next to godliness, had at last been made possible, even on a railway train.

The heating of cars was not successfully accomplished till a method was devised for circulating hot water through pipes running near the floor. The suffering from that bane of the traveller —cold feet—was then obviated and many a doctor's bill saved. The loss of human life from the destruction of trains by fires originating from stoves aroused such a feeling throughout the country that the legislatures of many States have passed laws within the

Dining-car (Chicago, Burlington, & Quincy Railroad.)

last three years prohibiting the use of stoves, and the railway managers have been devising plans for heating the trains with steam furnished from the boiler of the locomotive. The inventive genius of the people was at once brought into requisition, and several ingenious devices are now in use which successfully accomplish the purpose in solid trains with the locomotive attached, but the problem of heating a detached car without some form of furnace connected with it is still unsolved.

But notwithstanding the high standard of excellence which had been reached in the construction and operation of passenger trains, there was one want not yet supplied, the importance of which did not become fully recognized until dining-cars were introduced, and men. women, and children had to pass across the platforms of several cars in order to reach the one in which the meals were served. An act which passengers had always been cautioned against, and forbidden to undertake—the crossing of platforms while the train is in motion—now became necessary, and was invited by the railway companies.

It was soon seen that a safe covered passageway between the cars must be provided, particularly for limited express trains. Crude attempts had been made in this direction at different times. As early as the years 1852 and 1855 patents were taken out for devices which provided for diaphragms of canvas to connect adjoining cars and form a passageway between them. These were applied to cars on the Naugatuck Railroad, in Connecticut, in 1857, but they were used mainly for purposes of ventilation, to provide for taking in air at the head of the train, so as to permit the car windows to be kept shut, to avoid the dust that entered through them when they were open. These appliances were very imperfect, did not seem to be of any practical advantage, even for the limited uses for which they were intended, and they were abandoned after a trial of about four years.

In the year 1886 Mr. Pullman went practically to work to devise a perfect system for constructing continuous trains, and at the same time to provide for sufficient flexibility in connecting the passageways to allow for the motion consequent upon the rounding of curves. His efforts resulted in what is now known as the " vestibuled " train.

This invention, which was patented in 1887, succeeded not only in supplying the means of constructing a perfectly enclosed vestibule of handsome architectural appearance between the cars, but it accomplished what is even still more important, the introduction of a safety appliance more valuable than any yet devised for the pro-

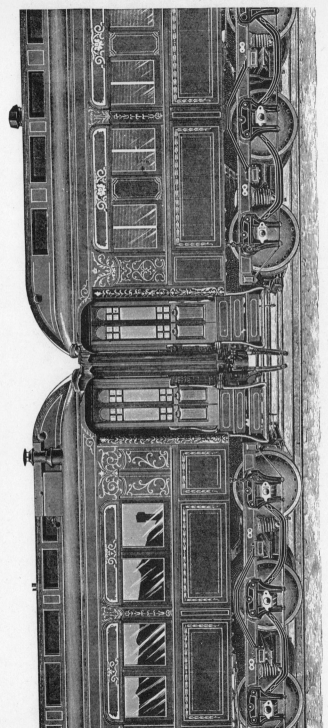

Pullman Vestibuled Cars.

tection of human life in case of collisions.   The elastic diaphragms
which are attached to the ends of the cars have steel frames, the
faces or bearing surfaces
of which are pressed firmly against each other by
powerful spiral springs,
which create a friction
upon the faces of the
frames, hold them firmly
in position, prevent the
oscillation of the cars, and
furnish a buffer extending
from the platform to the
roof which precludes the
possibility of one platform
"riding" the other and
producing telescoping in
case of collision.   The
first of the vestibuled
trains went into service

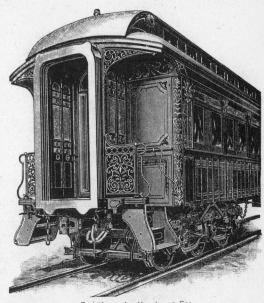

End View of a Vestibuled Car.

on the Pennsylvania Railroad in June, 1886, and they are rapidly
being adopted by railway companies.   The vestibuled limited trains
contain several sleeping-cars, a dining-car, and a car fitted up with a
smoking saloon, a library with books, desks, and writing materials,
a bath-room, and a barber-shop.   With a free circulation of air
throughout the train, the cars opening into each other, the electric
light, the many other increased comforts and conveniences introduced, the steam-heating apparatus avoiding the necessity of using
fires, the great speed, and absence of stops at meal-stations, this
train is the acme of safe and luxurious travel.   An ordinary passenger travels in as princely a style in these cars as any crowned
head in Europe in a royal special train.

The speed of passenger trains has shown steady improvement
from year to year.   In the month of June in our Centennial year,
1876, a train ran from New York to San Francisco, a distance of
3,317 miles, in 83 hours and 27 minutes actual time, thus averaging about 40 miles an hour, but during the trip it crossed four
mountain-summits, one of them over 8,000 feet high.   This train

ran from Jersey City to Pittsburg over the Pennsylvania Railroad, a distance of 444 miles, without making a stop. In 1882 locomotives were introduced which made a speed of 70 miles per hour.

Pullman Sleeper on a Vestibuled Train.

In July, 1885, an engine with a train of three cars made a trip over the West Shore road which is the most extraordinary one on record. It started from East Buffalo, N. Y., at 10.04 A.M., and reached Weehawken, N. J., at 7.27 P.M. Deducting the time consumed in stops, the actual running time was 7 hours and 23 minutes, or an average of 56 miles per hour. Between Churchville and Genesee Junction this train attained the unparalleled speed of 87 miles per hour, and at several other parts of the line a speed of from 70 to 80 miles an hour. The superior physical characteristics of this road were particularly favorable for the attainment of the speed mentioned.

The trains referred to were special or experimental trains, and while American railways have shown their ability to record the highest speed yet known, they do not run their trains in regular service as fast as those on the English railways. The meteor-like names given to our fast trains are somewhat misleading. When one reads of such trains as the " Lightning," the " Cannonball," the " Thunderbolt," and the " G—whiz-z," the suggestiveness of the titles is enough to make one's head swim, but, after all, the names are not as significant of speed as the British " Flying Scotchman " and the " Wild Irishman ; " for the former do not attain an average rate of 40 miles an hour, while the latter exceed 45 miles. A few American trains, however, those between Jersey City and Philadelphia, for instance, make an average speed of over 50 miles per hour.

The transportation of immigrants has recently received increased facilities for its accommodation upon the principal through lines. Until late years economically constructed day-cars were alone used, but in these the immigrants suffered great discomfort in long journeys. An immigrant sleeper is now used, which is constructed with sections

Immigrant Sleeping-car (Canadian Pacific Railway.)

on each side of the aisle, each section containing two double berths. The berths are made with slats of hard wood running longitudinally; there is no upholstery in the car, and no bedding supplied, and after the car is vacated the hose can be turned in upon it, and all the wood-work thoroughly cleansed. The immigrants usually carry with them enough blankets and wraps to make them tolerably comfortable in their berths; a cooking stove is provided in one end of the car, on which the occupants can cook their food, and even the long transcontinental journeys of the immigrants are now made without hardship.

View of Pullman, Ill.

The manufacture of railway passenger cars is a large item of industry in the country. The tendency had been for many years to confine the building of ordinary passenger coaches to the shops owned by the railway companies, and they made extensive provision for such work; but recently they have given large orders for that class of equipment to outside manufacturers. This has resulted partly from the large demand for cars, and partly on account of the excellence of the work supplied by some of the manufacturing companies. In 1880 the Pullman Company erected the most extensive car-works in the world at Pullman, fourteen miles south of Chicago; and, besides its extensive output of Pullman cars and freight equipment, it has built for railway companies large numbers of passenger coaches. The employees now number about 5,000, and an idea of the capacity and resources of the shops may be obtained from the fact that one hundred freight cars, of the kind known as flat cars, have been built in eight hours. The business of car-building has therefore given rise to the first model manufacturing town in America, and it is an industry evidently destined to increase as rapidly as any in the country.

The transportation of baggage has always been a most important item to the traveller, and the amount carried seems to increase in proportion to the advance in civilization. The original allowance of fourteen pounds is found to be increased to four hundred when ladies start for fashionable summer-resorts.

America has been much more liberal than other countries to the traveller in this particular, as in all others. Here few of the roads charge for excess of baggage unless the amount be so large that patience with regard to it ceases to be a virtue.

The earlier method, of allowing each passenger to pick out his own baggage at his point of destination and carry it off, resulted in a lack of accountability which led to much confusion, frequent losses, and heavy claims upon the companies in consequence. Necessity, as usual, gave birth to invention, and the difficulty was at last solved by the introduction of the system known as "checking." A metal disk bearing a number and designating on its face the destination of the baggage was attached to each article and a duplicate given to the owner, which answered as a receipt, and upon the presentation and surrender of which the baggage could be claimed. Railways soon united in arranging for through checks which, when attached to baggage, would insure its being sent safely to distant points over lines composed of many connecting roads. The check system led to the introduction of another marked convenience in the handling of baggage—the baggage express or transfer company. One of its agents will now check trunks at the passenger's own house and haul them to the train. Another agent will take up the checks aboard the train as it is nearing its destination, and see that the baggage is delivered at any given address.

The cases in which pieces go astray are astonishingly rare, and some roads found the claims for lost articles reduced by five thousand dollars the first year after adopting the check system, not to mention the amount saved in the reduced force of employees engaged in assorting and handling the baggage. Its workings are so perfect and its conveniences so great that an American cannot easily understand why it is not adopted in all countries; but he is forced to recognize the fact that it seems destined to be confined to his own land. The London railway managers, for instance, give many reasons for turning their faces against its adoption. They say that there are few losses arising from passengers taking baggage that does not belong to them; that most of the passengers take a cab at the end of their railway journey to reach their homes, and it costs but little more to carry their trunk with them; that in this way it gets home as soon as they, while the transfer company, or baggage express, would not deliver it for an hour or two later; that the cab system is a great convenience, and any change which would diminish its patronage would gradually reduce the number of cabs, and these " gondolas of London " would have to increase their charges or go out of business. It is very easy to find a stick when one wants to hit a dog, and the European railway officials seem never to be at a loss for reasons in rejecting the check system.

Coupon tickets covering trips over several different railways have saved the traveller all the annoyance once experienced in purchasing separate tickets from the several companies representing the roads over which he had to pass. Their introduction necessitated an agreement among the principal railways of the country and the adoption of an extensive system of accountability for the purpose of making settlements of the amounts represented by the coupons.

Like every other novelty the coupon ticket, when first introduced, did not hit the mark when aimed at the understanding of certain travellers. A United States Senator-elect had come on by sea from the Pacific Coast who had never seen a railroad till he reached the Atlantic seaboard. With a curiosity to test the workings of the new means of transportation, of which he had heard so much, he bought a coupon ticket and set out for a railway journey. He entered a car, took a seat next to the door, and was just beginning to get the " hang of the school-house " when the conductor, who was then not uniformed, came in, cried "Tickets!" and reached out his hand toward the Senator. "What do you want of me?"

In a Baggage-room.

Railway Station at York, England, built on a curve.

said the latter. "I want your ticket," answered the conductor. Now it occurred to the Senator that this might be a very neat job on the part of an Eastern ticket-sharp, but it was just a little too thin to fool a Pacific Coaster, and he said: "Don't you think I've got sense enough to know that if I parted with my ticket right at the start I wouldn't have anything to show for my money during the rest of the way? No, sir, I'm going to hold on to this till I get to the end of the trip."

"Oh!" said the conductor, whose impatience was now rising to fever heat, "I don't want to take up your ticket, I only want to look at it."

The Senator thought, after some reflection, that he would risk letting the man have a peep at it, anyhow, and held it up before him, keeping it, however, at a safe distance. The conductor, with the customary abruptness, jerked it out of his hand, tore off the first coupon, and was about to return the ticket, when the Pacific Coaster sprang up, threw himself upon his muscle, and delivered a well-directed blow of his fist upon the conductor's right eye, which landed him sprawling on one of the opposite seats. The other passengers were at once on their feet, and rushed up to know the

Outside the Grand Central Station, New York.

cause of the disturbance. The Senator, still standing with his
arms in a pugnacious attitude, said :

"Maybe I've never ridden on a railroad before, but I'm **not**
going to let any sharper get away with me like that."

"What's he done?" cried the passengers.

" Why," said the Senator, " I paid seventeen dollars and a half for a ticket to take me through to Cincinnati, and before we're five miles out that fellow slips up and says he wants to see it, and when I get it out, he grabs hold of it and goes to tearing it up right before my eyes." Ample explanations were soon made, and the new passenger was duly initiated into the mysteries of the coupon system.

The uniforming of railway employees was a movement of no little importance. It designated the various positions held by them, added much to the neatness of their appearance, enabled passengers to recognize them at a glance, and made them so conspicuous that it impressed them with a greater sense of responsibility and aided much in effecting a more courteous demeanor to passengers.

Many conveniences have been introduced which greatly assist the passenger when travelling upon unfamiliar roads. Conspicuous clock-faces stand in the stations with their hands set to the hour at which the next train is to start, sign-boards are displayed with horizontal slats on which the stations are named at which departing way-trains stop, and employ-

Boston Passenger Station, Providence Division, Old Colony Railroad.

ees are stationed to call out necessary information and direct passengers to the proper entrances, exits, and trains. A " bureau of information " is now to be seen in large passenger-stations, in which an official sits and with a Job-like patience repeats to the

curiously inclined passengers the whole railway catechism, and successfully answers conundrums that would stump an Oriental pundit

The energetic passenger-agent spares no pains to thrust information directly under the nose of the public. He uses every
means known to Yankee ingenuity to advertise his regular trains
and his excursion business, including large newspaper head-lines,
corner-posters, curb-stone dodgers, and placards on the breast and
back of the itinerant human sandwich who perambulates the streets.

Railway accidents have always been a great source of anxiety
to the managers, and the shocks received by the public when
great loss of life occurs from such causes deepen the interest
which the general community feels in the means taken to avoid
these distressing occurrences.

American railway officials have made encouraging progress in
reducing the number and the severity of accidents, and while the
record is not so good on many of our cheaply constructed roads,
our first-class roads now show by their statistics that they compare favorably in this respect with the European companies.

The statistics regarding accidents * are necessarily unreliable,
as railway companies are not eager to publish their calamities from
the house-tops, and only in those States in which prompt reports
are required to be made by law are the figures given at all accurately. Even in these instances the yearly reports lead to wrong
conclusions, for the State Railroad Commissioners become more
exacting each year as to the thoroughness of the reports called
for, and the results sometimes show an increase compared with previous years, whereas there may have been an actual decrease.

In 1880, the last census year, an effort was made to collect statistics of this kind covering all the railways in the United States,
with the following result :

To whom happened.	Through causes beyond their control.		Through their own carelessness.		Aggregate.		Total accidents.
	Killed.	Injured	Killed.	Injured.	Killed.	Injured.	
Passengers	61	331	82	213	143	544	687
Employees..................	261	1,004	663	2,613	924	3,617	4,541
All others..................	43	103	1,429	1,348	1,472	1,451	2,923
Unspecified................	..	...	....	....	3	62	65
Total.................	365	1,438	2,174	4,174	2,542	5,674	8,216

* See " Safety in Railroad Travel," page 191.

"Show Your Tickets!"
(Passenger Station, Philadelphia.)

Mulhall, in his " Dictionary of Statistics," an English work, uses substantially these same figures and makes the following comparison between European and American railways:

Accidents to Passengers, Employees, and Others.

	Killed.	Wounded.	Total.	Per million passengers.
United States............................	2,349	5,867	8,216	41.1
United Kingdom........................	1,135	3,959	5,094	8.1
Europe.............	3,213	10,859	14,072	10.8

That the figures given above are much too high as regards the United States, there can be no doubt. For the fiscal year 1880–81 the data compiled by the Railroad Commissioners of Massachusetts and published in their reports give as the total number of persons killed and injured in the United States 2,126, as against 8,216 upon which the comparisons in the above table are based. If we substitute in this table the former number for the latter, it would reduce the number of injured per million passengers in the United States to 10.6, about the same as on the European railways.

Edward Bates Dorsey gives the following interesting table of comparisons in his valuable work, " English and American Railroads Compared : "

Passengers Killed and Injured from Causes beyond their own Control on all the Railroads of the United Kingdom and those of the States of New York and Massachusetts in 1884.

	Total length of line operated.	Total mileage.		Killed.	Injured.
		Train.	Passengers.		
United Kingdom................	18,864	272,803,220	6,042,659,990	31	864
New York............................	7,293	85,918,677	1,729,653,620	10	124
Massachusetts........	2,852	32,304,333	1,007,136,376	2	42
In 1,000,000,000 ⎰ United Kingdom..	....	....	....	5.15	143
passengers trans- ⎱ New York........	....	....	....	5.78	70
ported 1 mile. ⎰ Massachusetts ...	....	....	....	2.00	42

			Miles.
The average number of miles a passenger can travel without being killed.	United Kingdom.................		194,892,255
	New York........................		172,965,362
	Massachusetts....		503,568,188
The average number of miles a passenger can travel without being injured.	United Kingdom.................		6,992,662
	New York		13,940,754
	Massachusetts...................		23,955,630

From this it will be seen that in the United Kingdom the average distance a passenger may travel before being killed is about equal to twice the distance of the Earth from the Sun. In New York he may travel a distance greater than that of Mars from the Sun; and in Massachusetts he can comfort himself with the thought that he may travel twenty-seven millions of miles farther than the distance of Jupiter to the Sun before suffering death on the rail.

The most encouraging feature of these statistics is the fact that the number of railway accidents per mile in the United States has shown a marked decrease each year. Taking the figures adopted by the Massachusetts commissions, the number of persons injured in the year 1880–81 was 2,126, and in 1886–87, 2,483, while in the same time the number of miles in operation increased from 93,349 to 137,986.

The amounts paid annually by railways in satisfaction of claims for damages to passengers are serious items of expenditure, and in the United States have reached in some years nearly two millions of dollars. About half of the States limit the amount of damages in case of death to $5,000, the States of Virginia, Ohio, and Kansas to $10,000, and the remainder have no statutory limit.

In the year 1840 the number of miles of railway per 100,000 inhabitants in the different countries named was as follows: United States, 20; United Kingdom, 3; Europe, 1; in the year 1882, United States, 210; United Kingdom, 52; Europe, 34.

In the year 1886 the total number of miles in the United States was 137,986; the number of passengers carried, 382,284,-972; the number carried one mile, 9,659,698,294; the average distance travelled per passenger, 25.27 miles.

In Europe the first-class travel is exceedingly small and the third class constitutes the largest portion of the passenger business, while in America almost the whole of the travel is first class, as will be seen from the following table:

	Percentage of passengers carried.		
	First Class.	Second Class.	Third Class.
United Kingdom........	6	10	84
France..........	8	32	60
Germany....	1	13	86
United States...	99	½ of 1	½ of 1

The third-class travel in this country is better known as immigrant travel. The percentages given in the above table for the United States are based upon an average of the numbers of passengers of each class carried on the principal through lines. If all the roads were included, the percentages of the second- and third-class travel would be still less.

That which is of more material interest to passengers than anything else is the rate of fare charged.

The following table gives an approximate comparison between the rates per mile in the leading countries in the world:

	First Class.	Second Class.	Third Class.
	Cents.	Cents.	Cents.
United Kingdom...	4.42	3.20	1.94
France	3.86	2.88	2.08
Germany..	3.10	2.32	1.54
United States...................	2.18	....	....

The rates above given for the United Kingdom, France, and Germany are the regular schedule-rates. An average of all the fares received, including the reduced fares at excursion rates, would make the figures somewhat less.

The rate named as the first-class fare for the railways in the United States is, strictly speaking, the average earnings per passenger per mile, and includes all classes; but as the first-class passengers constitute about ninety-nine per centum of the travel the amount does not differ materially from the actual first-class fare.

In the State of New York the first-class fare does not exceed two
cents, which is not much more than the third-class fare in some
countries of Europe, and heat, good ventilation, ice-water, toilet
arrangements, and free carriage of a liberal amount of baggage
are supplied, while in Europe few of these comforts are furnished.

On the elevated railroads of New York a passenger can ride
in a first-class car eleven miles for 5 cents, or about one-half cent a
mile, and on surface-roads the commutation rates given to suburban passengers are in some cases still less.

The berth-fares in sleeping-cars in Europe largely exceed those
in America, as will be seen from the following comparisons, stated
in dollars :

Route.	Distance in Miles.	Berth-fare.
Paris to Rome.............................	901	$12.75
New York to Chicago..	912	5.00
Paris to Marseilles...	536	11.00
New York to Buffalo...	440	2.00
Calais to Brindisi..	1,373	22.25
Boston to St. Louis................................	1,330	6.50

While it would seem that the luxuries of railway travel in America have reached a maximum, and the charges a minimum, yet in
this progressive age it is very probable that in the not far distant future we shall witness improvements over the present
methods which will astonish us as much as the present methods
surprise us when we compare them with those of the past.

THE FREIGHT-CAR SERVICE.

By THEODORE VOORHEES.

Sixteen Months' Journey of a Car—Detentions by the Way—Difficulties of the Car Accountant's Office—Necessities of Through Freight—How a Company's Cars are Scattered—The Question of Mileage—Reduction of the Balance in Favor of Other Roads—Relation of the Car Accountant's Work to the Transportation Department—Computation of Mileage—The Record Branch—How Reports are Gathered and Compiled—Exchange of " Junction Cards "—The Use of " Tracers "—Distribution of Empty Cars—Control of the Movement of Freight—How Trains are Made Up—Duties of the Yardmaster—The Handling of Through Trains—Organization of Fast Lines—Transfer Freight Houses—Special Cars for Specific Service—Disasters to Freight Trains—How the Companies Suffer—Inequalities in Payment for Car Service—The Per Diem Plan—A Uniform Charge for Car Rental—What Reforms might be Accomplished.

I.

THE WANDERINGS OF A CAR.

ON the 14th of December, 1886, there was loaded in Indianapolis a car belonging to one of the roads passing through that city. It was loaded with corn consigned to parties in Boston. The car was delivered to the Lake Shore road at Cleveland on the 16th ; but, owing to bad weather and various other local causes, it did not reach East Buffalo until December 28th. It was turned over by the New York Central & Hudson River Railroad to the West Shore road the next day, and by this company was taken to Rotterdam Junction, and there delivered on December 31st to the Western Division of the Fitchburg Railroad, or what was then known as the Boston, Hoosac Tunnel & Western. They took it promptly through to Boston. After a few days the corn was sold by the consignees for delivery in Medfield, on the New York & New England Railway. The car was delivered to this road on January 24, 1887, and taken down to Medfield. There it remained among a large number of other cars, until it suited the convenience of the purchaser to put the corn into his elevator.

On the 17th of March the car was unloaded, taken back to Boston, and delivered to the Fitchburg road to be sent West, homeward. That company took it promptly, but instead of delivering it to the West Shore road at Rotterdam Junction, as would have been the regular course, either through some mistake of a yardmaster at the junction station, or in pursuance of general instructions to load all Western cars home whenever practicable, the car was not delivered to the West Shore, but was turned over to the Delaware & Hudson Canal Co's. Railroad, taken down to the coal regions, and on March 31st delivered to the Delaware, Lackawanna & Western Railroad, by whom it was loaded with coal for Chicago. That company promptly delivered it to the Grand Trunk at Buffalo, and on April 10th the car reached Chicago. It was immediately reconsigned by the local agents of the coal company to a dealer in the town of Minot, 523 miles west of St. Paul, on the St. Paul, Minneapolis & Manitoba Railroad. To reach that point, it was delivered to the Chicago, Rock Island & Pacific on April 10th, then to the Burlington, Cedar Rapids & Northern, Minneapolis & St. Louis, St. Paul & Duluth, St. Paul, Minneapolis & Manitoba, arriving at its destination on the 14th of April.

Winter still reigned in that locality, and the car was promptly unloaded, and returned to St. Paul, where it was loaded with wheat consigned to New York. It left St. Paul on the 26th of April, was promptly moved through to Chicago, and delivered to the Grand Trunk. Coming east, in Canada, the train of which this car formed a part, while passing through a small station, in the night ran into an open switch. The engine dashed into a number of loaded cars standing on the siding, and the cars behind it were piled up in bad confusion, a number of them being destroyed, and the freight scattered in all directions. Our car, whose history we are tracing, suffered comparatively slight damage. The drawheads were broken, and some castings on one truck, not sufficient to affect in any way the loading of the car. It was sent to the shops of the road; and it became necessary for them, on examination, to send to the owners of the car for a casting to replace that broken on the truck. This resulted in serious detention. The requisition for this casting had to be approved by the Superintendent and by the General Manager, and was forwarded, after a considerable delay, to the officers of the road owning the car. There it was sent through a number of offices before it finally reached the hands of the man who was able to supply the required casting. This in turn was sent by freight, and passed over the intervening territory at a slow rate; the whole involving a detention which held the car from April 28th, when it was delivered at Chicago to the Grand Trunk, until July 18th, when finally the Grand Trunk delivered it to the Delaware, Lackawanna & Western at Buffalo. It came through promptly to New York, the grain was put in an elevator, the car was sent back once more to the mines at Scranton, and again loaded with coal for Chicago. On August 9th the record says the car was delivered by the Delaware, Lackawanna & Western to the Grand Trunk, and on the 12th of August it was in Chicago.

About this time the owners of the car began to make vigorous appeals to the various roads, urging them to send the car home. One of these tracers reached the Grand Trunk road while they still held the car in their possession; so that orders were sent that the coal must be unloaded at once, and the car returned. In order to unload it, it was necessary to switch it to the Illinois Central for some local consignee, and it was unloaded within four days and delivered back to the Grand Trunk at Chicago. This was on August 16th. During the few days that had elapsed since the order was given to send this car home, there had been an active demand for cars, and knowing that this one had to be sent to Buffalo in order to be delivered to the Lake Shore road, from which it had originally been received, the car was loaded for that point. This again resulted in detention, for we find that the car was held on the Grand Trunk tracks at Black Rock, awaiting the pleasure of the consignee to unload the freight, until the 27th of September; and then, instead of being unloaded and delivered to the Lake Shore road, as had been the intention of the Grand Trunk officials, the consignee sold the wheat in the car to a local dealer on the line of the Erie Railway, and the car was sent down on that road on October 1st, and not returned to the Grand Trunk again until the 10th day of October.

Unfortunately, the Erie was as anxious at that time to load cars west with coal as the other roads, and when they brought the car back to the Grand Trunk, they brought it once more filled with coal, and back the car went to Chicago, reaching there on the 13th of October.

It had now been away from home and diverted from its legitimate uses for nine months, and apparently was as far from home as ever. The delivery of the coal this time at Chicago put the car in the hands of the Louisville, New Albany & Chicago Railway, and they promptly gave it a lading by the southern route to Newport News; for we find the car delivered by the Louisville, New Albany & Chicago to the Chesapeake & Ohio route on October 28th, and at Newport News on the 10th of November. The owners of the car were meanwhile not idle. The occasional stray junction cards which came in notified them of the passage of the car by different junction points, giving them clews to work by, and they were in vigorous correspondence with the various roads over which the car had gone, urging, begging, and imploring the railway officers to make all efforts in their power to get the car back to its home road.

On its last trip from Chicago to Newport News, the car passed through Indianapolis, the very point from which it began its long journey and many wanderings. Unfortunately, however, it passed there loaded, without detention, and the owners of the car did not discover until it had been for some time at Newport News, that the car had been anywhere near its home territory. By the time they made this discovery the car had been unloaded, and had started west once more. The records of the movement of the car here become dim. It was apparently diverted from its direct route back, which would have taken it once more to Indianapolis, and so home, for we find, after waiting at Newport News for some time to be unloaded, it was delivered to the Nashville, Chattanooga & St. Louis, next on the Western & Atlantic, and so down into Georgia and South Carolina. Again, on January 14, 1888, the car was reported on the Richmond & Danville. They sent it once more down into South Carolina and Georgia. From there it was loaded down to Selma, Ala., on the Atlanta & West Point Railroad. They returned it promptly to Atlanta, and so to the Central Railroad of Georgia; and the car, after being used backward and forward between Montgomery and Atlanta and Macon, finally appeared at Augusta, Ga., where it stood on February 11, 1888. Here the car remained for some time, long enough for the owners to get advices as to its whereabouts, and communicate with the road on whose territory the car was, before it was again moved. An urgent representation of the case having been laid before the proper authorities, they agreed, if possible, to load it in such a way that it should go back to Indianapolis. This could not be done at once, however; but about the 12th of March the car was sent to a near-by point in South Carolina loaded, and worked back over the Georgia road and the Western Atlantic, delivered to the Louisville & Nashville on April 3d, and finally, after its many and long wanderings, was by that road delivered to the home road at Cincinnati on the 17th of April; having been away from home sixteen months and one day.

This is a case taken from actual records, and is one that could be duplicated probably by any railroad in the country.

II.

THE CAR ACCOUNTANT'S OFFICE.

THE WINNIPEG & ATHABASKA LAKE RAILWAY CO.,
General Superintendent's Office,
WINNIPEG, December 31, 1888.

To JOHN SMITH, ESQ.,
Supt. of Trans'n, L. & N. R. R. Co., Louisville, Ky.

SIR: Our records show forty-five of our box-cars on your line, some of which have been away from home over three weeks. I give below the numbers of those which have been detained over thirty days, viz. :

Nos.	28542	34210	34762	29421	28437	29842
	34628	34516	29781	28274	34333	28873

There is at this time a strong demand for cars for the movement of the wheat crop, and I must beg that you will send home promptly all that you have on your line.

I remain,
Yours very truly,
THOMAS BROWN.

LOUISVILLE & NORFOLK R. R. Co.,
Office of Superintendent of Transportation,
LOUISVILLE, KY., Jan'y 3, 1889.

To THOMAS BROWN, ESQ.,
   Gen'l Supt., W. & A. L. R. W. Co., Winnipeg, Canada.

SIR : Your favor of the 31st ulto. was duly received and contents noted.

I call your attention to the enclosed mem. from our Car Accountant, which shows that we have but seven of your cars now on our road ; of these but three are bad cases, Nos. 28437, 34516, and 28873. One of these cars was crippled, and is in the shops ; the other two are loaded with wheat consigned " to order."

The necessary instructions have been given our agents, and we will do all in our power to hurry the return of your cars.

I am,
Very truly yours,
JOHN SMITH.

(Mem. enclosed.)

MEMORANDUM.

W. & A. L. Nos.

28542 to Ohio Northern, Dec. 5th.
34210 " Ohio Northern, Dec. 10th.
34762 " Kanawha Junc., 12/15 crippled.
29421 " Elmwood, 12/15 unloading.
28437 " Norfolk Shops, Dec. 6th.
34628 " No account.
34516 " Blue Ridge, 12/4 ordered out.

29781 to Ohio Northern, Nov. 27th.
28274 " Niantic, Dec. 12th, loading home.
34333 " Louisville Belt, Dec. 8th.
29842 " Brockton, Dec. 14th, empty, will load home.
28873 " Blue Ridge, Nov. 18th, ordered out.

This is but an example of a correspondence that is constantly being exchanged between the officials who are in charge of the Transportation Department of the various railways of the country.

The demands of trade necessitate continually the transportation of all manner of commodities over great distances.

Thus, wheat is brought from the Northwest to the seaboard, corn from the Southwest, cotton from the South, fruit comes from California, black walnut from Indiana, and pine from Michigan. In the opposite direction, merchandise and manufactured articles are sent from the East to all points in the West, the North, and Southwest. The interchange is constant and steadily increasing in all directions.

In the early period of railways in this country, when they were built chiefly to promote local interests, and the movement of either freight or passengers over long distances was a comparatively small portion of the traffic, it was customary for all roads to do their business in their own cars, transferring any freight destined to a station on a connecting road at the junction or point of interchange of the two roads. While this system had the advantage of keeping at home the equipment of each road, it. resulted in a very slow movement of the freight. As the volume of traffic grew, and the interchange of commodities between distant points increased, this slow movement became more and more vexatious. Soon the railway companies found it necessary to allow their cars to run through to the destination of the freight without transfer, or they would be deprived of the business by more enterprising rivals. So that to-day a very large proportion of the freight business of the country is done without transfer ; the same car taking the load from the initial point direct to destination. The result of this is, however, that a considerable share of all the business of any railway is done in cars belonging to other companies, for which mileage has to be paid ; while, in turn, the cars of any one company may be scattered all over the country from Maine to California, Winnipeg to Mexico.

The problem that constantly confronts the general superintendent of a railway is, how to improve the time of through freight, thereby improving the service and increasing the earnings of the company ; and, at the same time, how to secure the prompt movement of cars belonging to the company, getting them home from other roads, and reducing as far as possible upon his own line the use of foreign cars, and the consequent payment of mileage therefor.

By common consent the mileage for the use of all eight-wheel freight cars has been fixed at three-quarters of a cent per mile run ; four-wheel cars being rated at one-half this amount, or three-eighths of a cent. This amount would at first sight appear to be insignificant, yet in the aggregate it comes to a very considerable sum. In the case of some of the more important roads in the country, even those possessing a large equipment, the balance against them for mileage alone often amounts to nearly half a million annually.

It becomes therefore of the first importance to reduce to a minimum the use of foreign cars, thereby reducing the mileage balance ; at the same time avoiding any action that will interfere with or impede in any way the prompt movement of traffic.

The first step toward accomplishing this result is to organize and fully equip the Car Accountant's Department. The importance of this office has been recognized only of late years. Formerly and on many lines even now, the Car Accountant was merely a subordinate in the Auditing Department of the company. His duties were confined strictly to computing the mileage due to other roads. This he did from the reports of the freight-train conductors, often in a cumbrous and mechanical manner, making no allowance for possible errors. At the same time, he received reports of foreign roads without question and without check. He was not interested in any way in the operations of the Transportation Department; and, as a consequence, it never occurred to him to make inquiries as to the proper use of the cars belonging to his own company. That he left entirely to the Superintendent. The latter, on the other hand, his time incessantly filled with many duties, could give but scant attention to his cars.

The Superintendent of a railway in this country who has, let us say, three hundred miles of road in his charge, has perhaps as great a variety of occupation, and as many different questions of importance depending upon his decision, as any other business or professional man in the community. Fully one-half of his time will be spent out-of-doors looking after the physical condition of his track, masonry, bridges, stations, buildings of all kinds. Concerning the repair or renewal of each he will have to pass judgment. He must know intimately every foot of his track and, in cases of emergency or accident, know just what resources he can depend upon, and how to make them most immediately useful. He will visit the shops and round houses frequently, and will know the construction and daily condition of every locomotive, every passenger and baggage car. He will consult with his Master Mechanic, and often will decide which car or engine shall and which shall not be taken in for repair, etc. He has to plan and organize the work of every yard, every station. He must know the duties of each employee on his pay-rolls, and instruct all new men, or see that they are properly instructed. He must keep incessant and vigilant watch on the movement of all trains, noting the slightest variation from the schedules which he has prepared, and looking carefully into the causes therefor, so as to avoid its recurrence. The first thing in the morning he is greeted with a report giving the situation of business on the road, the events of the night, movement of trains, and location and volume of freight to be handled. The last thing at night he gets a final report of the location and movement of important trains ; and he never closes his eyes without thinking that perhaps the telephone will ring and call him before dawn. During the day in his office he has reports to make out, requisitions to approve, a varied correspondence, not always agreeable, to answer. Added to this, frequent consultations with the officers of the Traffic Department, or with those of connecting lines, in reference to the movement of through or local business, completely fill his time.

It is not to be wondered at that such a man gives but slight attention in many cases to the matter of car mileage. He frequently satisfies himself by arranging a system of reports from his agents to his office that give a summary each twenty-four hours of the cars of every kind on hand at each station ; and leaves the distribution and movement of the cars in the hands of his agents. He will give some attention to the matter whenever he goes over his road on other and more pressing duties. Occasionally he will even take a day or two and visit every station, inquiring carefully as to each car he finds ; why it is being held, for what purpose, and how long it has stood. Then, satisfied with having, as he says, " shaken up the boys," he will turn his attention to other matters, and let the cars take care of themselves. When the monthly or quarterly statements are made up, and he sees the amount of balance against his road for car mileage, he gives it but little thought, regarding it as one of the items like taxes, important, of course, but hardly one for which he is responsible.

His General Manager, however, will note the car-mileage balance with more concern ; and, looking into the matter carefully, he will discover that the remedy is to put the Car Accountant into the Transportation Department; thus at once interesting him in the economical use of the equipment, and also placing in the hands of the Superintendent the machinery he needs to enable him to promptly control and direct the use of all cars.

The Car Accountant's Office may properly be divided into two main branches—mileage and record. The computation of mileage is made in most cases directly from the reports of each train.

These reports are made by the train conductors, and give the initials and number of each car in their train, whether loaded or empty, and the station whence taken and where left. To facilitate the computation of mileage of each car, the stations on the road are consecutively numbered, beginning at nought—each succeeding station being represented by a number equivalent to the number of miles it is distant from the initial station; excepting divisional and terminal stations, where letters are used, to reduce the work in recording. The conductors report the stations between which each car moves by their numbers or letters. So that all that is necessary for the mileage clerk to do is to take the difference between the station numbers in each case, and he has the miles travelled by that car. The mileage of each car having been so noted on the conductor's report, it is then condensed, the mileage of all cars of any given road or line being added together, and the results entered into the ledgers. At the close of the month these books are footed, and a report is rendered to each road in the country of the mileage and amount in money due therefor, in each case; and settlements are made accordingly, either in full or by balance. This is purely the accounting side of the Car Accountant's Office.

There remains the record branch, equally important, and to the operating department far more interesting. This consists broadly in a complete record being kept of the daily movement and location of every car upon the road, local or foreign. At first sight this may seem to be a difficult and complicated operation, but, in fact, it is simple. The record is first divided between local and foreign; local cars being all cars owned by the home road, foreign being all those owned by other roads. The local books are of large size, ruled in such a way as to allow space for the daily movement or location of each car for one month, and admit of twenty-five or fifty cars being recorded upon each page. The record books for foreign cars are similarly ruled, a slight change being necessary to allow for the numbers and initials of the foreign cars, which cannot well be arranged for in advance.

The train conductors' reports are placed in the hands of the record clerks, each one recording the movements of certain initials, or series of numbers, under the date as shown by the report; the reports being handed from one to another until every car has been entered and the report checked.

In addition to the conductors' train reports, the Car Accountant receives reports from all junction stations daily, showing all cars received from or delivered to connecting roads, whether loaded or empty, and the destination of each. He also has reports from all stations showing cars received and forwarded, from midnight to midnight, cars remaining on hand loaded or empty; and

A Page from the Car Accountant's Book.*

if loaded, contents and consignee, and also cars in process of load ing or unloading, and reports from shops or yards showing cars undergoing repairs, or waiting for the same. In fine, he endeav

* EXPLANATION. Each connecting road at each junction station is assigned a number, and when a car is received from a connection the record is shown by entering the road number in the upper space of the block under the proper date, followed by the character × if loaded; or, if empty, together with the time, as for example: Car 29421 is shown as received, Dec. 2d, from the Amherst & Lincoln Ry. at Port Chester (10), loaded (×), at 21 o'clock, or 9 P.M. A similar entry in the lower space of the block indicates a *delivery* to connecting line. The middle space of the block is used for the car move-ment, the first number or letter showing the station from which the car moved. The character × as a prefix to a station number indicates that the car is being loaded at that station. The —, when used as

ors to get complete reports showing every car that either may be in motion or standing at any point on his road. All of these are entered on his record books. The station reports check those of the conductor, and *vice versa*. It will thus be seen that the record gives a complete history of the movement and daily use of each car on the road.

In case of stock and perishable freight, or freight concerning whose movements quick time is of the utmost importance, this record is kept not only by days but by hours; that is, the actual time of each movement is entered on the record. This is done by a simple system of signs, so that an exact account of the movement, giving date and hour of receipt and delivery, can be taken from the record. This is frequently of the greatest value.

In addition to this, it is customary now for nearly all roads to exchange what are known as "junction cards." They are reports from one to another giving the numbers of all cars of each road passing junction stations. These junction reports when received are also carefully noted in the record, so that an account is kept in a measure of the movement of home cars while on foreign roads, and their daily location.

It would be difficult, and beyond the scope of this article, to tell of the great variety of uses these records are put to. They serve as a check upon reports of the mileage clerks, insuring their accuracy. The junction reports serve also in a measure to check the reports of foreign roads. Then, at frequent intervals, a clerk will go over the record and note every car that is not shown to have moved within, say, five days, putting down on a "detention report" for each station the car number and date of its arrival.

a prefix, shows that the car is being unloaded; as an *affix* it indicates a movement empty, or on hand empty. When the — is used *under* a station number it indicates a change date record, that is, leaving a station on one date and arriving at another on the following date. Station numbers or letters without other characters show that the car is loaded.

The sign (B) is used when a car is left at a station for repairs, while in transit. The sign (T) denotes that the lading was transferred to another car, a transfer record being kept showing to what car transferred; the sign (R), when a car is on hand at a station or yard for repairs. Shops are assigned numbers with an O prefix; the upper and lower spaces being used to show delivery to, or receipt from the shop, similar to the interchange record.

For convenience the twenty-four hour system is used for recording time, and is shown in quarter-hours; thus, 10, 12^1, 18^2, 21^3, representing 10 A.M., 12.15 P.M., 6.30 P.M., and 9.45 P.M. This, used in the movement record, shows the running time on each division, or detention at train terminals.

The "transfer" column shows the station at which the car was reported on the last day of the previous month, and the *arriving date;* also from what road received, with date.

These reports are sent to the agents for explanation, and then submitted to the Superintendent. In a similar manner reports will be made showing any use locally of foreign cars. From the record can be shown almost at a glance the location of all idle cars, information that is often very valuable, and that when wanted is wanted promptly. Also, from the record, reports are constantly being made out—" tracers," as they are termed—showing the location and detention of home cars on foreign roads. In turn, foreign tracers are taken to the record, and the questions therein asked are readily answered by the Car Accountant.

Whenever possible, the distribution of empty cars upon the line should be under the direct supervision of the Car Accountant. Where this matter is left to a clerk in the Superintendent's office, or, as has often been the case, is left to the discretion of yardmasters and agents, the utmost waste in the use of cars is inevitable. An agent at a local station will want a car for a particular shipment. If he has none at his station suitable he will ask some neighboring agent; failing there, he will ask the Superintendent's office, and frequently also the nearest yardmaster. Some other agent at a distant station may want the same kind of car; orders in this way become duplicated, and the road will not only have to haul twice the number of cars needed, but very often haul the same kind of cars empty in opposite directions at the same time. This is no uncommon occurrence even on well-managed roads, and, it is needless to say, is most expensive.

Where the cars are distributed under the direct supervision of the Car Accountant, he has the record at hand constantly, and knows exactly where all cars are, and the sources of supply to meet every demand. Not only that, but every improper use of cars is at once brought to light and corrected.

The *theory* of the use of foreign cars is that they are permitted to run through to destination with through freight, on condition that they shall be promptly unloaded on arrival at destination; that they shall be returned at once to the home road, being loaded on the return trip if suitable loading is available; but by no means allowed to be used in local service, or loaded in any other direction than homeward.

The *practice* of many agents, and many roads, too, unfortu-

Freight Pier, North River, New York.

nately, is hardly in keeping with this theory. Agents, especially if not closely watched, are prone to put freight into any car that is at hand, regardless of ownership, being urged to such course by the importunities of shippers and, at times, by the scarcity of cars. Frequently such irregularities are the result of pure carelessness, agents using foreign cars for local shipments, simply because they are on hand, rather than call for home cars which it may take some trouble and delay to procure. In this way at times a large amount of local business may be going on on one part of the road in foreign cars, while but a few miles distant the company's cars may be standing idle. The Car Accountant from his record can at once put a stop to this, and prevent its recurrence.

Another valuable use to which the Car Accountant's Office may be put is to trace and keep a record of the movement of freight, locating delays, and tracing for freight lost or damaged. By a moderate use of the telegraph wire the Car Accountant can keep track of the movement of special freight-trains concerning which time is important, and so insure regularity and promptness in their despatch and delivery. From the mileage records may be obtained the work of each engine in freight service, the miles run, the number of loaded and empty cars hauled; and by considering two, or perhaps three, empty cars as equivalent to one loaded car, the average number of loaded cars hauled per mile is obtained. The information is often valuable, as on many roads the ability of a Superintendent is measured to a considerable extent by the amount of work performed by the engines at his command.

In many other ways the resources of the Car Accountant's office will be found of the greatest value to the Superintendent. When the office is once fully organized and systematized, and all in good working order, the Superintendent will find that his capacity for control of his cars has been more than doubled, while the demands on his time for their care has been really lessened. He has all the information he needs supplied at his desk, far more accurate than any he was ever able to secure before, and in the most condensed form; while, at the same time, he will find his freight improving in time over his line, his agents will have cars more promptly and in greater abundance than ever, and last, and most gratifying of all, his monthly balance-sheets will show a steady decrease in the amount his road pays for foreign-car mileage, until probably the balance will be found in his favor, although his business and consequent tonnage may have increased meanwhile.

III.

USE AND ABUSE OF CARS.

A package of merchandise can be transported from New York to Chicago in two days and three nights. This is repeated day after day with all the regularity of passenger service. So uniform is this movement, that shippers and consignees depend upon it and arrange their sales and stocks of goods in accordance therewith. Any deviation or irregularity brings forth instant complaint and a threatened withdrawal of patronage. This is true of hun-

Hay Storage Warehouses, New York Central & Hudson River Railroad, West Thirty-third Street, New York.

dreds of other places and lines of freight service. To accomplish
it, there is necessary, first, a highly complicated and intricate organization, and, next, incessant watchfulness.

The shipper delivers the goods at the receiving freight-house
of the railway company. His cartman gets a receipt from the
tallyman. This receipt may be sent direct to the consignee, or
more frequently is exchanged for a bill of lading. There the responsibility of the shipper ends. His goods are in the hands of

the railway company, which to all intents and purposes guarantees their safe and prompt delivery to the consignee.

The tallyman's receipt is taken in duplicate. The latter is kept in the freight-house until the freight is loaded in a car, and is then marked with the initials and number of the car into which the freight has been loaded. After that it is taken to the bill clerk in the office, and from it and others is made the waybill or bills for that particular car.

Where the volume of freight received at a given station is large, it is customary to put all packages for a common destination, as far as possible, in a car by themselves, thus making what are termed "straight" cars. This is not always possible, however, or if attempted would lead to loading a very large number of cars with but light loads. So that it becomes necessary to group freight for contiguous stations in one car, and again often to put freight for widely distant cities in the same car. These latter are known as "mixed" cars.

We will assume the day's receipt of freight finished, and most of the cars loaded. About 6 P.M. the house will be "pulled," that is, those cars already loaded will be taken away, and an empty "string" of cars put in their place. An hour later, this "string" will in turn be loaded and taken out, and the operation repeated, until all the day's receipt of freight is loaded. Meanwhile other freight will have been loaded direct from the shippers' carts on to cars on the receiving tracks. For all cars, there is made out in the freight-office a running slip or memorandum bill, which gives simply the car number, initials, and destination. These are given to the yardmaster or despatcher, and from them he "makes up" the trains.

To a very great degree, the good movement of freight depends upon the vigilance of the yardmasters and the care with which they execute their duties. In an important terminal yard, the yardmaster may have at all times from one to two thousand cars, loaded and empty. He must know what each car contains, what is its destination, and on what track it is. To enable him to do this, he has one or more assistants, day and night. They, in turn, will have foremen in charge of yard crews, each of the latter having immediate charge of one engine. The number of engines employed will vary constantly with the volume of the freight handled, but it is safe to assume that there will be at all times nearly as many engines employed in shifting in the various yards and important stations on a line as there are road engines used in the movement of the freight traffic.

The work of the yard goes on without intermission day and night, Sundays as well as week-days. The men there employed know no holidays, get no vacations. The loaded cars are coming from the freight-houses all day long, in greater numbers perhaps in the afternoon and evening, but the work of loading and moving cars goes on somewhere or other, at nearly all times. As often as the yardmaster gets together a sufficient number of cars for a common destination to make up a train, he gathers them together, orders a road engine and crew to be ready, and despatches them. In the make up of "through" trains, care has to be exercised to put together cars going to the same point, and to "group" the trains so that as little shifting as possible may be required at any succeeding yard or terminal, where the trains may pass. To accomplish this, a thorough knowledge of all the various routes is necessary, and minute acquaintance with the various intermediate junction yards and stations.

The train once "made up" and in charge of the road crew, its progress for the next few hours is comparatively simple. It will go the length of the "run" at a rate of probably twenty miles per hour, subject only to the ordinary vicissitudes of the road. At the end of the division, if a through train, it will be promptly transferred to another road crew with another engine, and so on. Each conductor takes the running slip for each car in his train. He also makes a report, giving the cars in his train by numbers and initials, whether loaded or empty, how secured; and detailed information in regard to any car out of order, or any slight mishap or delay to his train. These reports go to the Car Accountant. The running slips stay with the cars, being transferred from hand to hand until the cars reach their destination. At junction yards where one road terminates and connects with one or more foreign roads, a complete record is kept, in a book prepared especially for the purpose, of every car received from and delivered to each connecting road. A copy of this information is sent daily to the Car Accountant.

Freight Yards of the New York Central & Hudson River Railroad, West Sixty-fifth Street, New York.

"Dummy" Train and Boy on Hudson Street, New York.

A road is expected to receive back from a connecting line any car that it has previously delivered loaded. It becomes very necessary to know just what cars have been so delivered. Without such a record a road is at the mercy of its connections, and may be forced to receive and move over its length empty foreign cars that it never had in its possession before, thus paying mileage and being at the expense of moving cars that brought it no revenue whatever. The junction records put a complete check on such errors, and by their use thousands of dollars are saved annually.

To still more expedite the movement of through freight, very many so-called fast freight lines exist in this country, as, for example, the Traders' Despatch, the Star Union, the Merchants' Despatch Transportation Company, the Red, the White, the Blue, the National Despatch, etc. Some of these lines are simply co-operative lines, owned by the various railway companies whose

roads are operated in connection with one another. Their organization is simple. A number of companies organize a line, which
they put in charge of a general manager. Each company will as-

sign to the line a number of cars, the quota
of each being in proportion to its miles of
road. The general manager has control
of the line cars. He has agents who so-
licit business and employees who watch the
movement of his line cars, and report the
same to him. He keeps close record of
his business, and reports promptly to the
transportation officer of any road in his
line any neglect or delinquency he may
discover. The earnings of the line and its
expenses are all divided *pro rata* among
the roads interested. Such a line is simply an organization to insure prompt service and secure competitive business, and the entire benefit goes to the railway companies.

Other lines are in the nature of corporations, being owned by
stockholders and operating on a system of roads in accordance
with some agreement or contract. Others, again, are organized
for some special freight, and are owned wholly by firms or individuals, such as the various dressed-beef lines and some lines of

live-stock cars. These are put in service
simply for the mileage received for their use,
and in many cases the railway companies have
no interest in them whatever.

The movement of "straight" cars and
"solid" trains is comparatively simple. But
there is a very large amount of through freight,
particularly of merchandise, that cannot be put
into a "straight" car. A shipper in New York
can depend on his goods going in a straight
car to St. Louis, Denver, St. Paul, etc., but he

can hardly expect a straight car to any one of hundreds of inter
mediate cities and towns. Still less is it possible for a road at a
small country-town, where there are perhaps but one or two factories, to load straight cars to any but a very few places. To over-

come this difficulty, transfer freight-houses have to be provided. These are usually located at important terminal stations.

To them are billed all mixed cars containing through freight. These cars are unloaded and reloaded, and out of a hundred

"mixed" cars will be made probably eighty straight and the balance local. This necessarily causes some delay, but it is practically a gain in time in the end, as otherwise every car would have to be reloaded, and held at every station for which it contained freight.

Coal Car, Central Railroad of New Jersey.

The variety of articles that is offered to a railway company for transportation is endless. Articles of all sizes and weights are carried, from shoe-pegs by the carload to a single casting that weighs thirty tons. The values also vary as widely. Some cars will carry kindling wood or refuse stone that is worth barely the cost of loading and carrying a few miles, while others will be loaded with teas, silks, or merchandise, where perhaps the value of a single carload will exceed twenty-five or thirty thousand dollars. The great bulk of all freight is carried in the ordinary box-cars, coal in cars especially planned for it, and coarse lumber and stone on flat or platform cars. But very many cases arise that require especial provision to be made for each. Chicago dressed beef has made the use of the refrigerator cars well known. These cars are also used for carrying fruit and provisions. They are of many kinds, built under various patents, but all with a common purpose; that is, to produce a car wherein the temperature can be maintained uniformly at about 40 degrees. On the other hand, potatoes in bulk are brought in great quantities to the Eastern seaboard in box-cars, fitted with an additional

or false lining of boards, and in the centre an ordinary stove in which fire is kept up during the time the potatoes are in transit.

An improvement on this plan is afforded by the use of cars known as the Eastman Heater Cars. They are provided with an automatic self-feeding oil-stove, so arranged that fire can be kept up under the car for about a fortnight without attention. These are largely used in the fruit trade.

For carrying milk, special cars have to be provided, as partic-

Unloading a Train of Truck-wagons, Long Island Railroad.

ular attention has to be given to the matter of ventilation in connection with a small amount of cooling for the proper carrying of the milk. Not only the cars but the train service has to be especially arranged for in particular cases.

As an instance, the Long Island Railroad Company makes a specialty of transporting farmers' truck-wagons to market. For this purpose they have provided long, low, flat cars, each capable of carrying four truck-wagons. The horses are carried in box-cars, and one farmer or driver is carried with each team, a coach being provided for their use. During the fall of the year, they frequently carry from 45 to 50 wagons on one train, charging a small sum for each wagon, and nothing for the horses or men. These trains run three times weekly, and are arranged so as to arrive in the city about midnight, returning the next day at noon. The trains by themselves are not very remunerative, but by furnishing this accommodation, farmers who are thirty or forty miles out on Long Island can have just as good an opportunity for market-gardening as those who live within driving distance of the city.

Freight from all Quarters—Some Typical Trains.

This builds up the country farther out on the island, which in turn gives the road other business.

The movement of freight is not always successfully accomplished. In spite of good organization, every facility, incessant watchfulness, accidents will occur, freight will be delayed, cars will break down, trains will meet with disaster. The consequences sometimes fall heavily on the railway companies. The loss is frequently out of all proportion to the revenue. The following instance is from the writer's own experience:

Some carpenters repairing a small low trestle left chips and shavings near one of the bents. A passing train dropped some ashes. The shavings caught fire and burnt one or two posts in one bent. The section men failed to notice the fire. Toward evening a freight train came to the trestle, the burnt bent gave way, and the train was derailed. Two men were killed, one severely injured, and eighteen freight cars were burned. The resulting loss to the railroad company was $56,113. Of this amount, the loss paid on freight was $39,613.12. As a matter of interest, and to show the disparity between the value of the commodities and the earnings from freight charges received by the railway company, the amount of each is given here in detail, taken from the actual records of the case:

Property destroyed.	Amount paid by railroad company.	Freight charges on the same.
Butter, 200 pounds at 35 cents	$70 00	$0 50
Ore, 75 9 tons at $3.50	265 80	56 91
Paper, 4,600 pounds	269 10	8 74
Pulp, 10,400 pounds	160 00	12 65
Shingles, 85 M	192 50	11 00
Horsenails	2,986 06	37 44
Lumber	252 00	18 40
Apples, 159 barrels	508 80	15 26
Hops, 209 bales, 37,014 pounds	34,908 86	59 22
	$39,613 12	$220 12

This was during the fall of 1882, when hops sold in New York for over $1 per pound.

The plan of payment for car service by the mile run, without reference to time, has the merit of simplicity and long-established usage.   It is, however, in reality, crude and unscientific, and has brought with it, in its train, numerous disadvantages.

The owner of a car is entitled, first, to the proper interest in his investment, that is, on the value of the car; second, to a proper amount for wear and tear or for repairs.   The life of a freight car may be reasonably estimated at ten years, so that ten per cent. on its value would be a fair interest-charge.   The average amount for repairs varies directly as to the distance the car moves, and may be put at one-half cent per mile run.

It will be seen that by the ordinary method of payment the car-owner is compensated for interest at the rate of $\frac{1}{4}$ of a cent for the time that the car is in motion, but receives nothing for all the time the car is at rest.   If cars could be kept in motion for any considerable portion of each twenty-four hours, this would prove ample. But in practice it is found that few roads succeed in getting an average movement of all cars for more than one hour and a half in each twenty-four.   This gives about five per cent. interest on the value of the car, only one-half of what is generally conceded to be a fair return.   Still further, there is no inducement to the road on which a foreign car is standing to hasten its return home.   On the contrary, there is a direct advantage in holding the car idle until a proper load can be found for it, rather than return it home empty. The most serious abuses of the freight business of the country have grown from this state of affairs.   It costs nothing but the use of the track to hold freight in cars; consequently freight is held in cars instead of being put in storehouses, frequently for weeks and months at a time.

There is but little earnest attempt made to urge consignees to remove freight; on the contrary, the consignees consider that they can leave their freight as long as they choose, and that the railroad companies are bound to hold it indefinitely.

One special practice has grown up as a result of this condition, that of shippers sending freight to distant points to their own order.   This practice is most prolific of detention to cars, and yet is so strongly rooted in the traffic arrangements of the country that it is most difficult to put an end to it.   Cars "to order" will frequently stand for weeks before the contents are sold and the consignee is discovered, during which time the cars accumulate,

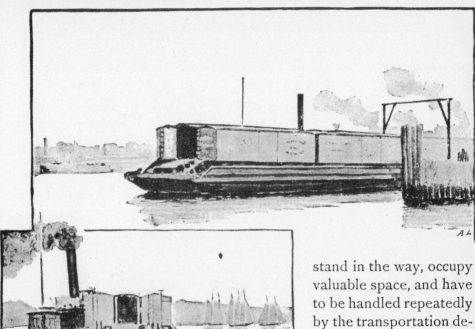

Floating Cars, New York Harbor.

stand in the way, occupy valuable space, and have to be handled repeatedly by the transportation department of the road, all at the direct cost of handling to the road itself, and loss of interest to the owner of the car.

Only two methods have so far been suggested to abate or put an end to the evils which have been but slightly indicated above. The first is a change in the method of payment for car service to a compensation based upon time as well as mileage, which is commonly known as the " per diem plan."

This plan consists in paying for the use of all foreign cars a fixed sum per mile run, based on the supposed cost of repairs of the car, and a price per day based upon what is estimated to be a fair return for the interest on its value. This plan was originally suggested by a convention of car accountants, and was brought up and advocated by Mr. Fink, the Chairman of the Trunk Line Commission, in New York, in the fall of 1887. At his suggestion, and largely through his influence, it was tried by a few of the roads (the Trunk Lines and some of their immediate connections) during the early part of the year 1888; the amounts as then fixed being one-half cent per mile run, and fifteen cents per day. The results of this experiment, while they were quite satisfactory to the friends of the proposed change, yet were not sufficiently conclusive to demonstrate the value of the plan to those who were indifferent or hostile to it.

For various reasons, chiefly local to the roads in question, the plan was discontinued after a few months' trial. The experiment resulted, however, in the collection of a large mass of statistics and other data, the study of which has led many to believe that the plan is the proper solution of the difficulties experienced, and, if adjusted so as not to add too much to the burden of those railway companies who are borrowers of cars, that it would meet with the approval of the railway companies throughout the country. It certainly provided a strong inducement to all roads to promptly handle foreign cars, and in that particular it proved a great advance over the existing methods of car service. The charge per day of fifteen cents was found too high in practice. Ten cents per day and a half-cent per mile would produce a net sum to the car-owner very slightly in excess of three-fourths of a cent per mile run. While this appears but small, yet it would be quite sufficient to amount in the aggregate to a considerable sum, and would serve to urge all railway companies to promptly unload and send home foreign cars. This plan would result, if generally adopted, in largely increasing the daily movement or mileage of all cars, or, what would be equivalent, would practically amount to a very considerable increase in the equipment of the country.

The plan has recently been approved by the General Time Convention, and there is strong probability that it will be very extensively adopted and given a trial by all the railways during the year 1890.

The second method of remedying the existing evils of car service is in a uniform and regular charge for demurrage, or car rental, to be collected by all railroad companies with the same regularity and uniformity that they now collect freight charges. This car rental, or demurrage charge, would not be in any sense a revenue to the car-owner; the idea of it being that it is a rental to the delivering company, not only for the use of the car but for the track on which it stands, and the inconvenience and actual cost that the

company is put to in repeated handling a car that is held awaiting the pleasure of the consignee to unload. The difficulty in the
way of making such a charge has been the unwillingness of any
railroad company to put any obstacle in the way of the free movement of freight to its line, and the fear that an equivalent charge
would not be made by some one of its competitors. Of late, however, the serious disadvantages resulting from the privileges given
to consignees at competing points, by allowing them to hold cars
indefinitely, have led the different railway companies to come together and agree upon a uniform system of demurrage charges at
certain competing points.

If these two plans could be put into operation simultaneously,
a fair and uniform method of charging demurrage, coupled with
the per diem and mileage plan for car service, the results would
be most satisfactory not only to the railway companies and car-
owners, but also to the community.

The matter of freight transportation is a vast one, and whole
chapters might be written on any one of the various topics that
have been but slightly mentioned in this sketch.

The subject is fraught with difficulties ; new complications
arise daily which, each in its turn, have to be met and mastered.
The publicity recently given to the various phases of the railway
problem has done much to enlighten the public mind in regard to
these difficulties.

The result has already been evident in the growing spirit of
mutual forbearance and good-will between the railway companies
and the public. 'Let us hope that this will continue, and that as
time goes on their relations will steadily improve, so that the public,
while yielding nothing of their legitimate demand for safe, prompt,
and convenient service, will at the same time see that this can only
be secured by allowing the railways a fair return for the services
rendered ; while the railways will learn that their true interest lies
in the best service possible at moderate, uniform rates.

HOW TO FEED A RAILWAY.

By BENJAMIN NORTON.

The Many Necessities of a Modern Railway—The Purchasing and Supply Departments—Comparison with the Commissary Department of an Army—Financial Importance—Immense Expenditures—The General Storehouse—Duties of the Purchasing Agent—The Best Material the Cheapest—Profits from the Scrap-heap—Old Rails Worked over into New Implements—Yearly Contracts for Staple Articles—Economy in Fuel—Tests by the Best Engineers and Firemen—The Stationery Supply—Aggregate Annual Cost of Envelopes, Tickets, and Time-tables—The Average Life of Rails—Durability of Cross-ties—What it Costs per Mile to Run an Engine—The Paymaster's Duties—Scenes during the Trip of a Pay-car.

HE commissary or supply department of a railroad is not unlike that of a large army. Like a vast army, its necessities are many, and the various departments which make up the whole system must be provided with their necessary requirements in order to accomplish the end for which it is operated. If, again, we regard a railroad as a huge animal, the quantity of supplies needed to fill its capacious maw is something overwhelming. It is always hungry, and the daily bill of fare (which includes pretty much everything known to trade) is gone through with an appetite as vigorous and healthy at the end as it exhibits in the beginning. Yet how few there are who realize the important part this one feature plays in the operation of the thousands of miles of railroad throughout the world! Upon the proper conduct of this department depends very largely the success of any road, so far as its relation to the stockholders is concerned; for while, as has been the case in the past, combinations and pools have aided in maintaining rates, and have served to increase the income, and attention has been paid to securing additional business in every possible way, the "out-goes" have often been over-

looked, to the detriment of dividends and the general welfare of the property.

The supplies must be furnished in any event, in order that the various departments may perform their allotted duties—coal for the engines, stationery for the clerks, ties and rails for the tracks, oils for the lubrication of the thousands of axles daily turning, passage-tickets for the travellers, and a thousand and one things which are absolutely necessary for the safe and efficient conduct of every railroad in active operation. Each item serves its purpose, and, properly assimilated, keeps alive all the functions of one vast and complicated system. It is easy to see, then, the importance, first, of proper economy in buying, and then a correct and systematic distribution of all supplies. On the Philadelphia & Reading Railroad, for instance, the annual supply bills aggregate more than $3,000,000, covering such supplies as those just mentioned, and, in fact, everything which is purchased and used in the operation of the road; so that on a large system like that, the commissary department requires no end of detail, both in the purchase and the distribution of all material.

The expenditure for lubricating oils, waste, and greases alone amounts to more than $150,000 per annum, while the outlay for fuel represents about $1,200,000, and this is comparatively a small sum, since that road is a coal road, so called, and the cost for fuel, as a matter of course, is reduced to a minimum. There the store-room system, which has now been pretty generally adopted by many of the larger roads, is fully exemplified. With a General Store-keeper in charge, all supplies purchased are accounted for through him, and distributions are made daily among the sub-store rooms, which are located at convenient points; and they in turn distribute among the various departments, for consumption, all accounting daily to the General Store-keeper at Reading.

To give an idea as to the quantity of material required in the service on such a road, it may be stated that from twelve to fif teen car-loads of supplies per day are shipped to various points. When we consider that an ordinary car will carry from fifteen to twenty tons of freight, we find that the annual requirements will average about four thousand car-loads, or, say, about fifty thousand tons, and if all the cars were made up into one solid train they would occupy fully twenty-five miles of track, and consume an hour and a half passing a given point running at the ordinary speed of freight-trains.

To account carefully for all this requires necessarily a large army of clerks and other assistants, though, with the fundamental principles correct, it is no more difficult to account for large quantities than for small. The supplies are purchased in the first instance, delivered at the General Storehouse, are there weighed or measured and receipted for, are then distributed on requisition, and finally delivered to the several departments when needed; are charged out to the various accounts, after consumption, and all returns and records are finally kept on the books of the General Store-keeper.

It would be a large army indeed which would require so much for its maintenance; and, remembering the hundreds of roads, small and large, throughout the country, the measure of one's comprehension is nearly reached in estimating the amount of money and the thousands of tons of material represented.

If the buyer of railroad stocks for investment, besides looking into the returns of freight and passenger business for his decision, would investigate carefully the method adopted for the purchase and distribution of supplies on any road in which he may be interested, he might get information enough to satisfy himself that a large portion of the earnings were dribbling out through this department, and that, as a result, his stock might eventually cease to be a dividend payer.

In the matter of buying, the result depends entirely upon the purchasing agent, and this position must necessarily be occupied by a man of honor and integrity, coupled with a reasonable amount of shrewdness and aptitude for such business. As this department covers to a greater or less degree pretty much all the known branches of trade, the buyer cannot, under ordinary circumstances, thoroughly master the whole field as an expert; but he can nevertheless inform himself in the most important articles of manufacture to the extent of preventing deception or fraud. The field is extensive, and the sooner railroad companies realize that the purchasing agent is not a mere order clerk, the sooner they will discover that their disbursements for supplies are very much less, and that the chief part of the leakage has found its source in this very department.

Exactly the same principles are involved in this matter as in the case of a thrifty proprietor of a country-store, whose profits each year depend materially upon the closeness and care with which his stock in trade is purchased from the wholesale dealers in a large city. A purchasing agent's experience is varied in the extreme, dealing as he does with all classes of salesmen and business houses. There is no end to the operations which skilful salesmen go through in offering their stock; but after some experience a sharp buyer will be able to fortify himself against the best of them—even against the clever vender of varnishes who disposed of one hundred barrels of his wares in small lots to different buyers, on a sample of maple-sirup. On the other hand, a salesman who, when a buyer asked him if his oil gummed, replied that "it gummed beautifully," lost the chance of ever selling any goods in that quarter.

As has been said, the ordinary or general supplies consumed in the operation of the average railroad include almost everything known to trade. Tobacco, for the gratification of the taste of a gang of men out on the road with the snow-plough, is not outside the list; and even pianos, for some trains (since the days of absolute comfort and possible extravagance have begun) for the benefit of passengers setting out on long journeys; nor do we lose sight of books, bath-tubs, and barbers. The practical feature involved, however, calls for an endless variety of expensive as well as inexpensive materials.

It is a safe rule to follow that anything which goes into the construction either of track, equipment, or buildings, should be the best. Care should always be exercised against the use of any material the failure of which might be the cause of loss of life, and consequently result in heavy damages to the company. Iron alone enters so extensively into railroad construction and operation that it is safe to say three-fourths of all manufactured in this country is consumed directly or indirectly in this way; and besides its use in rails and fastenings (the latter including spikes, fish-plates, and bolts and nuts), and in the many thousand tons of car-wheels and axles annually required, there must be reckoned the almost unlimited number of castings daily required in the way of brake-shoes, pedestals, draw-heads, grate-bars, etc. The lumber and timber for buildings, bridges, platforms, and crossings, and the large quantity of glass which is necessary, are among other large items of expenditure.

Lubricating and illuminating oils, paints and varnishes, soaps, chalk, bunting, hardware, lamps, cotton and woollen waste, clocks, brooms, and such metals as copper, pig tin, and antimony are only a few of the many articles of diet which a railroad requires to keep body and soul together, and give it strength to perform the great duty it owes to commerce and the public. After they have all served their purposes, such as cannot be worked over again in the shops, and are not entirely consumed, are consigned to the scrap-heap under the head of " old material "—an all-important consideration in the economical management of any road. On many roads very little attention is paid to the sale of scrap. As a general rule, the purchasing agent has charge of it, and if he shows any shrewdness in buying, he will exercise more or less ingenuity in selling. Most railroad scrap has a fixed value in the market. Quotations for old rails, car-wheels, and wrought iron are found in all the trade journals ; but as in buying one can usually buy of someone at prices less than market price, so in selling he can often find a buyer who is willing to pay more than the regular quotation. As it is found not wise in the long run to purchase ahead on some prospective rise, so in selling it is equally true that holding scrap over upon the possibility of a rise in prices is not always for the best advantage.

There has always been a demand for old iron rails, and recently use for old steel rails has been found. They are worked over at the rolling mills into crowbars and shovels, spikes, fish-plates, bolts, and other necessary things to be employed in construction and maintenance. Not long since an experiment with old steel rails was successfully performed, whereby they were melted and poured into moulds for use as brake-shoes. The result showed a casting of unusual hardness which would outwear three ordinary cast-iron shoes. This opens up an entirely new field in railroad economy, for with ordinary foundry appliances accumulations of old steel rails can be worked over and cast into all sorts of shapes and patterns to better advantage than selling them at a nominal

price to outside buyers. While worn-out car-wheels will generally bring more money from wheel manufacturers than they command in the open market, it has not always been found the best
policy to compel the mill from which the new wheels are purchased to take too many of them. It is apt to encourage the use
of too much old material in the manufacture of the new ; and while
the company may consider that it is realizing much more money
on sales of the old wheels than the market price, it does not take
into account the inferior stock it is getting back, or the fact that
possibly when the mileage is reckoned the wheels have signally
failed to run as long as they ought. In the aggregate about ten
per cent. of the original cost of all supplies purchased is realized
out of the sales of old material. From cast-iron wheels and old
rails, however, the percentage is much larger, for while at present
new passenger car-wheels of this class, weighing about five hundred and fifty pounds, are worth about ten dollars each, they will
bring in the market, when worn out after running say fifty thousand miles, about twenty dollars per ton. Four wheels go to the
ton, which represents five dollars per wheel, or fifty per cent.
of the original cost. With old rails the percentage is even higher,
in the present condition of the rail market. Old iron rails are
worth within four or five dollars of the price of new steel, and the
old steel about seventy per cent. of the price of the new. These
high percentages assist in making up for the materials which are
entirely consumed in the service, and which never form a part of
the ordinary scrap-heap, such as oils, waste, and paints.

While the majority of general supplies just mentioned briefly
may be arranged for as required and purchased from month to
month upon regular requisitions, there are certain staple articles
which are provided for in advance by contract. Among them
principally are the engine-coal, rails and ties, stationery, passage-
tickets, and time-tables. More money is expended for such supplies than for any others, and contracts with responsible business
houses, for their delivery at fixed prices for the limit of at least a
year, are generally made to insure, in the first place, the lowest
market rates and, again, to make the delivery certain.

Locomotive fuel is the largest single item of expense in the
operation of any road, the consumption of it running up as high as

a million tons per annum on some large roads ; and while there are a few exceptional cases where wood is used as fuel, coal is the necessary element in nearly every case in America to-day.

Of the two general varieties—bituminous or soft, and anthracite or hard—it is safe to say that bituminous coal is the more economical, assuming that the grade employed is the best, this economy lying both in the original cost and the fact that the bulk of it goes to serve its purpose, there being comparatively little waste in the way of ashes ; while the anthracite produces many ashes and clinkers, requires much more care and attention on the part of the stoker or fireman, and costs, as a general rule, about thirty per cent. more. Economy, however, should not be carried too far in any branch of the service, and if the passenger traffic be heavy the use of soft coal may be a great detriment. To a traveller there can be nothing more disagreeable than the smoke and cinders emanating from it ; and if, besides this, the road be an especially dusty one, the combination of dust, smoke, and cinders will be quite sufficient to turn the tide of travel in some other direction and over another route.

For freight service bituminous coal is decidedly the best, and perhaps might not be out of place on short local passenger trains ; but the company that provides hard-coal-burning engines for passenger trains, and soft-coal burners for freight, does about the right thing, and economizes as far as practicable in this particular. In making contracts for this important commodity the necessity of careful tests in advance is very apparent, and such trials are generally left with the best engineers and firemen ; otherwise it might be difficult to get at all the qualifications. On some roads inducements offered to firemen have brought the consumption of fuel down to the most economical point, and it is surprising how much depends upon their good judgment in this matter.

Now that heating cars direct from the engines is coming into general use, and State legislatures have given the subject their consideration, the consumption of the domestic sizes of coal as fuel in cars is growing less ; but this, too, is still a very important matter.

Stationery is not only a very significant item, but also an expensive one. This includes all the forms and blanks used in the conduct of the freight and passenger business, and there is an endless variety of them—the inks, pens, pencils, mucilage, sealing-wax, and envelopes, besides many other odds and ends. Perhaps the envelopes represent one of the largest single items of expense in this line. The hundreds of thousands of them used in the course of a year, even at low prices, mean an outlay of many thousands of dollars. Agents must send in daily reports, there must be covers for all the correspondence passing between the different departments, while the daily average amount of outside correspondence is very considerable. It is surprising how many dollars might be saved in this direction, not only by a judicious contract, but by a careful use of the supply.

When a railroad company takes up the question of time-tables, it has a matter of importance to handle which on many roads receives very little consideration. When the passenger traffic is heavy, the number of travellers during the year running into the millions, the demand for time-tables is very large. This refers directly to the time-table sheets or folders, which every company must keep on hand at its stations, and in other public places and hotels, for the convenience of the traveller, in addition to the printed schedules which are framed and hung up conspicuously on the walls of its waiting-rooms. A neat and attractive folder for general circulation is very desirable, particularly if competition is very strong. There is more virtue in a neatly made up schedule of trains than one would suppose. One in doubt is apt to reason that the road is kept up in a corresponding condition, and that the trains are made up on the same plan, and consequently would prefer to go by that route rather than by one whose trains were advertised on cheap leaflets.

Fifteen thousand to twenty thousand dollars per annum for envelopes alone is spent on some roads, and twice as much more perhaps for time-tables.

Passage-tickets, including all varieties of regular and special tickets, such as mileage books or coupons, family trip-books, and school-tickets are also an item of large expense, the annual consumption covering many tons, which once used are of no value save as waste paper; yet they are absolutely indispensable in the operation of the road. Yearly contracts for these are made, and while the actual cost of a single ticket may not exceed *one mill*, the aggregate on a road carrying fifteen millions to twenty millions or more passengers per annum is considerable.

To induce the public to travel, and encourage shippers to send their freight to market over any road, attention must first be paid to the condition of the track and rolling stock.

It is not economy to allow anything to be out of repair, on the supposition that it is less expensive than it would be to spend comparatively little from day to day to keep it up. The day of reckoning will come in the end, and the sacrifice will be considerable. As the track is the fundamental feature, the cross-ties or sleepers and rails should be the best. Iron rails are practically out of date, and it is fair to assume that the time is approaching when wooden ties will be things of the past. Where the traffic is light, heavy steel rails may not be necessary ; but it has been generally found economical to put in use rails which do not weigh less than sixty-seven or seventy pounds to the yard; an even greater weight than this is not ill-advised—they require fewer cross-ties to the mile, and in consequence the force of men required to keep the track in condition is less. Light rails are soon worn and battered out on a road over which heavy engines are run and large trains are hauled. The powerful locomotives now built require a well-kept track and a solid and substantial road-bed. Heavier and faster trains have tended to reduce the average life of rails, even though the weight of the rails has also been steadily increasing. Circumstances vary on the different roads, but it is safe to say that eight to ten per cent. of all rails in the track must be renewed every year. This brings the average life of the steel rails down to about twelve years, under ordinary conditions. On some divisions, however, where the traffic is frequent, and in yards where a good deal of switching is done, and the rails are under pressure constantly, the average is, of course, very much less—even as low as two or three years.

Aside from the durability of the timber employed, plenty of face for the rail bearings, and uniform thickness and length, are very important requirements in contracts for ties. While white oak is generally considered the most durable for this purpose, the growth of this timber is limited except in certain sections of the country, so that cedar, cypress, chestnut, and yellow pine are more commonly used than any other class. The millions of them used for renewals and new roads each year are gradually reducing our forests; and, like some of the European roads, we shall some day fall back upon metal, which (while its life may not be measured) will make so rigid a track that the traveller over long distances will be worn out with his journey, and the rolling stock will require frequent repairs and overhauling. The practice of creosoting cross-ties is growing rapidly, and this tends to increase their durability three or four times. While the first cost of such ties may be double that for the unprepared timbers, the result in the end is economical, for the labor alone required to take out an old tie and put in a new one costs at least twelve cents.

The general store-room is properly the intermediate stage, so far as supplies are concerned, between the different departments of the road and the Auditor, who charges up all material used to the different accounts into which his system is divided. Properly, everything in the nature of material, however small, directly or indirectly passes through the Store-keeper's books. An account is kept with each locomotive, station agent, switchman, and flagman, so that to a penny everything consumed in the operation of a road is accurately known. To accomplish this the Store-keeper, of course, must be a good accountant, and at the same time be more or less of an expert in railroad material. Under an economical administration of his affairs he is able to save a great deal of money for his company. By his system, with the aid of data from the mechanical department, he can tell the average number of miles run during the year to a pint of oil or a ton of coal; the number of pounds of coal consumed per mile run, as well as the number of pints of oil for the same distance. He can give in detail the cost in cents per mile run for all the oil, tallow, and waste, fuel, and other supplies consumed, and can account to a nicety for all the lanterns, brooms, hardware, and other material which he has received and distributed.

The following statement of averages represents fairly what it costs to run a locomotive under ordinary conditions:

Averages.

Number of miles run to pint of oil............................ 15.32
Number of miles run to ton of coal........................... 46.17
Number of pounds of coal per mile run........................ 48.62
Number of pints of oil per mile run.......................... 0.06

Cost in Cents per Mile Run.

	Cents.
For oil, tallow, and waste	0.32
For fuel	7.42
For engineers	3.60
For firemen	1.79
For wipers and watchmen	1.25
For water supply	0.49
For supplies (miscellaneous)	0.10
For repairs	2.40
Total	17.37

He will find that some engineers and firemen are more extravagant than others, and that some station agents and flagmen do not perform their respective duties with near so much regard for economy as others do under exactly similar circumstances. In such cases a report is made and a reminder from the Superintendent follows, calling attention to such carelessness. The result is apparent at the next monthly comparison.

Prompt payment of all supply bills helps to insure economy, and any company unable to make its payments promptly and regularly, suffers to a greater or less extent always ; for a firm not able to know whether its accounts are to be settled in thirty or ninety days cannot afford to allow all the discounts which it otherwise might, and this may mean an extra expense every year of many thousands of dollars.

So far as the employees are concerned, it is for the best interests of the company to have a fixed time for the pay-day. They need their money and should get it regularly. Any road on which the men are paid at uncertain times may be subject to incalculable losses. It is apt to provoke dishonesty and carelessness. The road which is bankrupt and forced to pass its pay-day to some indefinite time is always hampered by some of the most inferior class of servants in the market. Except in some instances where special laws have been passed requiring railroad companies to meet their pay-rolls oftener, once each month is generally recognized as pay-time, and on large roads it would be simply out of the question for the pay-rolls to be made up correctly and the men paid off sooner. The paymaster is the wage-distributing medium, and by virtue of his generosity will command as much respect as the

President of the road. No officer's face is more familiar than his, and surely no one connected with the institution is looked for with more eagerness by the hard-working employees. It is no easy task he has to perform, and the responsibility for the millions of dollars paid out in this way annually is very great. This responsibility, however, has been very much reduced on some roads, where wages are paid by checks entirely. Under some circumstances this system will not work satisfactorily, especially on a road running through a sparsely settled country. The employees may have to stand a good round discount to some store-keeper or tradesman in order to secure their money. The best and most satisfactory return for services can be nothing less than solid cash ; it encourages better attention to business and relieves the men from possible annoyance and inconvenience. The Paymaster's car, which is virtually a moving bank or cashier's office, and arranged conveniently for the payment of money to the men as they pass through, is generally run " special," upon notice in advance to all foremen or heads of departments, either by telegraph or, as on some roads, by the display of special signal flags, which are carried on the front end of the locomotive of some regular train the day before the car is run over any division. In this way all men employed along the line of the road, whether at or between stations, are notified of the Paymaster's coming, and it does not usually require any other inducement than this to bring them all out. There is nothing that will prompt them to jump higher and run faster than the whistle of the pay-train as it comes around the curve to the station. Men have been known to forget their names, and do other foolish things under the excitement of drawing their month's pay. The fellow who said he could not write all his name when requested by the Paymaster to sign the pay-roll, but offered to write as much of it as he could, after some deliberation made a cross on the sheet with all the care and nicety he could muster. Others who could not write have been very slow to admit it, and have pleaded haste as an excuse for not doing so. So far as Italians are concerned (and what railroad service is now complete without its gang of Italian laborers ?), they are usually designated by numbers, and in some cases their foremen have thought it well to name them after prominent statesmen or other public men, or possibly some of the head officials of the company. To run across twenty-five or thirty Daniel Websters on the same road is not surprising, and the President of the company himself is liable to have a half-dozen namesakes throughout the different divisions of his road. A cage of jabbering monkeys is not a more amusing spectacle than some gangs of Italian laborers receiving their month's pay.

The pay-department can be made very systematic, and to promote economy and accuracy it is absolutely necessary that it should be. The Paymaster is not simply a medium through whom wages are distributed. He may be one of the most important officers of his company, and ferret out frauds and dishonesty which otherwise might never be discovered. He knows all the men, and they, of course, know him. In fact, he is the only one connected with the road whose recognition among all the employees is absolutely certain.

Some idea of the enormous amount of money earned annually by the railroad men in this country may be formed from the statement that it requires about $1,000,000 per month to pay twenty thousand men, and there are a good many roads on which the average monthly pay-roll embraces from fifteen thousand to twenty thousand names ; in some cases even more.

When the pay-rolls are all turned over to the Paymaster, properly approved by each head of department, he notifies the Superintendent or Trainmaster of his proposed trip, mapping out in detail the route, which is usually the same each month. The signals or telegrams are sent ahead to the various foremen, and the car is ordered ready for the journey. The funds are arranged in denominations to suit the circumstances, with plenty of small change, and enough money for a day or two only at a time is provided. The pay for the flagmen at crossings, and switchmen on the road, as well as for the agents at small stations, is generally done up in envelopes, and, as the train speeds by, the packages are handed or thrown out at the proper places ; and sometimes, to warrant a safe delivery, a forked stick is used, into which the envelope is put, thus giving it plenty of weight and saving it from being tumbled about promiscuously on the ground. Much time is saved in this way, and the pay-train is able to keep well out of the way of any regular train which may be following. So the pay-car flies along, only stopping at some large station where the number of employees en-

gaged is sufficient to warrant it.   These are quickly paid off, however, and the journey is continued.   Perhaps at some junction a
freight crew is met ; and as these fellows have to get their money
when they can, a stop is made on the road to give them a chance
to do it.   At some stations are found two or three gangs of section
or track men, a watchman, an agent and his assistant, a pumper,
and possibly a mail-carrier.   Perhaps a discharged trainman will
turn up also, who may have part of a month's pay coming to him.

Later in the day it may be a shop gang of five hundred or one
thousand men, consisting of carpenters, painters, machinists, and
boiler-makers, and these are paid in order, each set of men by itself.   There is no noise or disturbance, everything goes like clock-
work, as all pass through in regular order, each gang or class preceded by its foreman, and the men arranged in line in the order in
which their names appear on the pay-rolls.   When night comes,
and two or three hundred miles of road have been covered, the
balance of the funds is carefully locked up in the safe on board, the
car run in upon some convenient siding, and the engine housed for
a wiping and a thorough preparation for the next day's run.   The
car is generally provided with comfortable beds for the Paymaster
and his clerks, and during the paying-off time they practically live
in the car.   This insures early starts in the morning, and on large
roads the necessity for haste is very apparent, where possibly two
or three weeks are consumed each month in paying off the rolls.

The average traveller, spinning across the country at forty
miles an hour, is not apt to think of the countless details involved
in the make-up of the train in which he rides or the track over
which he is wheeled ; but when he considers how safely the millions of passengers are annually carried over the one hundred and
fifty thousand miles or more of railroad in this country alone, he
may be brought to realize that quite as much depends upon the
quality of the material entering into the construction of the train
and tracks as upon the efficiency of the engineer in the cab, or the
conductor, brakeman, switchmen, and train-despatcher who perform their respective responsible duties in connection therewith.
Feeding a railroad, then, means a great deal more than the majority of mankind supposes.

THE RAILWAY MAIL SERVICE.

By THOMAS L. JAMES.

An Object Lesson in Postal Progress—Nearness of the Department to the People—The First Travelling Post-Office in the United States—Organization of the Department in 1789—Early Mail Contracts—All Railroads made Post-routes—Compartments for Mail Clerks in Baggage-cars—Origin of the Present System in 1862—Important Work of Colonel George S. Bangs—The " Fast Mail" between New York and Chicago—Why it was Suspended—Resumption in 1877—Present Condition of the Service—Statistics—A Ride on the " Fast Mail"—Busy Scenes at the Grand Central Depot—Special Uses of the Five Cars—Duties of the Clerks—How the Work is Performed—Annual Appropriation for Special Mail Facilities—Dangers Threatening the Railway Mail Clerk's Life—An Insurance Fund Proposed—Needs of the Service—A Plea for Radical Civil Service Reform.

AT the Centennial Exposition at Philadelphia, in the Post-Office exhibit, was a double picture showing the postal service at the beginning of the century and as it is to-day. On one side was a postman —perhaps Franklin—on horseback, jogging over a corduroy road, " through the forest primeval," making a mile or two an hour; and on the other a representation of the fast mail train, the " catcher " taking a pouch from the " crane " as it passes at the rate of fifty miles an hour ! Standing in the foreground is the pretty daughter of the village postmaster with the mail pouch just thrown from the car in her hand, a group of rustics, with ill-concealed admiration in their eyes, watching her as the swiftly passing train goes on its journey. This picture is not, perhaps, a work of art, but it is an " object lesson," giving at a glance the progress that our country has made in a hundred years.

Of all the executive departments of the Government, the Post-Office is the one nearest the people, and the one with which they are the most familiar. In addition to its work of collecting, trans-

porting, and delivering legitimate mail matter, viz., letters, newspapers, and magazines, it is the greatest express company of the

continent, since it has
an office at almost ev-
ery cross-roads, even
carrying merchandise
cheaper (considering
the distance) than its
rivals. Its registra-
tion system affords a
means of forwarding
valuable packages, at
a s l i g h t additional
cost, with almost ab-
solute security. It is
the greatest banking
institution on this side
of the Atlantic. The
transactions o f i t s
money-order system,
not only in our own
country, but with al-
most every nation in
the civilized w o r l d

Postal Progress, 1776–1876.
(Facsimile of a print in the Post-Office Department.)

(Russia and Spain excepted), run up to wellnigh fabulous sums.
Its drafts are easily obtained and cheap. Its notes are "gilt
edged," and have never been repudiated. With the creation of
the Postal Savings Bank system, the working people's department in its organization will approach perfection.

The first mention of a travelling post-office occurs in a me-
morial addressed to Congress in November, 1776, by Ebenezer
Hazard, Postmaster-General under the Continental Congress, in
which he states that, owing to the frequent removals of the Continental Army, he was subjected to extraordinary expense, difficulties, and fatigues, "having paid an exorbitant price for every
necessary of life, and having been obliged, for want of a horse—
which could not be procured—to follow the army on foot."

Directly after the inauguration of General Washington, in

April, 1789, the organization of the Post-Office Department followed, and Samuel Osgood, of Massachusetts, was appointed Postmaster-General. That the people might derive the greatest possible advantage from an institution peculiarly their own, this gigantic monopoly—for it is nothing else—was created, and all competition forbidden. The Postmaster-General had then but one clerk, and there were but 75 post-offices and 1,875 miles of post-roads in the United States; the cost of mail transportation being $22,081, the total revenue, $37,935, the total expenditures, $32,-140; leaving a surplus of $5,795. From this time until 1836 the contracts made for the transportation of the mails do not mention any kind of service on post-roads except stages, sulkies, four-horse post-coaches, horseback, packets, and steam-boats.

The growth of the Railway Mail Service has been coincident with that of the railway itself, and the importance of both cannot be underestimated in considering the future development of the

The Pony Express—The Relay.

country. Almost as soon as a railroad is fully organized it becomes a mail contractor with the Department.

The Act of Congress constituting every railroad in the United States a post-route was approved July 7, 1838. Postmaster-General Barry, in his annual report for 1836, speaks of the multiplication of railroads in many parts of the country, and suggests it as a subject worthy of inquiry, whether measures may not be taken to secure the transportation of the mail on them, and adds : " Al-

The Overland Mail Coach—A Star Route.

ready have the railroads between Frenchtown, in Maryland, and Newcastle, in Delaware, and between Camden and South Amboy, in New Jersey, afforded great and important facilities to the transmission of the great eastern mail." At this time a railroad between Washington and New York was in process of construction, and Postmaster-General Barry dwelt in his report on the importance of the facilities that would be afforded for speedy service between the two cities, predicting that the run between them would probably be made in sixteen hours. The service is now performed in about five hours.

At first the facilities for mail services were very limited. Postmaster-General Kendall, in 1835, suggested that the Baltimore & Ohio Railroad Company might be asked to close in some portion of their baggage-cars, a strong lock being placed on the apartment, to which only the postmasters at Washington and Baltimore should have keys. In the same report he adds : " If wheels can be constructed which can be used alike upon the railroads and the streets of the cities respectively, the Department will furnish an entire car containing the mail to be delivered at one depot, and received at the other, asking nothing of the company but to haul it." It was even proposed at this time that the Government should have its own locomotives, everything else on the road giving the right of way to the mail train. This proposition was not adopted. The

Mail Carrying in the Country.

fear was express-ed, however, that if the Department did not have ab-solute control over the road, the people would have to depend on stage or other horse transporta-tion for mail ser-vice. All these early troubles in time passed away, and, through con-cessions on both sides, the railways soon became the most impor-tant agent of the Post-Office Department.

This, of course, was not accomplished without many trials and tribulations. It seems strange, in the light of the present, to read in an official report a remonstrance from route agents that nearly every night dead bodies were placed in the mail crates between Philadelphia and New York, and the mails packed around the coffins. This breach of good order disappeared after that time, and with it came to an end the freight methods and the old stage-coach ideas of dealing with the mails.

A separate compartment in a baggage-car, fitted up with few conveniences necessary for the distribution of local way-mail, was the beginning of the system which has developed into the luxuri-ous postal cars of the present time. As a matter of history, how-ever, it is only fair to say that the system which we then adopted had been in use for some time by our northern neighbors of Canada, who had taken it from the mother country.

The credit of suggesting the first step toward the present sys-tem has generally been given to Colonel G. B. Armstrong, who in

1864 was Assistant Postmaster at Chicago. This is incorrect; Mr. W. A. Davis, a clerk of the St. Joseph, Mo., Post-Office, where the overland mail was made up, conceived the idea, in 1862, that if the letters and papers could be assorted on the cars between Quincy and St. Joseph, the overland mail could start promptly on time. He was given permission to carry out this idea, and there are vouchers on file in the Department at Washington showing that he was paid for that specific work. In 1864 Colonel Armstrong was authorized and encouraged by the Hon. Montgomery Blair, then Postmaster-General, to undertake the difficult task of arranging and introducing the service. On August 31, 1864, he wrote: " To-day I commenced the new distribution." Subsequently, Colonel Armstrong became the first General Railway Mail Superintendent, and held this office until ill-health compelled him to resign, in 1871. To Colonel George S. Bangs, of Illinois, and his successors, Theodore N. Vail, William B. Thompson, and John Jameson, is due the excellence of the present system. Colonel Bangs was a thoroughly equipped post-office man, energetic, courageous, and progressive. Brimful of ideas, he was ever on the lookout for improvement. Never satisfied with old ways, he was constantly striving to simplify and better the service. He forgot himself in his work, and died a martyr to his duty, leaving the Travelling Post-Office of to-day a monument to his memory. While to Colonel Armstrong is due the credit for the skeleton of the system, it was the genius of Colonel Bangs that clothed the bones with flesh, developed the sinew, put the blood in circulation, and breathed into its body the breath of life. Colonel Bangs found, in 1871, that everything was disjointed, disconnected, and sluggish. There was no attempt at " certainty, security, or celerity." It was a " go-as-you-please " condition of affairs. He grappled at once with it and brought order out of chaos. He introduced a system of emulation among the employees, rewarding those who displayed proficiency by promotion over the sluggish, and thus, in fact, was probably the father of what is now known as Civil Service Reform. In 1874 he discussed the propriety of establishing a fast and exclusive mail train between New York and Chicago, " this train " (quoting his report to the Postmaster-General) " to be under the control of the Department, so far as it is necessary for the purposes designed, and to run the distance in about twenty-four hours. It is conceded by railway officials that this can be done. The importance of a line like this cannot be overestimated. It would reduce the actual time of mail between the east and west from twelve to twenty-four hours. As it would necessarily be established upon one or more of the trunk lines, having an extended system of connections, its benefit would be in no case confined, but extended through all parts of the country alike."

This report met with the approval of Postmaster-General Jewell, who ordered Bangs to negotiate with the New York Central & Hudson River Railroad and the Lake Shore Railroad for a fast mail train, leaving New York at four o'clock in the morning, and arriving at Chicago in about twenty-four hours. It was the old story of making bricks without straw. The Post-Office Department had no appropriation to pay for such facilities, hence it had to depend at first on the public spirit of the railroad authorities. Commodore Vanderbilt, the president of the companies whose lines were to be used, had had dealings with the Department, and was perhaps not altogether sanguine as to the practical issue of the experiment, or in respect to the countenance it would receive from Congress; but Mr. William H. Vanderbilt, the vice-president, lent a willing ear to Mr. Bangs's proposition, and did his utmost to aid him in putting it into effect. There being no special appropriation available for the purpose in hand, "the devil was whipped around the stump" by Colonel Bangs stipulating that if Mr. Vanderbilt would have twenty cars built and the service performed, all matter originating at or coming into the New York Post-Office, which could reach its destination at the same time by this line, should be sent by this train, and that the railway companies could have the right to demand a weighing of the mail matter at will, all railroads being paid according to weight. When the details of the plan were communicated to Commodore Vanderbilt, he is reported to have said to his son: "If you want to do this, go ahead, but I know the Post-Office Department, and you will, too, within a year." Mr. Vanderbilt did "go ahead." He constructed and equipped the finest mail train ever seen on the planet, ran it for ten months, never missed a connection at Chicago, and was always on time at New York. He did not have to wait a year, however, for a realization of the sagacious old commodore's prophecy. Within three weeks, despite the indignant protest of Colonel Bangs, the mails of three States were ordered to be taken from this and given to another route. A grosser and more wanton breach of plighted faith it would be hard to find, and its results were far-reaching and disastrous.

This train was a marvel of completeness and efficiency. It was manned by picked men, and the only complaint ever made against it was that it ran so fast that the clerks had not time to sort the mails for the post-offices between New York and Poughkeepsie. To obviate this, Colonel Bangs requested the postmaster at New York to have two hundred mail-bags dyed red, which should contain the mail for those offices nearest together, so that the crew in the train could distribute them first. There was no complaint after that. But when the dyer's bill was sent by the postmaster to the Department, it was disallowed by a clerk of the Second Assistant Postmaster-General, who, in a letter announcing the fact, said that there was no necessity for the outlay if the postal clerks did their duty. Bangs, who had just arrived at the post-office from a day and night's ride on his favorite train, was lying on a sofa half asleep in the postmaster's private office, as that official was opening his mail. When he came to that letter he handed it to Bangs. He was wide-awake in an instant. " Mr. Postmaster," said he, " do you know the man who signed this letter ? He is a wheezy priest, a fool, and a Baptist, at that. Give me the letter." The bill was allowed as soon as Bangs reached the Department. He was wrong, however, in crediting the subordinate to the Baptist faith. He was an ornament of another persuasion.

So carefully had the project been considered and adapted that the service on the Central, from the start, moved with the precision of clock-work, and was an immediate success. It is proper to say that word of what was going on between the Department and the Vanderbilt system reached the Hon. Thomas A. Scott, President of the Pennsylvania Railroad, and he at once made up his mind that the corporation under his management could not afford to be behind its great rival. One Saturday morning he telegraphed to J. D. Layng (now General Manager of the West Shore and President of the C. C. C. & I.), then General Manager of the Pennsylvania lines west of Pittsburg, to know if by the following Monday week, the date on which the train was to start, four postal cars could be built and the first one be in Chicago ready to start on its eastern trip. The answer came back, " Yes." The order was given to the Allegheny shops on Saturday afternoon, and on the following Saturday the first of the cars, complete and equipped for mail service, started for Chicago, and began its east-bound trip on Monday morning. The second and third cars were finished on Monday night, and the fourth—thus fully equipping the line—on Tuesday.

Thus had been established two splendid fast trains, and the outlook was bright for the future, when Congress, in spite of the efforts of the Post-Office Department, passed an Act reducing the already inadequate compensation to the trunk lines, for the carrying of the mails. This action brought official notice from Messrs. Vanderbilt and Scott of the discontinuance of the fast mail trains between New York City and Chicago, and that service ended.

Colonel Bangs was greatly mortified at this result, but he stood his ground and remained at his post until the close of the year. Then, worn out with never-ending toil, and disheartened by the action of Congress, he tendered his resignation and insisted on its acceptance. Parted from the Post-Office, President Grant, knowing his worth and wishing to recognize his services, appointed him Assistant Treasurer of the United States at Chicago. He lived to perform the duties of this office only a few months, as death overtook him suddenly, while on a visit to Washington on official business, December, 1876. His work, however, was not permitted to drop. He had left in the service three assistants, Theodore N. Vail, William B. Thompson—afterward Second Assistant Postmaster-General—and John Jameson, who were fully imbued with the ideas of their late chief and were fully loyal to them. They, in the order named, became his successors, and never permitted opportunities to escape wherein there was a possible benefit to the service to be secured. Although the fast mail service was suspended for lack of support from Congress, its usefulness and practicability had been so thoroughly demonstrated that an appropriation of $150,000 was

At a Way-station—The Postmaster's Assistant.

made in March, 1877, for its resumption on the trunk lines. This victory was not reached without untiring efforts on the part of Mr. Vail, and by generous support in both houses of Congress; in the Senate by the Hon. Hannibal Hamlin and James G. Blaine, of Maine, and in the House of Representatives by such broad and liberal statesmen as Mr. Waddell, of North Carolina, Mr. Randall, of Pennsylvania, and Mr. Cox, of New York.

Since then, Messrs. Thompson and Jameson have watched the progress of the work with jealous eyes, and have succeeded in extending it practically to the whole country. The present service is due not alone to the liberality of Congress, because the appropriations have been parsimonious, but to the generosity of the railways, which have performed a valuable work for a price which in many cases does not pay the expense of the necessary additional labor involved.

The Railway Mail Service at the close of the fiscal year ending June 30, 1888, gave employment to 5,094 clerks. Matter was distributed on 126,310 miles of railway, and on 17,402 miles additional closed pouches were carried. There were also operated 41 inland steam-boat lines on which postal clerks were employed. The postal clerks travelled (in crews) 122,031,104 miles by railway, and 1,767,649 miles by steam-boats. They distributed 6,528,772,060 pieces of ordinary mail matter, and handled 16,001,059 registered packages and cases, and 1,103,083 through registered pouches and inner registered sacks. The service is in charge of one General Superintendent, who has his headquarters at Washington, and it is divided into eleven divisions with a superintendent in charge of each.

The majority of people who travel on railways (and how many Americans are there who do not?) have paid passing attention to the railway mail cars as they have stood at the station preparatory to the starting of the train, and have glanced through the open doors with more or less curiosity at the scene of energy and bustle witnessed within. At such a moment, no matter how great the curiosity, it is not feasible to investigate closely, for the workers must not be hampered by the prying public, however praiseworthy the motive. To supply this pardonable desire to know how it is done, I invite my readers to accompany me in spirit on a visit to

Loading for the Fast Mail, at the General Post-Office, New York.

the Grand Central Station, to witness the preparations for the departure of train No. 11, known in railway parlance as "the New York and Chicago Fast Mail," which leaves New York every night at nine o'clock.

It must not be supposed that everything has been left until the last moment, and that the mail matter has been tumbled into the cars on the eve of departure, to be handled as best it may in the short run to Albany; for under such conditions the task would be an impossibility even to an army of trained hands. Work has been in progress since four o'clock in the afternoon, and it has been steady, hard labor every minute of the time. The five cars have been backed down to the tracks opposite Forty-fifth Street, and have been so placed that they are convenient of access to the big lumbering mail wagons which are familiar sights in the streets of the metropolis. The crew of nineteen men, skilled in the handling of mail matter, and thorough experts in the geography of the country, reported to the chief clerk and took up their stations in the various cars at the hour named. At the same time the wagons began arriving from the General Post-Office with their tons of matter which had "originated" in New York, and were soon transferring their loads to the cars, where agile hands were in waiting to receive them. Since the removal of the deadly stoves from the railway trains the occupants of the postal cars have suffered to no small extent owing to the lack of heat. These cars are provided with steam-heating apparatus which is worked from the engine, but they are occupied for five hours before the engine comes near them, and in cold weather the hands of the men employed in distributing letters become numb with cold. This is a matter which should receive prompt attention.

Before we deal with the mail matter, let us look at the cars and the men who occupy them. The train, as it leaves New York, is made up of five cars which are placed immediately behind the engine, and are followed by express and baggage cars and one passenger coach. The car next to the engine is devoted entirely to letter mail, and the four following it to papers and packages. The letter car is fifty feet in length, while those for the newspaper mail are ten feet longer. All are uniform in width, nine feet eight inches, and are six feet nine inches high in the clear. When newly built, before long and hard service had told on their appearance, their outsides were white in color, with cream-tinted borderings and gilt ornamentations, and were highly varnished. Midway on the outside, and below the windows of each car, is a large oval gilt-finished frame within which is painted the name of the car, with the words, "United States Post Office" above and below. The cars used by the New York Central are named for the Governors of the State and the members of President Garfield's cabinet. Along the upper edge and centre are painted in large gilt letters the words, "The Fast Mail Train," while on a line with these letters at the other end, in a square, are the words, in like lettering, "New York Central" and "Lake Shore." The frieze and mi-nute trimmings around the windows are of gilt finish. The body of

At the Last Moment.

the car also contains other ornamentation, including the coat-of-arms of the United States. The running gear is of the most ap-proved pattern. The platforms are enclosed by swinging doors which, when opened, afford a protected passage between the cars. This arrangement no doubt suggested the modern improvement now known as the vestibuled train. The letter car is provided with a "mail catcher," which is placed at a small door through which mail pouches are snatched from conveniently placed posts at way-side stations where stops are not made. Each car is divided into three sections, all fitted up alike with conveniences for the service to be performed. The letter car, however, is somewhat differently

Transfer of Mail at the Grand Central Station, New York.

Pouching the Mail in the Postal Car.

arranged from the others, to meet the requirements of that particular branch of the work.

In the first section of the letter car are received the pouches from the General Post-Office, which when opened are found to contain letters done up in packages of about a hundred, marked for Michigan, Indiana, New York, Ohio, Western Pennsylvania, Montana, Dakota, and California. When this mass of matter has been emptied out of the pouches and, in the vernacular of the service, "dumped up" preparatory to distribution, the section is clear for the registered mail which is worked in it. Before this is accomplished, however, much work is done; in fact, a sort of rough distribution is made. All packages which are directed to one office are distributed into pouches, which are afterward stored away until the towns are reached. The other packages are carried into the letter department for distribution, where a rack, similar to those seen in almost every post-office, although space is thoroughly economized, is used for the purpose. To give a slight idea of the work done in this section, it may be mentioned that the distribution for New York State alone requires 325 boxes. Still there is plenty of space, otherwise the third section of the car would not be used, as it is, for the distribution of Montana and Dakota newspapers. How closely everything is packed, and all available space utilized, may be imagined when it is stated that for this newspaper mail ninety-five pouches are hung in the section, and that there is still sufficient room for the storage of pouches locked up and ready for delivery, and also for the sealed registered mail. A separation of the California mail is also made in this car, so that when it reaches Chicago the pouches into which the matter is placed are transferred without delay, thus saving twenty-four hours on the time to the Pacific Coast, not by any means an unimportant accomplishment.

There have been received in this car before it moves out of the Grand Central Station between 1,000 and 1,500 packages of letters and, in addition, forty or fifty sacks of Dakota and Montana papers. To handle this mass of correspondence there are six men in addition to the chief clerk, or superintendent. This official is not assigned to any particular duty, but he supervises the general work and lends aid where it is most required. The second clerk handles letters for Ohio, Dakota, and Montana; the third clerk takes charge of those for New York State; the fourth, Illinois; the fifth opens all pouches labelled, " New York and Chicago Railway Post-Office," distributes their contents, and afterward works on Dakota and Montana papers; the sixth, Michigan State letters, and the seventh, California letter mail. The salaries of these men, intrusted with so much responsibility and of whom so much is expected, range from $900 per annum for the lowest grade to $1,300 per annum for the superintendent.

The second, or " Illinois Car," is devoted, as are the others which follow it, to the newspaper and periodical mail. In it are handled papers for Ohio, Indiana, Illinois, New York, Oregon, and Wyoming. Two clerks and two assistants man this car. The

A Very Difficult Address—known as a "sticker."

first assistant, who "faces up" papers ready to be distributed, draws mails from stalls to case, and removes boxes as fast as they are filled, has gained the sobriquet of the "Illinois derrick," owing to the heavy nature of his duties. The second, who lends what aid he can in the heavy work on the run between New York and Albany, has become known on the train as "the short stop." The third section of the car is used for storing the bags of assorted matter.

The third car is used for storing through mail for San Francisco, Omaha, and points west of Chicago.   In it are also carried
stamped envelopes from the manufacturer at Hartford, Conn., to
postmasters in the West.   This car is frequently fully loaded with
matter from the New York office when the journey is begun, and
it is then found necessary to add a similar car to the train on its
arrival at Albany for the accommodation of matter taken on by the
way and bound for the same destination.

The Michigan paper car is the fourth.   In it are handled papers

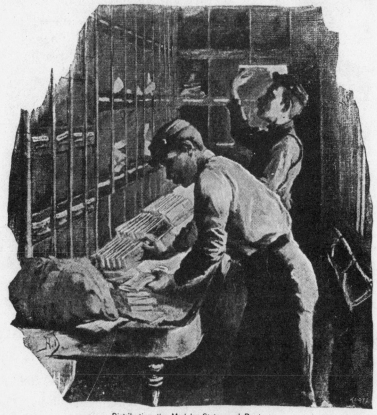

Distributing the Mail by States and Routes.

for Michigan, Iowa, and the mixed Western States.   In the first
section are piled the Iowa pouches and those for points out of
Utica, which have been distributed in the centre section, and in
the third section the distribution for Michigan, Nebraska, and
Minnesota, as well as for points reached from Buffalo, is made.

Sorting Letters in Car No. 1—The Fast Mail.

Two men perform the work of the car, one of whom has already handled the registered mail and Indiana letters in the first car.

The fifth, or California paper car, is the last mail coach on the train, as it is made up when leaving the Grand Central Station. Besides the papers for the Golden State the car carries through registered pouches to Chicago and the West, which have been made up in the New York office, and, as a usual thing, a large lot of stamped envelopes for postmasters in the West. The California letter man from the first car looks after the papers for the same State, and has an eye to the safety of the car. On reaching Albany another car is added to the train, making six in all from that point. This last addition comes from Boston, brings the morning mail from Bangor, Me., and is manned by four men.

Pouching Newspapers for California—in Car No. 5.

The run to Chicago for post-office purposes is divided into three divisions: from New York to Syracuse, from Syracuse to Cleveland, and from Cleveland to Chicago. Each division has its own crew, so that the men leaving New York are relieved at Syracuse by others, and these in turn at Cleveland. The New York crew go to work, as has been said, at 4 P.M., and if the train is on time at Syracuse, as it usually is, they arrive there at 5.35 A.M., after thirteen and a half hours of as hard work as men are called upon to do. The same evening at 8.40 they relieve the eastbound crew, and are in New York again at six o'clock on the following morning. Half an hour later they are to be found on the top floor of the General Post-Office building, comfortably ensconced in bunks and in a large and airy room, provided as a dormitory for their use by the postmaster of New York at the time of the inauguration of the fast mail service. Each crew makes three round trips and is then laid off for six days, but its members are all this time subject to extra duty, which they are called upon to perform with unpleasant frequency, particularly in holiday times.

After leaving New York, the first stop the train makes is at Poughkeepsie, but no mail is taken on there. At Albany the second halt is made, and there twenty minutes are spent in taking on the mail from New England and northeastern New York. At Palatine Bridge there is a brief stop, and after that comes Utica, where the Delaware, Lackawanna & Western, the Ontario & Western, and the Rome, Watertown & Ogdensburg roads exchange mail matter. At Syracuse more mails come, this time from the Oswego, Binghamton & Syracuse, and the Auburn & Rochester branch of the New York Central. Here also comes welcome relief for the crew which left New York. Those who follow have much to keep them busy, but the heaviest part of the work has been already performed.

From Syracuse to Cleveland there are several distributing points where mail matter is also received on the train, and the routine is continued much as already described until the crew is relieved at Cleveland. There the men of the Western Division take charge and continue the work until Elkhart, Ind., is reached. There a special force from Chicago meets the train, takes possession of a portion of the letter car, and makes the distribution for the main office and stations of the city of Chicago, thus saving much time. When the train arrives in Chicago, it makes connection with a fast mail train on the Chicago, Burlington & Quincy, as also on a like train on the Chicago, Milwaukee & St. Paul. The former train arrives at Council Bluffs about 7 P.M., and there overtakes the train which left Chicago on the previous evening. The Pacific Coast mail is thus expedited just twenty-four hours. A similar train on the St. Paul road also saves twenty-four hours' time on the trip to the northwestern portion of the Pacific Coast.

The appropriation for special facilities for the year ending June 30, 1889, was $295,987.53. The uses to which the appropriation referred to is put are explained in the following table.

Termini.	Railroad Company.	Miles.	Pay.
New York to Springfield..	New York, New Haven & Hartford..	136	$17,647 06
4.35 A.M. train...........	New York Central & Hudson River .	144	25,000 00
Philadelphia to Bay View.	Philadelphia, Wilmington & Baltimore	91.80	20,000 00
Bay View to Quantico....	Baltimore & Potomac.......	79.80	21,900 00
Quantico to Richmond....	Richmond, Fredericksburg & Potomac	81.50	17,419 26
Richmond to Petersburg..	Richmond & Petersburg...........	23.39	4,268 67
Petersburg to Weldon. ..	Petersburg	64	11,680 00
Weldon to Wilmington...	Wilmington & Weldon............	162.07	29,541 27
Wilmington to Florence ..	Wilmington, Columbia & Augusta...	110	20,075 00
Florence to Charleston Junction	Northeastern...	95	17.337 50
Charleston Junction to Savannah..............	Charleston & Savannah............	108	19,710 00
Savannah to Jacksonville .	Savannah, Florida & Western	171.50	31,309 70
Baltimore to Hagerstown..	Western Maryland...	86.60	15,804 50
Jacksonville to Tampa....	Jacksonville, Tampa & Key West & South Florida......	242.57	43,962 42
Total...			$295,655 38

A careful perusal of this table develops the fact that the greater portion of this money is expended south of Philadelphia, the railroad companies in that section not having sufficient weight of mails to warrant fast trains without some additional compensation. It will also be noted that with the exception of the sum of $25,000 for a special train to Poughkeepsie, which leaves New York City at 4.35 in the morning, the New York Central receives no compensation except that earned by them as common carriers of so many pounds of freight-mail matter carried, being paid for in accordance with its weight. It will also be observed that the Pennsylvania Railroad, on its trunk line, is not even so fortunate as its great rival.

There may be more dangerous pursuits in life than that of the railway post-office clerk, but there are not many so, and there are few in which the risk to life and limb is so constant. The everyday citizen who is called upon occasionally to make a railroad journey of a few hundred miles feels it to be incumbent upon himself on such occasions to make special provision for those dependent on him in case injury or death should come while riding in the thoroughly appointed and luxurious coach placed in a portion of the train least likely to suffer from accident. But too little thought is devoted to the safety of those poorly paid but efficient servants of the State, in the forward cars, without whose services the business of the country, as conducted to-day, would come to a stand-still. To show that the importance of this service is not here exaggerated, it is only necessary to recall the condition of affairs in New York City, and other cities as well, in March, 1888, when the great blizzard fell upon the land. There were then no mails for several days, and the prostration which came upon the community is too well remembered to need comment. The danger to those within the postal cars, however, is recognized by the railway people, and efforts have been made in the way of providing safety appliances, but it is, of course, impossible to lessen the danger to any great extent. All that American ingenuity suggests in the way of construction, both inside and outside of the cars, is provided. The body of the car is most substantially built, the platforms and couplings are of the most approved patterns, the trucks are similar to those used under the best passenger coaches, and the air-brakes and other safety apparatus are all brought into requisition. Within the cars are saws, axes, hammers, and crowbars conveniently placed in case of wreck, and safety-bars extend the length of the cars overhead to which the clerks may cling when the cars leave the track and roll down embankments, as they often do. In the year ending June, 1888, there were 248 accidents to trains upon which postal clerks were employed. In these wrecks four clerks were killed; sixty-three were seriously, several of the number permanently, and forty-five slightly injured. The official report of the accidents shows that the majority of them resulted from collisions, while others were due to the spreading of the rails, the failure of air-brakes to work at critical moments, and obstructions on the track.

In every case where cars were wrecked the postal car was among the number.

In many instances the cars were telescoped, and on such occasions the clerks were found buried in the wreckage or pinned under the engine or its tender. And many times true heroism was shown by the injured men. Over and over again the General Superintendent reports that, notwithstanding severe injuries received by the clerks, the scattered mail matter was collected by them and transferred either to another train or to the nearest post-office. Several times trains in the West were held up by robbers, who, after sacking the express car, visited the postal car, introducing themselves with pistol-shots. One clerk was seriously wounded in the shoulder. An instance of self-possession is reported in Arkansas, where the robbers, before visiting the postal car, had secured $10,-000 from the express safe. When they came to clerk R. P. Johnson he suggested that they had secured booty enough, and that under the circumstances they might let the mail matter alone. The masked men agreed with him, and did not molest the mails.

In view of the dangers to which employees of the Railway Mail Service are exposed, it may be permitted to quote from the last annual report of General Superintendent Bancroft on the subject of insurance. No action, he points out, has ever been taken by Congress toward providing for the care of clerks permanently injured in the service, or those dependent upon them in case of death, notwithstanding frequent recommendations by the Department. He attributes this to insurmountable objections on the part of the people's representatives to the creation of anything of the nature

Catching the Pouch from the Crane.

of a civil pension-roll.   He therefore suggests that there shall be deducted from the pay of each and every railway postal clerk ten cents per month, to be paid into " The Railway Postal Clerks' Insurance Fund," the custodian of which is to be the United States Treasury.   In case of death from injuries while on duty, $1,000 is to be paid to the clerk's heirs.   While this proposition is in the right direction, it hardly goes far enough.   Provision should be made for the disabled, and to do so, the clerks doubtless would not object to an assessment of double the amount suggested.   That they should be compelled to resort to such a mode of relief, however, is a reflection upon the Government of the United States.

The first great need of the Railway Mail Service is an adequate appropriation by Congress to extend its usefulness, and to keep it up to the demands and the needs of the public.   Where speed is required to make connections, the Department should have the cash on hand to buy what is necessary.   The railways are business institutions, managed as such, and when the Department desires extra facilities it should be prepared to pay in coin and not in talk.   In this connection it is a pleasant duty for the writer of this very imperfect sketch to say that during his term of service in the post-office at New York, and at the Department, he always found Mr. William H. Vanderbilt, Mr. Cornelius Vanderbilt, Mr. J. H. Rutter, of the New York Central; Mr. John Newell, of the Lake Shore; Mr. George B. Roberts, Mr. A. J. Cassatt, and Mr. Frank Thomson, of the Pennsylvania system; Mr. R. R. Bridgers and Mr. H. B. Plant, of the Atlantic Coast Line, ready to grant any reasonable request for the improvement and extension of the service.   Time after time Mr. Roberts has run a special train with the Australian transcontinental mail from Pittsburg to New York, that it might catch an outgoing steamer; and he and Mr. Vanderbilt practically re-established the fast mail, by taking letters on their limited trains.   Mr. Roberts gave, in addition, an extra mail train from Philadelphia west at four o'clock in the morning, and Mr. Vanderbilt placed a postal car on the 4 P.M. train from New York, receiving in return —what they had a right to demand—an extra weighing of the mails, and, what was not a matter of surprise to them, unmeasured abuse on the floor of Congress for giving these additional facilities to the people of the country.

The last and greatest need of the postal service is the total and complete elimination of partisan considerations as affecting appointments and removals in the working force. The spoils method invariably brings into the service a lot of do-nothings or a race of experimenters, whose performances never fail to breed disaster and to crush out substantial progress.

There is no position in the Government more exacting than that of a postal clerk, and none that has so many requirements. He must not only be sound " in wind and limb," but possessed of more than ordinary intelligence, and a retentive memory. His work is constant, and his only recreation, study. He must not only be proficient in his own immediate work, but he must have a general knowledge of the entire country, so that the correspondence he handles shall reach its destination at the earliest possible moment. He must know no night and no day. He must be impervious to heat or cold. Rushing along at a rate of forty or fifty miles an hour, in charge of that which is sacred—the correspondence of the people—catching his meals as he may ; at home only semi-occasionally, the wonder is that men competent to discharge the duties of so high a calling can be found for so small a compensation, and for so uncertain a tenure of official life. They have not only to take the extra-hazardous risks of their toilsome duties, but they are at the mercy of the practical politicians who believe that "to the victor belong the spoils." There are no public offices which are so emphatically " public trusts " as those whose duties comprise that of handling the correspondence of the people, because upon the proper and skilful performance of that duty depend —to a far greater degree than in the care of any other function accomplished through government agency—the business and social welfare of the entire community. The effects of ignorance, carelessness, and dishonesty in any other branch of the public service, although to be deplored, are not to be compared to those which follow the existence of such evils in the Post-Office. Can there be a more flagrant abuse of a " public trust " than the perversion of a branch of the public service into an agency for furthering the ambitious ends of local politicians and their partisans by allowing them to distribute its " patronage " as rewards for party services among those who, by reason of inexperience—if for no graver cause—are incompetent to replace the skilled workman who must be routed out in order to give them room ?   This evil should be corrected at once.   The Railway Mail Service must no longer be left at the mercy of the local partisans.   The reform is not only a present necessity, but it was one in the past and will be in the future, until the force of public sentiment shall compel acquiescence in the reasonable demand that what was so eminently meant for mankind shall not be given up to party; that the non-political business of letter-carrying, which the Government has monopolized, shall be conducted by it solely with a view to prompt and expeditious carrying of mail matter, and not with the object of bolstering up local " statesmen" or carrying elections.

At the coming in of Mr. Cleveland's administration, William B. Thompson was Second Assistant Postmaster-General—in charge of the contract office—and John Jameson was General Railway Mail Superintendent.   Both of these gentlemen had worked their way from the ranks by sheer merit.   In private business the value of their services would have been so highly appreciated that, no matter who became senior partner of the firm, under no circumstances would they have been permitted to retire.   The case of these gentlemen is mentioned now simply to illustrate an idea and not to found a complaint.   On the incoming of the new administration, General Thompson, in accordance with precedent, promptly tendered his resignation, and it was as promptly accepted ; while General Superintendent Jameson struggled along doing his work until, to relieve his chief from embarrassment, he, too, tendered his resignation.   The country was thus deprived of the services of two men who were experts in their profession, simply to give place to others, of high character, no doubt, but with no knowledge and special aptitude for the great trust that was committed to them.   And now, in the first year of another administration, the experience that many valuable officials have gained has counted for nothing, and they have been rotated out. In no other civilized country would such an atrocity be possible. An attempt to remove, for similar reasons, such postal authorities as Messrs. Rich, of Liverpool, Johnston, of Manchester, or Hubson, of Glasgow, all of whom, under a sound, logical, just, and economical business system, have reached their present positions by merit and efficiency from more or less inferior places, would hurl an administration in Great Britain from power, and justly too. The possession of the immense patronage of the Government did not save the Republican party from defeat in 1884, or keep the Democratic party in power in 1888. Ideas are stronger than " soap," and principles more potent than spoils. It is due to President Cleveland to state that toward the close of his administration he recognized the importance of permanency in the Railway Mail Service, and that he made a long step in advance by approving a series of rules submitted by the Civil Service Commission having for its object the removal of the service from the influences of politicians. It needs more than this, however ; it needs the sanctity of the statute law, declaring that the clerks should not only keep their offices during good behavior, but that after twenty years of faithful and efficient service, or before that time, if injured in the discharge of their duty, they should retire on half-pay. In case of death from accident while on duty, proper provision should be made for the family of the official. Whenever justice is done by Congress in these particulars, the United States will have the best and most efficient Railway Mail Service in the world.

THE
RAILWAY IN ITS BUSINESS RELATIONS.

By ARTHUR T. HADLEY.

Amount of Capital Invested in Railways—Important Place in the Modern Industrial System—The Duke of Bridgewater's Foresight—The Growth of Half a Century—Early Methods of Business Management—The Tendency toward Consolidation—How the War Developed a National Idea—Its Effect on Railroad Building—Thomson and Scott as Organizers—Vanderbilt's Capacity for Financial Management—Garrett's Development of the Baltimore & Ohio—The Concentration of Immense Power in a Few Men—Making Money out of the Investors—Difficult Positions of Stockholders and Bondholders—How the Finances are Manipulated by the Board of Directors—Temptations to the Misuse of Power—Relations of Railroads to the Public who Use Them—Inequalities in Freight Rates—Undue Advantages for Large Trade Centres—Proposed Remedies—Objections to Government Control—Failure of Grangerism—The Origin of Pools—Their Advantages—Albert Fink's Great Work—Charles Francis Adams and the Massachusetts Commission—Adoption of the Interstate Commerce Law—Important Influence of the Commission—Its Future Functions—Ill-judged State Legislation.

HE railroads of the world are to-day worth from twenty-five to thirty thousand million dollars. This probably represents one-tenth of the total wealth of civilized nations, and one-quarter, if not one-third, of their invested capital. It is doubtful whether the aggregate plant used in all manufacturing industries can equal it in value. The capital engaged in banking is but a trifle beside it. The world's whole stock of money of every kind—gold, silver, and paper—would purchase only a third of its railroads.

Yet these facts by no means measure the whole importance of the railroad in the modern industrial system. The business methods of to-day are in one sense the direct result of improved means of transportation. The railroad enables the large establishment to reach the markets of the world with its products; it enables the large city to receive its food-supplies, if necessary, from a distance of hundreds or thousands of miles. And while it thus favors the concentration of capital, it is in itself an extreme type of this concentration. Almost every distinctive feature of modern business, whether good or bad, finds in railroad history at once its chief cause and its fullest development.

As befits a nineteenth century institution, the railroad dates from 1801. In that year Benjamin Outram built in the suburbs of London a short line of horse railroad—or tramroad, as it was named in honor of the inventor. Other works of the same kind followed in almost every succeeding year. They were recognized as a decided convenience, but nothing more. It was hard to imagine that a revolution in the world's transportation methods could grow out of this beginning. Least of all could such a result be foreseen in England, whose admirable canal system seemed likely to defy competition for centuries to come. And yet, curiously enough, it was a man wholly identified with canal business who first foresaw the future importance of the railroad. The Duke of Bridgewater had built canals when they were regarded as a hazardous speculation; but they proved a success, and in the early years of the century he was reaping a rich reward for his foresight. One of his fellow-shareholders took occasion to congratulate the Duke on the fact that their property was now the surest monopoly in the land, and was startled by the reply, "I see mischief in these —— tramroads." The prophecy is all the more striking as coming from an enemy. Like Balaam, the Duke of Bridgewater had a pecuniary interest in cursing, but was so good a prophet that he had to tell the truth in spite of himself, even though his curse was thereby turned into a blessing.

George Stephenson.

It is hardly necessary to tell in detail how this prediction was realized. Thanks to the skill and perseverance of George Stephenson, the difficulties in the use of steam as a mode of propulsion were rapidly overcome. What was a doubtful experiment as late as 1815 had become an accomplished fact in 1830. The successful working of the Liverpool & Manchester Railway gave an impulse to similar enterprises all over the world. In 1835 there were 1,600 miles of railroad in operation—more than half of it in the United States. In 1845 the length of the world's railroads had increased to more than 10,000 miles; in 1855 it was 41,000 miles; in 1865, 90,000; in 1875, 185,000; in 1885, over 300,000.

There were perhaps a few men who foresaw this growth; there were almost none who foresaw the changes in organization and business methods with which it was attended. People at first thought of the railroad as merely an improved highway, which should charge tolls like a turnpike or canal, and on which the public should run cars of its own, independent of the railroad company itself. In many cases, especially in England, long sheets of tolls were published, based on the model of canal charters, and naming rates under which the use of the road-bed should be free to all. This plan soon proved impracticable. If independent owners tried to run trains over the same line, it involved a danger of collision and a loss of economy. The former evil could perhaps be avoided; the latter could not. The advantages of unity of management were so great that a road running its own trains could do a much larger business at lower rates than if ownership and carriage were kept separate. The old plan was as impracticable as it would be for a manufacturing company to own the buildings and engines, while each workman owned the particular piece of machinery which he handled. Almost all the technical advantages of the new methods would be lost for lack of system. The railroad company, to serve the public well, could not remain in the position of a turnpike or canal company, but must itself do the work of carriage.

This was not all. The same economy which resulted from the union of road and rolling-stock under one management was still further subserved by the consolidation of connecting lines. This change did not come about so suddenly as the other. Half a century had elapsed before it was fully carried out. At first there was no need of it. The early railroads were chiefly built for local traffic, and especially for the carriage of local passengers. They were like the horse railroads of the present day in the simplicity of their organization and the shortness of their lines. England in 1847 had chartered 700 companies, with an average authorized length of hardly fifteen miles each. The line from Albany to Buffalo and Niagara Falls was in the hands of a dozen independent concerns. These were but types of what existed all over the world. As through traffic, and especially through freight traffic, grew in importance, this state of things became intolerable. Frequent transshipment was at once an expense to the railroad and a burden to the public. Even when this could be avoided, there was a multiplication of offices and a loss of responsibility. The system of ownership and management had to adapt itself to the technical necessities of the business. The change was not the result of legislation; nor was it, except in a limited sense, the work of men like Vanderbilt or Scott. It occurred in all parts of the world at about the same time. It was the result of business necessity, strong enough to shape legislation, and to find administrative leaders who could meet its demands.

From the very first there were some men who felt the importance of the railroads as national lines of communication. The idea was present in the minds of the projectors of the Baltimore & Ohio, of the Erie, and of the Boston & Albany. But it was not until 1850 that it became a controlling one; nor was it universally accepted even then. As late as 1858 we find that there was a violent popular agitation in the State of New York to prohibit the New York Central from carrying freight in competition with the Erie Canal. It was gravely urged that the railroad had no business to compete with the canal; that the latter had a natural right to the through traffic from the West, with which the railroads must not interfere. It is less than thirty years since a convention at Syracuse, representing no small part of the public sentiment of New York, formally recommended "the passage of a law by the next Legislature which shall confine the railroads of this State to the business for which they were originally created."

But matters had gone too far for effective action of this kind. Besides the New York Central, the Erie and the Pennsylvania were in condition to handle the through traffic which Western connections were furnishing. These connections themselves were rapidly growing in importance. Prior to 1850 there were very few railroads west of the Alleghanies. In 1857 there were thousands of miles. The policy of land-grants acted as an artificial stimulus to the building of such roads; and a land-grant road, when once built, was almost necessarily dependent on through traffic for its support. It could not be operated locally; it was forced into close traffic arrangements which paved the way for actual consolidation.

The war brought this development to a stand-still for the time being; but it was afterward resumed with renewed vigor. It is probable that the final effect of the war was to hasten rather than to retard the growth of large systems. In the first place, it familiarized men's minds with national ideas instead of those limited to their own State. It is hard for us to realize that our business ideas were ever thus confined by artificial boundaries; but if we wish proof, we have only to look at the original location of the Erie Railway from Piermont to Dunkirk. Both were unnatural and undesirable terminal points; but people were willing to submit to inconvenience and to actual loss in order that the railroad might run as far as the New York State limits would allow, and not one whit farther. Similar instances can be found in other States. Hard as it is to understand, there seems to have been a positive jealousy of interstate traffic. The war did much to remove this by making the different sections of the country feel their common interest and their mutual dependence. It also had more direct effects. It produced special legislation for the Pacific railroads as a measure of military necessity; and this was but the beginning of a renewal of the land-grant policy, no longer through the medium of the States, but in the Territories and by the direct action of Congress. All the results in the way of extension or consolidation which had been noted in the first land-grant period were more intensely felt in the second. Never was there a time when business foresight and administrative power were more needed or more richly rewarded than in railroad management during the third quarter of the century.

J. Edgar Thomson.

In 1847 J. Edgar Thomson, an engineer of experience, entered the service of the Pennsylvania Railroad, of which he afterward became president. Three years later, a young man without experience in railroad business applied to him for a position as clerk in the station at Duncansville, and was, with some hesitation, accepted. Not long after—so runs the story—an influential shipper entered the station, and demanded that some transfers should be made in a manner contrary to the rules of the company. This the clerk refused to do ; and when the influential shipper tried to attend to the matter himself, he was forcibly ejected from the premises. Indignant at this, he complained to the authorities, demanding that the obnoxious employee be removed from his position. He was —and was promoted to a much higher one. This is said to have been the beginning of the railroad career of Thomas Alexander Scott.   Edgar Thomson was a sufficiently able man to appreciate Scott's talent at its full worth, and took every opportunity to make

Thomas A. Scott.

it useful in the service of the company.   Both before and after the war the system was extended in every direction; and the man who in 1850 had need of all his nerve to defy a single influential shipper was a quarter of a century later at the head of 7,000 miles of the most valuable railroad in the country.

As an enterprising and active railroad organizer, Scott was probably unrivalled—especially when aided by the soberer judgment of Thomson ; nor has the operating department of any other railroad in the country reached the standard established on the Pennsylvania by Scott and Thomson and the men trained up under their eyes.   But in business sagacity and those qualities which pertain to the financial management of property, Scott was surpassed by Vanderbilt.   The work of the two men was so totally different in character that it is hard to compare them. Vanderbilt was not so distinctively a railroad man as Scott. He had already made his mark as a ship-owner before he went into railroads. But he was a man who was bound to take the lead in the business world ; and he saw that the day for doing it with steamships was passing away, and that the day of railroads was come. He therefore presented his best steamship to the United States Government in a time when it was sorely needed, disposed of the others in whatever way he could, and turned his undivided attention to railroads.

In 1863 Vanderbilt began purchasing Harlem stock on a large scale. The road was unprofitable, but he at once improved its management and made it pay. Speculators on the other side of the market had not foreseen the possibility of this course of action, and were badly deceived in their calculations. Vanderbilt had begun buying at as low a figure as 3 ; within little more than a year he had forced some of its opponents to buy it of him at 285. He soon extended his operations to Hudson River, and somewhat later to New York Central. Defeated in an attempt to gain control of Erie, he turned his attention farther west; and was soon in virtual possession of a system which, in his hands at any rate, was fully a match for all competitors.

These systems did not long remain without rivals. The Baltimore & Ohio, whose development had been interrupted by the war, soon resumed, under the leadership of John W. Garrett, its old commanding position in the railroad world. Farther west, in the years succeeding, systems were developed and consolidated which surpassed their eastern connections in aggregate mileage. The combined Wabash and Missouri Pacific system in its best days included about 10,000 miles of line under what was virtually a single management. The Southern Pacific, the Atchison, the Northwestern, and the St. Paul systems control each of them in one way or another decidedly over 5,000 miles ; and a half-dozen others might be named, scarcely inferior either in magnitude or in commercial power.

The result of all this was to place an enormous and almost irresponsible power in the hands of a few men. The directors of such a system stand for thousands of investors, tens of thou-

Cornelius Vanderbilt.

sands of employees, and hundreds of thousands of shippers.   They
have the interests of all these parties in their hands for good or ill.
If they are fit men for their places, they will work for the advantage
of all.   A man like Vanderbilt gave higher profits, larger employment, and lower rate as the result of his railroad work.   But if the
head of such a system is unfit for his trust intellectually or morally,
the harm which he can do is almost boundless.

Of intellectual unfitness the chance is perhaps not great.   The
intense competition of the modern business world makes sure that
any man, to maintain his position, must have at least some of the
qualities of mind which it exacts.   But of moral unfitness the danger is all the greater, because some of the present conditions of
business competition directly tend to foster it.   A German econo-
mist has said that the so-called survival of the fittest in modern industry is really a double survival, side by side, of the most talented

on the one hand and the most unscrupulous on the other.   The
truth of this is already apparent in railroad business.   A Vanderbilt on the Central meets a Fisk on the Erie.   In spite of his superior power and resources he is virtually beaten in the contest—
beaten, as was said at the time, because he could not afford to go
so close to the door of State's prison as his rival.

The manager of a large railroad system has under his control a
great deal of property besides his own—the property of railroad
investors which has been placed in his charge.   Two lines of action
are open to him.   He may make money *for* the investors, and
thereby secure the respect of the community ; or he may make
money *out* of the investors, and thereby get rich enough to defy
public opinion.   The former course has the advantage of honesty,
the latter of rapidity.   It is a disgrace to the community that the
latter way is made so easy, and so readily condoned.   A man has
only to give to charitable objects a little of the money obtained by
violations of trust, and a large part of the world will extol him as a
public benefactor.   Nay, more ; it seems as if some of our financial
operators really mistook the *vox populi* for the *vox Dei*, and believed that a hundred thousand dollars given to a theological semi-
nary meant absolution for the past and plenary indulgence for the
future.   It is charged that one financier, when he undertook any
large transaction which was more than usually questionable, made
a covenant that if the Lord prospered him in his undertaking he
would divide the proceeds on favorable terms.   But—as Wamba
said of the outlaws and "the fashion of their trade with Heaven"
—"when they have struck an even balance, Heaven help them
with whom they next open the account ! "

A word or two as to the methods by which such operations are
carried on, and the system which makes them possible.   From the
very first, railroads have been built and operated by corporations.
A number of investors, too large to attend personally to the management of the enterprise, took shares of stock and elected officers
to represent them.   These officers had almost absolute power ;
but while matters were in this simple stage, there was no great
opportunity for its abuse.   The losses of investors were due to
bona fide errors of judgment rather than to misuse of power.   But
soon the corporations found it convenient to borrow money by

mortgaging their property. We then had two classes of investors —stockholders and bondholders, the former taking the risks and having the full control of the property, the latter receiving a relatively sure though perhaps smaller return, but having no control over the management as long as their interest was regularly paid.

Of course there is always some danger when the men who furnish the money do not have much control of the enterprise; but as long as the relations of stock and bonds were in practice what they pretended to be in theory, the resulting evils were not very great. Matters soon reached another stage. The amount of money furnished by the bondholders increased out of all proportion to that furnished by the stockholders. Sometimes the nominal amount of stock was unduly small; more commonly only a very small part of the nominal value was ever paid in.* The stock was nearly all water, simply issued by the directors as a means of keeping control of the property. After the crisis of 1857, people had become shy of buying railroad stock; but they bought railroad bonds because they thought they were safe. This was the case only when there was an actual investment of stockholders behind them; without this assurance, bonds were more unsafe than stock had been, because the bondholders had still less immediate control over the directors and officials. If there was money to be made at the time, the directors made it; if there was loss in the end, it fell upon the bondholders.

Let us take a specific case. An inside ring issues stock certificates to the value of a million dollars, on which perhaps a hundred thousand is paid in. They then publish their prospectus and place on the market two million of bonds with which the road is to be built. They sell the bonds at 80, reimburse themselves for

---

* In 1886 the capital stock and the indebtedness of the railroads of the United States amounted to about four thousand million dollars each. Most of the debt represents money actually paid in; but a very large fraction of the stock is a merely nominal liability on which no payments have been made. Some was issued as here described merely as a means of keeping control of the property; some, as the easiest method of balancing unequal values in reorganization; some, to represent increased value of the property, so as to be able to divide all the current earnings without calling public attention too prominently to the very profitable character of the business. On the other hand, some stock on which money was actually paid has been wiped out of existence; and something has been paid out of earnings for capital account without corresponding issue of securities. The net amount of " water," or excess of nominal liabilities over actual investments, in the capital account of the railroads of the country can only be made the subject of guesswork. Estimates of responsible authorities vary all the way from nothing to $4,000,000,000.

John W. Garrett.

the $100,000 advanced by charging the moderate commission of 5 per cent. for services in placing the loan, and have at their disposal $1,500,000 cash. These same directors now appear as a construction company, and award themselves a contract to pay $1,500,000 for work which is worth $1,200,000 only. The road is finished, and probably does not pay interest on its bonds. It passes into the hands of a receiver. Possibly the old management may have an influence in his appointment. At the worst, they have got back all the money they put in, *plus* the profits of the construction company; in the case supposed, 300 per cent. The bondholders, on the other hand, have paid $1,600,000 for a $1,-200,000 road.

But the troubles of the bondholders and the advantages of the old directors by no means end here. When the receiver takes possession he discovers that valuable terminals, necessary for the successful working of the road, are not the property of the company, but of the old directors. He finds that the road owns a very inadequate supply of rolling-stock, and that the deficiency has been made up by a car-trust—also under the control of the old directors. Each of these things, and perhaps others, must be made the subject of a fight or of a compromise. The latter is often the only practicable alternative, and almost always the cheaper one; by its terms the ring perhaps secures hundreds of thousands more, at the expense of the actual investors.

These are but a few of the many ways in which a few years' control of property may be made profitable to the officials at the expense of legitimate interests. In a case like this, all depends upon the possibility of selling bonds. It is usually impossible to place the whole loan before construction; and if the market-price falls below the cost of the work undertaken, as was the case with the West Shore, the loss falls upon the construction company. Such accidents were for a long time rare. It took the public nearly twenty years to learn the true character of imperfectly secured railroad bonds. Within the past five years it seems to have become a trifle wiser. The crisis of 1873 was insufficient to teach the lesson; but that of 1885 has been at least partially successful in this respect.

In cases like the one just described the bondholders are largely to blame for their own folly. But sometimes the loss falls on those who are in no way responsible for it. A railroad may be built as a blackmailing job. If a company is sound and prosperous, speculators may be tempted to build a parallel road, not with the idea of making it pay, but because they can so damage the business of the old road as to force it to buy them out. They build the road to sell.

It is but fair to say that operations as bad as those just described are the exception rather than the rule. But the fact that they can exist at all is by no means creditable to our financial methods. The whole system by which directors can use their positions of trust to make contracts in which they are personally interested puts a premium on dishonesty. Such contracts are forbidden in England. It may be true, as is urged by many railroad officials of undoubted honesty, that it would be inconvenient to apply the same law here; but on the whole, the gain would far outweigh the loss.

At the very best, a railroad president is subject to temptations to misuse his financial powers, all the more dangerous because it is impossible to draw the line between right and wrong. He knows the probable value of his railroad and of the property affected by its action a great deal better than any outsider possibly can. The published figures of earnings of the road are the result of estimates by himself and his subordinates. Out of the current earnings he pays current expenses, and probably charges permanent expenditures to capital account. But what expenditures are current and what are permanent? This division is itself the result of an estimate, and a very doubtful one at that. There are some well-established general principles, but none which will apply themselves automatically. With the best will in the world he cannot make his annual reports give a thoroughly clear idea of what has been done. Is he to be forbidden to buy stock when it seems too low, or sell it when it is high? Shall we refuse him the right to invest in other property which he sees will advance in value? Apparently not; and yet, if we allow this, we open the door for some of the worst abuses of power which have occurred in railroad history. The line between good faith and bad faith in these matters is a narrow one, and the average conscience cannot be trusted to locate it with accuracy.

But the relations to the investors cover but a small part either of the work or of the responsibility of the railroad authorities. They are managing not merely a piece of property, but a vast and complicated organization of men, and an instrument of public service. In all these capacities their cares are equally great. The operating and the traffic departments are not less important than the financial department. The relations of the railroad to its employees, and to the business community at large, are even more perplexing than its relations to the investors.

Of the questions arising between the railroad and its employees we are just beginning to realize the full importance. They are not matters to be settled by private agreement or private war. If they involve a serious interruption of the business of the community they concern public interests most vitally. The community cannot afford to have its business interrupted by railroad strikes. On the other hand, it cannot allow the men to make this public duty of the railroads a means of enforcing their own will on every occasion, to the detriment of all discipline and responsibility, or in disregard of investors' rights. How to compromise between these two conflicting requirements is one of the most serious problems of the immediate future.* Little progress in this direction has as yet been made, or even systematically attempted.

The questions arising from the relations of the railroads to those who use them are wider and older. From the very outset attempts were made to regulate railroad charges by law in various ways. The fear at that time was that they might be made unreasonably high. This fear proved groundless. From the outset the rates were rather lower than had been expected, and much lower than by many of the means of transportation which railroads superseded. These low rates caused a great development in business; and this, in turn, gave a chance for such economy in handling it that rates went still lower. Each new invention rendered it easier to do a large business at cheap rates. The substitution of steel rails for iron, which began shortly after the close of the war, had an enormous influence in this respect. This was not merely due to the direct saving in repairs, which, though appreciable, was moderate in amount. It was due still more to improvements in transportation which followed. It was found that steel rails would bear heavier rolling-stock. Instead of building ten-ton cars to carry ten tons of cargo, companies built twelve-ton cars to carry twenty tons of cargo, or fourteen-ton cars to carry thirty tons; and they made the locomotives heavy enough to handle correspondingly larger trains. A given amount of fuel was made to haul more weight; and of the weight thus hauled, the freight formed a constantly increasing proportion as compared with the rolling-stock itself. The system of rates was adopted to meet the new requirements. Charges were made incredibly low in order to fill cars that would otherwise go empty, or to use the road as nearly as possible to its full capacity. In the twenty years following the introduction of steel rails the traffic of the New York Central increased from less than 400,000,000 ton-miles to decidedly over 2,000,000,000; while the average rates fell from 3.09 cents per ton per mile in 1866 to 0.76 cent in 1886. This is but a sin-

* See following article on " The Prevention of Railway Strikes."

gle instance of a process which has gone on all over the country. The average freight charge on all railroads of the country to-day is a little over one cent per ton a mile : less than half what would have been deemed possible on any railroad a few years ago.

The progress of railroad consolidation contributed greatly to this economy. It saved multiplication of offices ; it saved re-handling of freight ; it enabled long-distance business to be done systematically. So great were its advantages that co-operation between connecting lines was carried far beyond the limits of act-ual consolidation. Through traffic was handled without transship-ment, sometimes by regularly incorporated express companies or freight companies on the same plan, but more commonly by what are known as fast-freight lines.* These are little more than com-binations for keeping account of through business ; they are by no means ideal in their working, but they have the advantage of few expenses and no income, so that the temptation to steal, which is the bane of such organizations, is here reduced to a minimum.

But all these things, while they increased the efficiency of the service, also increased the power of the railroad authorities and rendered the shipper more helpless. The very cheapness of rates only made a recourse to other means of transportation more diffi-cult. If *A* was charged 30 cents while his competitor *B* was pay-ing only 20 cents for the same service, he was worse off than when they were both paying a dollar ; and the fact that no other means of conveyance could be found to do the work for less than a dollar simply put *A* all the more completely at the mercy of the railroad freight-agent. In other words, the fact that rates were so low made any inequality in rates all the more dangerous. The lower the rate and the wider the monopoly, the less was the chance of relief.

Such inequalities existed on a large scale : and they were all the more difficult to deal with because there was a certain reason for some of them arising from the nature of railroad business. The expenses of a railroad are of two kinds. Some, like train and station service, locomotive fuel, or repairs of rolling-stock, are pretty directly chargeable to the different parts of the traffic. It costs a certain amount in wages and in materials to run a particu-

* See " The Freight-car Service," page 287.

lar train ; if that train is taken off, that part of the expense is saved. But there is another class of items, known as fixed charges, that do not vary with the amount of business done. Interest on bonds must be paid, whether the volume of traffic be large or small. The services of track-watchmen must be paid for, whether there be a hundred trains daily or only a dozen. In short, most of the expenses for interest and maintenance of way are chargeable to the business as a whole, but not to particular pieces of work done. The practical inference from this is obvious. In order that the railroad as a whole may be profitable, the fixed charges must be paid somehow. The railroad manager will try to get them as he can from different parts of his traffic. But if, for any reason, a particular piece of business cannot or will not pay its share of the fixed charges, it is better to secure it at any price above the bare expense of loading and hauling, without regard to the fixed charges. For if the business is lost, these charges will run on just the same, without any added means of meeting them.

The consequence is that there is no natural standard of rates ; or, rather, that there are two standards, so far apart that the difference between the two is quite sufficient to build up one establishment or one locality and ruin another, in case of an arbitrary exercise of power on the part of the freight-agent. In the use of such a power it was inevitable that there should be a great many mistakes, and some things which were worse than mistakes. Colbert once cynically defined taxation as " the art of so plucking the goose as to secure the largest amount of feathers with the least amount of squealing." Some of our freight-agents have taken Colbert's tax theories as a standard, and have applied them only too literally. It is this short-sighted policy which has made the system of charging " what the traffic will bear " a synonyme for extortion. Interpreted rightly, this phrase represents a sound principle of railroad policy—putting the burden of the fixed charges on the shipments that can afford to pay them. But practically—in the popular mind at least—it has come to mean almost exactly the opposite.

The points which got the benefit of the lowest rates were the large trade centres, which had the benefit of competing lines of railroad, and often of water competition also. The threat to ship goods by a rival route was the surest way of making a freight-agent give low rates. The result was that the growth of such places was specially stimulated. In addition to their natural advantages they had an artificial one due to the policy of competing lines of railroad. It may well be the case, as is argued by railroad men, that sound railroad economy demands that goods in large masses should be carried much more cheaply than those which are furnished in smaller quantities. But it is certain the practice went far beyond the limits of any such justification. There was a time when cattle were carried from Chicago to New York at a dollar a car-load; and many other instances, scarcely less marked, could be cited from the history of trunk-line competition. The fact was, that in an active railroad war freight-agents would generally accede to a demand for reduced rates at a competing point, whether well founded or not, and would almost always turn a deaf ear to similar demands from local shippers, however strongly supported by considerations of far-sighted business policy.

But this was not the worst. Inequalities between different places might after some hardship correct themselves; differences of treatment between individuals could not be thus adjusted. And the system of making rates by special bargain almost always led to differences between individuals, where favors were too often given to those who needed or deserved them least. The fluctuation of rates was first taken advantage of by the unscrupulous speculator. Often, if he controlled large sources of shipment, he might receive the benefit of a secret agreement by which he could obtain lower rates than his rivals under all circumstances. A more effective means for destroying straightforwardness in business dealings than the old system of special rates was never devised. Sometimes, where one competitor was overwhelmingly strong, the pretence of secrecy was thrown aside, and the railroad companies so far forgot their public duties as almost openly to assist one concern in crushing its rivals. The state of things in this respect twelve or fifteen years ago was so bad that it is painful to dwell upon; but the reformation to-day is not so complete that we can wash our hands of past sins.

Less was said or felt of similar evils in passenger traffic, be-cause the passenger business of the country generally is of much less importance than its freight business, either to the railroad investors or to the producers themselves. But there was the same fluctuation in passenger rates ; and there was an outrageous form of discrimination in the development of the free-pass system ; a practice which would have fully deserved the name of systematic bribery, had it not become so universal that most men hardly recognized any personal obligation connected with the acceptance of a pass. Officials and other citizens of influence had come to regard it as a right; it was not so much bribery on the part of the companies as blackmail levied against them.

The remedies proposed for all these evils have been various. From the very beginning until now there have been some who held that such abuses could be avoided only by State railroad own-ership. Such experiments in the United States have not gone far enough to furnish conclusive evidence either way ; but the experience of other countries indicates that State railroads, as such, do not avoid these evils. Where they have been worked in competition with other lines, they have been as deeply involved in these abuses as their private competitors—perhaps more so. Where the government has obtained control of all the railroads of the country, and made such arrangements with the water-routes as to render competition impossible, the abuses have vanished, because there was no longer any conceivable motive to continue them. But this was the result of the monopoly, not of the State ownership ; and the advantage was purchased by a sacrifice of all the stimulus of competition toward the development of new facilities.

Many people assume that, because the government represents the nation as a whole, therefore government officials will not be under the same temptations to act unjustly which are felt by the representatives of a private corporation. This is a mistake. It is not as representatives of the investor that railroad agents do much injustice; this motive has practically nothing to do with it. Most of the abuses complained of are positively injurious to the investor in the long run. When officials really represent the interests of the property with wise foresight, they, as a rule, give the public no ground to complain. The question reduces itself to this : Will the

State choose better representatives and agents than a private corporation? Will it secure a higher grade of officials, more competent, more honest, and more enterprising? The difference between state and private railroads is not so much on matters of policy as on methods of administration. The success of government administration varies with different countries. In Prussia, where it is seen at its best, the results are in some respects remarkably good; yet even here the roads are not managed on anything like the American standard of efficiency, either in amount of train service, in speed, or in rapidity of development. And what is barely successful in Prussia, with its trained civil service on the one hand and its less intense industrial demands on the other, can hardly be considered possible or desirable in America. No one who has watched the workings of a government contract can desire to have the whole trade of the country put to the expense of supporting such methods in its transportation business.

A more easy method of trying to regulate railroad charges has been by forced reductions in rates. This was tried on the largest scale in the Granger movement fifteen years ago. A fall in the price of wheat had rendered it difficult for the farmers to make money. The Patrons of Husbandry, in investigating the causes, saw that the larger trade centres, where there was competition, were getting lower rates than the local producer. They reasoned that if all the farmers could get such low rates, they could make money; and that, if the roads could afford to make these low rates for any points, they could afford to do it for all. The railroad agents, instead of foreseeing the storm and trying to prevent it, assumed a defiant attitude. The result was that legislatures of the States in the upper Mississippi Valley passed laws of more or less rigidity, scaling down all rates to the general level of competitive ones. After a period of some doubt, the right of the States to do this was admitted by the courts. But before the legal possibility had been decided, the practical impossibility of such a course had been shown. If all rates were reduced to the level of competitive ones, it left nothing to pay fixed charges. On such terms, foreign capital would not come into the State; nor could it be enticed by such a clumsy effort as that of one of the States, which provided "that no road *hereafter constructed* shall be subject to the provisions of this act." The goose which laid the golden eggs was not such a goose as to be deceïved by this. The untimely death of several of her species meant more than any promises of immunity to those who should follow in her footsteps. In those States which had passed the most severe laws capital would not invest; railroads could not pay interest, their development stopped, and the growth of the community was seriously checked thereby. The most obnoxious laws were either repealed or allowed to remain in abeyance. Where the movement was strongest in 1873 it had practically spent its force in 1876. There have been many similar attempts in all parts of the country since that time; just now they are peculiarly active; but nothing which approaches in recklessness some of the legislation of 1873 and 1874. The lesson was at least partly learned.

We had hardly passed the crisis of the effort to level down, when some of the more intelligent railroad men made an effort to level up. Recognizing that discriminations and fluctuating rates were an evil, they sought to avoid it by common action with regard to the business at competing points. A mere agreement as to rates to be charged was not enough to secure this end. Such an agreement was sure to be violated. Even if the leading authorities meant to observe it, their agents could always evade its requirements to some extent. Such evasion was favored by loose arrangements between connecting roads, and by the somewhat irresponsible system of fast freight lines. Wherever it existed, it gave rise to mutual suspicion. *A* believed that his road did it because he could not help it, but that *B* and *C* were allowing their roads to do it maliciously; while *B* and *C* had the same consciousness of individual rectitude and the same unkind suspicions with regard to *A*. It was at best a rather hollow truce, which did not really accomplish its purpose, and which might change to open war on very slight provocation.

To avoid this difficulty a pool, or division of traffic, was arranged. It is a fact that, whatever wars of rates there may be, the percentage of traffic carried by the different lines varies but little. If an arbitrator can examine the books and decide what these percentages have been in the past, he can make an award for the future, under which the competitive traffic of the different roads may be fairly divided. The arrangements for doing this are various. Sometimes the roads carry such traffic as may happen to be offered, and settle the differences with one another by money balances; sometimes they actually divert traffic from one line to another. But the advantage of either of these arrangements over a mere agreement to maintain rates is that they cannot be violated without direct action on the part of the leading authorities of the roads concerned—either in open withdrawal, or in actual bad faith. The ordinary irregularities of agents do not, under a pooling system, give rise to much suspicion, because they do not benefit the road in whose behalf they are undertaken. Its percentage being fixed there is no motive for rate-cutting. So great is this advantage that pooling is accepted in almost all other countries as a natural means of maintaining equality of rates; the state railroads of Central Europe entering into such contracts with competing private lines and even with water-routes. In America itself, pools have had a longer and wider history than is generally supposed. In New England they arose and continued to exist on a moderate scale without attracting much attention. In the Mississippi Valley, the Chicago-Omaha pool was arranged as early as 1870, and formed the model for a whole system of such arrangements extending as far as the Pacific Coast. But, as involving wider questions of public policy, the activity of the Southern and the Trunk Line Associations has attracted chief attention.

The man whose name is most prominently identified with both these systems is Albert Fink. A German by birth and education, his long experience as a practical railroad engineer did not deprive him of a taste for studying traffic problems on their theoretical side. As Vice-President of the Louisville & Nashville, he had given special attention to the economic conditions affecting the Southern roads; and when, in the years 1873–75, a traffic association was formed by a number of these roads to secure harmony of action on matters of common interest, he became the recognized leader. His success in arrangements for through traffic was so conspicuous that when, in 1877, the trunk lines were exhausted with an unusually destructive war of rates, they looked to him as he only man who could deliver them from their trouble. In some lines, division of traffic had already been resorted to; but it was in the hands of outside parties, like the Standard Oil Company or the cattle eveners, and was made a means of oppression against shippers not in the combination itself.

Albert Fink

The conditions were not favorable; the result of Fink's efforts to bring order out of chaos was slow and by no means uninterrupted. Yet on the whole, as was admitted even by opponents of the pooling system, it contributed to steadiness and equality of rates. The arrangement of these agreements was hampered by their want of legal status. While the law did not at that time actually prohibit them, it refused to enforce them. Existing thus on sufferance, they depended on the good will of the contracting parties. None but a man of Fink's unimpeached integrity and high intellectual power could have kept matters running at all; and even he could not prevent the adoption of a policy of making hay while the sun shines, more or less regardless of the future. The results of the trunk-line pool were unsatisfactory—most of all to those who believed in pools as a system; but it is fair to attribute a large part of this failure to the absence of legal recognition, which in a manner compelled the agreements to be arranged to meet the demands of the day rather than of the future.

Meantime an equally important contribution to the solution of the railroad question was being worked out in another quarter. In the year 1869 the Massachusetts Railroad Commission was established. Its powers were so slight that it was not regarded as likely to be an influential public agency. Fortunately it numbered among its members Charles Francis Adams, Jr. ; a man whose efficiency more than made up for any want of nominal powers. In his hands the mere power to report became the most effective of all weapons. Representing at once enlightened public judgment and far-sighted railroad policy, he did much to bring the two into harmony and protect the legitimate interests on both sides from short-sighted misuse for the benefit of either party. The detail of his work is matter of past history ; perhaps its most prominent result was to introduce to State legislation the idea of a railroad commission as an administrative body. Those States which had no stringent laws appointed commissions to take their place; those which had overstringent ones appointed commissions to use discretion in applying them. In either case, the existence of a body of men representing the State, but possessing the technical knowledge to see what the exigencies of railroad business demanded, was a protection to all parties concerned.

Charles Francis Adams.

But matters were rapidly passing beyond the sphere of State legislation. Each new consolidation of systems, each additional development of through traffic, made it more impossible to control railroad policy by the action of individual States. It could only be done by a development of the law in the United States courts or by Congressional legislation. The former result was necessarily slow ; each year showed an increased demand for pecial action on the part of Congress. But such action was hindered by divergence of opinion in that body itself. One set of men wished a moderate law, prohibiting the most serious abuses of railroad power, and enforced under the discretionary care of a commission. These men were for the most part not unwilling to see pools legalized if their members could thereby be held to a fuller measure of responsibility. On the other hand, the extremists wished to prescribe a system of equal mileage rates ; they would hear of no such thing as a commission, and hated pools as an invention of the adversary. Between the two lay a large body of members who had no convictions on the matter, but were desirous to please everybody and offend nobody—a hard task in this particular case. It was nearly nine years from the time Mr. Reagan introduced his first bill when a compromise was finally effected— largely by the influence of Senator Cullom. As compromises go, it was a tolerably fair one. The extremists sacrificed their opposition to a commission, but secured the prohibition of pools ; the disputed points with regard to rates were left in such a shape that no man knew what the law meant, and each was, for the time being, able to interpret it to suit the wishes of his Congressional district.

The immediate effects of the law were extremely good. There were certain sections of it, like those which secured publicity of rates and equal treatment for different persons in the same circumstances, whose wisdom was universally admitted. Indeed it was rather a disgrace, both to the railroad agents and to the courts, that we had to wait for an act of Congress to secure these ends ; and most of the railroads made up for past remissness in this respect by quite a spasm of virtue. In some instances it was even thought that they " stood up so straight as to lean over backward." But this was not the only part of the law which proved efficient. The very vagueness of the clause concerning the relative rates for through and local traffic, which under other circumstances might have proved fatal, put a most salutary power into the hands of the Interstate Commerce Commission, and one which they were not slow to use.

The President was fortunate in his selection of commissioners ; above all in the chairman, Judge T. M. Cooley, of Michigan, a

man whose character, knowledge of public law, and technical familiarity with railroad business made him singularly well fitted for the
place. The work of the Interstate Commission, like that of its
Massachusetts prototype, shows
how much more important is
personal power than mere technical authority. It was supposed
at first that the commission would
be a purely administrative body,
with discretion to suspend the
law. Instead of this, they have
enforced and interpreted it; and
in the process of interpretation
have virtually created a body of
additional law, which is read and
quoted as authority. With but
little ground for expecting it from

Thomas M. Cooley.

the letter of the act, they have become a judicial body of the highest importance. Their existence seems to furnish a possibility for
an elastic development of transportation law, neither so weak as
to be ineffective nor so strong as to break by its own rigidity.

But the final test of their success is yet to come. They have
laid down a few principles as to the cases when competition justi-
fies through rates lower than those at intermediate points. But
the application of these principles is as yet far from settled; and it
is rendered doubly hard by the clause against pools, which does
much to hamper the roads in any attempt to secure common action
on the matter of through rates. Each ill-judged piece of State
legislation, and each reckless attempt to attack railroad profits, increases the difficulty. There was a time when the powers of railroad managers were developed without corresponding responsibility. In many parts of the country we are now going to the
other extreme—increasing the responsibility of railroad authorities
toward shipper and employees, State law and national commission,
and at the same time striving to restrict their powers to the utmost.
Such a policy cannot be continued indefinitely without a disastrous
effect upon railroad service, and, indirectly, upon the business of
the country as a whole.

THE PREVENTION OF RAILWAY STRIKES.

By CHARLES FRANCIS ADAMS.

Railways the Largest Single Interest in the United States—Some Impressive Statistics—
Growth of a Complex Organization—Five Divisions of Necessary Work—Other
Special Departments—Importance of the Operating Department—The Evil of
Strikes—To be Remedied by Thorough Organization—Not the Ordinary Relation
between Employer and Employee—Of what the Model Railway Service Should
Consist—Temporary and Permanent Employees—Promotion from One Grade to
the Other—Rights and Privileges of the Permanent Service—Employment during
Good Behavior—Proposed Tribunal for Adjusting Differences and Enforcing Discipline—A Regular Advance in Pay for Faithful Service—A Fund for Hospital
Service, Pensions, and Insurance—Railroad Educational Institutions—The Employer to Have a Voice in Management through a Council—A System of Representation.

IN 1836—fifty years ago—there were but a little more than
1,000 miles of railroad on the American continents, representing an outlay of some $35,000,000, and controlled by
a score or so of corporations. There are now (1886) about 135,-
000 miles in the United States alone, capitalized at over eight
thousand millions of dollars.

The railroad interest is thus the largest single interest in the
country. Probably 600,000 men are in its employ as wage-earners. It is safe to say that over two millions of human beings are
directly dependent upon it for their daily support. The Union
Pacific, as a single and by no means the largest member of this
system, controls 5,150 miles of road, represented by stock and
bonds to the amount of $275,000,000. More than 15,000 names

NOTE.—The following paper was prepared for a special purpose in June, 1886, and then submitted
to several of the leading officials directly engaged in the local management of the lines operated by
the Union Pacific Railway Company, of which the writer had been president for two years. It drew
forth from them various criticisms, which led to the belief that the publication of the paper at that time
might easily result in more harm than good. It was accordingly laid aside, and no use made of it.

Nearly three years have since elapsed, and the events of the year 1888—with its strike of engineers
on the Chicago, Burlington & Quincy—seem to indicate that the relations of railroad employees to the
railroad companies have undergone no material change since the year 1886, when the strike on the

are borne upon its pay-rolls. Its yearly income has exceeded $29,000,000, and in 1885 was $26,000,000. Large as these aggregates sound, there are other corporations which far exceed the Union Pacific both in income and in capitalization, and not a few exceed it in mileage. The Pennsylvania, for instance, either owns or directly controls 7,300 miles of road. It is represented by a capitalization of $670,000,000; its annual income is $93,000,000; it carries 75,000 names on its pay-rolls.

This has been the outgrowth of a single half-century. The vast and intricate organization implied in the management of such an interest had, as it were, to be improvised. The original companies were small and simple affairs. Some retired man of business held, as a rule, the position of president; while another man, generally a civil engineer, and as such supposed to be more or less acquainted with the practical working of railroads, acted as superintendent. The superintendent, in point of fact, attended to everything. He was the head of the commercial department; the head of the operating department; the head of the construction department; and the head of the mechanical department. But there is a limit to what any single man can do; and so, as the organization developed, it became necessary to relieve the railroad superintendent of many of his duties. Accordingly, the working management naturally subdivided itself into separate departments, at the head of which men were placed who had been trained all their lives to do the particular work required in each department. In the same way, the employees of the company—the wage-earners, as they are called—originally few in number, held toward the company relations similar to those which the employees in factories, shops, or on farms, held to those who employed them. In other words, there was in the railroad system

Missouri Pacific took place. The same unsatisfactory condition of affairs apparently continues. There is a deep-seated trouble somewhere.

No sufficient reason, therefore, exists for longer suppressing this paper. Provided the suggestions contained in it have any value at all, they may at least be accepted as contributions to a discussion which of itself has an importance that cannot be either denied or ignored.

The paper is printed as it was prepared. The figures and statistics contained in it have no application, therefore, to the present time; nor has it been thought worth while to change them, inasmuch as they have little or no bearing upon the argument. That is just as applicable to the state of affairs now as it was to that which existed then. The only difference is that the course of events during the three intervening years has demonstrated that the paper, if it does no good, will certainly do no harm.

BOSTON, February 4, 1889.   C. F. A.

no organized service.   As the employees increased until they were numbered by hundreds, better organization became a necessity.   The community was absolutely dependent upon its railroad service for continued existence, for the running of trains is to the modern body politic very much what the circulation of blood is to the human being.   An organized system, therefore, had to grow up.   This fact was not recognized at first ; and, indeed, is only imperfectly recognized yet.   Still the fact was there ; and inasmuch as it was there and was not recognized, trouble ensued.   No rationally organized railroad service—that is, no service in which the employer and employed occupy definite relations toward each other, recognized by each, and by the body politic—no such service exists.   Approaches to it only have been made.   A discussion, therefore, of the form that such a service would naturally take if it were organized, cannot be otherwise than timely.

It has already been noticed that in the process of organization the railroad, following the invariable law, naturally subdivides itself into different departments.*   In the case of every corporation of magnitude there are of these departments, whether one man is at the head of one or several of them, at least five.   These are :

1st. The financial department, which provides the ways and means.

2d. The construction department, which builds the railroad after the means to build it are provided.

3d. The operating department, which operates the road after it is built.

4th. The commercial department, which finds business for the operated road to do, and regulates the rates which are to be charged for doing it.

5th. The legal department, which attends to all the numerous questions which arise in the practical working of everyone of the other departments.

These five divisions of necessary work exist in the organization of every company, no matter how small it may be, or how few officers it may employ.   In the larger companies the need is found for yet other special departments.   In the case of the Union Pacific, for instance, there are two such: First, the comptroller's

* See " Railway Management," page 151.

department, which establishes and is responsible for the whole method of accounting; second, a department which is responsible for all the numerous interests which a large railroad company almost of necessity develops outside of its strict, legitimate work as a common carrier.

When it comes to dealing with the employees of the company, it will be found that the vast majority of those whose names are on the pay-rolls belong to the operating department. This department is responsible not only for the running of trains and, usually, for the maintenance of the permanent way, but also for the repairs of rolling stock. All the train-hands, all the section-men and bridge-gangs, and all the mechanics in the repair shops thus belong to the operating department. The accounting department employs only clerks. The same is true of the commercial department, though the commercial department has also agents at different business centres who look after the company's interests and secure traffic for it. The construction department is in the hands of civil engineers, and the force employed by it depends entirely upon the amount of building which may at any time be going on. As a rule, the bulk of the employees in the construction department are paid by contractors, and not directly by the railroad company. The legal department consists only of lawyers and the few clerks necessary to aid them in transacting their business.

In the operating department of the Union Pacific at the present time (1886) about 14,000 names are carried upon the pay-roll. The number varies according to the season of the year and the pressure of traffic. In January, and during the winter months, the average will fall to 12,000, while in June and during the summer it rises to 14,000.

Of these, 2,800, or 20 per cent., are engaged in train movement; 4,200, or 30 per cent., are in the machine-shops and in charge of motive power and rolling-stock; 7,000, or 50 per cent., are employed in various miscellaneous ways, as flag-men, section-hands, station agents, switch-men, etc., etc.

So far as the wage-earner is concerned, it is, therefore, this portion of the force of a railroad company which may be called distinctively "the service." If good relations exist between the men employed in its operating department and the company no serious trouble can ever arise in the operation of the road. The clerks in the financial department, or the engineers in the construction department, might leave the company's employ in a body, and their places could soon be filled. In point of fact, they never do leave it; but should they do so, the public would experience no inconvenience. The inconvenience—and it would be very considerable—would be confined to the office of the company, and their work would fall into arrears. It is not so with the operating department. So far as the community at large is concerned, whatever difficulties arise in the working of railroads develop themselves here. All serious railroad strikes take place among those engaged in the shops, on the track, or in handling trains. That these difficulties should be reduced to a minimum is therefore a necessity. They can be reduced to a minimum only when the railroad service is thoroughly organized.

How then can this service be better organized than it is? It is usually maintained that only the ordinary relation of employer and employed should exist between the railroad company and the men engaged in operating its road. If the farmer is dissatisfied with his hands, he can dismiss them. In like manner, if the laborer is dissatisfied with the farmer, he can leave his employ. It is argued that exactly the same relation should exist between the great railroad corporation and the tens of thousands of men in its operating department. The proposition is not tenable. The circumstances are different. In the first place, it is of no practical consequence to the community whether difficulties which prevent the work of the farm from going on arise or do not arise between an individual farmer and his laborers. The work of innumerable other farms goes on all the same, and it is a matter of indifference what occurs in the management of the particular farm. So it is even with large factories, machine-shops—in fact, with all industrial concerns which do not perform immediate public functions. A railroad company does perform immediate public functions. The community depends upon it for the daily and necessary movements of civilized existence. This fact has to be recognized. For a railroad to pause in its operation implies paralysis to the community which it serves.

Such being the fact, it is futile to argue that the ordinary relations of employer and employed should obtain in the railroad service. Something else is required; and because something else is required but has not yet been devised we have had the numerous difficulties which have taken place during the present year—difficulties which have occasioned the community much inconvenience and loss.

The model railroad service, therefore, is now to be considered. Of what would it consist? At present, there is practically no difference between individuals in the employ of a great railroad corporation. All the wage-earners in its pay stand in like position toward it. There should be a difference among them; and a marked difference, due to circumstances which should receive recognition. Take again the case of the Union Pacific. The Union Pacific, it has already been mentioned, numbers 14,000 employees in its operating department as a maximum, and 12,000 as a minimum. They vary with the season of the year, increasing in summer and diminishing in winter. Consequently there is a large body of men who are permanently in its employ; and there is a smaller body, although a very considerable portion of the whole, who are in its employ only temporarily. Here is a fact, and facts should be recognized. If this particular fact is recognized, the service of the company should be organized accordingly, and each of the several divisions of the operating department would have on its rolls two classes of men: First, those who have been admitted into the permanent service of the company; and, second, those who for any cause are only temporarily in that service. And no man should be admitted into the permanent service until after he has served an apprenticeship in the temporary service. In other words, admission into the permanent service would be in the nature of a promotion from an apprenticeship in the temporary service.

Those in the temporary service need not, therefore, be at present considered. They hold to the companies only the ordinary relation of employee to employer. They may be looked upon as candidates for admission into the permanent service—they are on probation. So long as they are on probation they may be engaged and discharged at pleasure. The permanent service alone is now referred to.

The permanent service of a great railroad company should in

many essential respects be very much like a national service, that of the army or navy, for instance, except in one particular, and a very important particular : to wit, those in it must of necessity always be at liberty to resign from it—in other words, to leave it.   The railroad company can hold no one in its employ one moment against his will.   Meanwhile, to belong to the permanent service of a railroad company of the first class, so far as the employee is concerned, should mean a great deal.   It should carry with it certain rights and privileges which would cause that service to be eagerly sought.   In the first place, he who had passed through his period of probation and whose name was enrolled in the permanent service would naturally feel that his interests were to a large extent identified with those of the company ; and that he on the other hand had rights and privileges which the company was bound to respect.   It has been a matter of boast in France that every private soldier in the French army carried the possibility of the field-marshal's baton in his knapsack.   It should be the same with every employee in the permanent service of a great American railroad company.   The possibility of his rising to any position in that service for which he showed himself qualified should be open before him and constantly present in his mind.   Many of the most remarkable and successful men who have handled railroads in the United States began their active lives as brakemen, as telegraph operators, even as laborers on the track.   Such examples are of inestimable value.   They reveal possibilities open to all.

Beyond this, the man who is permanently enrolled should feel that, though he may not rise to a high position, yet, as a matter of right, he is entitled to hold the position to which he has risen just so long as he demeans himself properly and does his duty well. He should be free from fear of arbitrary dismissal.   In order that he may have this security, a tribunal should be devised before which he would have the right to be heard in case charges of misdemeanor are advanced against him.

No such tribunal has yet been provided in the organization of any railroad company ; neither, as a rule, has the suggestion of such a tribunal been looked upon with favor either by the official or the employee.   The latter is apt to argue that he already has such a tribunal in the executive committee of his own labor organization ; and a tribunal, too, upon which he can depend to decide always in his favor. The official, on the other hand, contends that if he is to be responsible for results he must have the power of arbitrarily dismissing the employee. Without it he will not be able to maintain discipline. The two arguments, besides answering each other, divide the railroad service into hostile camps. The executive committees of the labor organizations practically cannot save the members of those organizations from being got rid of, though they do in many cases protect them against summary discharge ; and, on the other hand, the official, in the face of the executive committee, enjoys only in theory the power of summary discharge. The situation is accordingly false and bad. It provokes hostility. The one party boasts of a protection which he does not enjoy ; the other insists upon a power which he dares not exercise. The remedy is manifest. A system should be devised based on recognized facts ; a system which would secure reasonable protection to the employee, and at the same time enable the official to enforce all necessary discipline. This a permanent service, with a properly organized tribunal to appeal to, would bring about. Meanwhile the winnowing process would be provided for in the temporary service. Over that the official would have complete control, and the idle, the worthless, and the insubordinate would be kept off. The wheat would there be separated from the chaff. Until such a system is devised the existing chaos, made up of powerless protection and impotent power, must apparently continue. None the less it is a delusion on the one side and a mockery on the other.

How the members of such a court as has been suggested would be appointed and by whom is matter for consideration. It would, of course, be essential that the appointees should command the confidence of all in the company's service, whether officials or employees. The possible means of reaching this result will presently be discussed.

Not only should permanent employees be entitled to retain their position during good behavior, but they should also look forward to the continual bettering of their condition. That is, apart from promotion, seniority in the service should carry with it certain rights and privileges. Take the case of conductors, brakemen, engineers, machinists, and the like ; there seems to be no reason why length of faithful service should not carry with it a stipulated increase of pay. If conductors, for example, have a regular pay of $100 a month, there seems no good reason why the pay should not increase by steps of $5 with each five years' service, so that when the conductor has been twenty-five years in the service his pay should be increased by one-quarter, or $25 a month. The increase might be more or less. The figures suggested merely illustrate. So also with the engineer, the brakeman, the section-man, the machinist. A certain prospect of increased pay, if a man demeans himself faithfully, is a great incentive to faithful demeanor. This is another fact which it would be well not to lose sight of.

There ought likewise to be connected with every large railroad organization certain funds, contributed partly by the company and partly by the voluntary action of employees, which would provide for hospital service, retiring pensions, sick pensions, and insurance against accident and death. Every man whose name has once been enrolled in the permanent employ of the company should be entitled to the benefit of these funds ; and he should be deprived of it only by his own voluntary act, or as the consequence of some misdemeanor proved before a tribunal. At present the railroad companies of this country are under no inducement to establish these mutual insurance societies, or to contribute to them. Their service, in principle at least, is a shifting service ; and so long as it is shifting the elaborate organizations which are essential to the safe management of the funds referred to cannot be called into existence. A tie-up, as it might be called, between the companies and their employees is a condition precedent. Were this once effected the rest would follow by steps both natural and easy. For a company like the Union Pacific to contribute $100,-000 a year to a hospital fund and retiring pension and insurance associations would be a small matter, if the thing could be so arranged that the permanent employees themselves would contribute a like sum ; and permanent employees only would contribute at all. Once let the growth of associations like these begin, and it proceeds with almost startling rapidity. At the end of ten years the accumulated capital on the basis of contribution suggested would probably amount to millions. Every man who was so fortunate as to become a permanent employee of the company would then be assured of provision in case of sickness or disability, and his family would be assured of it in case of his death.

The moment a permanent service was thus established it would also involve further provision of an educational nature. That is, the companies must continually provide a stock of men for the future. Where a boy—the son of an employee—grows up always looking forward to entering the company's service, he becomes to that company very much what a cadet at West Point or Annapolis is to the army or the navy of the United States ; the idea of loyalty to the company and of pride in its service grows up with him. Railroad educational institutions of this sort have already been created by at least one corporation in the country, and they should be created by all railroad corporations of the first class. The children of employees would naturally go into these schools, and the best of them would at the proper age be sent out upon the road to take their places in the shops, on the track, or at the brake. From those thus educated the higher positions in the company would thereafter be filled. The cost of maintaining these schools, at least in part, would become a regular item in the operating expenses of the road. Properly handled, a vast economy would be effected through them. The morale of the service would gradually be raised, and the morale of a railroad is, if properly viewed, no less important than the morale of an army or navy. It is invaluable.

But it is futile to suppose that such a service as that outlined could be organized, in America at least, unless those concerned in it were allowed a voice in its management. Practically the most important feature of the whole is therefore yet to be considered. How is the employee to be assured a voice in the management of these joint interests, without bringing about demoralization ? No one has yet had the courage to face this question ; and yet it is a question which must be faced if a solution of existing difficulties is to be found. If the employees contribute to the insurance and other funds, it is right that they should have a voice in the management of those funds. If an employee holds his situation during good behavior, he has a right to be heard in the organization of the board which, in case of his suspension for alleged cause, is to pass upon his behavior. No system will succeed which does not recognize these rights. In other words, it will be impossible to establish perfectly good faith and the highest morale in the service of the companies until the problem of giving this voice to employees, and giving it effectively, is solved. It can be solved in but one way: that is, by representation. To solve it may mean industrial peace.

It is, of course, impossible to dispose of these difficult matters in town-meeting. Nevertheless, the town-meeting must be at the base of any successful plan for disposing of them. The end in view is to bring the employer—who in this case is the company, represented by its president and board of directors—and the employees into direct and immediate contact through a representative system. When thus brought into direct and immediate contact, the parties must arrive at results through the usual method: that is, by discussion and rational agreement. It has already been noticed that the operating department of a great railroad company naturally subdivides itself into those concerned in the train movement, those concerned in the care of the permanent way, and those concerned in the work of the mechanical department. It would seem proper, therefore, that a council of employees should be formed, of such a number as might be agreed on, containing representatives from each of these departments. In order to make an effective representation, the council would have to be a large body. For present purposes, and for the sake of illustration merely, it might be supposed that, in the case of the Union Pacific, each department in a division of the road would elect its own members of the employees' council. There are five of these divisions and three departments in every division. The operating-men, the yard and section-men, and the machinists of the division would, therefore, under this arrangement choose a given number of representatives. If one such representative was chosen to each hundred employees in the permanent service those thus selected would constitute a division council. To perfect the organization, without disturbing the necessary work of the company, each of these division councils would then select certain (say, for example, three) of their number, representing the mechanical, the operating, and the permanent way departments, and these delegates from each of the departments would, at certain periods of the year, to be provided for by the articles of organization, all meet together at the head-quarters of the company in Omaha. The central council, under the system here suggested, would consist of fifteen men ; that is, one representing each of the three departments of the five several divisions. These fifteen men would represent the employees. It would be for them to select a board of delegates, or small executive committee, to confer directly with the president and board of directors. Here would be found the organization through which the voice of the employees would make itself heard and felt in matters which directly affect the rights of employees, including the appointment of a tribunal to pass upon cases of misdemeanor, and the management of all institutions, whether financial or educational, to which the employees had contributed and in which they had a consequent interest.

There is no reason whatever for supposing that, within the limits which have been indicated, such an organization would lead to difficulty. On the contrary, where it did not remove a difficulty it might readily be made to open a way out of it. The employees, feeling that they too had rights which the company frankly recognized and was bound to respect, would in all cases of agitation proceed through the regular machinery, which brought them into easy and direct contact with the highest authority in the company's service. They would not, therefore, be driven into outside organizations. Meanwhile, on the other hand, the highest officers of the company, including the president and the board of directors, would be brought into immediate relations with the representatives of the employees on terms of equality. Each would have an equal voice in the management of common interests ; and it would only remain to make provision for arriving at a solution of questions in case of deadlock. This would naturally be done by the appointment of a permanent arbitrator, who would be selected in advance.

The organization suggested includes, it will be remembered, only those employees whose names are on the permanent rolls of the operating department. For reasons which have been sufficiently referred to, those whose names are on the rolls of the other four departments have not been considered. But there would be no difficulty in making provision for them also, should it be found expedient or desirable so to do. Through the system of represen-tation the organization could in fact be made to include every employee in the permanent service of the company, not excepting the president, the general manager, or the general counsel. Each employee included would have one vote, and each division and department its representatives. The organization in other words is elastic. No matter how large it might be it would never become unwieldy so long as it resulted in the small committee which met in direct conference face to face with the board of directors.

Could such a system as that which has been suggested be devised and put in practical operation there is reason to hope that the difficulties which have hitherto occurred between the great railroad companies and those in their pay would not occur in future. The movement is the natural and necessary outcome of the vast development referred to in the opening paragraphs of this paper. It is based on a simple recognition of acknowledged facts, and fol-lows the lines of action with which the people of this country are most familiar. The path indicated is that in which for centuries they have been accustomed to tread. It has led them out of many difficulties. Why not out of this difficulty?

THE EVERY-DAY LIFE OF RAILROAD MEN.

By B. B. ADAMS, Jr.

The Typical Railroad Man—On the Road and at Home—Raising the Moral Standard— Characteristics of the Freight Brakeman—His Wit the Result of Meditation—How Slang is Originated—Agreeable Features of his Life in Fine Weather—Hardships in Winter—The Perils of Hand-brakes—Broken Trains—Going back to Flag— Coupling Accidents—At the Spring—Advantages of a Passenger Brakeman— Trials of the Freight Conductor—The Investigation of Accidents—Irregular Hours of Work—The Locomotive Engineer the Hero of the Rail—His Rare Qualities— The Value of Quick Judgment—Calm Fidelity a Necessary Trait—Saving Fuel on a Freight Engine—Making Time on a Passenger Engine—Remarkable Runs—The Spirit of Fraternity among Engineers—Difficult Duties of a Passenger-train Conductor—Tact in Dealing with Many People—Questions to be Answered—How Rough Characters are Dealt with—Heavy Responsibilities—The Work of a Station Agent—Flirtation by Telegraph—The Baggage-master's Hard Task—Eternal Vigilance Necessary in a Switch-tender—Section-men, Train Despatchers, Firemen, and Clerks—Efforts to Make the Railroad Man's Life Easier.

THE typical railroad man "runs on the road;" he is not the one whose urbane presence adorns the much-heralded offices of the railroad companies on Broadway, where the gold letters on the front window are each considerably larger than the elbow-room allowed the clerks inside; nor, indeed, is he, generally speaking, the one with whom the public or the public's drayman comes in contact when visiting a large city station to ship or receive freight. These and others, whose part in the complex machinery of transportation is in a degree auxiliary, are indeed largely imbued with the *esprit de corps* which originates in the main body of workers; but their duties are such that their interest is not especially lively. Even the men employed at stations in villages and large towns acquire a share of their railroad spirit at second hand, as life on a train is necessary to get the experience which embodies the true fascination which so charms Young America.

The railroad man's home-life is not specially different from other people's. There have been Chesterfields among conductors, and mechanical geniuses have grown up among the locomotive engineers, but these were products of an era now past. Station-men are a part of the communities where their duties place them. Trainmen and their families occupy a modest though highly respectable place in the society they live in. Trainmen who live in a city generally receive the same pay that is given to their brothers, doing the same work, whose homes are in the country. The families of the latter therefore enjoy purer air, lessened expenses, and other advantages which are denied the former.

On most railroads the freight trainmen—engineers, conductors, brakemen, and firemen—are the most numerous and prominent class, as the number of freight trains is generally larger than that of passenger trains ; and among these men there are more brakemen than anything else, because there are two or more on every train, while there is but one of each of the other classes. And as the ranks of the passenger-train service are generally recruited from the freight trainmen, it follows that the *freight brakeman* impresses his individuality quite strongly upon not only the circles in which he moves but the whole train-service as well. Freight conductors are promoted brakemen, and most (though not by any means all) passenger conductors are promoted freight conductors ; so that the brakeman's prominent traits of character continue to appear throughout the several grades of the service. As he is promoted he of course improves. The general character of the *personnel* of the freight-train service has undergone a considerable change in the last twenty years. Whiskey drinkers have been weeded out, and pilferers with them. Improved discipline has effected a general toning up, raising the moral standard perceptibly. One reforming superintendent, a few years ago, on undertaking an aggressive campaign found himself compelled to discharge three-fifths of all his brakemen before he could regard the force as reasonably cleared of the rowdy element.

The brakeman, like the "drummer," is a characteristic American product. Each has his wits sharpened by peculiar experiences, and, while important lines of intellectual training are almost wholly neglected, there is contact with the world in various directions, which develops qualities that tend to elevate the individual in many ways. Although freight brakemen do not have any intercourse with the public, they somehow learn the ways of the world very quickly, and the brightest ones among them need very little training to fit them for a place on a passenger train where they are expected to deal with gentle ladies and fastidious millionaires, and bear themselves with the grace of a hotel clerk. Perhaps one reason why brakemen impress their characteristics on the whole *personnel* of the service is because they have abundance of opportunity for meditation. Many of them have a superfluity of hours and half-hours when they have nothing to do but ride on the top of a car and keep a general watch of the train, and they have ample time to think twice before speaking once. Even a circus clown or the vender of shoestrings or ten-cent watches has to study the arts of expression ; why should not the intelligent trainman, who wishes to let people know that he is of some account in the world ? If he wants a favor from a superior he knows just the best way of approach to secure success. If he deems it worth while to complain of anything, he formulates his appeal in a way that is sure to be telling. Everyone knows the old story of the brakeman who was refused a free pass home on Saturday night with the argument that his employer, if a farmer, could not be reasonably expected to hitch up a horse and buggy for such a purpose. The reply that, admitting this, the farmer who had his team already harnessed up and was going that way with an empty seat would be outrageously mean to refuse his hired man a ride, is none too 'cute to be characteristic. The brakeman who is not able to puncture the sophistries of narrow-souled or disingenuous superiors is the exception and not the rule.

The brakeman gives the prevailing tone to the "society" of despatchers' lobbies and other lounging places which he frequents. If he be profane or fault-finding or sour, he can easily spread the influence of these unpleasant traits. A lazy brakeman becomes more lazy, because his work is in many respects easy. Having little to do he demands still less. A foul-mouthed one gives himself free rein because many usual restraints are absent. The

prevalence of profanity, which, aside from the question of sinful-
ness, hampers a man in any aspirations he may have toward more
elevating society, is perhaps the worst blot on the reputation of
brakemen as a class.   Many worthy men among them, and especially among conductors and engineers, have, however, done much
to improve the tone of conversation in trainmen's haunts, and on
the better disciplined roads decorum is the rule, and rowdyism the
exception.   There is abundance of humor and spirit, however.   The
brakeman originates whatever slang may be deemed necessary to
give spice to the talk of the caboose and round-house.   He calls a
gravel train a " dust express," and refers to the pump for compress-
ing air for the power-brakes as a " wind-jammer."   The fireman's
prosaic labors are lightened by being poetically mentioned as the
" handling of black diamonds," and the mortification of being called
into the superintendent's office to explain some dereliction of duty
is disguised by referring to the episode as " dancing on the carpet."

The disagreeable features of a freight brakeman's life are chiefly

" Dancing on the Carpet."

those dependent upon
the weather.   If he
could perform his du-
ties in Southern Cali-
fornia or Florida in
winter, and in the
Northern States in
summer, his lot would
ordinarily be a happy
one, though the an-
noyance of tramps is
almost universal in
mild climates, and in
many cases takes the
shape of positive dan-
ger.   These vaga-
bonds persist in riding
on or in the cars, while
the faithful trainman
must, according to his instructions, keep them off.   In some sections
of the country they will board a train in gangs of a dozen, armed

Trainman and Tramps.

with pistols, and dictate where a train shall carry them. Not long ago in Chicago a conductor, while ejecting a tramp from the caboose, was shot and killed by the ruffian.

The hardships of cold and stormy weather are serious, both because of the test of endurance involved and the added difficulties in handling a train. The Westinghouse automatic air-brake, which has served so admirably on passenger trains for the past fifteen years, has only recently been adapted and cheapened so as to make it available for long freight trains, but it is now so perfected that in a few years the brakeman who now has to ride on the outside of cars in a freezing condition for an hour at a time will be privileged to sit comfortably in his caboose while the speed of the train is governed by the engineer through the instantaneous action of the air-brake. On the steep roads of the Rocky Mountains, and a few other lines, this brake is already in use.

But "braking by hand" is still the rule. In running on ascending grades or at slow speeds, the brakemen can ride under cover, but in descending grades, or on levels when the speed is high, they must be on the tops of the cars ready to instantly apply the brakes, for the reason that there are generally only three or four men to a long train weighing from 500 to 1,000 tons, whose momentum cannot be arrested very quickly. In descending steep grades, only the most constant and skilful care prevents the train from rushing at breakneck speed to the foot of the incline, or to a curve, where it would be precipitated over an embankment and crushed into splinters. One of the mountain roads in Colorado which now uses air-brakes is said to be lined its whole length with the ruins of cars lying in the gorges, where they were wrecked in the former days of hand-brakes. Even on grades much less steep than those in Colorado the danger of this sort of disaster is one that has to be constantly guarded against. Take the case of a 40-car train descending a $1\frac{1}{2}$ per cent. grade ($79\frac{2}{10}$ feet per mile). Before all of the cars have passed over the summit and commenced to descend, the forward part of the train will have increased its velocity very perceptibly and will thus by its weight exert a strong pull on the rear portion, "yanking" it very roughly sometimes, and if one of the couplings between the cars chances to be weak it breaks, separating the train into two parts. Mishaps of this kind are frequent, and two or more breakages often occur at the same time, dividing the train so that one of the parts—between the two end portions—is perhaps left with no brakeman upon it. The engineman then has the choice of slackening his speed and allowing the unmanageable cars to violently collide with his portion, or of increasing his own speed to such a rate that he is soon in danger of suddenly overtaking a train ahead of him. To avoid this breaking-in-two the brakemen must be wide awake on the instant and see that their brakes are tightened before the speed even begins to elude control. As soon as the whole train has got beyond the summit, and the speed is reduced to a proper rate by the application of the brakes on, say, one-third or one-half the cars, it will perhaps be found that one or two brakes too many have been put

Braking in Hard Weather.

on and that the train is running too slowly. Some of them must
then be loosened. Or perhaps some are set so tightly that the
friction heats the wheels unduly or causes them to slide along the
track instead of rolling; then those brakes must be released and
some on other cars applied instead; and all this must be done
(sometimes for an hour) when the temperature is 20 degrees below
zero, or the wind is blowing a gale, just as under more favorable

circumstances.   A train moving at 20 miles an hour against a wind
with a velocity of 30 miles increases the latter to 50, so far as the
brakeman is concerned ; and if rain or sleet is falling, the force of
it on his hands and face is very severe.   If we add to this the danger attendant upon stepping from one car to another over a gap of
27 to 30 inches, in a dark night, when the cars are constantly moving up and down on their springs and are swaying to one side or
the other every few seconds, we get some idea of, though we cannot realize, the sensations that must at such times fill the minds of
the men whose pleasant berth seems so enjoyable on a mild summer's day.   And this is not an overdrawn picture or the worst that
might be given ; for rain and snow combined often coat the roofs
of cars so completely and solidly that they are worse than the
smoothest skating-pond, and moving upon them is attended with
danger at every step.   Jumping—it cannot be called walking—from
one car to another is in such cases positively reckless.   The brake-
apparatus will in a snow-storm be coated with ice so rapidly that
vigorous action is required to keep it in working condition.   Even
a wind alone, in dry weather, sometimes compels the men to *crawl*
from one car to another, grasping such projections as they may.
The brakeman who forgets to take his rubber coat and overalls
sometimes suffers severely from sudden changes of temperature.
In spring or fall a lively shower will be encountered in a sheltered
valley, and the clothing be completely drenched, and then within
perhaps half an hour the ascent of a few hundred feet brings the
train into an atmosphere a few degrees below the freezing point, so
that with the aid of the wind, fanned by the speed of the train, the
clothes are very soon frozen stiff.

Another feature which often involves discomfort, and occasionally positive suffering and danger, is " going back to flag."   When
a train is unexpectedly stopped upon the road, the brakeman at
the rear end must immediately take his red flag or lantern and go
back a half-mile or more to give the " stop " signal to the enginemen of any train that may be following.   This rule is sometimes
disregarded in clear weather on straight lines, and is even evaded
by lazy or unfaithful brakemen where the neglect is positively dangerous, but still many a faithful man has to go out and stand for a
long time in a severe snow-storm or risk his life in walking several

miles to a station. The record of individual perils and heroisms in the New York blizzard of March, 1888, are paralleled, or at least repeated, on a slightly milder scale, by brakemen every winter.

Flagging in Winter.

Even in the blizzard country of the Northwest, where a half hour's exposure is often fatal, the system of train-running is such that the stopping of a train at an unexpected place involves danger of collision if the brakeman does not at once go back and *stay back.* A "tail-end" brakeman has various anxieties, which cannot be detailed here. Often there is a possibility that the advancing engineer will not see his red lantern. One brakeman in New Brunswick several years ago ignominiously deserted his post, leaving his train to look out for itself, because of a visit from a huge bear whose residence was in the woods near the point on the railroad where the brakeman was keeping his lonely night-vigil.

Coupling.

The danger of sudden accidental death or maiming is constant and great, and the bare record of the numerous cases is acutely suggestive of inexpressible suffering ; but, strange to say, it does not worry the average brakeman much. Though probably a thousand trainmen are killed in this country every year, and four or five thousand injured, by collisions and derailments, in coupling cars, falling off trains, striking low overhead bridges, and from other causes, no one brakeman, from what he sees in his own experience, realizes the danger very vividly. As in other dangers which are constant but inevitable, familiarity breeds carelessness which is closely akin to contempt. Falling from trains is really a serious danger, because the most ceaseless caution—next to impossible for the average man to maintain—is necessary to avoid missteps. This will be practically abolished when the long-wished-for air-brake comes into use, as that will obviate the necessity of riding on the tops of the cars.

Coupling accidents are practically unavoidable because, although the necessary manipulations *can* be made without going between the cars or placing the hands in dangerous situations, the men as a general thing prefer to take the risk of the more dangerous method. With the ordinary freight-car apparatus (which, however, is destined to be superseded by an automatic coupler) the link by which the cars are connected is retained by a pin in the drawbar of either car ; as one car approaches another at considerable speed, this link, which hangs loosely down at an angle of thirty degrees, must be lifted and guided into the opening in the opposite drawbar. This operation must, according to the regulations of most roads, be performed by the aid of a short stick ; but, disregarding the regulation, partly to save time and partly because of fear of the ridicule that would be called out by the exhibition of a lack of dexterity, the average brakeman uses his fingers. He must lift the link and hold it horizontally until the end enters the opening, and then withdraw his hand before the heavy drawbars come together. A delay of a fraction of a second would crush the hand or finger as under a trip-hammer. And, in point of fact, this delay does, for various reasons, frequently happen, and the number of trainmen with wounded hands to be found in every large freight-yard is sad evidence of the fact. But again, assuming that this part of the operation is accomplished in safety, there is another and worse danger in the possibility of being crushed bodily. Cars are built with projecting timbers on their ends at or near the centre, for the purpose of keeping the main body of each car twelve or fifteen inches from its neighbor ; but cars of dissimilar pattern sometimes meet in such a way that the projections on one lap past those on the other, and the space which should afford room for the man to stand in safety is not maintained. If the brakeman, in the darkness of night or the hurry of his work, fails to note the peculiarities of the cars, he is mercilessly crushed, the ponderous vehicles often banging together with a force of many tons. A constant danger in coupling and uncoupling is the liability to catch the feet in angles in the track.* Freight conductors are peculiarly liable to this, as the duty of uncoupling (pulling out the coupling-pin) generally devolves upon them, and must be done while the train is in motion. Walking rapidly along, in the dark, with the right hand holding a lantern and grasping the car, while the left is tugging at a pin which sticks, involves perplexities wherein a moment's hesitation may prove fatal.

The dangers here recounted are those which only brakemen (or those acting as brakemen) have to meet. The liability of all trainmen to be killed by the cars tumbling down a bank, colliding with another train, and a hundred other conditions, is also considerable. The horror which the public feels on the occurrence of such a disaster as that at Chatsworth, Ill., in the summer of 1887,

* See " Safety in Railroad Travel," page 222.

or the half-dozen other terrible ones within the past few years, could reasonably be repeated every month if railroad employees instead of passengers were considered.   There are no accurate official statistics kept of the train accidents in the country, but the accounts compiled monthly by the *Railroad Gazette* always show a large number of casualties to railroad men from causes *beyond their own control* (collisions, running off the track, etc.), no mention being made of the larger number resulting from the victims' own want of caution.   In the month of March, 1887, in which occurred the terrible Bussey Bridge disaster, near Boston, 25 passengers were killed in the United States ; but the same month recorded 34 employees killed.   At Chatsworth 80 passengers were killed ; but in that and the following month the number of employees killed in the country reached 97.   In both of these comparisons the number of passengers is exceptional, while that of employees is ordinary.   But, as already intimated, these dangers and discouragements are distributed over such a large territory and among such a large number of individuals that the general serenity of the brakeman's life is not much disturbed by them.   In spite of them all, he enjoys his work and, if he is adapted to the calling, he sticks to it.

The brakeman must be on hand promptly at the hour of his train's preparation for departure, and generally he must do his part in 15, 30, or 60 minutes' lively work in assembling cars from different tracks, changing them from the front to the rear or middle of the train, and setting aside those that are broken or disabled ; but, once on the road, by far the greater portion of his time is his own, for his own enjoyment, almost as fully as that of the passenger who travels for the express purpose of entertaining himself. In mild weather and in daylight, life on the top of a freight train is almost wholly devoid of unpleasant features, and it takes on the nature of work only for the same reason that any routine becomes more or less irksome after a time.   Much of the time there are a few bushels of cinders from the engine flying in the air, which a novice can get into his eyes with great facility, but the brakeman gets used to them.   He sees every day (on many roads) the beauties of nature in great variety.   Much of the scenery of the adjoining country is 500 per cent. more enjoyable from the brake-

The Pleasant Part of a Brakeman's Life.

man's perch on the roof than from the car windows, for the reason that the increased height gives such an enlarged horizon. This education from nature is an element in railroad men's lives not to be despised. The trainman whose daily trips take him past the panoramic charms of the Connecticut Valley in summer, through the gorgeous-hued mountain-foliage along the Erie in autumn, or the perennial grandeur of the Rocky Mountains in Colorado, certainly enjoys a privilege for which many a city worker would gladly make large sacrifices.   But to trainmen the refining influence of these surroundings is often an unconscious influence, and with the majority of them is perhaps generally so, because of the prosaic round of every-day thoughts filling their minds.   There are also some other advantages, not wholly unæsthetic, which a millionaire might almost envy the freight trainman.   Every twenty miles or so the engine must stop for water, and it often happens that this is in a cool place where the men can at the same time refresh themselves with spring water whose sparkling purity is unknown in New York or Chicago.   Though brakemen who love beer are not by any means scarce, an accessible spring or well of pure water along the line always finds appreciative users during warm weather; and the Kentuckian who sojourned six months in Illinois without thinking to try the water there is not represented in the ranks of level-headed brakemen.   A certain railroad president regales himself in summer on spring water brought in jugs from 100 miles up the road by trainmen who find in this service an opportunity to "make themselves solid" at headquarters.   Freight trainmen get all the delicious products of the soil at first hands.   In their stops at way-stations they get acquainted with the farmers, and can make their selection of the best things at low prices, thus (if they keep house) living on fruits, vegetables, etc., of a quality fit for a king.

The passenger-train brakeman differs from the freight trainman chiefly in the fact that he must deal with the public, and so must have a care for his personal appearance and behavior, and in the fact that he is *not a brakeman*, the universal air-brake relieving him of all work in this line.   His chief duties are those of a porter, though the wide-awake American brakeman, with an eye to future promotion to a conductorship, maintains his dignity and is not by any means the servile call-boy that the English railway porter is.   The wearing of uniforms has been introduced here from England and is, in the main, a good feature, though some roads, whose discipline is otherwise quite good, allow their men to appear in slovenly and even ragged clothes.   Superintendents should give

more care to this matter, as it is not an unimportant one. It
affects the men's self-respect and influences their usefulness in other
ways. The frugal brakeman can-
not wear his blue suit on Sunday
or a-visiting, and his Sunday
suit when old cannot
be used up by week-
day wear, so he nat-

At the Spring.

urally concludes that his
employer is guilty of a little
undue severity toward him. Brakemen on the modern "limited"
trains (a three hours' run without a stop constituting a day's
work) have in some respects too easy a task, and their minds are
more likely to rust out than to wear out. They have a constant
care, to be sure, and sometimes must "go back to flag," the same

as a freight trainman, but, in the main, their berth would about fill the ideal of the Irish shoveller who confided to his fellow-workman that "for a nice, clane, aisy job" he would like to be a bishop.

Brakemen have had the reputation of doing a good deal of flirting, and many a country-girl has found a worthy husband among them ; but there is not so much of this method of diversion as formerly ; both passenger and freight men now have to attend more strictly to business, and they cannot conveniently indulge in side play.   There are still, however, enough short branch-lines and slow-going roads in backwoods districts to insure that flirting shall not become a lost art in this part of the world.

The freight conductor is simply a high grade of brakeman. His work is almost wholly supervisory and clerical, and so, after several years' service, he becomes more sober and business-like in his bearing, the responsibilities of his position being sufficient to effect this change ; but he generally retains his sympathies with his old associates who have become subordinates.   His duties are to keep the record of the train, the time, numbers of cars, etc. ; to see that the brakemen regulate the speed when necessary, and to keep a general watch.   The calculations necessary to make a 75-mile trip and get over the line without wasting time are often considerable, and an inexperienced conductor can easily keep himself in a worry for the whole trip.   Often he cannot go more than ten miles after making way for a passenger train before another overtakes him ; so that he must spend a good share of his time sitting in his caboose with the time-table in one hand and his watch in the other, calculating where and when to side-track the train.   On single-track roads perplexities of this kind are generally more numerous than on double lines, because trains both in front and behind must be guarded against, and because the regulations are frequently modified by telegraphic instructions from headquarters.   A mistake in reading these instructions, which are written in pencil, often by a slovenly penman, and on tissue-paper, may, and occasionally does, cause a disastrous collision.   These duties of conductors are especially characteristic of trains that must keep out of the way of passenger trains, so that in this particular line it will be seen that the passenger conductor has much the easier berth.   The freight and "work-train" conductor must really be a better calculator, in many ways, than the wearer of gilt badges and buttons, though the latter receives the higher pay.

The *bête noire* of the freight conductor is an investigation at headquarters concerning delinquencies in which the blame is divided. A typical case of this kind is that of a freight train which has stopped at some unusual place and been run into by a following train, doing some hundreds of dollars damage, if not killing or injuring persons. " Strict adherence to rules will avert all such accidents," the code says ; but they do happen, and the inquiry as to whether the conductor used due diligence in sending a man with a red flag to warn the oncoming train, or the engineer of the latter was heedless, or what was the trouble, is the occasion of much anxiety.

Conductors, concerning whose life I have only noted a few of the duties and perplexities, are not so much subject to the vicissitudes of cold and wet weather, and therefore have in many respects better opportunities than the brakemen to avail themselves of the enjoyments of a trainman's life. The risk to life and limb from coupling cars, etc., is also somewhat less, though many a faithful conductor has lost his life in the performance of a dangerous duty which he had assumed out of generous consideration for an inexperienced or overworked subordinate. The beneficial influences on health, mind, and morals coming from contact with nature are, as before remarked, largely unconscious influences, because of the counteracting effect of the immediate surroundings. The irregular hours are unfavorable to health. The crews run in turn ; if there are forty crews and forty trains daily, each crew will start out at about the same hour each day. But if on Monday there are forty trains, on Tuesday thirty, and on Wednesday fifty, it will be seen that the starting time must be very irregular. Ten of the crews which worked on Monday will have nothing to do on Tuesday, but on Wednesday or Thursday will have to do double service. The first trip will be all in the daytime, and the next all in the night, perhaps. This irregularity is constant, and it is impossible to tell on Monday morning where one will be on Wednesday. All the week's sleep may have to be taken in the daytime or all at night. There may be five days' work to do between Monday morning and the following Monday morning, or there may be nine. The trainman has to literally board in his "mammoth" dinner-pail, and his wife or boarding mistress knows less about his whereabouts than if he were on an Arctic whaling vessel.

The locomotive engineer is the popular " hero of the rail," and the popular estimate in this respect is substantially just. Others have to brave dangers and perform duties under trying circumstances; but the engine-runner has to ride in the most dangerous part of the train, take charge of a steam-boiler that may explode and blow him to atoms, and of machinery that may break and kill him, and try to keep up a vigilance which only a being more than human could successfully maintain. He must be a tolerably skilful machinist—he cannot be too good—and have nerves that will remain steady under the most trying circumstances. If running a fast express through midnight darkness over a line where a similar train has been tipped off a precipice (and a brother runner killed) by train-wreckers the night before, he must dash forward with the same confidence that he would feel in broad daylight on an open prairie. But he does not " heroically grasp the throttle" in the face of danger, when the throttle has been already shut, nor does he " whistle down brakes," in order to add a stirring element to the reporter's tale, when by the magic of the air-brake he can, with a turn of his hand, apply every brake in the train with the grip of a vise in less time than it would take him to reach the whistle-pull. When there is danger ahead there is generally just one thing to do, and that is to stop as soon as possible. An instant suffices for shutting off the steam and applying the brake. With modern trains this is all that is necessary or can be done. Reversing the engine is necessary on many engines, and formerly was on all; this would, in fact, be done instinctively by old runners, in any case, but this also is done in a second. After taking these measures there is nothing for the engineman to do but look out for his own safety. In some circumstances, as in the case of a partially burned bridge which may possibly support the train even in a weakened condition, it may be best to put on all steam. The runner is then in a dilemma, and a right decision is a matter of momentary inspiration. Many lives have been saved by quick-witted runners in such cases, but there is no ground for censure of the engineer who, in the excitement of the moment, decides to slacken instead of quicken his speed. The rare cases of this kind are what show the value of experience, and of men of the right temperament and degree of intelligence to acquire experience-lessons readily. The writer recalls an instance several years ago where an alert, steady, and experienced runner found himself on the crossing of another railroad with a heavy train rushing toward him on the transverse track at uncontrollable speed. It was too late to retreat, and in less than ten seconds the oncoming train would crash broadside into his cars, filled with passengers. A frantic effort to increase the speed and clear the crossing would have either broken the weak couplings then in use or would have simply whirled the driving-wheels with such excessive force as to slacken the speed of the train rather than accelerate it. In point of fact, the rear car just escaped being struck by the ponderous engine bearing down upon it at the rate of twenty or thirty feet a second; and the preservation of the lives of the passengers was due to the fact that the engineer was well-balanced, quick to act, and not excitable. What did he do? He instantly put on more steam, but with unerring judgment opened the valve just far enough and no more.

But the terrible cloud constantly hanging over the engineer and fireman of a fast train is the chance of encountering an obstacle which cannot possibly be avoided, and which leaves them no alternative but to jump for their lives, if, indeed, it does not take away even that. To the fact that this cloud is no larger than it is, and that these men have sturdy and courageous natures, must be attributed the lightness with which it rests upon them. On one road or another, from a washout, or inefficient management, or a collision caused by an operator's forgetfulness, or some one of a score of other causes, there are constantly occurring cases of men heroically meeting death under the most heart-rending circumstances. Every month records a number of such, though happily they are not frequent on any one road. The case of Engineer Kennar, a year or more ago, is a typical one. Precipitated with his engine into a river by a washout which the roadmaster's vigilance had failed to discover, his first thought, as zealous hands tried to rescue him, was for the safety of his train; and, forgetting his own anguish, he warned those about him to attend first to the sending of a red lantern to warn a following train against a collision. The significance of facts like this is not so much in the service to humanity done at the time, or even in the example set for those who shall meet such crises in the future, but rather in the evidence they give of the firm and lofty conscientiousness that inspires the everyday conduct of thousands of engineers all over the land. As has already been said, the critical occasions on which engineers are supposed to be heroic often allow them no chance at all to be either heroic or cowardly, and their heroism must be, and is, manifested in the calm fidelity with which they, day after day and year after year, perform their exacting and often monotonous round of duties while all the time knowing of the possibilities before them.

On the best of roads a freight train wrecked by a broken wheel under a borrowed car may be thrown in the path of a passenger train on another track, just as the latter approaches. This has happened more than once lately. No amount of fidelity or forethought (except in the maker of the wheels) can prevent this kind of disaster. There is constant danger, on most roads, of running off the track at misplaced switches, many switches being located at points where the runner can see them only a few seconds before he is upon them; but the chance is so small—perhaps one in ten or a hundred thousand—that the average runner forgets it, and it is only by severe self-discipline that he can hold himself up to compliance with the rule which requires him to be on the watch for every switch-target as long before reaching it as he possibly can. He finds the switches all right and the road perfectly clear so regularly, day after day and month after month, that he may easily fall into the snare of thinking that they will always be so. But, like other trainmen, the engineman finds enough more agreeable thoughts to fill his mind, and reflects upon the hazards of his vocation perhaps too little.

The freight engineman's every-day thoughts are largely about the care of his engine and the perplexities incident to getting out of it the maximum amount of work with the minimum amount of fuel. The constant aim of his superiors is to have the engine draw every pound it possibly can. To haul a train up a long and steep grade when the cars are so heavily loaded that a single additional one would bring the whole to a dead stand-still requires a knack that can be appreciated only by viewing the performance on the spot. Failure not only wastes time and fuel (it may necessitate a return to the foot of the hill or going to the top with only half the load), but it raises a suspicion that some other runner might have succeeded better. The runner whose engine "lays down on the road" (fails to draw its load because of insufficient fire and consequent low steam-pressure) is

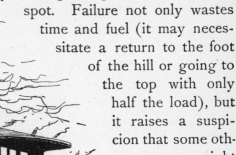

Just Time to Jump.

liable to the jeers of his comrades on his return home, if not to some sharp inquiries from his superior.

The passenger runner's greatest concern is to "make time." Some trains are scheduled so that the engineman must keep his locomotive up to its very highest efficiency over every furlong of its journey in order to arrive at his destination on time. A little carelessness in firing, in letting cold water into the boiler irregularly, or in slackening more than is necessary where the right to the track is in doubt for a few rods; these and a score of similar circumstances may make five minutes' delay in the arrival at the terminus and necessitate an embarrassing interview with the trainmaster. A trip on a crowded line may involve watching for danger-signals every quarter of a mile and the maintenance of such high speed that they must be obeyed the instant they are espied in order to avoid the possibility of collision.*

* The New York elevated roads run 3,500 trains a day, each one passing signals (likely to indicate danger) every hundred rods, almost. Who can expect engineers never to blunder in such innumerable operations?

The passenger runner finds himself now and then with a disabled engine on his hands, and two or three hundred passengers standing around apparently ready to eat him up if he does not remedy the difficulty in short order. Often in such cases he is in doubt himself whether the repairs necessary to enable his engine to proceed will occupy fifteen minutes or an hour. This, with the knotty question of where the nearest relief engine is, causes the brow to knit and the sweat to start, and to the young runner proves an experience which he long remembers.

Stories of fast running are common but unreliable; and when truthful, important considerations are often omitted. There are so many elements to be considered, that usually the verdict can be justly rendered only after a careful comparison with previous records. Most regular runs include a number of stops, and are subject to numerous slackenings of the speed, thus dimming the lustre of the record of the trip as a whole. Frequently, quick runs which have been reported as noteworthy have had favoring circumstances not told of. The most remarkable single run on record was that of Jarrett & Palmer's special train chartered to carry their theatrical company from New York to San Francisco (Jersey City to Oakland), June 1–4, 1876, which is well known to all Americans. Perhaps the fastest long run ever made in this country was that of a special train over the West Shore Railroad from East Buffalo to Frankfort, N. Y., two hundred and one miles, on July 9, 1885, which ran this distance in four hours, including several stops. This train ran thirty-six miles in thirty minutes, and ran many single miles in forty-three seconds each. An engine with two cars ran over the Canada Southern Division of the Michigan Central from St. Clair Junction to Windsor, Ont., on November 16, 1886, a distance of one hundred and seven miles, in ninety-seven minutes; and this included two or three stops. The average rate of speed was about sixty-nine miles an hour, and in places it rose to seventy-five and over. The engineers and their firemen, and all connected with the handling of the trains, certainly deserve credit for performances like these, and they receive it; but the supplying of the perfect machine, the smooth and safe roadway comparatively clear of other trains, and other conditions, is so manifestly beyond their control, while at the same time constituting such an important fac-

A Breakdown on the Road.

tor in the result, that praise should be given discriminatingly. An engineer who makes a specially quick trip feels proud of his engine, and of the honor of having been chosen for an important run, and he shares with the passengers the exhilaration produced by such a triumph of science and skill in annihilating space; but in the matter of credit to himself for experience and judgment, patience and forethought, he feels and knows that many a trip in his every-day service is worthy of greater recognition. Many a runner has to urge his engine, day after day, with a load twenty-five per cent. heavier than it was designed for, over track that is fit only for low speeds, at a rate which demands the most constant care. He must run fast enough over the better portions of the track to allow of slackening where prudence demands slackening. The tracks of many roads are rendered so uneven by the action of frost in winter that with an unskilful runner the passengers would

Timely Warning.

be half-frightened by the unsteady motion of the cars. This condition is not common on the important trunk-lines, of course; but it does prevail on roads that carry a great many passengers, nevertheless; and engineers who guide trains over such difficult journeys, gently luring the passengers, with the aid of the excellent springs under the cars, into the belief that they are riding over a track of uniform smoothness, should not be forgotten in any estimate of the fraternity as a whole.

The engineer whose humanity is not hardened has his feelings harrowed occasionally by pedestrians who risk their lives on the track. Tramps and other careless persons are so numerous that the casual passenger in a locomotive cab generally cannot ride fifty miles without seeing what seems to him a hair-breadth escape, but which is nevertheless treated by the engineer as a commonplace occurrence.   These heedless wayfarers do, however, occasionally carry their indifference to danger too far, and they are tossed in the air like feathers.*   Doubtless there are those who, like the fireman who talked with the tender-hearted young lady, regret the killing of a man chiefly "because it musses up the engine so ;" but, taking the fraternity as a whole, warmth of heart and tenderness of feeling may be called not only well-developed but prominent traits of character.   The great strike on the Chicago, Burlington & Quincy road in 1888, which proved to have been ill-advised, would have been possible only in a body of men actuated by the most loyal friendship.   Undoubtedly a large conservative element in the Brotherhood of Engineers believed the move injudicious, but they joined in it out of an intense spirit of fidelity to their brethren and leaders.

The passenger-train conductor has in many respects the most difficult position in the railroad ranks.   He should be a first-class freight conductor and a polished gentleman to boot.   But in his long apprenticeship on a freight train he has very likely been learning how *not* to fulfil the additional requirements of a passenger conductorship.   In that service he could be uncouth and even boorish, and still fill his position tolerably well; now he feels the need of a life-time of tuition in dealing with the diverse phases of human nature met with on a passenger train.   He must now manage his train in a sort of automatic way, for he has his mind filled with the care of his passengers and the collection of tickets. He must be good at figures, keeping accounts, and handling money, though the freight-train service has given him no experience in this line.   Year by year the clerical work connected with the taking up of tickets and collecting of cash fares has been increased until now, on many roads, an expert bank clerk would be none too proficient for the duties imposed.   The conductor who grumblingly averred that "it would take a Philadelphia lawyer

* Mr. Porter King, of Springfield, Mass., who has run an engine on the Boston & Albany road for forty-five years, and who served on the Mohawk & Hudson, the Long Island, and the New Jersey Railroads in 1833-44, when horses were the motive power and the reverse lever consisted of a pair of reins, ran until December, 1887, before his engine ever killed a person.

with three heads " to fill his shoes was not far out of the way. Every day, and perhaps a number of times a day, he must collect fares of fifty or a hundred persons in less time than he ought to have for ten   Of that large number a few will generally have a

The Passenger Conductor.

complaint to make, or an objection to offer, or an impudent asser-tion concerning a fault of the railroad company which the con-ductor cannot remedy and is not responsible for.   A woman will object to paying half-fare for a ten-year-old girl or to paying full rates for one of fifteen.   A person whose income is ten times larger than he deserves will argue twenty minutes to avoid paying ten cents more (in cash) than he would have been charged for a ticket.   Passengers with legitimate questions to ask will couch them in vague and backhanded terms, and those with useless ones will take inopportune times to propound them.   These are not oc-casional but every-day experiences.   The very best and most intel-ligent people in the community (excepting those who travel much) are among those who oftenest leave their wits at home when they

take a railroad trip. All these people must be met in a concilia-
tory manner, but without varying the strict regulations in the least
degree. The officers of the revenue department are inexorable
masters, and passengers offended by alleged uncivil treatment are
likely to make absurd complaints at the superintendent's office. A
conductor dreads an investigation of this sort, however unreason-
able the passengers' complaints may be, because it may tend to
show that he lacked tact in handling the case. But after becoming habituated to this sort of dealings, there are still left the oc-
casional disturbances which no amount of philosophy can make
pleasant. These are the encounters with drunken and disorderly
passengers. The conductor, starting at the forward end of his
train, finds, perhaps, in the first car one or two " toughs " who refuse payment of fare and are spoiling for a fight. Care must be
taken with this sort of character not to punish him or use the least
bit of unnecessary severity, for he will, when sobered off, quite
likely be induced by a sharp lawyer to sue the railroad company
for damages by assault. The conductor, however, if he be one
who has (in his freight-train experience) dealt with tramps, is able
to cope with his customer and confine him to the baggage-car or
put him off the train. But a tussle of this kind is at best far from
soothing to the temper, and the very next car may contain the
wife of a nabob, who will expect the most genteel treatment
and critically object to any behavior on the part of the conductor
which is not fully up to the highest drawing-room standard. Experiences of this kind, it can be readily imagined, are exceedingly
trying. The conductor cannot give himself up completely to learning gentility, for he still has need for his old severity.

The difficulty of always finding the ideal person when wanted
has led to the employment of men of good address who have had
little or no training on freight trains ; so that we find some conductors who are able to deal with all sorts of passengers with a
good degree of success, but who are far from brilliant as managers
of trains, technically speaking ; while others, who from their early
experience have first-class executive ability, are slow in discarding
the somewhat rough habits of the freight train. While there are
not wanting those who strive faithfully to reach the ideal, and succeed admirably, it may be said that the average conductor retains

more of the severe than of the gentle side of his character, at least so far as outward behavior goes. The rigid requirements of his financial superiors, which compel him to actually fight for his rights with dishonest and stingy passengers, make it almost impossible that he should be otherwise. Ignorant foreigners, poor women and girls who have lost their way, and other unfortunates are, however, encountered often enough to preclude the conductor's forgetting how to be compassionate.

The heroic element is not wholly lacking in the conductor's life. The temporary guardianship of several hundred people is an important trust even in smooth sailing, but the conductor's possibilities are entirely different from the engineer's. He has so much to do to attend to the petty wants of passengers that their remoter but more important interests are not given much thought. The anxieties of a hundred nervous passengers who terribly dread the loss of an hour by a missed connection are much more likely to weigh down a conductor's mind than any thoughts of his duty to them in a possible emergency that will happen only once in five years. And yet the last-mentioned contingency is a real one. Only last year, in the great Eastern blizzard, conductors risked their lives in protecting their passengers. One spent three or four hours in travelling a mile and a half to a telegraph-office; in consequence of the six feet of snow, the blinding storm, and the darkness, he had to constantly hug a barbed-wire fence to avoid losing his way, and was on the point of exhaustion when he reached the station.

The term "station-agent" means, practically, the person in charge of a small or medium-sized station. When one of these men is promoted to the charge of a large city station, either freight or passenger, he becomes really a local superintendent, his duties then consisting very largely in the supervision of an army of clerks and laborers who must, each in his place, be as capable as the agent himself. The agent at a small station has a great multiplicity of duties to perform. He must sell tickets, be a good book-keeper, and a faithful switch-tender. He generally must be a telegraph-operator and must be vigorous physically. He must be ready, like the conductor, to submit to some abuse from ill-bred customers, and should be the peer of the business men of his town.   He often encounters almost as great a variety of knotty problems as the superintendent himself, though he has the advantage that he can generally turn them over to a superior if he feels unequal to them.   The practical difficulties that most beset him are those incident to doing everything in a hurry.   People who buy tickets wait until the train is about to start before presenting themselves at the office.   Then the agent has a dozen other things to attend to, and must therefore detect counterfeit ten-dollar bills with the expertness of a Washington treasury-clerk.   Just as a train reaches his station the train despatcher's click is heard on the wires, and he must drop everything and receive (for the conductor) a telegram in which an error of a single word would very likely involve the lives of passengers. At a very small station the checking of baggage devolves on the agent, his overburdened back being thus loaded with one more straw.   He is in many cases agent for the express company, and so must count, seal, superscribe, and way-bill money packages and handle oyster-kegs and barrels of beer at a moment's notice. Women with wagon-loads of loose household effects to go by freight, and shippers of car-loads of cattle, for which a car must be specially fitted up, will appear just as the distracted station-man is receiving a telegram with one side of his brain and selling a ticket with the other.   The household goods must be weighed and tagged, the sewing-machine tied up, and tables repaired ; the cattle-shipper must be given a short lecture on the legal bearings of the bargain for transportation which he is about to make, and his demand that his live-stock shall be carried 500 miles more quickly than human animals are taken over the same road is to be gently repressed.   It is not every day that a small station is enlivened by this sort of excitement, yet it is common, and is familiar to every station agent.   The variety in the duties of this position is, however, a great advantage to the ambitious young man, because it serves to give him a good lift toward a valuable business education.   He can learn about the methods and knacks and tricks of many different kinds of business, and can profit by the knowledge thus gained.   Thomas J. Potter, the lately deceased vice-president of the Union Pacific Railway, whose memory it is proposed to per-

In the Waiting Room of a Country Station.

petuate by a bronze statue, began his railroad career as agent at a small station in Iowa. Others of equal ability and perfection of character have risen from similar places and by the same means.

The agent at a small station catches his breath between trains. There is then generally ample time for calming the nerves and preparing for the next onslaught. If he is a telegraph-operator he can chat with the operators at other stations—a common resource if the wires are not occupied with more important affairs. In the class periodicals of operators and railroad men, reference to this phase of their life may be constantly seen, and incidents of even romantic interest are not infrequent. Many of the men at small stations are young and unmarried, while at places where the business has increased enough to warrant the employment of an assistant, a young woman to do the telegraphing is frequently the first helper engaged. With this combination it is unnecessary to tell what follows. If iron bars and stone walls are things which Cupid holds in contempt, an electric telegraph wire is the thing which makes him " snicker right out," if we may use the language of the circus ring. A distance of 100 miles, instead of being a barrier, is, under these circumstances, an advantage. There is, to be sure, a slight disadvantage in the fact that any tender communication confided to the wires will be liable to fall on the ears of unfeeling persons at intermediate offices, but the overcoming of this obstacle provides the agreeable incidental excitement which is always necessary in genuine love-making. Young persons (or old, either) can study each other's characters, in important phases at least, at a distance better than at short range. The telegraphic mode of sending communications discloses one's disposition far better than does handwriting. Working on the same wire with another for a few months enables one to form judgments of that other's generosity or narrowness, serenity or excitability, industry or laziness, refinement or boorishness, kindliness of heart or otherwise, which are quite sure to be correct judgments. Judgments ripen into attachments, and romances of the wire are common.

At the railroad station next larger in size, the work is more divided. One man sells tickets, another attends to the freight office, another to the baggage, and so on. The ticket-seller must make five-cent bargains with the same urbanity that is given to a $100 trade, and must be able to toss off the latter in two minutes if occasion requires, or to spend an hour in helping the passenger choose the best route among a score of possible ones.   The fusilade of questions that must be met by the ticket-seller every time he opens his window is familiar to everyone who has ever watched a place of the kind for ten minutes.   The inexperienced traveller wants to be fully posted as to the exact hour of departure of a tri-weekly stage with which he is to connect at a railroad station a thousand miles away, and the more intelligent ones demand an oral time-table covering the trains for the ensuing week on all railroads within a radius of 50 miles.   Those who cannot read or understand the time-tables are too modest to ask aid, and their misfortune is disclosed only after their train has gone and they are found in tears ; while those who can read the table ignore it and ask questions simply to be sociable.

The station baggage-master has an important but rather thankless place.   He must handle 200-pound trunks with as much ease as though they contained feathers, and, if he break a moulding off

Station Gardening.

one, must meet the reproaches of the owner, who imagines that the time available for handling the trunk was five minutes instead of two seconds.   He must handle much dirty and otherwise unpleasant stuff, and on the whole pursue a very unpoetic life.   He has little to do with train-handling, but he " keeps in with " the trainmen and furnishes them with a share of their entertainment.   They lounge in his room sometimes and he keeps on tap a supply of jokes such as that about the new brakeman who sent to headquarters for a supply of red oil for his red lantern, and the engineer who lost time with an excursion train on

The Trials of a Baggage-master.

In the Yard at Night.

the Fourth of July because the extremely hot weather had elongated the rails and thus materially increased the distance to be travelled over. When "hot boxes" (friction-heated axles) are given as the cause of a delay the real cause of which is concealed (by the conductor who is ashamed of it), the baggage-master gently punctures the deception by suggesting that perhaps a hot *fire*-box (in the engine) is what is meant. Whether the roguish clerk of an inexperienced general manager, who slyly induced his chief to issue an order to station agents directing that "all freight cars standing for any length of time on side tracks must be occasionally moved a short distance in order to prevent flattening of the wheels," had formerly been a baggage-master, history does not state.

The switch-tender, whose momentary carelessness has many a time caused terrible disaster, but whose constant faithfulness outweighs a million-fold even that painful record, is one of the essential figures around a station. Nothing but eternal vigilance will suffice to keep switches always in safe position, and the conscientious custodian of these always possible death-traps often takes his burden of care to his pillow. The mishaps which do occur strikingly illustrate the practical impossibility of holding the human brain always to the highest pitch. A conductor in New Jersey (trainmen have to set switches at many places where no switchmen are employed) recently caused a slight collision by misplacing a switch, and on seeing the consequences exclaimed, "I deserve to be discharged ; my mistake was inexcusable." And yet an honest man of that type is the kind demanded for such a place. The interlocking of switches and signals (the arrangement in a frame of the levers moving the switches and those moving signals in such a way that the signal which tells the engineer to come on *cannot be given* until the switch is actually in proper position) is one of the notable improvements of the last twenty years, and is a great boon to switchmen, as well as to passengers and the owners of railroads.* By the aid of this apparatus and its distant signals, connected by wire ropes, the switchman's anxieties are reduced immeasurably. By concentrating the levers of a number of switches in a single room one man can do the work of several, and to the looker-on the perplexities of the position seem to have been increased instead of diminished. But the switchman's task now is of a different sort. Under the old plan he was constantly on guard lest he make a mistake and throw an engine or car off the track. Under the new, his calculations are chiefly about saving time and facilitating the work of the trainmen. Questions of danger rarely come up, being provided against by the perfection of the machinery. By long familiarity with the ground and the ways of

* See " Safety in Railroad Travel," page 204.

handling the trains, the switch-tender in an " interlocking tower "
is enabled to safely conduct a score of trains through a labyrinth
of switches in the time that the novice would take to make the first

A Track-walker on a Stormy Night.

move for a single train. Without this admirable apparatus, and
skilful and experienced attendants, the business of great stations
like the Grand Central at New York would be impossible in the
space allowed.

One of the habitués of every station is the section-master, who
looks after three, five, or ten miles of track and a gang of from five

to twenty-five men who keep it in repair. He is not much seen, because he is out on the road most of the time ; and his duties are not of a kind that the reader could study, on paper, to much advantage ; but he deserves mention because his place is a really important one. Railroad tracks cannot be made, like a bridge, five times as strong as is necessary, and thus a large margin be allowed for deterioration ; they must be constantly watched to see that they do not fall even a little below their highest standard. This care-taking can be intrusted only to one who has had long experience at the work. In violent rain-storms the trackman must be on duty night and day and patrol the whole length of his division to see that gravel is not washed over the track or out from under it. Though roughly dressed and sunburnt, he is an important personage in the eye of the engineer of a fast express train, and if he be the least bit negligent, even to the extent of letting a few rails get a quarter of an inch lower than they ought to, he hears a prompt appeal from the engine-runner. The latter could not feel the confidence necessary to guide his 50-ton giant over the road at lightning speed with its precious human freight if he had not a trusty trackman every few miles ; and passengers who feel like expressing gratitude for a safe railroad journey should never forget this unseen guardian.

A number of classes of men in the railroad service must be turned off with a word for lack of space. The train despatcher, with his constant burden of care, deserves a chapter. The locomotive fireman, who has not been directly alluded to, is practically an apprentice to the engineer, and, like apprentices in some other callings, has a good deal of hard work to do. He generally has longer hours than the engineer, as he has to clean a portion of the polished brass- and iron-work of the engine. He has to throw into the fire-box several tons of coal a day, and gets so black that his best friends would not know him when washed up. Those who begin young and are intelligent, and conserve their strength, are at length promoted to be engineers. The fireman's twin brother is the "hostler," who is employed at the larger termini to get the iron horse out of its stable, lead it to the watering place and feed-trough (coal-bin), and harness it to the train.

The clerk in the freight office has almost as much variety of work as the ticket-seller, and is by no means a mere book-keeper. The workmen at the freight station are not common laborers. Their work requires peculiar skill and experience, and they have diversions worth tell-ing of, if there were space. The men in the shops, and those who go out with derricks and chains to pick up wrecks, are an im-portant class by themselves, and bridge - builders, gate - tenders, and various others bring up the rear.

A Crossing Flagman.

In conclusion, railroad men as a body are industrious, sober when at work, and lively when at play, using well-trained minds, in their sphere, and possessing capacity for a high degree of further training. The public is not without its duty toward the million or so of men in the railroad service. The liability to death or maiming from accident is such a real factor in railroad men's lives that the public, and especially shareholders in railroads, are bound to not only uphold officers in providing every possible ap-pliance and regulation for safety, but to demand the introduction of such devices. Some of the State railroad commissioners have done and are doing noble service in this direction, and should be vigorously supported by their constituencies. The demands of the public, re-enforced by the exigencies of competition, have made Sunday trains in many localities almost as common as on week-days, so that many train and station men work seven days in the week. In addition to this, holidays oftener increase their work than diminish it, so that there is room for a considerable reform in this regard.

The general moral welfare of railroad men has received much attention in late years, and affords a wide field for work by all who will. Many railroads have co-operated with the Young Men's Christian Association branches, started by a few of the employees, in building and equipping reading-rooms, libraries, etc., and the companies give many hundred dollars annually toward the support of these resorts, which serve to keep many a young trainman away from loafing places of a question-able character or worse. Mr. Cornelius Vanderbilt, whose mil-lions came largely out of the pro-fits of the New York Central & Hudson River Railroad, has set a good example to other railroad millionaires in the erection of a building for the employees of that road in New York City, whose luxuriousness is an evidence that he loves his neighbor as himself, even if that neighbor be a plain brakeman earning but low wages.

A Little Relaxation.

That the resorts provided for railroad men are appreciated is evi-denced by their records. Of the trainmen who regularly come into the Grand Central Station in New York, 46 per cent. are members of the Association occupying the building given by Mr. Vanderbilt, and 65 per cent. make use of the rooms more or less regularly. Rooms in numerous other cities also make encourag-ing showings.

Railroad officers, with their great advantages for enlighten-ment, owe it to themselves and their men to see that the thou-sands under them have fair opportunities for rising in the world, and that the owners of the immense corporations which stand as masters of such vast armies fully understand their measure of re-sponsibility in the premises. Science and invention, machinery and improved methods, have effected great changes in the railroad art, but the American nation, which travels more than any other, still recognizes the fact that faithful and efficient *men* are an essen-tial factor in the prosecution of that art. People desire to deal with a personality, and therefore wish to see the *personnel* of the railroad service fostered and perfected.

STATISTICAL RAILWAY STUDIES.*

By FLETCHER W. HEWES.

Railway Mileage of the World—Railway Mileage of the United States—Annual Mileage and Increase—Mileage Compared with Area—Geographical Location of Railways — Centres of Mileage and of Population — Railway Systems—Trunk Lines Compared : By Mileage ; Largest Receipts ; Largest Net Results—Freight Traffic —Reduction of Freight Rates—Wheat Rates—The Freight Haul—Empty Freight Trains—Freight Profits—Passenger Traffic—Passenger Rates—Passenger Travel —Passenger Profits—General Considerations—Dividends—Net Earnings per Mile and Railway Building—Ratios of Increase—Construction and Maintenance—Employees and their Wages—Rolling Stock—Capital Invested.

 LTHOUGH the United States was the second nation to open a line of railway, it operates to-day nearly half the mileage of the world, and it has so many miles of double, triple, and quadruple track that, were the data of trackage available, such a comparison would undoubtedly show it to more than equal all the rest of the world combined.

Below is given a chart comparing the mileage of the principal railway countries. The list contains all countries having a mileage of over ten thousand kilometers.

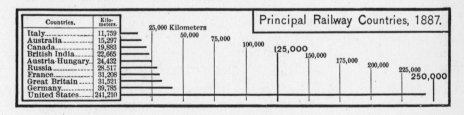

Countries.	Kilometers.
Italy	11,759
Australia	15,297
Canada	19,883
British India	22,665
Austria-Hungary	24,432
Russia	28,517
France	31,208
Great Britain	31,521
Germany	39,785
United States	241,210

Principal Railway Countries, 1887.

The most prominent fact is impressed by the very long line representing the mileage of the United States. A second impres-

* Data drawn from " Poor's Manual of Railroads," 1889, and the " Statistical Abstract of the United States," 1888, and carefully revised, form, in large part, the basis of the several studies ; and the writer hereby expresses obligation to Mr. John P. Meany, editor of the " Manual," for kindly aid in his work.

sive fact is that the United States has more than six times the mileage of any other country. A third, that there are but five other countries that have even a tenth as much railway.

RAILWAY MILEAGE OF THE UNITED STATES.

Total Annual Mileage and Increase.—On page 429 is given a chart which, beginning with the 23 miles of 1830 and ending with the 156,082 miles of 1888, delineates our ever-increasing total mileage. It also portrays the fluctuations in the number of miles built annually. This latter study is the more interesting, especially during the last twenty-five years, which cover the periods of extreme activity.

Mileage Compared with Area.—The shaded map on the same page pictures the railway mileage of each State as compared with its total area. The eleven States bearing the deepest shade (5) are those having the larger proportions of mileage to area. Of these, New Jersey stands first, having almost exactly one-fourth of a mile of railroad for each square mile of land. The proportion of total area occupied by this mileage is measured to the eye by the accompanying diagram.

The entire square stands for one square mile of land, and the space at the upper left-hand corner stands for that part of the square mile which the railroad occupies, counting from fence to

Mileage to Area in New Jersey.

fence on each side of the road. This comparison is made on the basis of one hundred feet for the "right of way" (the width allowed in government grants), and is useful in connection with the study of the historical maps, especially those of 1880 and 1889, on which the area of some of the States seems to be nearly all taken up with roads, owing to the small scale of the maps. Iowa has the smallest proportion of any in Group 5. The figures show her proportion to be a little over one-seventh of a mile of road to one square mile of area. (Nevada has the smallest proportion of all the States and Territories, viz., a trifle over $\frac{1}{117}$ of a mile of line to one square mile.)

That part of the map bearing the deepest shade shows at a glance that an unbroken belt, averaging some two hundred miles wide, stretching from Cape Cod to beyond the Mississippi River, is that part of the country best supplied with railways.

The lighter shades grouped on either side of this belt show how the mileage grades away north and south.

GEOGRAPHICAL LOCATION OF RAILWAYS.

On pages 430 to 433 is a series of historical maps showing the location of railway lines at each census-year from 1830 to 1880, and in 1889. Charts comparing and ranking the mileage by States accompany the maps of 1870, 1880, and 1889. These maps and charts give a better idea of the location and extent of progress than could be given by a dozen pages of description and a hundred columns of figures.

Centre of Mileage and of Population.—The space for notes on the maps permits the bare mention of the meaning of the series of stars in the 1889 map (page 433), which mark the centres of mileage and of population. It is well to state the manner of determining the centres of mileage, that it may have its proper bearing in any study of the subject into which the showing may enter.

The locations are necessarily approximate. Each centre was determined by selecting, on the proper map, a line running east and west which seemed, to the eye, to nearly divide the mileage into equal parts. The sum of the mileage of the States north, was then compared with that of the States south of the line. By this means the position of the line chosen by the eye was corrected and the right parallel determined. The meridian dividing the total mileage into equal parts was ascertained in like manner. The point of intersection of the parallel and meridian is marked in the map by a star, having the proper date printed to the right of it.

The upper series of stars locates the centres of railway mileage, and the lower series the centres of population, as given by the returns of the census of 1880.

The following table describes the several locations thus ascertained:

Centres of Railway Mileage.

Date.	Latitude.	Longitude.	Approximate location by towns.
1840..	40° 50′ N.	76° 10′ W.	Twenty miles west of Mauch Chunk, Pa.
1850..	41° 30′ N.	77° 27′ W.	Twenty-five miles northwest of Williamsport, Lycoming County, Pa.
1860..	40° 40′ N.	82° 30′ W.	Ten miles south of Mansfield, O.
1870..	41° 10′ N.	84° 35′ W.	Paulding, Paulding County, O.
1880..	41° 05′ N.	86° 50′ W.	Thirty miles northwest of Logansport, Ind.
1888..	39° 50′ N.	88° 40′ W.	Pontiac, Ill., about ninety miles S. S. W. of Chicago.

The remarkable movement of the centre of mileage from 1850 to 1860 is easily understood when one turns to the maps of those dates (page 430) and locates the fields of activity. The wonderful increase in Ohio, Indiana, Illinois, Wisconsin, and Iowa gave the Western impulse, while the growth in Tennessee and the States south of it furnishes the principal explanation of the southerly motion.

Although the study of this period is the most interesting of the series, in the space passed over, yet each period has its points of special interest, which the reader will easily solve by referring to the proper maps on pages 430 to 433.

Railway Systems.—The consolidation of separate lines under central controlling interests has resulted in several "systems" of great extent. Five such are mapped on pages 434 and 435. The roads controlled by them are printed in broad lines, while all others are printed in narrow lines. It needs but a glance to see whether any of them has so far absorbed the roads of a given region as to be able to control rates. The systems selected are believed to be representative ones, and the mapping of a dozen others would not tell the story any more plainly.

TRUNK LINES COMPARED.

Compared by Mileage.—At present there are twenty-four corporations reporting over one thousand miles of line each. A comparison of these roads by mileage is profitless, as it furnishes no just clew to their importance in point of business transacted. Several of the shorter of these twenty-four lines largely exceed some of the longer ones in the volume of business transacted. As

Compared with Area, 1888.

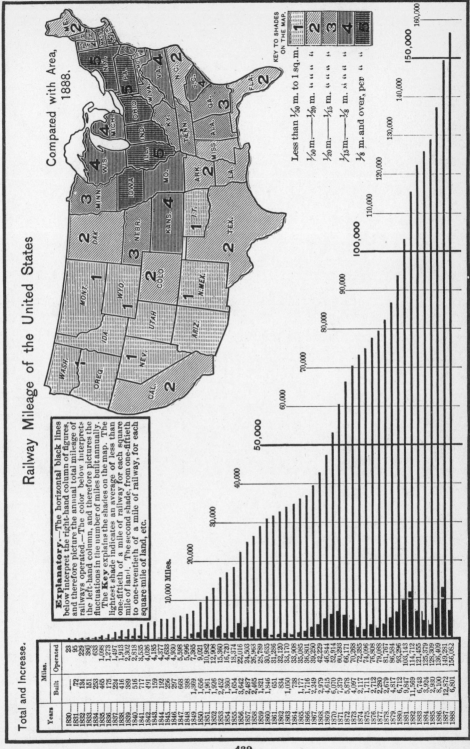

Explanatory.—The horizontal black lines below interpret the right-hand column of figures, and therefore picture the annual total mileage of railways operated.—The color below interprets the left-hand column, and therefore pictures the fluctuations in the number of miles built annually. The **Key** explains the shades on the map. The lightest shade indicates an average of less than one-fiftieth of a mile of railway for each square mile of land. The second shade, from one-fiftieth to one-twentieth of a mile of railway, for each square mile of land, etc.

KEY TO SHADES ON THE MAP.

1	Less than 1/50 m. to 1 sq. m.
2	1/50 m.——1/20 m. " " " "
3	1/20 m.——1/15 m. " " " "
4	1/15 m.——1/8 m. " " " "
5	1/8 m. and over, per " "

Total and Increase.

Years	Miles Built	Miles Operated
1830	——	23
1831	72	95
1832	134	229
1833	151	380
1834	253	633
1835	465	1,098
1836	175	1,273
1837	224	1,497
1838	416	1,913
1839	389	2,302
1840	516	2,818
1841	717	3,535
1842	491	4,026
1843	159	4,185
1844	192	4,377
1845	256	4,633
1846	297	4,930
1847	668	5,598
1848	398	5,996
1849	1,369	7,365
1850	1,656	9,021
1851	1,961	10,982
1852	1,926	12,908
1853	2,452	15,360
1854	1,360	16,720
1855	1,654	18,374
1856	3,642	22,016
1857	2,487	24,503
1858	2,465	26,963
1859	1,821	28,789
1860	1,846	30,635
1861	651	31,286
1862	834	32,120
1863	1,050	33,170
1864	738	33,908
1865	1,177	35,085
1866	1,716	36,801
1867	2,249	39,250
1868	2,979	42,229
1869	4,615	46,844
1870	6,070	52,914
1871	7,379	60,293
1872	5,878	66,171
1873	4,097	70,268
1874	2,117	72,385
1875	1,711	74,096
1876	2,712	76,808
1877	2,280	79,088
1878	2,679	81,767
1879	4,817	86,584
1880	6,712	93,296
1881	9,847	103,143
1882	11,569	114,712
1883	6,743	121,455
1884	3,924	125,379
1885	2,930	128,309
1886	8,100	136,409
1887	12,872	149,281
1888	6,801	156,082

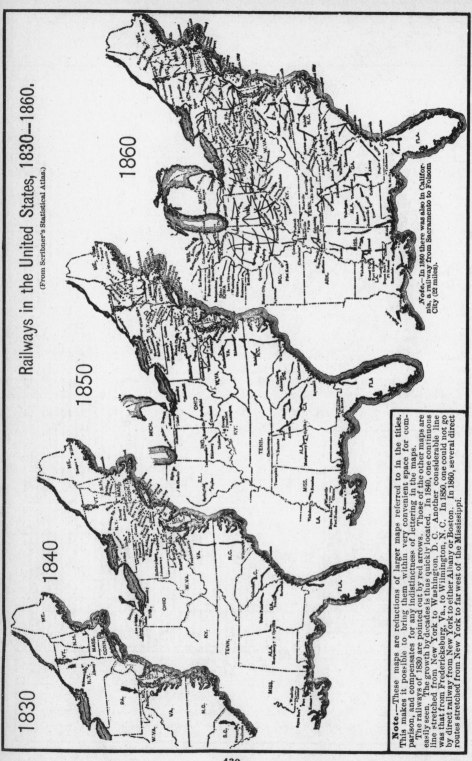

Railways in the United States, 1830—1860.

(From Scribner's Statistical Atlas.)

1830   1840

1850

1860

Note.—In 1860 there was also in California, a railway from Sacramento to Folsom City (22 miles).

Note.—These maps are reductions of larger maps referred to in the titles. This makes it possible to bring them within very convenient space for comparison, and compensates for any indistinctness of lettering in the maps. The railways of 1830 are pointed out by red arrows. Those of the other maps are easily seen. The growth by decades is thus quickly located. In 1840, one continuous line stretched from New York to Washington, D. C. Another considerable line was that from Fredericksburg, Va., to Wilmington, N. C. In 1850, one could not go by direct railway from New York to either Albany or Boston. In 1860, several direct routes stretched from New York to far west of the Mississippi.

430

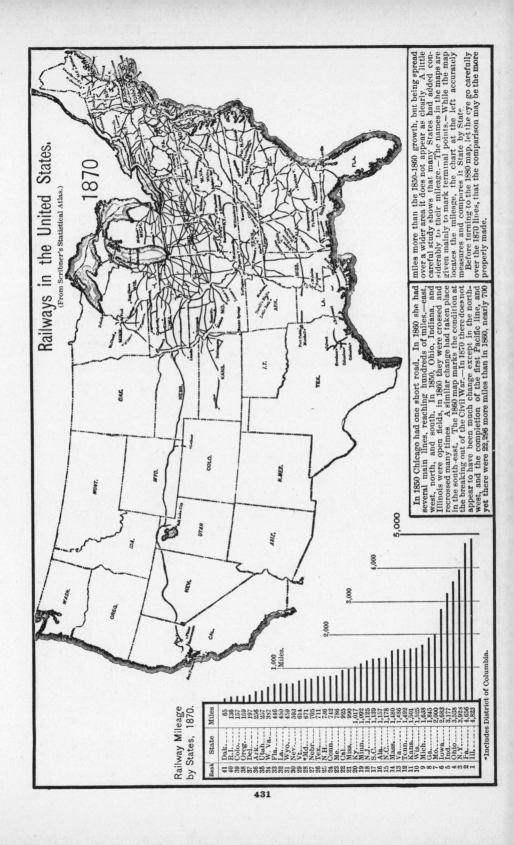

Railways in the United States.

(From Scribner's Statistical Atlas.)

1870

In 1850 Chicago had one short road. In 1860 she had several main lines, reaching hundreds of miles,—east, west, north, and south. In 1850, Ohio, Indiana, and Illinois were open fields, in 1860 they were crossed and recrossed many times. A similar change had taken place in the south-east. The 1860 map marks the condition at the breaking out of the Civil War.—In 1870 there does not appear to have been much change except in the north-west, and the completion of the first Pacific line, and yet there were 22,296 more miles than in 1860, nearly 700 miles more than the 1850-1860 growth, but being spread over a wider area it does not appear as clearly. A little careful study shows that many States had added considerably to their mileage.—The names in the maps are given mainly to mark terminal points.—While the map locates the mileage, the chart at the left accurately measures and compares it State by State.

Before turning to the 1880 map, let the eye go carefully over the 1870 lines, that the comparison may be the more properly made.

Railway Mileage by States, 1870.

Rank	State	Miles
41	Dak.	65
40	R.I.	136
39	Colo.	157
38	Oreg.	159
37	Del.	197
36	Ark.	256
35	Utah	257
34	W. Va.	387
33	Fla.	446
32	Wyo.	459
31	Nev.	593
30	Vt.	614
29	*Md.	671
28	Nebr.	705
27	Tex.	711
26	N.H.	736
25	Conn.	742
24	Me.	786
23	Cal.	925
22	Miss.	990
21	Ky.	1,017
20	Minn.	1,092
19	N.J.	1,125
18	S.C.	1,139
17	Ala.	1,157
16	N.C.	1,178
15	Mass.	1,480
14	Va.	1,486
13	Tenn.	1,492
12	Kans.	1,501
11	Wis.	1,525
10	Mich.	1,638
9	Ga.	1,845
8	Mo.	2,000
7	Iowa	2,683
6	Ind.	3,177
5	Ohio	3,538
4	N.Y.	3,928
3	Pa.	4,656
2	Ill.	4,823

*Includes District of Columbia.

5,000

4,000

3,000

2,000

1,000 Miles.

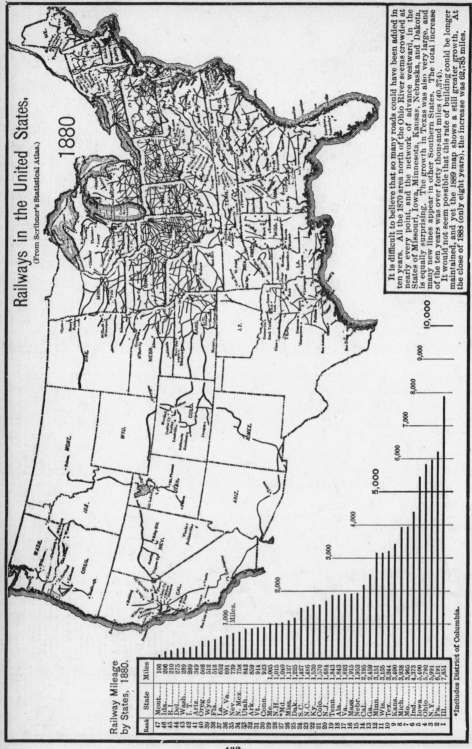

Railways in the United States,

1880

(From Scribner's Statistical Atlas.)

It is difficult to believe that so many roads could have been added in ten years. All the 1870 area north of the Ohio River seems crowded at nearly every point, and the network of advance westward, in the States of Missouri, Iowa, Minnesota, Kansas, Nebraska, and Dakota, is equally surprising. The growth in Texas was also very large, and many new lines appear in other Southern States. The total increase of the ten years was over forty thousand miles (40,374).

It would not seem possible that this rate of building could be longer maintained, and yet, the 1889 map shows a still greater growth. At the close of 1883 (only eight years), the increase was 62,785 miles.

Railway Mileage by States, 1880.

Rank	State	Miles
47	Mont...	106
46	Ida...	206
45	R.I.	210
44	Del...	275
43	Wash...	289
42	I. T.	289
41	Ariz.	349
40	Oreg.	508
39	Wyo.	512
38	Fla.	518
37	La.	652
36	W. Va.	691
35	Nev.	739
34	N. Mex.	758
33	Utah.	842
32	Ark.	859
31	Vt.	914
30	Conn.	923
29	Me.	1,005
28	N.H.	1,015
27	*Md.	1,040
26	Miss.	1,127
25	Dak.	1,225
24	S.C.	1,427
23	N.C.	1,486
22	Ky.	1,530
21	Colo.	1,570
20	N.J.	1,684
19	Tenn.	1,843
18	Ala.	1,843
17	Va.	1,893
16	Mass.	1,915
15	Nebr.	1,953
14	Cal.	2,195
13	Ga.	2,459
12	Minn.	3,151
11	Wis.	3,155
10	Tex.	3,244
9	Kans.	3,400
8	Mich.	3,938
7	Mo.	3,965
6	Ind.	4,373
5	Iowa	5,400
4	Ohio	5,792
3	N.Y.	5,991
2	Pa.	6,191
1	Ill.	7,851

*Includes District of Columbia.

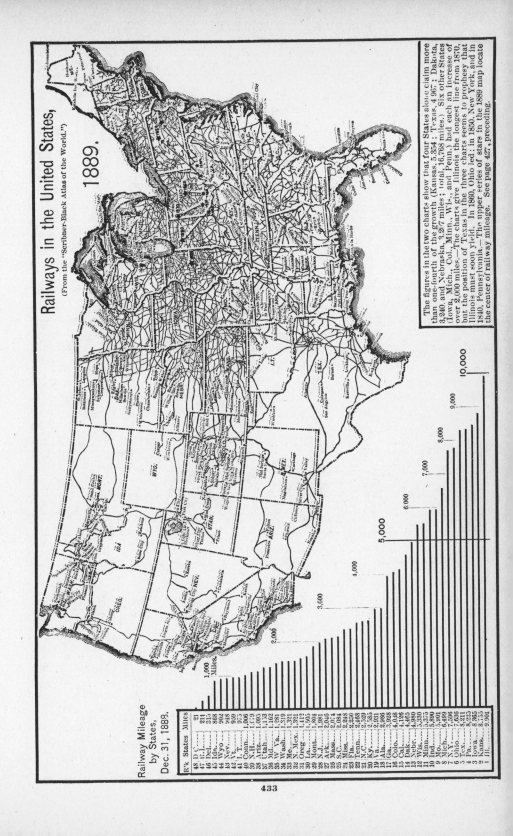

Railways in the United States,

(From the "Scribner-Black Atlas of the World.")

1889.

The figures in the two charts show that four States alone claim more than one-fourth of the growth (Kansas, 5,354; Texas, 4,967; Dakota, 3,240 and Nebraska, 3,267 miles; total, 16,768 miles.) Six other States (Iowa, Mich., Col., Minn., Wis-., and Penn.) had each an increase of over 2,000 miles.—The charts give Illinois the longest line from 1870, but the position of Texas in the three charts seems to prophesy that Illinois must soon yield. In 1860, Ohio led; in 1850, New York, and in 1840, Pennsylvania.—The upper series of stars in the 1889 map locate the center of railway mileage. See page 427, preceding.

Railway Mileage by States, Dec. 31, 1888.

R'k	States	Miles
48	D.C.	211
47	R.I.	214
46	Del.	315
45	Ida.	868
44	Wyo.	902
43	Nev.	948
42	Vt.	939
41	I.T.	973
40	Conn.	1,006
39	N.H.	1,079
38	Utah	1,095
37	Ariz.	1,133
36	Md.	1,162
35	W. Va.	1,281
34	Wash.	1,319
33	Me.	1,321
32	N. Mex.	1,321
31	Oreg.	1,412
30	S.C.	1,505
29	Mont.	1,804
28	N.J.	1,981
27	Ark.	2,046
26	Mass.	2,074
25	S.C.	2,084
24	Miss.	2,243
23	Fla.	2,250
22	Tenn.	2,468
21	N.C.	2,329
20	Ky.	2,585
19	Va.	2,931
18	Ala.	2,986
17	Ga.	3,928
16	Colo.	4,038
15	Cal.	4,128
14	Dak.	4,465
13	Nebr.	4,980
12	Wis.	5,330
11	Minn.	5,375
10	Ind.	5,890
9	Mo.	5,901
8	Mich.	6,499
7	N.Y.	7,596
6	Ohio	7,636
5	Pa.	8,211
4	Tex.	8,225
3	Iowa	8,365
2	Kans.	8,755
1	Ill.	9,901

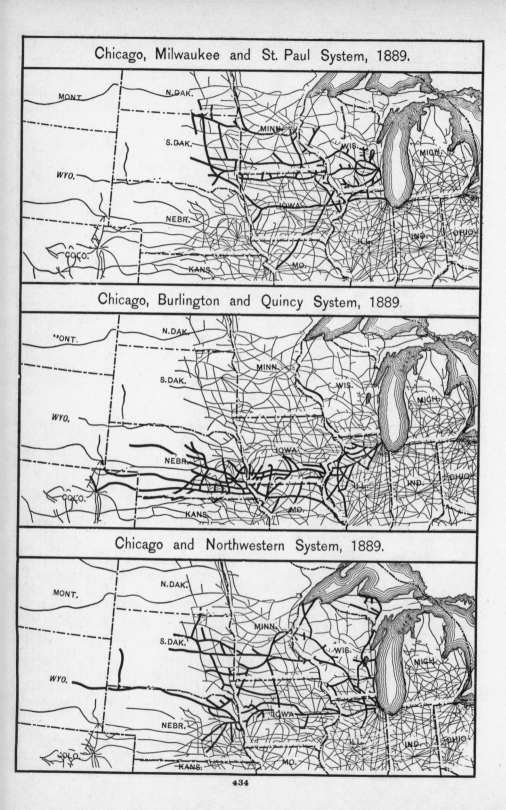

Chicago, Milwaukee and St. Paul System, 1889.

Chicago, Burlington and Quincy System, 1889.

Chicago and Northwestern System, 1889.

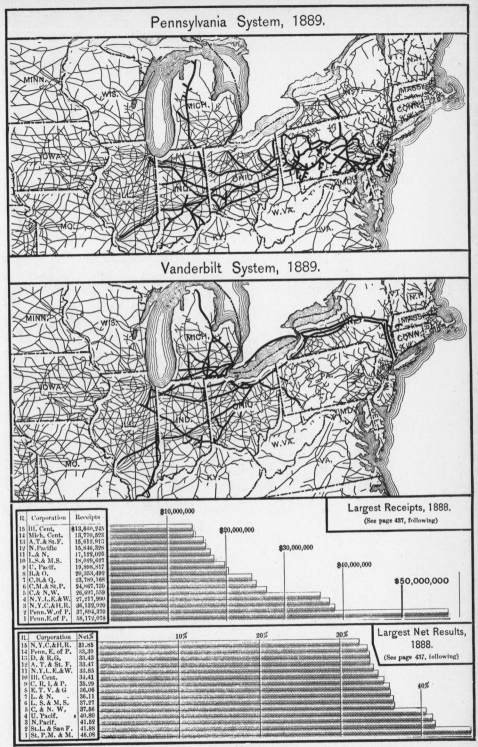

Pennsylvania System, 1889.

Vanderbilt System, 1889.

Largest Receipts, 1888.
(See page 437, following)

R.	Corporation	Receipts
15	Ill. Cent.	$13,660,245
14	Mich. Cent.	13,770,523
13	A.T.& St.F.	15,612,913
12	N.Pacific	15,846,328
11	L.& N.	17,122,026
10	L.S.& M.S.	18,029,627
9	U. Pacif.	19,898,817
8	B.& O.	20,353,492
7	C.B.& Q.	23,789,168
6	C.M.& St.P.	24,867,730
5	C.& N.W.	26,697,559
4	N.Y.L.& W.	27,217,990
3	N.Y.C.&H.R.	36,132,920
2	Penn.W.of P.	37,894,370
1	Penn.E.of P.	58,172,078

$10,000,000 $20,000,000 $30,000,000 $40,000,000 $50,000,000

Largest Net Results, 1888.
(See page 437, following)

R.	Corporation	Net%
15	N.Y.C.&H.R.	31.85
14	Penn. E. of P.	33.39
13	D. & R.G.	33.43
12	A. T. & St. F.	33.47
11	N.Y.L.E.&W.	33.85
10	Ill. Cent.	34.41
9	C. R. I. & P.	35.29
8	E. T. V. & G	36.06
7	L.& N.	36.11
6	L. S. & M.S.	37.27
5	C. & N. W.	37.56
4	U. Pacif.	40.80
3	N.Pacif.	41.52
2	St.L. & San F.	41.88
1	St.P.M. & M.	46.08

10% 20% 30% 40%

AVERAGE CHARGE PER MILE FOR EACH TON OF FREIGHT HAULED.

TRUNK LINES.	1870	1871	1872	1873	1874	1875	1876	1877	1878	1879	1880	1881	1882	1883	1884	1885	1886	1887	1888

Chicago and Northwestern
Chicago, Milwaukee and St. Paul
Chicago, Rock Island and Pacific
Av. of 6 Lines West of Chicago
Chicago, Burlington and Quincy
Illinois Central
Chicago and Alton

Boston and Albany
Michigan Central
New York Central
Av. of 7 Lines East of Chicago
Pennsylvania
Lake Shore and Michigan Southern
New York, Lake Erie and Western
Pittsburgh, Fort Wayne and Chicago

Scale values: 2.8c. 2.6c. 2.4c. 2.2c. **2.0c.** 1.8c. 1.6c. 1.4c. 1.2c. 0.8c. 0.6c. 0.2c.

Explanatory.—The upper edge of the deep shade marks the fluctuations of the average rate charged by the seven lines east of Chicago.—The upper edge of the light shade marks the fluctuations of the average rate charged by the six lines west of Chicago.—Each particular road has a distinctive line, which makes it easy to trace it among other lines.—All Western lines are accompanied by lines of color, to distinguish them plainly from the Eastern lines, and to make their relation to their own average more easily discovered. The Boston and Albany is the only Eastern line whose rate places it near the Western lines, but the absence of color prevents it from being taken for a Western line, which it might otherwise be, especially during the last three years, in its journey through and above them all.—The C. B. & Q. Road makes no report later than 1879.— The Chicago and Alton report begins at 1874.

Explanatory.—The diagram upon which the rates are charted (like all such diagrams) is constructed of perpendicular and horizontal lines. Each line, and each space between lines, has a particular meaning. The perpendicular spaces represent years, indicated by the figures at the top of each space. The horizontal spaces represent money values, each space representing 2c (two mills). Each horizontal line represents a particular money value, marked by the figures at the end of the line. Each black dot represents the average annual rate of some particular road. For example, take the Boston and Albany Road. Starting with the name and following the tracing line, the 1870 dot is found just below the 2.2c (2 cents and 2 mills) line. This indicates that the average rate charged by that road in 1870 was a trifle less than 2.2c. Following the line leading from the 1870 dot into the 1871 space, the 1871 dot is found a little below the center of the space between the 2c line and the 2.2c line, indicating a rate of a little less than 2 cents and 1 mill for 1871. The next year it is lower still. In this way the history of any road is quickly traced.

436

an example of the little value of comparison by mileage, the New York Central & Hudson River Road, with but 1,421 miles of line, reports $63,132,920 receipts, while the Union Pacific, with 6,288 miles, reports but $19,898,817. Two of the twenty-four roads, viz., the Southern Pacific Railroad (5,931 miles) and the Richmond, West Point & Terminal Railroad (6,869 miles) report neither gross or net earnings. The remaining twenty-two report both, and these reports furnish a satisfactory basis for study.

Largest Receipts.—A comparison on the basis of gross receipts gives the best means of judging of the financial importance of the several roads, for it measures the volume of business done. On page 435 is given such a comparison of the fifteen roads (of the twenty-two referred to above) reporting the largest gross receipts.

Largest Net Results.—While the gross receipts measure the volume of business they may not give any indication of net results. A chart, immediately under that comparing gross receipts, compares the net receipts of the fifteen roads (of the same twenty-two) which report the highest per centages.

Of the ten reporting largest net results, seven are west of Chicago. This fact, coupled with the desire of the great western systems to possess new territory in advance of others, suggests a reason for the large railway growth in that part of the country.

FREIGHT TRAFFIC.

The gross traffic receipts of the railways of the United States are divided between freight and passenger business in very nearly the proportion of three to one in favor of the freight traffic. For this reason, and because the data are still more largely available on the same side, the freight service receives herein the fuller treatment.

Reduction of Freight Rates.—On the opposite page is a chart delineating the fluctuations in freight rates since 1870. To one not familiar with the subject the picture presented is a most remarkable one. It looks as though the roads are all in a mad scramble to see which can reach the bottom of the hill first. To railway managers the picture is a painful reminder of a serious struggle, the end of which no one can yet predict.

The lines selected are representative lines of the east and west divisions of the country, north of the Ohio River, where the great number of competing roads has induced sharp competition.

The history of the *averages* is very clear, and it is easy to see that they are steadily approaching common ground, for while in 1870 the eastern average marked almost exactly one cent six mills, the western marked two cents four mills, a separation of eight mills ; in 1888 they recorded seven mills and a trifle over nine mills, a separation of about one-quarter of the 1870 record.

Wheat Rates.—The chart below repeats the lesson of the larger chart as to reduction of rates. The persistency with which water rates have kept below rail rates, emphasizes the fact that wherever water-ways exist, they are stubborn competitors for such freight traffic as will not suffer by the longer time required for the journey.

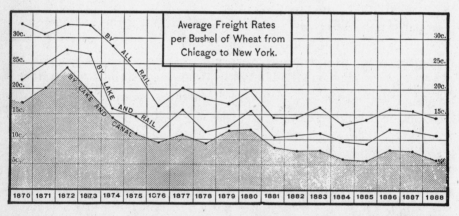

Average Freight Rates per Bushel of Wheat from Chicago to New York.

The Freight Haul.—It costs as much to load and unload a train that hauls its freight ten miles as it does one that carries it a thousand miles. In other words, the longer the haul the less the proportional cost to the carriers. The great extension of long lines westward in the last few years naturally raises the question whether the average freight haul has increased. The largely diminished rates suggest that probably producers have been led thereby to ship both agricultural and manufactured products greater distances to market. One or both of these conditions may have operated favorably for some roads, but, plausible as the theories seem, the facts prove that neither of them is sup-

ported in a study of the average haul of the country. The available figures permit us to go back only to 1882. Within that period the little chart given herewith deline-
ates the fluctuations, but indicates no permanency in either direction. It is a matter of regret that in this, as in many other studies, the history is not available for earlier years, as the more extended the view the better the judgment of such questions becomes.

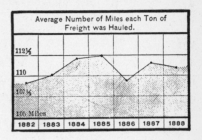

Empty Freight Trains.—One of the considerable items of expense in the freight traffic is that of returning empty cars to their point of starting. Just how large an item this is depends chiefly upon the demands of the population at either end of the operating line for the product of the population at the opposite end. Thus the carriage of the great agricultural product of the West to feed the denser population of the East, and for export to foreign countries, may or may not be met by the demand of the western people for the manufactures of the East and the imports from foreign countries arriving at the eastern seaboard. It is scarcely probable that any line, short or long, running east and west or north and south, finds its traffic in opposite directions balanced.

An interesting study of this problem is presented in the accompanying chart, the road selected for the illustration being one

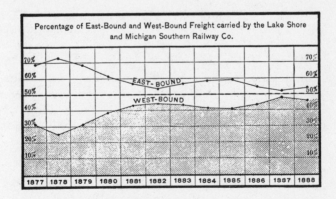

of the large carriers between Chicago and Buffalo. The upper chart-line marks the proportion of freight carried from west to east, while the lower line (at the top of the shaded part of the dia-gram) marks the portion carried from east to west. It is readily seen that in 1877 the west-bound freight was less than half as much as the east-bound, for they stand 30.8 per cent. and 69.2 per cent., respectively; and in 1878 the difference is still greater. From that year, however, there has been great improvement, so that now it would appear that there is on that road a much diminished need for hauling empty cars. The history of the Pennsylvania Road is similar to that shown in the chart, but the ratios have not come so nearly together. That of the New York Central & Hudson River Road shows very little change in the ratios since 1870, and all the time both these roads report a very large excess of east-bound freight.

Freight Profits.—The change in rates are of great moment to the producer; that of profits is the important one to the carrier. No matter how great the reduction of rates, if the reduction of ex-pense is as great, the profits are not disturbed. This question can be studied best by examining the figures which measure the actual profits. But few corporations furnish such figures, and the two whose history is delineated on the accompanying chart are among those giving the most readily available data. It will be

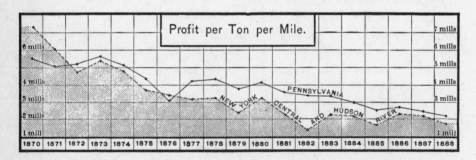

seen that the reduction of profits is no less remarkable than the re-duction of rates, which shows that the reduction of rates has far exceeded that of expense of carriage; for, had the reduction of ex-penses kept pace with that of rates, the profits would have remained level. As it is, the reduction of profits in the history of these roads, as shown, is from about six mills per ton per mile in 1870, to about two mills in 1888. These two roads are probably good represent-

atives of the experience of the general freight service of all railways north of the Ohio River.   If so, the prospect of the future
of freight traffic is not cheerful.

PASSENGER TRAFFIC.

The study of passenger traffic is less satisfactory than that of
freight traffic.   Fewer lines furnish a history of their passenger
rates, and ordinarily those histories cover shorter periods.   The
study is therefore confined to narrower limits and its lessons are
necessarily less conclusive.

Passenger Rates.—Below is given a chart interpreting the available data of six representative lines.   The first lesson impressed is

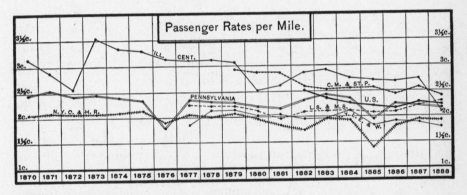

that no such reduction marks the history of passenger rates as is
shown in freight rates, although the general trend of the chart-lines
is plainly downward.   The line indicating the average rate for all
the roads in the country (marked U. S. in the chart) shows a reduction of over one-fourth of a cent per passenger per mile since
1882.

Certain features of this chart attract special attention.   The reduction of rates by the Pennsylvania, and the New York Central
& Hudson River roads in 1876, and that by the same roads in
1885, are suggestive.   Equally noticeable are the reductions of
the Illinois Central in 1871, 1872, 1880, and 1888.

This chart would seem to indicate that competition has not
operated as sharply on passenger as on freight traffic.

Passenger Travel.—The average distance that passengers ride
is not as important an element of railway business as is the aver-

age freight haul, for the passengers load and unload themselves; so that, whether they ride few or many miles, the cost of loading and unloading is neither increased nor diminished. On the contrary, if a thousand tons of freight, once loaded, is to be hauled one hundred miles instead of fifty, the proportional cost of loading and unloading is reduced one-half.

Still, the average distance passengers ride is important; for, if the number of passengers remains the same and their ride is shorter, the receipts are diminished. The returns show that while the number of passengers has increased since 1882 about fifty-six per cent., the total miles travelled have not increased quite fifty per cent., marking a falling off in the average number of miles each

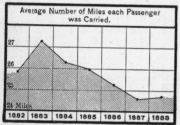

passenger rode. The reduction is graphically shown in the little chart given herewith. This result is no doubt largely due to the great increase of suburban travel which has developed about our large cities within in the past few years.

It is necessary to state, however, that the figures embraced in this study do not include the traffic of the elevated roads of New York and Brooklyn.

Passenger Profits.—Again a marked difference between freight and passenger traffic appears in comparing the chart given below with the corresponding chart on page 440.

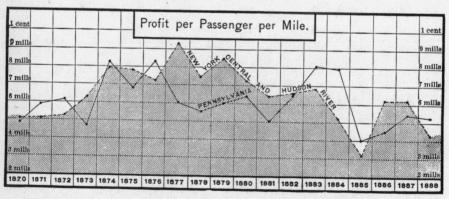

The study covers the history of the same roads in each case. The history of freight profits shows a persistent falling off, which in the nineteen years amounts to four mills per ton per mile, a loss of two-thirds of the six mills of 1870. The history delineated on this chart shows the average profit of the two roads to be almost exactly at the same point that it was in 1870, while the profits for most of the intervening years have been much greater.

Were this the record of the freight traffic, it would be much more gratifying to the managers of the roads, for the New York Central & Hudson River Railway receives about twice as much, and the Pennsylvania Railway receives four times as much, from freights as from passengers. Attention is invited to the opposite results of the same policy on these two roads in 1876. The chart of passenger rates on page 441 marks a decided reduction of rates by the Pennsylvania Road, and a slight reduction by the New York Central & Hudson River Road. The chart of profits records an increase for the former and a decrease for the latter. This year (1876) is the date of the Centennial World's Fair at Philadelphia. The Pennsylvania Road had an enormous increase of passenger traffic (double that of the following year), a record which it did not equal until 1887. The New York Central & Hudson River Road had but a slightly increased traffic, the record of which it passed in 1881.

GENERAL CONSIDERATIONS.

Dividends.—While many readers are probably not holders of railway stocks, yet a look at the dividends received by those who are will not be without interest. The little chart given below tells an interesting, although a not over-attractive story.

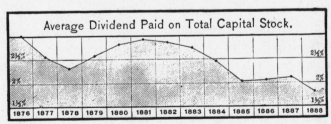

It shows that, comparing the aggregate of all the railroad stocks of the country with the aggregate of all dividends paid, the holders of stock realized an average of 3.03% on their investment in 1876. In 1878 it had fallen to less than 2½%. From that date to 1885 the record makes a curve ending just above 2%. A slight rally is indicated for 1886 and 1887, but 1888 carries it down to 1.81%. The stock of many roads has paid no dividend whatever these later years, and the lines whose stock proves a good investment at par are very few.

Net Earnings per Mile.—Although the studies of the financial question already made undoubtedly point out the true drift of

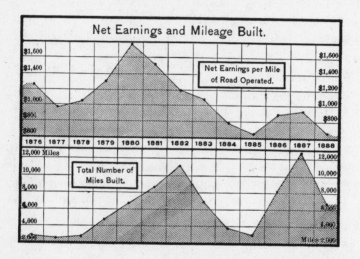

railway business, yet one more comparison is worth making, both for its bearing on the question of profits and the study of the influence of profits on railway building. The upper one of the two charts given herewith is the record of net earnings per mile of road in operation, and is based on the reported net earnings less the interest-charge. It therefore shows the average number of dollars each mile had earned, after paying all expenses and the interest on its debt. This money, then, is the clear amount each mile could apply each year to pay the principal of its debt and the dividends on its capital stock, or to use for improvements, such as rolling stock, stations, better road-bed, new rails, or any other betterments which might seem advisable.

In 1876 this sum was $1,264; in 1880 it was $1,798, since which time it has suffered a serious decline, until in 1888 it was only $650. It is the story of the previous studies repeated, and needs no further reiteration.

Railway Building.—The larger chart given on page 429, gives the history of railway building from 1831 to 1888. The lower chart of the two given together on page 444, repeats the annual record from 1876, for the purpose of studying the influence of profits on the progress of building. The net earnings per mile show a reduction in 1877. The following year shows an increase of earnings, and the building responded somewhat feebly the same year. The next two years (1879 and 1880) show great gains in net earnings, and the impetus given thereby to building, carries its increase steadily forward even two years beyond the turning-point of the earnings. The decline is then mutual to 1885. In 1886 the advance in earnings was responded to by such a remarkable increase in building that the stimulus is to be sought for partly outside of the increase of earnings, and is undoubtedly found in the desire to occupy the newly opening fields of western settlement; for the records mark unparalleled activity among the great trunk lines of the West in pushing their advances in Dakota, Kansas, Nebraska, and Colorado, in 1886 and 1887. This is graphically shown in the map of 1889, when compared with that of 1880 (pages 432 and 433).

Ratios of Increase.—It is difficult to obtain a just impression of values when expressed by figures alone. It is easy when these values are expressed in lines or colors. The greater difficulties come in the effort to compare values expressed in differing terms. To read that the increase of population was 23,400,000 from 1870 to 1888; and that of railway mileage was 62,785 miles; and that of freight traffic was nearly 30,000,000,000 tons, in the same period, and then to attempt the comparison of increase without further aid, is a hopeless task.

As a study of financial economy the comparison is worth making, for evidence of the over-development of an industry or a financial interest, rightly considered, may prevent suicidal development. The chart given on the next page makes the comparison easy. The actual increase in each instance is reduced to percentages, and the several chart-lines measure the progress. The increase of population is estimated on the basis of 62,000,000 persons in 1888. (So far as the lesson conveyed by the chart is concerned, the estimate might as well have been 60,000,000, the variation in the location of the line would be trifling.)

It appears, then, that railway mileage has increased nearly two hundred per cent. and that the rate of increase of freight traffic (as measured by ton-miles *) has been enormously larger, considering the history of the thirteen trunk lines as indicative of the whole. It further appears that the freight traffic of the West has developed much more rapidly than that of the East, during the last eight years.

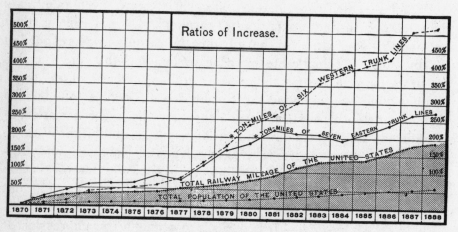

Ratios of Increase.

Construction and Maintenance.—The tabulated statistics of these subjects are not of special interest, as the annual variation of cost is slight. In both these elements the wage-question is so large a factor that a comparative level is maintained from year to year. The available figures touching these subjects are few. The first table on the opposite page gives the average cost of construction per mile of the *total mileage of the country ;* and the cost of maintenance per mile as reported by the New York, Lake Erie & Western Road. The second table furnishes interesting *details* of the cost of maintenance.

Employees.—This item is also one touching which railways make few reports. The New York Central & Hudson River Road reports as follows : " Average number of employees, 20,659, being at the rate of 14.54 per mile of road worked ; aggregate wages,

---

* A ton-mile means a ton of freight hauled one mile ; ten ton-miles, a ton of freight hauled ten miles, or two tons hauled five miles.

Construction and Maintenance for Ten Years.

Years	Cost of construction per mile.	Cost of maintenance per mile.	Years	Cost of construction per mile.	Cost of maintenance per mile.	Years	Cost of construction per mile.	Cost of maintenance per mile.
1879	$57,730	$1,671	1883	$61,800	$1,533	1886	$61,098	$1,496
1880	58,624	1,371	1884	61,400	1,281	1887	58,603	1,533
1881	60,645	1,448	1885	61,400	1,082	1888	60,732	1,226
1882	61,393	1,335						

Comparative Statement of Maintenance of Way of the Illinois Central Road for Ten Years.

Year.	Miles of road at end of year.	Labor on track.	New rails.		Cross-ties.		Repairs of bridges.	Other items.	Total.	Expense per mile run by engines.	Repairs of fences.	Repairs of station buildings and water-works.
		$	Tons.		Number.	$	$	$	$	Cents.	$	$
1879	1,286.72	297,363 40	9,276.00	125,062 70	264,520	93,107 51	73,119 56	125,041 92	640,575 53	11.73	$33,416 86	45,755 09
1880	1,320.35	343,982 23	9,767.49	215,365 32	260,116	93,330 32	105,551 62	49,399 09	807,628 58	12.39	36,981 94	80,887 34
1881	1,320 35	411,018 91	10,098.47	169,718 80	345,260	127,279 76	114,193 18	30,399 46	852,610 11	12.16	36,690 33	70,699 58
1882	1,908.65	690,112 59	8,438.00	128,521 48	604,096	201,648 26	114,826 24	17,277 34	1,212,385 91	11.87	31,032 57	87,588 26
1883	1,927.99	742,476 20	8,191.79	183,239 65	425,627	153,739 00	121,101 03	72,294 71	1,272,850 59	11.89	30,084 49	87,291 93
1884	2,066.35	706,751 86	6,342.73	193,446 25	462,665	154,083 19	173,831 23	107,236 13	1,235,348 66	12.20	21,394 71	94,122 03
1885	2,066.35	749,254 19	8,747.31	87,331 95	508,756	176,835 69	164,586 39	88,126 28	1,266,134 50	11.27	21,932 48	94,518 19
1886	2,149.07	705,553 82	6,376.40	63,238 84	492,524	174,515 72	172,144 65	63,976 69	1,179,429 72	10.15	26,668 91	123,519 83
1887	2,355.12	760,093 33	6,092.66	79,917 84	573,898	197,989 47	250,337 47	61,441 88	1,349,779 99	9.95	31,905 46	129,526 76
1888	2,552.55	847,806 67	8,172.36	106,372 94	654,141	214,130 73	310,908 42	115,898 04	1,595,116 80	10.74	40,423 39	170,023 85

$12,460,708.89, or $603.16 each. Payments in wages equalled 50.60 per cent of the total working expenses, against 51.90 per cent. in 1886–87." Reckoning that each employee's wages supports an average of three persons, we have a total of 61,977 persons clothed, housed, and fed by this one corporation.

" Poor's Manual " discusses this subject at some length, but mainly on theoretical ground.

Rolling Stock.—A table showing the history of the growth of the rolling stock of the country is given on page 148 ; it is therefore unnecessary to repeat it here.

Capital Invested.—It is folly for the human mind to attempt to grasp the immensity of the financial interest expressed in the statement, that the combined capital invested in the railways of the United States is $9,369,398,954. No more can it comprehend that this vast aggregate has been the growth of about fifty years in a single interest, in a single country.

Capital Invested.

Year.	Capital.	Year.	Capital.
1876	$4,468,592,000	1883	$7,477,866,000
1877	5,106,202,000	1884	7,676,399,000
1878	4,772,297,000	1885	7,842,533,000
1879	4,872,017,000	1886	8,163,149,000
1880	5,402,038,000	1887	8,673,187,000
1881	6,278,565,000	1888	9,369,399,000
1882	7,016,750,000		

The first date in the table marks the close of the first century of our national life. Since that time the investment has more than doubled ; an increase of nearly five billion dollars in twelve years— an average of over four hundred million dollars per year. More exactly expressed, this means $1,118,906 per day, or $46,621 for every hour, day and night, during the first twelve years of our second century.

It is safe to say that no other financial interest shows a total of such wonderful magnitude. And with greater emphasis may it be said, that the finances of the world, record, in all the ages, to the present day, no such astounding increase of investment.

INDEX.

ACCIDENTS, chances of, 191
  at crossings, 408
  from coupling cars, 223, 392
  investigation of, 399
  to railway bridges, 26
  South Norwalk, 221
  statistics of, 260
  to trainmen, 393
  to trains, origin of, 167
Adams, Charles Francis, 104, 367
Air-brake, 193, 195
Allen, Horatio, 2, 4, 102
Arbitration between railways and their employees, 376, 381
Armstrong, Colonel G. G., 316
Atkinson, Edward, 43
Auditor's duties, 180, 183

BAGGAGE-CHECK SYSTEM, 253
Baggage-master, work of, 416
Baggage service, abuses in, 179
Baggage transportation, 253
Baldwin Locomotive Works, 132
Ballast of a railway, 37
Baltimore & Ohio, the, 103
  cars, 139
  early passenger-trains, 230
  in 1830, 101
Bangs, George S., 317
Bell-cord train-signal, 237
Bessemer, Sir Henry, 37
Bessemer steel, invention of, 37
Blaine, James G., 323
Blair, Montgomery, 317
Block-signal, automatic, 215
  system, 168, 213
Boilers, construction of, 114
Bonds and stock, relative position of, 354

Brake, air-, 193, 195
  advantages of air-, 387
  improvements suggested to air-, 199
  American, 202
  and coupler, 237
  Beals, 202
  chain, 193
  continuous, 195
  early forms of, 192
  electric, 194
  hand, 193 ; perils of, 387 ; how to manage, 388
  hydraulic, 193
  steam driver-, 192
  trials at Burlington, 200
  vacuum, 193, 195
  water, 202
  Westinghouse air-, 193, 195
Brakemen, characteristics of, 384
  duties of, 394
  life, agreeable and disagreeable features of, 386, 389
  passenger-train, advantages of, 396
  pleasures of, 394
  wit of, the result of meditation, 385
Bridges, railway, accidents to, 26
  American iron, 28
  American, development of, 27 ; length of, 24, 26
  American wooden, 27
  and culverts, how built, 22
  Bismarck, 86
  Britannia, 79
  builders, 423
  cantilever, 33, 88
  connecting two tunnels, 55
  connections, types of, 85
  foundations by crib or open caisson, 75

Bridges, foundations by pneumatic caisson, 69
  foundations, how made, 32, 67
  foundations under water, 67
  gangs, work of, 155
  great, over cañons and valleys, 55
  guard-rails and frogs for, 221
  Hawkesbury River, 32
  Howe truss, 27
  how to build safe, 31
  Kentucky River, 34, 55, 88
  Kinzua, 30
  Lachine, 92
  masonry arch, 76
  Niagara cantilever, 34, 90
  Portage, 78
  Poughkeepsie, 32, 34
  steel truss, development of, 85
  strength of, 29
  St. Louis, 93
  trusses, types of, 86
  tubular, 80
  typical American truss, 86
  Verrugas, 55
  Victoria, 80
  Washington, over Harlem River, 77, 94
  wooden, 78
  wood, stone, and iron, 25, 26
Bridgers, R. R., 340
Bridgewater, Duke of, 345
Broken trains, dangers of, 388
Burr & Wernwag, 27

CAISSONS FOR BRIDGE FOUNDATIONS, how made, 32, 69
  open, 75
  pneumatic, 69
Camden & Amboy locomotives, 106
Cameron, Simon, prediction of, 232
Campbell, Henry R., 109
Cantilever bridges, 33, 88
Capital invested in railways, 344, 448
Car-accountant, and the transportation department, 275
  office of, 271
Car-accounting, benefits of a good system, 280
Car-builders' dictionary, 147
Car-couplers, imperfections of, 140
  need of uniformity in, 141

Car-coupling, accidents from, 223, 392
Cars, American and English, 7
  American, evolution of, 139
  Baltimore & Ohio freight-, 139
  different kinds of, 146
  old, discomforts of, 234
  distribution of, 171, 279
  empty, distribution of, 279
  first American passenger-, 139
  first sleeping-, 140
  for special uses, 289
  freight-, wanderings of a, 267
  heating by gas, 226
  heating by steam, 226
  heating, methods of, 245
  lighting safely, 226
  mileage and records, 158
  mileage charges, 273
  Mohawk & Hudson passenger-, 139
  number of, in the United States, 148
  records of movement, 171
  service charges, per-diem plan, 29
  service of, payment for, 293
  service records and reports, 276
  tracers for, 279
  trucks, 7 ; invention of, 108
  use and abuse of, 281
Car-wheels, European, 144
  how made, 142
  paper, 145
Cassatt, A. J., 340
Check system for baggage, 253
Chief engineer, duties of, 154
Chimbote Railway in the Andes, 50, 53
Civil service reform in the mail service, 340
Classifications of freight, 176
Clerks, railway, 422
Coffer-dam foundations for bridges, 67
Commissions to passenger agents, 179
Competing points and pools, 364
Concentration of power, 351
Conducting transportation, 159
Conductors, freight, trials of, 398
  heroism of, 411
  passenger, 408
Consolidation, effects of, 351
  tendency to, 346
Construction companies, 355
Contractors, railway, work of, 21
Conveniences at stations, 259

Cooley, Judge Thomas M., 368
Cooper, Peter, 104, 231
Council, proposed railway, 380
Couplers and brakes, 237
  imperfections of, 140
  uniform automatic, 223
Coupling cars, accidents from, 223, 392
Coupon tickets, 254
  misunderstood, 254
Cox, S. S., 323
Cranes, large travelling, in locomotive shops, 132
Crib foundations for bridge piers, 75
Crises of 1873 and 1885, effects of, 356
Crossings, accidents at, 408
  protection for, 216
Cullom, Senator S. M., 368
Culverts, building of, 22
  log, 25
  masonry, 76
  on American railways, 24, 26
Curves, American and European railway, 8
  least, 8
Cutting, largest ever made, 56
Cylinders, locomotive, construction of, 117

DARWIN, ERASMUS, 2
Davis & Gartner, 106
Davis, Phineas, 106
Davis, W. A., 317
Death and accident provisions for postal clerks, 343
Delays in a long journey, 267
Delaware & Hudson Canal Company, 101
Demurrage charges, 296
Derailing switches, use of, 207
Derailments of trains, causes of, 218
Destructive force of a locomotive at high speed, 187
Detector-bar for switches, 205
Differentials, 175
Dining-cars, introduction of, 243
Discipline necessary on a railway, 377
Distribution of cars, 171, 279
Dividends, average, on railway stock, 443
Drawbridge accidents, 221
Driving-wheels, large and small, 128

EADS, CAPTAIN JAMES B., 64, 93
Eames vacuum brake, 195

Eccentric, operation of, 118
Educational institutions for railway employees, 379
Electric annunciator for signals, 209
Electric lights for cars, 226
Electricity applied to brakes, 194
Elevated Railroad, New York, 97
Employees, railway, benefit funds, 378
  permanent and temporary, 375
  promotion of, 376
  number of, in the United States, 43, 370
  permanency of service during good behavior, 376
  relations of, to the railway, 357
  representative system for, 380
  rights and privileges of permanent, 376
  to have a voice in management, 379
  wages of, 448
Engineer, the, as a public benefactor, 46
  civil, qualifications of, 15
  responsibilities and duties of, 98
Engineering, good, true test of, 60
Ericsson, John, 2

FACING AND TRAILING POINT SWITCHES, 219
Facing-point locks, 205
Fast freight lines, 287
Fast mail service, appropriations for, 337
Fast mail train, trip with, 323
Fast runs, remarkable instances, 404
Fast time on railways, conditions of, 128
Field & Hayes, 34
Fink, Albert, 365
Fisk, James, Jr., 353
Flagging trains, 390
Foot-guard for frogs, 222
Foreign cars, theory and practice in their use, 279
Foster, Rastrick & Company, 102
Free-pass system, 362
Freight-car wanderings, 267
  classifications and rates, 176
  conductor and his trials, 398
  department, organization of, 282
  engines, saving fuel on, 402
  empty trains of, 439
  handlers at stations, 423
  movement, accidents in, 293; cost of delays in, 293

Freight profits, 440
  rates, reduction of, 358 ; 438
  traffic, 437 ; how handled, 180
Freight trains, air-brakes for, 200
  transportation, needs of the service, 297
Fuel, saving, on freight-engines, 402

GARRETT, JOHN W., 351
Gate-tenders on the railway, 423
General Freight Agent, 172
General Manager, duties of, 154
General Passenger Agent, 172
Geographical location of railways in the
  United States, 427
Goold, James, 139
Grades, limit of, 8
Grand Central Station interlocking signals,
  208
Grand River cañon, 54
Granger movement, 363
Guard-rails and frogs for bridges, 221

HAMLIN, HANNIBAL, 323
Hampson, John, 231
Harrison, Joseph, Jr., 4
Hawkesbury River bridge, 32
Heater-cars, Eastman, 289
Heating cars, 245
Highway crossing accidents, 216
  crossing gates, 217
Holley, Alexander L., 37
Hoosac Tunnel, 63
Hospital funds for railway employees, 378
Hotel-cars, 244
Howe-truss bridges, 27

IMMIGRANT SLEEPING-CARS, 251
Inclined planes for overcoming elevations,
  58
Injectors, principle of, 116
Insurance funds for railway employees, 378
Interchange of cars, methods of, 272
Interlocking bolts, uses of, 221
  signals and switches, 204
Interstate commerce law, 173, 368
  Commerce Commission and its work, 368
Investigation of accidents, 399
Investors and managers, relations of, 357
  difficult position of, 354
Irregular hours of work, 399

JAMESON, JOHN, 317, 323, 342
Janney car-coupler, 237
Jervis, John B., 4, 107
Johnson, R. P., 339
Judgment, value of, in a locomotive runner,
  407
Junction-cards and car-reports, 278

KENTUCKY RIVER CANTILEVER BRIDGE,
  34, 55, 88
King, Porter, 408
Kinzua Bridge, 30

LACHINE BRIDGE, 92
Latimer, Charles, 221
Latrobe, Benjamin H., 8
Layng, J. D., 319
Legal department of a railway, duties of,
  152
Lighting cars, safe methods, 226
Lincoln, Abraham, in the first sleeping-
  car, 240
Link motion for locomotive valves, 119
Location, approximate, 15
  final, 18
  how governed, 16
  in old and new countries, 17
  importance of, 15
Locomotives, ability to climb grades, 8
  American type, origin of, 109
  Baltimore & Ohio "grasshopper," 106
  boiler construction, 115
  cab, what is in it, 131
  capacity to draw loads, 120
  consolidation, 122
  cost of running, 307
  cylinders, how supplied with steam, 117
  decapod, 122
  destructive force of, at high speed, 187
  "DeWitt Clinton," 105
  driving-wheels, how made, 142
  earliest American, 2
  early eight-wheeled, 105
  engineer, the duties and qualifications of,
    137 ; peculiarities of, 134 ; duties and
    dangers of, 400 ; spirit of fraternity of,
    408
  English type of, 3
  equalizing levers, 4
  fireman, 422

Locomotives, first trial of, in America, 103
   fuel, 303 ; consumption, 135
   hostler, 422
   how to start and stop, 120
   "John Bull," 106
   Mogul, 122
   number of, in the United States, 148
   Peter Cooper's, 104
   prize offered for, by the Baltimore & Ohio, 105
   pumps and injectors, 116
   "Rocket," 1
   running, systems of, 134 ; cost of, 158, 159
   running gear, adjustment of, 114 ; flexible, 113
   shops, 132
   size, weight, and price, 126
   speed, law of, 127
   suburban traffic, 124
   ten-wheeled, 122
   trials, Liverpool & Manchester Railway, 2, 3
   truck, invention of, 4, 107
   types of, 109
   valve motion, 118
London Underground Railway, 97
"Long and short haul," 173

MAIL SERVICE, railway, civil service reform in, 340
Mail train, fast, 317
Managers and investors, relations of, 357
Masonry arch bridges, 76
Massachusetts Railroad Commission and traffic questions, 367
Master Car Builders' Association brake-trials, 200
   type of car-coupler, 223
Master car-builder's duties, 158
Master mechanic's work, 157
Master of transportation, duties of, 159, 171
Mexican Central Railway, 56
Mileage balances, reduction of, 273
Miller coupler and buffer, 237
Miller, Ezra, 237
Milling in transit, 175
Model railway service, 375
Mohawk & Hudson passenger-cars, 139

Mont Cenis Tunnel, 63
Moral standard on the railway, improvement in, 384
Mount Washington Railway, 58
Mountain climbing by rack railways, 58
   railways, 49

NATIONAL REGULATION of railways, 367
Newell, John, 340
New York Elevated Railways, 97
Niagara cantilever bridge, 34, 90
   suspension bridge, 81
Nochistongo cut, 56

OPERATING DEPARTMENT OF A RAILWAY, importance of, 373
Oroya Railway in the Andes, 50, 53
Outram, Benjamin, 345

PAPER CAR-WHEELS, 145
Passenger advertisement, first, 229
   brakeman, 396
   burned in wrecks, 225
   cars, early, 231 ; English and American, 232 ; first American, 139 ; manufacture of, 252 ; Mohawk & Hudson, 139
   conductor, 408
   fares, comparative rates, 265
   profits, 442
   rates and commissions, 17
   tickets, old, 236
   traffic, 442
   trains, first, 228 ; early American, 230 ; making time on, 403
   travel, 362 ; amount of, 264 ; safety of, in England and America, 260 ; speed of, 249
Pay-car, trip of the, 309
Pay, increase of, for faithful service, 378
Paymaster's work, 308
Parallel roads, 356
Pensions for railway employees, 378
Pennsylvania Railroad shops at Altoona, 132
   maintenance of track, 41
   system, 371
Permanent service of a railway, 375
Pile-driver, work of a, 22
Pile foundations for bridges, 68
Plant, H. B., 340

Pneumatic caissons for bridge foundations, 69
  interlocking apparatus, 210
Pœtsch method of building foundations for bridge piers, 32
Pooling rates, 184
Pools and competing points, 364
  railway, origin and nature of, 364
Pope, Thomas, 33
Portage Bridge, 78
Postal cars, 325
  first used, 316
  provision against accident in, 338
Postal clerks, accidents to, 338
Postal progress, object lesson in, 312
Postal service, early history, 313
Potter, Thomas J., 412
Poughkeepsie cantilever bridge, 32, 34
Predecessors of the railway, 101
Premiums to section-men, 41
Promotion of employees, 376
Pullman, George M., 239
  Palace Car Company, 242
  sleeper, first, 241
Purchasing agent's varied duties and experience, 300

RAILS, development of, 47
  increased weight of, 122
  iron, first used, 1, 37
  joints for, 37
  steel, first introduction, 37
  supply and renewal of, 306
  weight which they will carry, 121
Railroading fifty years ago, 100
Railways, American, key to the development of, 3 ; rolling stock of, 148 ; and English, essential differences, 10
  amount of capital invested in, 344
  and their employees, nature of relations, 374
  and democracy, 45
  and their customers, 358
  beginning of, 345
  building, cost of, 43 ; example of rapid, 44 ; history of, 445
  competition of, 174 ; with canals, 347
  consolidation, 174, 346
  council, proposed, 380
  division of expenses on, 359

Railways, earnings, average net, per mile, 444
  earliest, 1 ; in America, 103
  early systems of management, 346
  economic view of, 45
  educational institutions, 379
  employees, permanent and temporary, 375 ; general characteristics of, 423 ; moral welfare of, 423 ; a typical, 383 ; wages of, 448
  growth of, 346
  income, sources of, 180
  influence on the world, 149
  mail first carried on, 314
  mail service, growth of, 314 ; importance of, 323 ; needs of, 341 ; organization of, 323 ; party injury to, 341
  management, development of, 150 ; in Europe, 184 ; organization and division of authority, 151 ; results expected from, 184 ; special departments of, 372 ; stability of, 184 ; subdivisions of, 372
  men's building in New York, 424
  mileage, comparative, of the principal countries, 425 ; of the United States, 426
  national idea developed by, 348
  national regulation, 367
  officers' duties and responsibilities, 151
  organization analyzed, 185 ; complex, 183 ; growth of, 371
  personnel, importance of, 424
  place in the modern industrial system, 344
  postal clerks' dangers, 337 ; just claims, 343 ; need of provision against disability, 339 ; work, 334
  relations of, to their employees, 357
  shop-men, 423
  State ownership of, 362
  statistics of, 425
  systems, 428
  the largest single industrial interest, 370
  United States, extent of, 43
  " wars " between, 361
Randall, Samuel J., 323
Rates and rebates, 173
  causes of reduction, 358
  combinations and adjustments, 176

Rates, forced reductions, 363
  how made and regulated, 176
  inequalities of, 359
  passenger, and commissions, 178
  plans for regulating, 362
  special, wars over, 177
  without a natural standard, 360
Reagan, John H., 368
Reconnoissance, 13
Refrigerator cars, 289
Representation for railway employees, 380
Restriction of railways, tendency to, 369
Ride on a locomotive at night, 188
Righi Railway, 59
Road-bed of a railway, how made, 21
Roadway department of a railway, 154
Roberts, George B., 340
Roebling, John A., 82
Rolling stock, growth of, 448
Routine of the railway mail service, 325
Rutter, J. H., 340

SAFETY APPLIANCES, railway, 191
  devices needed, 423
St. Gothard Tunnel and spirals, 63
St. Louis Bridge, 64, 93
Schneider, C. C., 34
Scott, Thomas Alexander, 319, 349
Scrap-heap, value of, 302
Section-master's duties, 421
Section-men's work, 156
Semaphore signals, 203
Shepard, General D. C., 44
Signals and switches, interlocking, 168, 204
  automatic block, 215
  block system, 168, 213
  semaphore, 203
  torpedo, 213
Sleeping-car rates, comparative, 266
Sleeping-cars, first experiments, 239
  immigrant, 251
  Pullman, 239, 242
Smith, Colonel C. Shaler, 34, 88
Snow-sheds and fences, 18
South American mountain-railways, 50
South Carolina Railway, 104
  early passenger trains, 231
Special rates, 177, 361
Spoils system, how it works in the railway
  mail service, 342

Spreading of rails, 220
State ownership of railways, 362
State regulation of railways, 362, 363
Station agent's duties, 411
Station indicators, 259
Station, large, work at, 415
  small, work at, 411
Stationery and blanks, quantity used on a
  railway, 304
Statistics, railway, 425
Steam driver-brake, 192
  how distributed to the cylinders, 117
  shovel, work of, 21
  supply and speed, relations of, 129
Steel bridges, 29
Steel rails, first introduction, 37
Steel truss-bridges, development of, 85
Stephenson, George, 1, 2, 3, 228, 346
  Robert, 1, 2, 3, 79, 192
Stock and bonds, relative position, 354
Storekeeper's duties on a railway, 307
Stockton & Darlington passenger train, 228
" Stourbridge Lion," 102
Strikes, evils of, 374
Superintendent, duties of, 274
  of machinery, powers and duties, 157
Supply department, 298
  importance of, 311
Supplies, aggregate of, on a railway, 299
  variety required for a railway, 301
Surveying party, life of, 13
  from a rope-ladder, 50
Surveys, preliminary, 13
Suspension bridges, 81
Switchbacks and loops, 8 ; types of, 9, 10
Switches, interlocking, 420
  stub, accidents caused by, 218
Switch-tender's work, 420

TELEGRAPH IN RAILROADING, 238
Thompson, William B., 317, 322, 342
Thomson, Frank, 43, 340
Thomson, J. Edgar, 349
Through and local freight, 288
Through lines, growth of, 348
Tickets, cost of, on a railway, 305
  coupon, 254
  old, 236
  sales and reports, 182
Ties and timber supplies, 306

Time, fast, instances of, 404
  making, on passenger trains, 403
Time-tables, cost of, 305
  earliest American, 235
  how made, 160
Torpedo signals, 213
Track, early experiments with, 36, 37
  how laid, 36
  how maintained and kept in order, 38
  inspection on the Pennsylvania Railroad, 41
  laid on stone, 36
  standards of excellence, 41
Trackmen's duties, 38
  organization and officers, 41
Track-walker's duties and trials, 422
Trade centres, advantages of, 360
Traffic, how influenced and secured, 172
  manager, duties of, 172
  questions and the Massachusetts Railroad Commission, 367
  receipts, how returned and accounted for, 182
Train despatcher and his work, 163, 422
Train despatching, 162
  old and new, 187
Train orders and rules, 164
Train signals, bell-cord and other, 237
Train work, irregularity of, 399
Trainmen, accidents to, 393
  and tramps, 386
Trains, rules for running, 162
Tramways, Roman, of stone, 1
Transfer freight stations, 288
Transportation, cost of, 43
  conducting, 159
  department and the car-accountant, 275
Trestles, wooden, 78
Trevithick, Richard, 2
Tribunal, proposed, for adjusting differences between railways and their employees, 376
Trucks for cars, 7, 108
  for locomotives, 4, 107, 109
Trunk lines compared, 428
Trunk-line pool, origin and history, 365
Truss-bridge, typical American, 86
Tubular bridges, 80
Tunnels, 59

Tunnels, American, 23
  connected by a bridge, 55
  difficulties of construction, 62
  great, 62
  how avoided, 23
  located by triangulation, 53
  Mont Cenis, 63
  St. Gothard, 63

UNDERGROUND RAILWAY, London, 97
Union Pacific Railway system, extent of, 370

VACUUM-BRAKE, 193, 195
Vail, Theodore N., 317, 322
Valleys, how crossed by a railway, 49
Valve-motion arrangements, 118
Vanderbilt business methods, 351
Vanderbilt, Commodore, 318, 340
Vanderbilt, Cornelius, 350, 424
Vanderbilt, William H., 318, 340
Verrugas Viaduct, 55
Vestibule train, luxury of, 248
  as a safety device, 224
Viaducts, American metal, 79
Victoria Bridge, 80

WADDELL, A., 323
Wagner Palace Car Company, 242
Wagon cars, 290
War, the late, effect of, on railway growth, 348
Washington Bridge over the Harlem River, 77, 94
Waste and saving in supplies, 302
Water-jet method of sinking piles, 68
Watt, James, 1
Way-bill and its theory, 181
Westinghouse air-brake, 195, 196
Westinghouse, George, Jr., 200, 237
West Point Foundry as a locomotive shop, 104
Whipple, Squire, 28
Winans, Ross, 7, 108

YARDMASTER'S DUTIES, 283
Young Men's Christian Association, Railway Department, 424